Time Out

1000

things for kids to do in the holidays

timeout.com

Published by Time Out Guides Ltd, a wholly owned subsidiary of Time Out Group Ltd.
Time Out and the Time Out logo are trademarks of Time Out Group Ltd.

© **Time Out Group Ltd 2009**

10 9 8 7 6 5 4 3 2 1

This edition first published in Great Britain in 2009 by Ebury Publishing
A Random House Group Company
20 Vauxhall Bridge Road, London SW1V 2SA

Random House Australia Pty Limited 20 Alfred Street, Milsons Point, Sydney, New South Wales 2061, Australia
Random House New Zealand Limited 18 Poland Road, Glenfield, Auckland 10, New Zealand
Random House South Africa (Pty) Limited Isle of Houghton, Corner Boundary Road & Carse O'Gowrie,
Houghton 2198, South Africa

Random House UK Limited Reg. No. 954009

Distributed in USA by Publishers Group West
1700 Fourth Street, Berkeley, California 94710

Distributed in Canada by Publishers Group Canada
250A Carlton Street, Toronto, Ontario M5A 2L1

For further distribution details, see www.timeout.com

ISBN: 978-1-84670-090-3

A CIP catalogue record for this book is available from the British Library

Printed and bound by Firmengruppe APPL, aprinta druck, Wemding, Germany

The Random House Group Limited supports The Forest Stewardship Council (FSC), the leading international forest
certification organisation. All our titles that are printed on Greenpeace approved FSC certified paper carry the FSC
logo. Our paper procurement policy can be found at http://www.rbooks.co.uk/environment.

Time Out carbon-offsets all its flights with Trees for Cities (www.treesforcities.org).

Time Out Guides Limited
Universal House
251 Tottenham Court Road
London W1T 7AB
Tel + 44 (0)20 7813 3000
Fax + 44 (0)20 7813 6001
Email guides@timeout.com
www.timeout.com

Editorial
Editor Ronnie Haydon
Deputy Editor Elizabeth Winding
Listings Checkers Alex Brown, Cathy Limb,
Gemma Pritchard, Kohinoor Sahota
Proofreader John Pym
Indexer Jackie Brind

Managing Director Peter Fiennes
Editorial Director Sarah Guy
Series Editor Cath Phillips
Business Manager Dan Allen
Editorial Manager Holly Pick
Assistant Management Accountant Ija Krasnikova

Design
Art Director Scott Moore
Art Editor Pinelope Kourmouzoglou
Senior Designer Henry Elphick
Graphic Designers Kei Ishimaru, Nicola Wilson
Ad Designer Jodi Sher

Picture Desk
Picture Editor Jael Marschner
Deputy Picture Editor Lynn Chambers
Picture Researcher Gemma Walters
Picture Desk Assistant Marzena Zoladz
Picture Librarian Christina Theisen

Advertising
Commercial Director Mark Phillips
Sales Manager Alison Wallen
Advertising Sales Ben Holt, Philippa Johnson, Jason Trotman
Copy Controller Alison Bourke

Marketing
Marketing Manager Yvonne Poon
Sales & Marketing Director,
North America & Latin America Lisa Levinson
Senior Publishing Brand Manager Luthfa Begum
Marketing Designer Anthony Huggins

Production
Group Production Director Mark Lamond
Production Manager Brendan McKeown
Production Controller Damian Bennett
Production Coordinator Kelly Fenlon

Time Out Group
Chairman Tony Elliott
Chief Executive Officer David King
Group General Manager/Director Nichola Coulthard
Time Out Communications Ltd MD David Pepper
Time Out International Ltd MD Cathy Runciman
Time Out Magazine Ltd Publisher/
Managing Director Mark Elliott
Group IT Director Simon Chappell
Head of Marketing Catherine Demajo

Contributors Nuala Calvi, Kate Fuscoe, Derek Hammond, Bruce Jones, Rick Jones, Kaye McAlpine, Fiona McAuslan, Eleanor McKee, Cath Phillips, Andrew Shields, Helen Stiles, Buzz Stokes, Teresa Trafford, Tony Trafford, Jill Turton, Elizabeth Winding.

Interviews Nuala Calvi, Ronnie Haydon, Rick Jones, Sarah Thorowgood.

The Editor would like to thank all contributors to Time Out Guides and *Time Out London* magazine (whose work forms the basis for part of this book), as well as: Bevin, Orla, Liadan, Fintan, Sarah and Anto Anandarajah; Fiona Cumberpatch; Ros Esposito, Anthony Felstead, Susannah Felstead, Janet Hockney; Sarah Guy; Franny and Jimmy Hammond; James, Miles and Joseph Johnson; Jane Jones; Cathy Limb, Finn Jordan; Eleanor and Esther Mannoukas; Rory Pagan, Ralph Kemp; Buzz, Dom and Hannah Stokes; Mary Trafford.

Cover photography Sam Atkins, Elisabeth Blanchet, Don Brownlow, Nadin Dunnigan, Tim Mitchell, Fabio De Paola, Jonathan Perugia, Christina Theisen and Marzena Zoladz

Photography by pages 5 (middle top), 5 (bottom right), 7 (left), 76, 77, 78, 273, 294 Marzena Zoladz; pages 5 (top left), 65, 66, 187, 188, 275 Elisabeth Blanchet; pages 5 (bottom middle), 133, 218, 267 Andrew Brackenbury; pages 7 (bottom right), 120, 155, 163, 203, 236, 237, 241, 250, 251, 268, 269, 290 Heloise Bergman; pages 7 (top right), 29, 30, 103, 104, 112, 113, 159, 203, 243, 244, 285, 286, 287 Jonathan Perugia; pages 9, 139, 140, 141 Fabio De Paola; page 15 Dave Willis; page 27 Alys Tomlinson; page 31 Jon Bowers; pages 32, 33 Howard Barlow; pages 39, 40, 50, 206, 299 Susannah Stone; page 48 Don Brownlow; pages 58, 185 Tove Breistein; pages 68, 69, 92, 123, 174, 175, 216, 217, 249 Rob Grieg; page 74 www.hackney.gov.uk; page 75 (top) Tim Mitchell; page 75 (bottom) Talula Sheppard; pages 84, 85, 86, 190, 191, 263, 264 Christina Theisen; page 91 Rebecca Lewis; page 91 Richard Eaton; pages 94, 95, 130, 131 Sam Atkins; pages 125, 126 Chris Barber; page 128 Jane Airey; page 143 Arsenal Football Club/Niall O'Connor; page 146 Alan R Thomson; pages 152, 153, 197, 198 Nadin Dunnigan; page 156 Tony Gibson; page 157 Justin Downing/A Chance To Shine; page 158 Andrew Shields; page 160 Scott Wishart; page 164 (right) David Levenson; page 164 (left) Andy Hay; page 208 The National Trust/Lee Searle; page 209 Getty Images; page 219 Freia Turland/Bath Fashion Museum; pages 221, 222 Hugh Palmer; page 226 Eamonn McGoldrick; page 228 Olivia Rutherford; page 235 John Hooper/Hoopix; page 253 Debbie Bragg/Underage festival; page 257 Paul Box; page 260 Extreeme Adventure; page 288 Tricia de Courcy Ling; page 290 Martyn J Brooks.

The following images were provided by the featured establishments/artists: pages 3, 5 (bottom left), 5 (top right), 7 (bottom middle), 10, 11, 14, 16, 20, 21, 22, 23, 34, 35, 41, 47, 52, 54, 55, 62, 63, 79, 88, 97, 99, 108, 110, 111, 116, 117, 135, 145, 150, 151, 162, 166, 167, 170, 172, 176, 180, 181, 182, 184, 193, 195, 199, 202, 205, 210, 211, 213, 215, 225, 227, 230, 231, 233, 239, 259, 275, 276, 279, 280, 293, 295, 300, 301, 302, 303.

Illustrations mrhenryfisher.com.

Contents

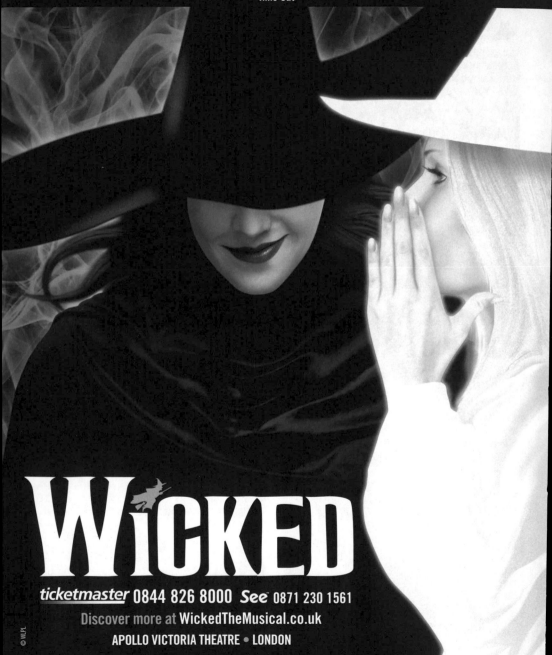

About the guide

Telephone numbers

All phone numbers listed in this guide assume that you are calling from within Britain. If you are calling from abroad, dial your international access code, then 44 for the UK; follow that with the phone number, dropping the first zero of the area code.

Disclaimer

While every effort has been made to ensure the accuracy of information within this guide, the publishers cannot accept responsibility for any errors it may contain. Businesses can change their arrangements at any time so, before you go out of your way, we strongly advise you to phone ahead to check opening times, prices and other particulars.

Advertisers

The recommendations in *1000 Things for kids to do in the holidays* are based on the experiences of Time Out journalists. No payment or PR invitation of any kind has secured inclusion or influenced content. The editors select which venues and activities are listed in this guide, and the list of 1,000 was compiled before any advertising space was sold. Advertising has no effect on editorial content.

Let us know what you think

Did we miss anything? We welcome tips for 'things' you consider we should include in future editions and take note of your criticism of our choices. You can email us at guides@timeout.com.

5 HUGE FLOORS OF THE WEIRD WACKY & WONDERFUL!

PEEL 50

NEW FOR 2009 – THE WORLD'S SMALLEST CAR!

The p-50 holds the record for being the smallest road-legal car ever produced as seen on Top Gear!

You Won't Believe Your Eyes!

Ripley's
Believe It or Not!®

Welcome to the world of Ripley's Believe It or Not! London's Biggest New Attraction. Situated in the heart of the West End at 1 Piccadilly Circus, the attraction houses over 800 authentic, original and unbelievable exhibits spread over 5 floors, from a four-metre long model of Tower Bridge made out of matchsticks and an upside-down tea party to the world's tallest man and a Mini Cooper encrusted with 1,000,000 Swarovski crystals. Ripley's Believe It or Not! presents a unique mixture of entertainment, education and fun for the entire family - appealing to anyone with a basic sense of curiosity.

YOU WON'T BELIEVE YOUR EYES!

OPEN UNTIL MIDNIGHT EVERYDAY!

RIPLEYSLONDON.COM | 1 PICCADILLY CIRCUS | LONDON W1J 0DA | 020 3238 0022

Introduction

Way back, in prehistoric times (the 1970s) there was a children's television programme, broadcast on school-holiday mornings, entitled *Why don't you just switch off your television set and go out and do something less boring instead?* A confusing title for a TV programme if ever there was one. These days, of course, kids can choose from any number of screen-based entertainments to while away those long empty days between school terms. And grown-ups, more often than not the very people who have bought said screens, are still exhorting their offspring to switch off and get some fresh air. No wonder children are still confused.

We compiled this book because we believe school holidays are precious. They're a time when families can escape from the rigours of school runs, homework horrors, after-class activities, PE-kit remembering, SATs-panicking and all the other irritations that term-time brings. The holidays are a time for parents and children to relax a bit, enjoy each other's company, go on excursions, or get creative in the kitchen or the garden. Our collection of 1,000 things is all about making the most of that relatively brief period of life when you're given about ten weeks off a year in which to play.

We've consulted people of all ages about what to include. The range of suggestions is vast, but we've made sure that every one of them is fun, whether they're simply dotty or (whisper it) quite educational – but not in a school way. There are places to go and things to see throughout the country: festivals and spectacles, workshops and beauty spots, beaches, farms, cityscapes, stately homes and spooky caverns. Then there's the stuff to be done at home: baking, making, sewing, growing, cutting, sticking and letting your imagination run riot. So go on, then, switch off your television set, and the computer, and go and do something – 1,000 things – less boring instead.

Ronnie Haydon, Editor

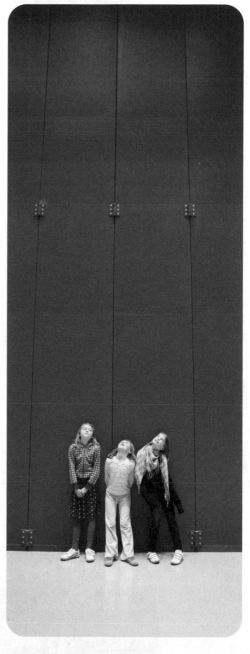

1

Wallow in the mud in Wales

Getting grubby is inevitable if you're attending September's National Mud Festival – a weekend of mud worshipping at Wales's National Wetland Centre (01554 741087, www.wwt.org.uk). Building mud huts, fashioning mud sculptures and taking part in a tug of war or welly-wanging contest are all on the agenda – though a serious environmental message is imparted if you take a guided tour of the centre's salt marshes and mud flats.

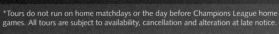

2 Attend a masterclass in magic

Chorley's Camelot Theme Park has tough jousting knights, scary rides, a petting farm and play areas, but the top priority for would-be sorcerer's apprentices is enrolling at Merlin's School of Wizardry. Sadly, turning teachers into toads or parents into a puff of smoke isn't on the curriculum, but the great man does promise to reveal some sleight-of-hand secrets, card tricks and illusions. Workshops last 20 minutes and take place twice daily.
Camelot Theme Park *Park Hall Road, Chorley, Lancashire PR7 5LP (01257 453044/ www.camelotthemepark.co.uk).*

3 Raid Scotland's best dressing-up box

In the National Museum of Scotland, you can be a dapper Georgian gent, a Viking girl, a Roman soldier, a couple set for emigration or a medieval lord or lady. That is, if you're around ten or under (boo!). You can still fit the medieval gear and the Roman helmet if you're an adult, though (hurray!). There are also dozens of hands-on games and interactive exhibits, which are an engaging introduction to history, including the great Connect Gallery.
National Museum of Scotland *Chambers Street, Edinburgh EH1 1JF (0131 225 7534/ www.nms.ac.uk).*

4 Unleash a giant slinky

Perched on Whitby's West Cliff, this quirky little science museum is an unexpected gem. Hand-built by Whitby's very own resident Viking, Norwegian explorer and teacher Dag Kjelldahl, it features almost 100 hands-on and highly entertaining science experiments; and what's more, they work. Visitors queue to push that slinky, defy the magnet, examine a skeleton and disappear like the Cheshire Cat.
Whitby Wizard *West Cliff, Whitby, North Yorkshire YO21 1RR (01947 810470/ www.whitbywizard.com).*

5-6 Go scrumping (legally)

Norfolk was once famous for its orchards, but since 1960 the county has lost a huge percentage of its apple trees. In recent years, though, campaigners have been on a mission to bring back the apples. Recently planted community orchards are maturing nicely, and visitors are encouraged to help tend them, and to pick the fruit. You'll find an organically managed orchard about 30 kilometres north-east of Norwich at Pigney's Wood (Hall Lane, Knapton, www.pigneys-wood.co.uk), where the first heritage orchard trees – all Norfolk varieties – were planted in 2007 by the North Norfolk Community Woodland Trust. Come in early October and enjoy old varieties you'll never see in a supermarket. Another community orchard – open at all times – has been planted in nearby Coltishall (off Kings Road and Wroxham Road).

For more on where to scrump for apples, or just admire the blossom-covered boughs, in community orchards, contact the East of England Apple Orchards Project (www.apples andorchards.org.uk).

7 Hang out the bunting

Pep up party decor by draping the walls with bunting – a length of string hung with little triangular penants. First, draw a triangle on some card, using a ruler. Make the base of the triangle 23cm, and the two sides 28cm. Cut this out, and use it as a template to make more triangles from wrapping paper, newspaper, crêpe paper or tissue. Pattern-wise, anything goes, from cut-up old Christmas cards for yuletide feasts to fresh spring florals or jaunty union jacks. Next, take two of the matching triangles and sandwich them together, using glue or sticky tape at the top with a drinking straw cut to size in between. Thread a length of string through the straws at the top of each triangle, and you're ready to go.

A few of my favourite things

8-13

Carole Smillie, TV presenter

We eat together as a family around the table almost every day of the week, and I think that's really important. We used to have a nanny when the kids were very small, and that was fantastic, but you can easily slip into a routine where you're on different time zones. When you eat together, you get time to chat to the kids; find out what's going on in their lives and what's concerning them. And, of course, you can get them into the same food you like. We went to China at Easter and it made a huge difference to the kids in terms of introducing them to different kinds of cuisine. Now they love Chinese takeaways – though I try to limit it to once every two or three weeks. **My daughters are nine and 13 now, and their retail therapy gene has kicked in. Glasgow is fantastic for shopping – try St Enoch Shopping Centre (Management Street, 35 St Enoch Square, G1 4BW, 0141 204 3900, www.stenoch.co.uk) and Princes Square (38-42 Buchanan Street, G1 3JX, 0141 221 0324, www.princes square.co.uk). I try not to give the girls too much advice – if your mum likes something, you'll never want to wear it – that's the law of the jungle. I'm always** flattered when my 13-year-old wants to borrow my stuff. Depressingly, she's already two inches taller than me and her feet are two sizes bigger.

I find more and more that my teenager, Christie, likes to do her own thing, which is tricky. If she's got one of her friends round she'll be more sullen and grumpy, but if she's on her own she is still capable of being part of the group. I like to take them to Kelvingrove (Argyle Street, G3 8AG, 0141 276 9599, www.glasgowmuseums.com). It's a stunning art gallery and museum, with everything from dinosaurs to things like the Kylie exhibition. We go there a lot because it's educational, but not in a stuffy way. **My son Robbie likes to go off and do his own boyish things. We've discovered Unit 23 (45-50 The Old Bond, Castlegreen Street, Dunbarton G82 1JD, 01389 768 333, www.unit23skatepark.co.uk), an indoor skate park just out of town. It's an awesome place, which has helped reduce crime in the area by 35 per cent. Robbie got one of the older boys there to show him how to do all the tricks on his BMX. He's more of a surfer at heart, but he loves it.** Another place he enjoys is Xscape (Kings Inch Road, Braehead, Renfrew PA4 8XQ, 0871 200 3222, www.xscape.co.uk), an indoor ski slope with real snow. It's also got a crazy-golf range, bowling alley, rock climbing and Skypark – an aerial assault course. I hate skiing, so my husband does that with Robbie, but he's terrified of heights, so I have to do the Skypark. **If we want to get away, we go to our holiday cottage in Ayrshire. It's by the sea, so the kids can go rock pooling and pony trekking and build beach bonfires. We refuse to have cable TV or computers there, so they have to entertain themselves in old-fashioned ways. They might moan about it, but secretly they know it's more fun than anything else they could do.**

14 *Make edible 'stained glass'*

Make pretty edible Christmas decorations out of boiled sweets – but take care, the molten syrup you're working with can deliver a nasty burn. First, preheat your oven to 170°C. Take some boiled fruit sweets and some metal cookie-cutter shapes. Line a baking sheet with foil, spray the surface with cooking oil and place the cookie-cutters on it, then pop in the oven for about six minutes until the sweets have melted. Take out the tray and swirl the molten liquid with a cocktail stick to fill up the cutter shape. Let it cool a little and make a hole in each shape while they're still soft.

When cool, but not cold, peel the shapes from the foil, string thread or ribbon through the hole and hang them on the Christmas tree.

15 Go back to back in Brum

Who'd have thought a cluster of humble, 19th-century workers' house would make it on to the National Trust's books? Carefully restored and spanning 1840 to 1977, Birmingham's last surviving court of back-to-back housing is unexpectedly fun for kids. For one, the stand-on-ceremony rules of grander properties don't apply – so you can flick through the 1970s menswear catalogue in the tailor's shop, ogle the freaky drawers of glass eyes in the 1870s house, check how soft the beds are and spot the three resident stuffed mice (Louis, Nibbles and Squishy). Visits are by guided tour only, with crafts sessions in the school holidays that range from making rag rugs to fashioning eyeballs from table tennis balls. Stock up on rhubarb and custard or sherbet pips at the sweet shop.
Birmingham Back to Backs *50-54 Inge Street & 55-63 Hurst Street, Birmingham B5 4TE (0121 666 7671/www.nationaltrust.org.uk).*

16 Have a cream tea while the cows come home

After following the three-kilometre trail through Low Sizergh Farm, admiring its 400-year-old hedgerow, ancient woodland and feisty, free-roaming hens, you'll work up quite an appetite. Happily, there's an excellent tea room, with most unusual views – its windows look out over the milking yard. Time your visit right (12.30-3.30pm) and you can watch the cows ambling in to chew on their tea while they're being milked. The organic milk they provide makes the cream teas served here all the more delicious. Freshly baked scones, home-made jam and cream, big pots of tea – all go down a treat as you admire the animals that make it all possible. The farm shop is equally mouth-watering, with artisan cheeses for the grown-ups and glorious creamy ice-creams for kids: the cinder toffee flavour is a treat.
Low Sizergh Farm *Sizergh, Kendal, Cumbria LA8 8AE (01539 560426/www.lowsizerghbarn.co.uk).*

Low Sizergh Farm

17 Enjoy a green playdate

The Centre for Alternative Technology, one of the world's best known eco-parks, sits high on a wooded clifftop above the Dulas Valley on the edge of Snowdonia National Park. First, you ascend the 60 metres to the Upper Station via a remarkable cliff railway, powered entirely by water. At the top, you're treated to fabulous views to Tarren-y-Gesail, the southernmost peak in Snowdonia. From here on in, the ecological education – and the fun – begins, with all sort of interactive displays for children. There's the mole hole, which they can dive down to explore underground chambers with lit displays of over-large soil inhabitants. The busiest area, though, is all about recycling, composting and renewable energy. Here, kids can light up bulbs while pedalling on a bike-generator, slide merrily into the composting area, indulge in splashy water play and really get stuck into the eco-interactive thing.

Leave plenty of time for the kids to monkey around in the eco-adventure playground and, during school holidays, take in a workshop or show in the straw-bale theatre.

Centre for Alternative Technology *Machynlleth, Powys SY20 9AZ (01654 705950/www.cat.org.uk).*

18 Sprout your beans

If you love bean sprouts in stir-fries and salads, get some mungs and see them sprout. Forget expensive commercial sprouters, and do it the old-fashioned way. Take a mixing bowl and place a layer of beans (about two beans thick; 1-2cm) at the bottom of the bowl. This will give them plenty of room to sprout. Submerge the beans in a few centimetres of warm water.

Cover the bowl with a layer of cheesecloth or muslin, fastened with a large rubber band around its edge. (It's important to use a fabric that lets the air circulate, and allows you to rinse the beans through it.) Leave the bowl to stand overnight, so that the beans can absorb most of the water and bulk up.

Next morning, drain the beans by inverting the bowl over the sink, then rinse them in tepid water through the cheesecloth. You need to keep them moist, but not in standing water. Put the bowl in a warm, dark place (a kitchen cabinet will do), and keep them damp by rinsing them several times a day. Continue this process for three or four days, until the sprouts are tender. Rinse the sprouts before using them; they will stay fresh in the salad section of the fridge for several days.

Centre for Alternative Technology

19 *Run a mini marathon*

Keen to encourage future champions, London's famous marathon also mounts a separate race for 11- to 17-year-old distance runners. The five-kilometre course runs from Old Billingsgate to the Mall, ending underneath the Flora London Marathon gantry. Find out how to qualify for the team to represent your borough or region by going online at www.minimarathon.co.uk. Local running clubs also operate similar events, such as the hotly contested Minithons and Time Trials organised by the Poole Runners in Dorset (www.poolerunners.com).

20-24 *Watch Punch and Judy squabble*

Seaside resorts just wouldn't be the same without donkey rides and a riotous Punch and Judy show on the sands, bemoan those of a certain generation. And they're right. While this dwindling seaside tradition might no longer be a guaranteed attraction along our shores (with only around a dozen resorts having a resident show), some traditions die hard. Despite the PC brigade's complaints about Punch and Judy's undoubtedly violent tendencies, children still relish the simple slapstick. The Codman family has run a Punch and Judy pitch at Llandudno Pier (Promenade, Llandudno, Conwy LL30 2LP, www.visitconwy.org.uk) since 1860, when 'Professor' Bert Codman ran the show. Nowadays it's his great-granddaughter who orchestrates the time-honoured anarchy, using puppets carved from local driftwood. Alternatively, there are Punch and Judy booths to be found on Clacton Beach (01473 831365), Exmouth Sands (01626 891328), Weymouth and Paignton (01803 529737, www.poulton puppets.co.uk), among others; or you can check www.punchandjudy.org for details. Altogether now: 'He's behi-i-ind you!'

25 *Sit in the Devil's Chair*

Towering over Shropshire's wild and eerie Stiperstone hills is an ancient rocky outcrop known as the Devil's Chair (www.shropshire tourism.co.uk). Legend has it, the devil was travelling across the county with a weighty apronful of rocks, when he stopped here for a breather. The apron strings snapped and out tumbled the stones, leaving them strewn across the ridge. Head up there to see for yourself and admire the views – though not on foggy days, when the route can be treacherous, and it's said the Prince of Darkness returns to his throne with a coven of cackling witches. In hot weather, meanwhile, locals swear the rocks smell of brimstone.

26 *Get ye to the workhouse*

Until the Welfare State was established in 1948, families who couldn't support themselves had only one choice – to live and work in the workhouse. The market town of Southwell, in Nottinghamshire, has the best surviving example of such an institution: an imposing, red-brick building, erected in 1824 and in its day considered a model of its kind. Today it's maintained by the National Trust as a tourist attraction, though it's a funny sort of attraction. Its very bareness, and the worn floors of the austere dormitory, speak volumes of the privation endured by its many inhabitants, about half of whom were children.

Slice-of-life audio-guide commentaries from supposed inhabitants really help you get a feel for the bleakness of the daily grind, when three meals of bread, gruel and thin soup were all residents had to look forward to during days filled with hard work and humiliation. There are also interactive displays charting the spread of 19th-century poverty, and a game based around the punishments meted out by the master of the workhouse to its inhabitants. It's a chilling, revealing trip.

The Workhouse *Upton Road, Southwell, Nottinghamshire NG25 0PT (01636 817250/ www.nationaltrust.org.uk).*

27-33 *Be a Harry Potter spotter*

Once upon a time there was a boy called Harry Potter, who also happened to be a junior wizard at a magical boarding school called Hogwarts. When the great and the good heard about him they decided to make six or more films of his life, so they hunted around for suitable movie locations all over Britain. It has become a popular holiday pastime with Harry's friends to visit these places too.

For Hogwarts, the film-makers chose the 600-year-old cloisters at Gloucester Cathedral (2 College Green, Gloucester GL1 2LR, 01452 528095, www.gloucester cathedral.org.uk), where the original monks would meditate and write. On the left of the North Walk is the lavatorium, where Harry and Ron hid behind a pillar from a computer-generated troll. The red door in the north-east corner is Hogwarts' Dark Entry, through which gushed the flood from the girls' toilets. In fact, it was pumped from a lorry into a huge plastic container, held in place by extra-strong tape – bits of which are still stuck to the ground. In the film, the door in the West Walk leads to the Gryffindor Common Room – it actually leads down a flight of steps. Of much less interest, obviously, is the 1,000-year-old Norman cathedral itself, with its stained-glass windows, fan-vaulting, misericords and the tomb of King Edward II, who was assassinated nearby in the nastiest way possible.

Other Hogwarts scenes were filmed at Alnwick Castle, 640 kilometres away (Alnwick, Northumberland NE66 1NQ, 01665 510777, www.alnwickcastle.com). The outer bailey was where the practice games of quidditch were played and Harry first learnt to pilot a broomstick, while the inner bailey was where Ron crash-landed his flying car. The castle is the home of the Percy family. The castle also has a Knights' School and holds a Country Fair with ducking stools, bumper cars and stocks.

For Hogwarts' classrooms, the film company favoured Lacock Abbey near Bath (Lacock, Chippenham, Wiltshire SN15 2LG, 01249 730227, www.nationaltrust.co.uk). Although it has kept its religious name, the Abbey has been a country house since 1540, and a National Trust property since the 1940s – so filming a story about sorcery here wasn't as controversial as the filming at Gloucester Cathedral. Three Gothic chambers off the abbey's 14th-century cloisters were used.

The steam-engine that the students take at the beginning and end of term is the Jacobite Steam Train (01524 737751, www.steamtrain.info). It was built in 1937 and apart from accepting occasional roles in films, still runs every day during the summer holidays from Fort William to Mallaig in Scotland. The film company changed its name to the Hogwarts Express and painted it cherry red for the films – it spent hours in make-up, darling. On its daily journey in July and August, it crosses the 21 arches of the Glenfinnan Viaduct 25 kilometres west of Fort William just as it does in the film. Thomas the Tank Engine is still jealous.

London also stars in the movies. The scene in which Harry discovers he can talk to snakes was shot in London Zoo's reptile house (Regent's Park, London NW1 4RY, 020 7722 3333, www.londonzoo.co.uk). On Fridays visitors can take part in the feeding (if not the conversations) that the snakes hold in their chat room.

Harry and his schoolfriends also famously catch the Hogwarts Express from platform 9¾ at London's King's Cross Station. It really exists, and there's a sign and part of a luggage trolley on platform 4. Somehow the film company got its cameras through, but it's not advisable to try.

The school station is at Hogsmeade, which is actually the unspoilt village of Goathland on the North Yorkshire Moors. It looks pretty much as it appeared on screen – the view of Hogwarts school in the background was computer-generated.

Harry Potter lives with the Dursleys in the town of Little Whinging, Surrey. The dubious honour of representing that settlement went to the real town of Martins Heron near Bracknell in Berkshire. The Dursleys' house at 4 Privet Drive is not identified among the rows of boring, identical semis.

34 Flip a pancake

You need:

110g flour
pinch of salt
2 eggs
200ml milk mixed with 75ml water
2tbsp butter (melted)

Put the flour and water into a mixing bowl, make a little hole in the middle, and drop in the eggs. Then start whisking, slowly drawing in the flour from the sides, until it has a thin, creamy consistency. Once that's done, heat your pan, pour in the melted butter and make sure the entire pan bottom is covered, then pour in a ladleful of batter. When you see bubbles form, flip! How high can you go without a grown-up shouting? As you know, pancakes can be eaten with almost anything. The classic accompaniment is lemon juice and sugar; we love chopped nuts, chocolate spread and bananas, or you can make them into a square meal by using savoury fillings.

Donkey Sanctuary

35 Earn your Lego driving licence

Get up early to hit Legoland before the queues – although, as the park fills up, you can't avoid waiting ages for your turn on the popular rides. One such is the delightful Driving School, which many children become quite obsessed with. First, the kids watch a safety video, learning how to control the cars and absorbing the rules of the road. Then they are unleashed on the electric cars, amid roundabouts, traffic lights and much confusion. Some drivers favour going round and round the roundabouts in dizzying circles, while others spend their time immobilised after a crash, or seized with uncertainty at the traffic lights. When the horn sounds it's all over, and they receive their Legoland driving licence. It's strictly for six to 13s, so bring photo ID to avoid tears; there's also a less demanding scaled-down version for three- to five-year-olds.

Legoland Windsor *Winkfield Road, Windsor, Berkshire SL4 4AY (0871 222 2001/ www.legoland.co.uk).*

36 Meet Eeyore and friends

Sidmouth in east Devon is donkey heaven, with more than 400 asses in residence at its Donkey Sanctuary. This five-star seaside retirement home is for animals who have worked hard all their lives, and need a rest from being beach donkeys and general beasts of burden. The sanctuary also works as a rescue centre, and has taken in more than 13,000 animals since it opened in 1969. Meet some of the residents wandering around in the main yard – they love to be hugged and patted by visitors. In the paddocks you'll see donkeys of all ages, colours, shapes and sizes, from pint-sized miniature donkeys and foals to elderly jennies. During the school holidays, children can join staff in the Hayloft paddock to help groom and walk the donkeys. The Sanctuary is open 365 days a year from nine until dusk, with free entry and parking; donations are welcome.

Donkey Sanctuary *Sidmouth, Devon EX10 0NU (01395 578222/www.thedonkeysanctuary.org.uk).*

37 Gaze at lazing lizards

Lizard hunting requires patience and stealth – and one of the best spots to do it is Branksome Dene Chine in Dorset (www.poole.gov.uk). When the sun shines, warming the concrete steps and paths, rare sand lizards slither out to soak up the heat, favouring the beach huts away from the promenade. Creep carefully, stay quiet and you'll be rewarded by the sight of *Lacerta agilis*, a shy, fast-moving creature that's now endangered. In the car park, there's a useful guide to help identify lizards and other wildlife.

38 Climb a turbine

Set in organically managed grounds, the crowning glory at Norfolk's Ecotech Centre is its 97-metre wind turbine. After super-charging your energy levels with a slice of homemade cake in the Orchard Café, take a guided tour of the viewing platform – 305 steps up a narrow spiral staircase. Once you've made it to the top, see if you can spot the distant dot of Ely Cathedral, 42 kilometres away. Tours run on weekdays, and are open to anyone aged over seven and at least 1.2 metres tall.
Ecotech Centre *Turbine Way, Swaffham, Norfolk PE37 7HT (01760 726100/www.ecotech.org.uk).*

39 Plant a family tree

The Woodland Trust (www.woodland-trust. org.uk) is gradually greening up everyone's neighbourhood. Established in 1972, it has planted over 4.5 million trees, and created 3,200 hectares of new native woodland. There's plenty a family can do to help the Trust in its mission. You can plant a tree together by joining in one of the events listed on its website – or, if you have a little patch of land to call your own, buy one of the many native saplings sold by the Trust, follow its instructions on how to give it the best start in life, then watch your investment grow.

Ecotech Centre

40 Set up camp at Eden

During the summer hols the Eden Project comes alive with families competing in the Den Challenge. It's part of Eden's 'Mud Between Your Toes' programme, designed to get children playing outside. Eden provides everything you need to design and build your family fortress, and a gang of expert den-builders to help. Before long, fabulous dens emerge from old sails, inner tubes, bamboo, sheets, poles, rope, rugs, clothes-horses, scraps of fabric and washing lines. Keen survival experts can learn about knot-tying and making a fire without matches, and there's a magical base camp to explore and be inspired by. Throughout August, a granite-walled fire pit serves campfire grub to get families in the outdoor mood. Eden has the biggest greenhouses in the world: the Rainforest Biome and Mediterranean Biome, which are well worth a visit during your den building.
Eden Project *Bodelva, Cornwall PL24 2SG (01726 811911/www.edenproject.com).*

41

Take the Angel bus

The Angel of the North is one of Britain's most dramatic, daring landmarks – 200 tonnes of steel, silhouetted against the sky at the head of Team Valley. The sculpture was designed by Antony Gormley and erected in 1998 on a hilltop overlooking the A1. Though most people simply speed past, we recommend taking a closer, more contemplative look: catch the Angel bus (Go North East services 21 & 22) from Eldon Square bus station in Newcastle or Gateshead Interchange (www.simplygo.com) and stand at its feet, gazing skywards.

42

Make your own liquorice laces...

You either like liquorice, or you loathe it – but if it's the former, you can mix up a batch of your own. Natural and additive-free, it's made from molasses, powdered liquorice and anise roots – available from good herbalists such as G Baldwin & Co (020 7703 5550, www.baldwins.co.uk). Take one cup of molasses, warm it, then add one teaspoon each of the liquorice and anise powders. Mix with some flour to make a dough that you can roll out, then roll into thin tubes. Cut the tubes into the lengths you want and dust them with icing sugar – or leave them bare. The liquorice hardens as it cools. Don't eat too much of the finished product, as it's mildly laxative.

Liquorice Festival

43

...or eat your fill at the festival

Pontefract, home of the Pontefract cake and Bertie Bassett's Liquorice Allsorts, celebrates the town's proud history every year in mid July at the Liquorice Festival (0845 6018353, www.pontefractliquorice.co.uk). Expect street theatre, hands-on craft activities, all kinds of weird ands wonderful characters made from the lovely black stuff – the Dalek (pictured) caused quite a stir – historic re-enactments, trails, tours and story-telling; all sorts, in fact.

44-48 *Find out where your food comes from*

The farmer's lot – all those animals, tractors, open spaces and lashings of mud – often appeals to children (especially those who've never had to get up at 5am for milking). There are any number of farm-related theme parks across the land, but to see day-to-day agriculture in action you need to pull on your wellies and head for a working farm.

In Paignton, South Devon, Occombe Farm (01803 520022, www.occombe.org.uk) is an 60-hectare organic open farm that aims to reconnect visitors with food, farming and the countryside. Family-friendly events run throughout the year, from letterboxing trails to Meet the Farmer sessions, when kids can help feed the livestock and collect the chickens' still-warm eggs. There are vintage tractors to be climbed upon and the farm shop is full of local produce, including meat, eggs and home-cured bacon.

Another Devonshire operation is Riverford Farm, near Buckfastleigh (0845 600 2311, www.riverford.co.uk). Regular farm tours are followed by lunch in the Field Kitchen. School holiday Pick & Cook Days encourage kids to learn to love their veg by harvesting their own cabbage and kohlrabi. 'Taking them into the fields, touching stuff and getting involved makes them much more open to trying things,' says Rachel Watson, whose family owns the farm. The fruit and veg are taken back to the Field Kitchen, where the children cook it under the supervision of chef Russell Goodwin before sitting down to eat. 'Children enjoy food more if they understand how it's produced,' says Rachel. 'It's that final connection from the field to the plate.' Pick & Cook days cost £24 per child, and are open to seven- to 16-year-olds. Check online for dates and seasonal events such as Pumpkin Day.

In the heart of the countryside north of Peterborough is Sacrewell Farm (01780 782254, www.sacrewell.org.uk), which offers tractor rides and day-to-day farming activities, along with a campsite and 18th-

Riverford Farm

century watermill. In spring, you can stroke the chicks and help feed the young calves, or watch lambs race full-pelt in the Lamb National. Sacrewell charges admission.

Stockley Farm, on the Arley Estate in Cheshire (01565 777323, www.stockley farm.co.uk) is a working organic farm, open most weekends and throughout the school holidays. As well as taking a tractor ride, meeting the farm animals and bottle-feeding the lambs, you can watch the farm's 200 cows being milked, then buy a pint in the shop. You can even have a party here.

Farmers Julian and Rose Harris offer children the opportunity to be real farmers at Warleigh Lodge Farm in Bathford, Somerset (01225 859 065). 'They're not coming here to pet the animals, they're here to look after them, come rain or shine,' says Julian. 'They bed up the piglets and feed the chickens, and the older children help clean out the pigs. In winter, I take them out on the trailer to throw root crops to the cattle. It's a totally unique experience for them.'

49 *Get beading!*

Set in London's Covent Garden, the Bead Shop is irresistible to magpie-eyed children, who love sifting through the trays of beads. You take a little plastic container and work your way around the trays of treasure. There are more than 5,000 different beads in stock, and an afternoon can fly by as you're dawdling over the chunky wooden spheres, shiny bugle beads and glowing glass baubles (though the indecisive can always plump for a mixed bag or the kids' kit). You're always surprised by the amount you've spent when your haul is totted up at the till. Staff are happy to advise, and there are free instruction sheets on how to create your own beaded beauties. Pocket-money-friendly prices start at 2p a bead – though a ginormous Swarovski crystal will set you back around a tenner. If London's too far away, check out the princely array of beads on the website: they're available by mail order.

Bead Shop *21A Tower Street, London WC2H 9NS (020 7240 0931/www.beadworks.co.uk).*

50

Sleep with the dead

Besides its ancient war booty and priceless holiday souvenirs, the British Museum has a large number of 5,000-year-old dead people, mostly in the Egyptology department. Some of them are cursed. Just the place to spend the night, then – which you can do on four weekends a year, provided you join the British Museum Young Friends first. (Joining costs £20 for a year, then a place on the sleepover is £27.50.) After arriving at 6pm on the Saturday, you spend the evening exploring the museum and doing themed activities until you feel weary enough for a long, undisturbed sleep. Then, at midnight, you get in your sleeping bag and pull the cord tight. The lights go out. What's that creaking sound? If you make it through to dawn, breakfast is provided. Bring your own mummy, guardian or carer.

British Museum *Great Russell Street, London WC1B 3DG (020 7323 8000/ www.britishmuseum.org).*

51 Spot eagles and jellyfish in Calgary

As beautiful as it is remote, the Isle of Mull's Calgary Bay (www.calgarybay.co.uk) is a half-kilometre stretch of dazzling white-gold sand – without an ice-cream kiosk in sight. Bring your own picnic and wetsuits (even in high summer, the water rarely reaches even a chilly 14°C), then set off on a shell-collecting, jellyfish-spotting expedition. There's bonus points for anyone who glimpses a white-tailed sea eagle – the biggest and rarest bird of prey in the UK, with a wingspan of up to 2.4 metres. Look out for its pale head and the flash of its white tail feathers – and count yourself lucky you're too big to be swooped up in its talons.

52 Join the Woodcraft Folk

Established in 1925, the Woodcraft Folk (www.woodcraft.org.uk) is a voluntary organisation working with young people. It has been called 'Brownies for socialists', with no uniform, no salutes or and no swearing of allegiance to any religious or political body. Kids might experience bat-watching, camping trips and stimulating discussion about world peace or gender equality. Hiking, hostelling and summertime camping are a big part of the picture. All ages are catered for, from Woodchips (under-sixes) to Venturers (13-16s). There are about 500 groups around the UK.

53 See doves nesting

Take a look at the 14th-century Kinwarton Dovecote in Warwickshire. Standing just north of the Saxon parish church, it's a curious-looking circular structure, with walls over a metre thick. Inside, through the tiny door, you'll find row upon row of snug nesting boxes; more than 500 in all. Many are still occupied by doves – and the odd pigeon.
Kinwarton Dovecote *Kinwarton, near Alcester, Warwickshire B49 6HB (01789 400777/ www.nationaltrust.org.uk).*

54 Exercise your facial muscles after dinner

After a dinner party, grown-ups are horribly prone to sitting round the table for hours, wittering on over wine. Children are advised to appropriate the nearest box of After Eight mints, and play this game (allowing any grown-up who's not averse to getting a chocolately face to join in). The rules are simple.

All players take an After Eight or any square-shaped thin chocolate mint, and place it on their forehead. Using only your facial muscles, make it move down to your mouth, then eat it with maximum lip-smacking. The winner in the face race gets another After Eight. Continue until someone tells you off.

55 Guess the age of the shell grotto

Margate's most mysterious attraction is its shell grotto – a subterranean chamber, covered with intricate mosaics made from more than 4.5 million carefully glued-on shells. It was discovered by a local man, James Newlove – or, more accurately, his son, Joshua – while digging a duck pond in 1835. Newlove lowered Joshua into the hole that opened up, and the lad emerged with wild stories of tunnels covered in shells. The Shell Grotto became a local attraction, and as such has puzzled visitors ever since. Is it a pagan temple, a Regency folly or a secret underground meeting place? Some people believe that the grotto was a sun temple, because the sun enters the dome (which extends up to ground level, with a small circular opening) to form a dramatic alignment at midday on the summer solstice. Even its age remains a mystery, as the soot from the oil lamps that lit it in Victorian times means it can't be carbon-dated. Shells' bells.
Shell Grotto *Grotto Hill, Margate, Kent CT9 2BU (01843 220008/www.shellgrotto.co.uk).*

56 *Go crabbing...*

The North Norfolk coast offers rich pickings for crustacean-hunters, with an abundance of edible brown crabs. Fishing them out of the ocean from the quayside at high tide is a time-honoured pursuit, with the best hauls found at Wells-next-the-Sea and Blakeney.

First, you need to invest in some equipment: a crab line, a decent-sized bucket to contain your catch (half-fill it with seawater for the crabs to splash in), and a landing net to scoop up the crustaceans, so they can't drop off your line as you're hauling them up. Next, choose your bait. For minimum outlay, ask for bacon off-cuts at a butcher's: Arthur Howell's (01328 710228) at 53 Staithe Street in Wells, for instance.

Find a space, lower your line, then wait for the fun to start. Take care not to get too close to the edge in the thrill of the chase, though: the water is deep, and the currents are strong. Once your catch has been gawped at by passing tourists, gently tip out the bucket and allow the crabs to scuttle back into the sea.

57 *...then compete in the Crabbing Championship at Walberswick*

Every August, the riverbanks in the pretty Suffolk village of Walberswick are taken over by would-be crabbing champions, angling to win the gold medal and £50 cash prize. Armed with a single line and their bait of choice, competitors have 90 minutes to lure and land the heftiest crab. Entry costs a pound, proceeds go to charity (www.explorewalberswick.co.uk).

58 *Play inside a flower*

Grown-ups may wax lyrical about the landscaping at Kew Gardens, but children love Climbers & Creepers, the indoor and outdoor adventure playground, where they can climb right inside a big purple flower, through a blackberry tangle and dig for 'fossilised' plants. It's gardening, but not as you know it.

Royal Botanic Gardens, Kew *Richmond, Surrey TW9 3AB (020 8332 5655/www.kew.org).*

Climbers & Creepers, Kew

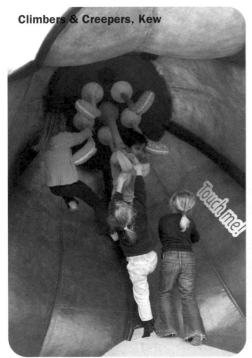

Science
boffins

*Rick Jones **uncovers the mystery of Mentos with an enthusiastic boffin
and a few GCSE chemistry hopefuls.***

Although most parents experience great joy if their children show interest in any subject, it is when the desire for science manifests itself that they really get excited. They know how rare a thing it is, how sought after scientists are and, unless it turns out to be archaeology, how lucrative a career it might lead to.

The creation of explosions is the traditional hook. One scientist who is happy to explain how to set off a few reactions is the white-coated David Hammerson, whose 'lab' is in a secret cave in hills on the end of the Northern tube line outside London. It is disappointing that his lair contains no line of gurgling test-tubes or steaming bell jars, and although there is a body in the corner, it is only Hammerson's secretary. She's busy fielding calls from parents wishing to book the services of one of the 21 Science Boffins whom Hammerson has successfully cloned and stationed in towns from Portsmouth to Edinburgh, ready to be activated and sent to children's parties as science entertainers at a moment's notice.

'The difference between us and magicians,' says Hammerson, preparing to ignite a piece of nitro-cellulose with a kitchen lighter, 'is that we say how we do it. Magicians keep everything a secret. We explain the explosions. And we don't do tricks, we do experiments. This one's called Flash Paper.'

'Wow!' say the three GCSE science students, who have been persuaded to give up a day of their half-term to be guinea pigs for the prospective master of the universe. They are wearing special Day-Glo, defraction-grating goggles. These multiply and sustain the effect when the cellulose, which, as Hammerson explains, has been dipped in nitro-glycerine, bursts into a fireball, floats briefly towards the ceiling and then disappears so completely that not even a speck of ash remains.

'It's amazing how many kids think I've got it up my sleeve,' says Hammerson, now sliding his hand down a thin strip of plastic attached to a polystyrene beaker, which amplifies the noise made as his thumb catches on a series of

notches. An eerie voice croaks out, 'science is fun', although it takes some prompting before anyone can decipher it. Hammerson reveals this to be the principle of the old-fashioned record-player, with a light needle rubbing against the fine grooves of a fast-spinning disc. This is one that anyone could make, and I manage to manufacture a version when I get home – although I cannot get it to say anything but 'have a banana'.

Outside on Hammerson's concrete rocket launch pad, which has been cleverly disguised as a car park, the fiendish scientist prepares to demonstrate how spectacularly volatile the reaction is when an entire packet of Mentos mints (45p from corner shops) is emptied into a two-litre bottle of Diet Coke (£1.67, according to the label). 'Diet Coke is better than non-Diet, and the sooner you can get the mints into the bottle after opening it, the more violent the reaction,' enthuses Hammerson.

His mints are in a plastic see-through tubular dispenser fixed to the opening of the Coke bottle. Such a device is obtainable through the internet, but the experiment is not impossible without one. A red stopper like a grenade pin is

attached to a piece of cord, which one of the guinea pigs pulls so that ten sweets plunge like depth charges into a sea of fizzy drink. Two seconds later – ay caramba! – a nine-metre, khaki-brown fountain shoots into the sky. Apparently it's to do with nucleation, by which process brainier scientists have been able to create artificial rainfall and fog. The full explanation passes me by, however, as I have to rescue one of the guinea pigs. He's being held down by his companions as they prepare to funnel more Mentos into his open mouth, after he has swallowed a beakerful of Coke.

Fortunately, they abandon this in favour of the ping-pong pipes, to see who can keep a ball in the air the longest. Hammerson says this is the principle of flight: when one current of air is faster than another, as happens over and under the curve of an aeroplane wing, pressure is reduced and you have lift. But the GCSE candidates know this already and their attention drifts to the Balloon Kebabs. 'Twist and push,' Hammerson instructs, as the youths attempt to impale inflated balloons on to wooden skewers without bursting them. 'Latex has molecular memory,' says Hammerson instructively. I am not sure I understand. Still, the experiment looks good – success is possible, provided the skewer is pushed through near the nipple and out through the top.

Out in the Atlantic, Hammerson almost certainly has a submarine waiting as he is suspiciously well informed on how such vessels work. He demonstrates this with 'Squiddy', who rises and falls in a plastic bottle of water, apparently at Hammerson's command. Squiddy's head is full of air, which is compressed when Hammerson squeezes the bottle – and according to one of the more useful scientific principles, compressed air sinks. 'Fish know all about it,' says Hammerson, as if he has asked them. 'They have a swim-bladder, which does the same job.'

But the GCSE boys are acting as if they know this too. In their heads, they have already constructed their own submarine, with nuclear warheads in the shape of Coke bottles aimed at all the capitals of the world. Hammerson's experiments have fired their imaginations – and mine too. Later on, in the bath, I am trying to work out how a plastic duck might be adapted to carry tanks of compressed air underwater from tap end to my end. Try it at home, kids.

60-66 *Get up a head of steam*

Bluebell Railway

The romance of the steam era lives on in Sussex, where the Bluebell railway line puffs through the countryide for 14 kilometres. There are Santa Specials every Christmas for younger fans, who couldn't care less about the stunning 1920s Sussex Belle Pullman (which serves old-fashioned cream teas) and just want Thomas and his friends.

Sheffield Park Station, East Sussex TN22 3QL (01825 720825/www.bluebell-railway.co.uk).

Ffestiniog & Welsh Highland Railways

Ffestiniog & Welsh Highland Railways is currently reinstating the railway link between Caernarfon and Porthmadog, so passengers can travel from Caernarfon through to Blaenau Ffestiniog: 64 kilometres of narrow-gauge steam (check the website to see if the work has been completed). Halloween specials include the Ghostly Train from Porthmadog to spooky Tan-y-Bwlch station in the woods; Santa Trains run at Christmas.

Harbour Station, Porthmadog, Gwynedd LL49 9NF (01766 516000/www.festrail.co.uk).

Gloucestershire Warwickshire Railway

Looking like a historic train set with its dinky tea rooms and shiny engines, the 16-kilometre line between Toddington and Cheltenham Racecourse is a delight. There are Thomas the Tank Engine events, fish and chips evenings and Cheltenham race-meeting specials.

Railway Station, Toddington, Gloucestershire GL54 5DT (01242 621405/www.gwsr.com).

Keighley & Worth Valley Railway

This eight-kilometre run visits Haworth (home of the Brontë sisters) and Oakworth (the setting for the 1970s adaptation of *The Railway Children*). Hop on board at any one of six stations from Oxenhope to Keighley, where the line connects with the national rail network. On summer Vintage Train days, cream teas are served in the Old Gentlemen's Saloon Car.

Haworth, Keighley, West Yorkshire BD22 8NJ (01535 645214/ www.kwvr.co.uk).

South Devon Railway

Dating from 1872, the South Devon Railway runs from Buckfastleigh to just outside Totnes.

The Station, Dart Bridge Road, Buckfastleigh, South Devon TQ11 0DZ (0845 345 1420/www.southdevonrailway.org).

Talyllyn Railway

Take to the tracks on this 11-kilometre stretch of historic narrow-gauge railway, running from Tywyn Wharf to Nant Gwernol. There are Duncan Days for Thomas the Tank Engine fans, plus Santa Specials.

Wharf Station, Tywyn, Gwynedd LL36 9EY (01654 710472/www.talyllyn.co.uk).

Watercress Railway

A 'Day out with Thomas' on the Watercress Railway is a must for fans of the little blue tank engine. It includes all-day travel on steam-hauled trains such as Henry, as well as rides on Thomas, Diesel and Toad and brake-van rides by Percy at Alresford.

New Alresford, Hampshire SO24 9JG (01962 733810/www.watercressline.co.uk).

67

Learn to play on a piece of junk

Freelance composer Michael Freeman's junk music workshops tick many boxes. First, there's the fun of making music and learning about sound, then there's the arty-crafty activity of making the instruments. Finally, there's a message about recycling and looking after the environment as the band plays on their rubbish orchestra.

Junk music performances and workshops are popular half-term attractions in museums around the country, or Freeman can be hired for pre-school groups, youth clubs and parties. For more information, call 01434 618842 or 07903 173615.

68 *Support wolves*

Especially if they've been rescued from a fur farm in eastern Europe, as were two of the 14-strong pack in Kent's Wildwood. This wildlife park aims to show visitors the animals that used to live in the woodlands of Britain before we hunted them to extinction. There are wild boar, lynx and beavers too, but it's the wolves that have the glamour. Only 350 years ago they were wandering around the Kent countryside and scaring little girls in red hoodies, but now they must be safely confined in Wildwood's enclosures. Half-term here often brings a wolf special, when children are encouraged to find out how wolves communicate, using faces, tails, posture and granny's clothing.

Wildwood's main lupine mission is, however, to reintroduce wolves to the wilder parts of Britain. They wouldn't last long in built-up Kent, but in Scotland wolves would help keep the marauding deer down. Not sure what it would do to the tourist footprint, however.
Wildwood Wildlife Park *Herne Common, Herne Bay, Kent CT6 7LQ (01227 712 111/ www.wildwoodtrust.org).*

69

Encourage butterflies to flutter by

The cold wet summers Britain has been enduring in recent years have made life very difficult for butterflies. Try to improve their lot by growing the shrubs and flowers they love. Top of the list comes buddleia, which grows like stink and is a magnet for butterflies on hot days. It flourishes almost everywhere, so you can dig up a seedling from any patch of waste ground; for a picture, check out the RSPB's wildlife garden guide at www.rspb.org.uk. Smaller butterfly-friendly plants, which can grow in pots on window sills and balconies, if you don't have a garden, include wallflowers (often available as bunches of seedlings from flower stalls in early spring), honesty (easily grown from seed) and michaelmas daisies (you only need buy one plant from a garden centre, as it spreads like wildfire).

Wildwood Wildlife Park

A few of my favourite things

70-75

Michael Morpurgo, writer

My children are grown up, so most of the activities we do are with the grandchildren. We usually take them out in London, Devon or in the Scilly Isles. I'll tell you about London first. One of our favourite things is a walk on the north bank of the Thames all the way from Putney Bridge past Fulham's football ground to Hammersmith Bridge. We go over the bridge, turn left and walk to the London Wetland Centre (Queen Elizabeth's Walk, London SW13 9WT, 020 8409 4400, www.wwt.org.uk/london), which is lovely to explore all the way through. When we've spent some time there, it's grandpa's choice, which is a drink in a pub nearby (child-tolerant pubs with outdoor seating in Barnes include the Red Lion, 2 Castelnau, SW13 9RU, 020 8748 2984, the Sun Inn, 7 Church Road, SW13 9HE, 020 8876 5256, and Ye White Hart, The Terrace, Riverside, SW13 0NR, 020 8876 5177). **Alternatively, we'll head to the Fulham Palace & Museum (Bishop's Avenue, London SW6 6EA, 020 7736 8140, www.fulhampalace.org) near Putney Bridge. It's a Tudor house that used to be the official residence of the Bishops of London; it's like a mini Hampton Court. The café is a good spot for a cup of tea or coffee. It's always busy with families, and** the children can run around and play in the grounds. Summertime is wonderful as you can sit out on the terrace and watch the children race around. It's a treat to have Sunday lunch there – they do a good sausage and mash. That's about it for London, although we often come up to go to the theatre.

My next thing is on the Scilly Isles (www.simplyscilly.co.uk). We love to take the children to an island called Samson (the largest uninhabited island). I have a little boat, so we chug across in that. It's just like a Famous Five adventure. We like to have barbecues there. I'm always in charge of the cooking because I'm very macho with barbecues. Sometimes we share the beach with other people, but often the island is deserted. Samson has a ghostly history too; it's full of abandoned cottages, which the kids like to count. You get fabulous views from the topmost cottage. **Another thing we love to do in the Scillies is collect shells, particularly looking out for cories, known as guinea money. They're hard to spot, so it's wonderful to find them. We also love sailing and generally messing about with our boats around all the islands.** Here in Devon, our favourite walk is Lydford Gorge, a spectacular deep valley with waterfalls the like of which you wouldn't expect to see in England. It's precarious enough a walk to interest the grandchildren – it takes about one and a half hours and has loads to occupy the walker, such as streams to poke about in. **On rainy days when the children have to stay indoors, one of their favourite activities is sitting down with their granny and knitting blanket squares. I can't see the attraction myself, but the children love it and sit for hours. How on earth they can do that and watch *The Lord of the Rings* DVD at the same time is beyond me. Cooking is another favourite rainy day activity; the children love to make pancakes and what not with granny.**

76 *Visit Mr Morpurgo's farms*

As well as entertaining his own grandchildren, Michael Morpurgo and his wife run a charity that creates the opportunity for 1,000 inner-city schoolchildren to stay, and work, on a farm every year. There are now three Farms for City Children in Britain (Nethercott Farm near Dartmoor in Devon, Treginnis Isaf on the Pembrokeshire coast in Wales and Wick Court in Gloucestershire). Outside term time, the farm properties are let to holiday makers and there's an annual open day for public visiting. For details, contact www.farmsforcitychildren.org.

77 Memorise the Periodic Table

The songwriter Tom Lehrer provides an excellent list of the elements in his song 'The Elements', rhyming germanium with uranium, rhenium and selenium and so on. Unfortunately, his song doesn't include the chemical symbols, so you'll have to learn those separately. They'll come in handy for solving cryptic crosswords: 'Au' is gold, for instance, 'Ag' silver, and 'Fe' iron. Thus 'Iron alien smells of cheese (4)'. The answer? 'Feet', of course.

78 Make your own pasta and build up some muscle

You don't need a machine to make your own pasta – but you do need to knead like crazy. Take 600g of flour and half a dozen eggs. Place the flour in a bowl, make a well in it, and add the eggs. Take a fork and mix them all together, then use clean fingers to mix it a bit more, rubbing the flour and eggs between your fingers until it's all bound together in a big doughy ball. Then knead and knead until your arms ache. Once the dough is smooth, cover it with clingfilm and put it in the fridge for an hour or so. Next, roll out the dough on a floury surface until it's as thin as card. Cut the pasta sheets to the shape you want (try tagliatelle or stracci – ragged ribbons) and cook for about three minutes in boiling water.

79 Buy a lorikeet a drink

There may be lions and tigers and bears at Woburn Safari Park, but for us, the most enchanting experience is Rainbow Landing. This is an indoor aviary where you can spend 60p on a little cup of nectar, then enjoy the exquisite sensation of having a colourful lorikeet perch on your hand to drink it with his brush-tipped tongue. The simplest pleasures are often the best.
Woburn Safari Park *Woburn Park, Bedfordshire MK17 9QN (01525 290407/ www.woburnsafari.co.uk).*

80 Follow the teddy bear trail

The Polka Theatre, in Wimbledon, south London, is a favourite destination for families. They don't come just to see a show, however. The friendly folk at Polka are also happy to welcome children to their café, playground (indoors and out) and teddy bear collection. To follow the Polka Teddy Bear trail, pay a suggested £1 donation, pick up your leaflet, then meet the bears, taking in ted celebs such as Rupert, Fozzie, Nookie and that funny knitted bear beloved of one Mr Bean. Seen them all? Then repair to the café for some cocoa and an iced bun, just like You Know Who.

81 Sit on a white horse

The white horse of Uffington is no ordinary steed. Galloping across the Berkshire Downs and measuring 114 metres from nose to tail, its dramatic, chalk-filled outline has been a local landmark since the Bronze Age. At close range it's hard to make sense of the sweeping white chalk lines, so climb flat-topped Dragon Hill or drive a little further away to appreciate its undulating curves (OS grid ref SU301866). There are more white horses on the hills of Wiltshire, but they're much later additions to the landscape, having been carved in the 18th and 19th centuries.

82 Make it snow

To make realistic-looking snow for Christmas modelling, all you need is soap flakes and water. Use two mugs full of soap flakes to half a cup of water, then whisk them together with an electric mixer until the gloop is as thick as whipped cream. Add more soap or water until the consistency is right, then leave the mixture overnight before modelling it into balls for snowmen or using it to give cardboard a frosty finish. It dries out once shaped, and lasts for several weeks.

Special branch

Nuala Calvi **and friends build a des res in the woods.**

'Sign your child's life away here, please,' a jovial woman named Jackie tells the haggard half-term mums and dads. They sign the waivers with a grateful look, give their little darlings a pat and rush off to the forest café.

The faces of 15 tweenies – deprived of televisions, mobile phones and iPods – gaze up at us. These under-12s have been returned to nature for the afternoon, and my partner and I are going with them. 'It's better if the parents don't come,' Jackie tells me. 'Otherwise, you get the precious mummies saying, "Oh don't do that, dear, you'll have to wash your hands now".' There will be no point trying to keep hands clean today: the assigned task is den-building, and in less than two hours we must build a shack that could see us through an unscheduled night in the forest.

The session is one of a huge range of holiday-time activities at Alice Holt Forest in Surrey (about six kilometres south of Farnham). This morning, Jackie has already been playing Professor Mushroom for a Fun with Fungi

workshop, while our other guide, Louise, has been wriggling like a worm in Animal Antics. Den-building is clearly a favourite, however. When Louise asks the group – mainly boys – whether any has been to the session before, at least five hands go up.

'Today, we'll be judging your dens on four things,' she informs us. 'Safety, stylishness, teamwork – and how waterproof it is. We've ordered rain for 2.30pm, so you've been warned.' There are a few knowing chuckles from the second-timers. 'You lot at the front keep quiet,' she winks, and marshals us into line.

It's a steep walk from the visitors' centre to the beech glade, where we're filled in on the den-building basics. First, we must find a good 'Y tree' (one with a branch sticking out of its side). Next, a large, sturdy log must be found for the 'spine' and positioned with its thin end resting in the 'Y' – and then more logs. 'Put the other logs against your spine log like a dinosaur's tummy, leaning in towards the tree,' Louise instructs us. The analogy is lost on me,

but the kids, split into three groups and assigned different corners of the glade, seem to know what they're doing.

I'm sent to join a group of young, fair-haired boys who've decided to call our gang Stealth. One adventurer has spotted a long, wibbly log for our spine, and the other five set to work carrying it like marching ants. But we've fallen at the first hurdle, as Louise condemns our spine as too wobbly.

I cast a jealous eye over to the boyfriend's team, whose self-styled Hideaway Hollow already has a ribcage, if not a tummy. Louise puts this down to the fact that he's scored the only team with girls in it – Amber and Imogen, who, at 12, take no nonsense. 'Girls are always more organised,' she reassures me. 'You tend to find they have it all planned out in their heads.'

Our group seems to lack a clear leader, but a division of labour has wordlessly occurred; one tiny architect is gurning over his plans, a couple of scavengers are off fetching logs, and two labourers are merrily building.

No one is allowed inside the dens until a Wobbleocity Test has been carried out; a skilful manoeuvre involving Jackie's behind being shoved against the inner walls of each den. We cringe to witness just how many branches could have landed on our co-workers' heads, had her posterior not taken the brunt.

The next stage is thatching, to protect us from the promised rainstorm. Unfortunately, the other two teams have already snapped up most of the bracken. On entering our den, eight-year-old Luke tells me it has 'lots of windows'; a worrying state of affairs.

We're determined to make up ground at the next stage: decoration. To that end, we launch an espionage mission to Hideaway Hollow. Reports come back of compost heaps, fire exits, satellite TV and all manner of domestic innovations. Undeterred, the boys and I install a three-piece suite (one big log and two little ones), a toilet (hole in the ground) and a secret hideaway for weapons (don't ask).

The whistle blows and it's results time. We gather round nervously as Louise marks us out of ten. Wobbleocity: seven – not bad. Teamwork: six and a half, owing to our lack of leadership. Style: a disappointing six – reduced after our 'toilet' caved in. Next it's time for the waterproof test. We huddle in our den while Louise summons the rain clouds (as it turns out, two litre-bottles of tap water, which fall straight through the numerous skylights on to our heads). A five.

At 24.5 points we fare better than the next group, Haunted Hideaway, who score 23.5, despite having a twiggy telescope. An opportunist group member offers to flog the lot for a tenner, to no avail.

Then it's over to the girls' group. A budding estate agent gives us the guided tour. 'Here we have our nice, comfy, padded-leather armchairs and sofa,' he squeaks. 'And next to that, an extra seat for company. Here's the french window on to the garden, overlooked by a majestic tree.' As a final insult, they score 9.5 on the waterproof test and win with 31 points. Beaten by the girls' team! We roll our eyes in disbelief.

But as we march back home singing army songs, rivalries are quickly forgotten. The kids are swapping MySpace addresses and doing what they do best: forming life-long friendships in the space of two hours.

Back at the visitors' centre, the parents are waiting, caffeinated and re-energised, to return their reluctant offspring to the world of Wii and Wi-Fi.

As we stagger home exhausted, Louise and Jackie bounce off to their next session, this time entitled There Be Dragons and involving a search for monsters' feet.

Alice Holt Forest *Bucks Horn Oak, Farnham, Surrey GU10 4LS ((www.forestry.gov.uk/aliceholt).*

84 *Test out your vet skills*

'Veterinary surgeon' scores pretty highly in children's lists of dream jobs, and at this little museum, kids can see if they've got what it takes. It's based in the original surgery of the country's premier celebrity vet, the late James Alfred Wight, aka James Herriot. His stories based on his experiences as a farm vet in Yorkshire (*All Creatures Great & Small, It Shouldn't Happen to a Vet*) became bestsellers and dominated telly screens in the 1970s. Of most interest to children are the interactive games about the role of vets past and present. They can don stethoscopes and test their veterinary mettle by diagnosing, operating on and prescribing for their (thankfully model) patients. Say 'baaaa!'

The World of James Herriot *23 Kirkgate, Thirsk, North Yorkshire YO7 1PL (01845 524234/ www.worldofjamesherriot.org).*

85 *Be a drama queen*

Having recently changed its name from the Scottish International Children's Festival, the Bank of Scotland Imaginate Festival (0131 228 1404, www.imaginate.org.uk) is still the UK's largest performing arts festival specifically for children and young people. It runs for a week at the end of May into the beginning of June, with 14 or 15 companies offering around 100 performances in venues across Edinburgh and the Lothians. Past attractions have included Michael Morpurgo's wonderful adaptation of Aesop's Fables, a pair of Croatian parachutists and, for teenagers, TAG Theatre Company's *Yellow Moon*, a modern Bonnie and Clyde story written by one of Scotland's leading playwrights, David Greig. Certainly, there's something for all ages, from babies through to 18-year-olds – though as most of the baby- and toddler-focused events have an interactive element, parents and carers should be ready to get their groove on too.

Imaginate Festival

Sông Quê Café
Authentic Vietnamese Food

134 Kingsland Road, London E2 8DY
Tel: 020 7613 3222

'Definitely worth a visit and one of my favourite restaurants ever.'
Restaurant-Guide.com

"At this moment, it has to be the best Vietnamese food in London....
Our meals at this new Vietnamese Restaurant have been thrilling & memorable"
Guy Dimond, Time Out
Winner of the Best Cheap Eats category
Time Out Eating & Drinking Awards 2003

Time Out's top 50 places you must eat before you leave London
January 2008

Time Out's 50 Greatest Restraunts 2009
25 Song Que

Eat-in or Takeaway Available
Open 7 days a week
Lunch: 12:00 - 3:00
Dinner: 5:30 - 11:00 (last orders)
Sun: 12:00 - 11:00

86 Sweat it out at the Winter Festival

In days of yore – 1564 – when Christmas-time was properly cold, the River Thames in London froze o'er. The tradition of the Frost Fair began when stallholders set up their wares on the frigid river. No such luck these days, but for the past eight or nine years, a modern style of Frost Fair, now called the Winter Festival, has been held in the second week of December. It comprises seasonal attractions such as mulled wine stalls, ice slides and huskies to make everyone pretend that Jack Frost is nipping at their nose, even though they're invariably gently perspiring in today's mild, wet conditions. Still, it's a great way to start the Christmas holidays.

Bankside Winter Festival *Bankside Riverwalk, by Shakespeare's Globe, London SE1 9DT (020 7928 3998/www.visitsouthwark.com).*

87 See the cliffs come alive

One of the most rewarding places to admire seabirds is Bempton Cliffs, an RSPB reserve on the East Yorkshire coast. Climb up to one of the special clifftop viewing points between April and August and you're rewarded with a quite spectacular sight as thousands of gannets, guillemots, kittiwakes and fulmars build nests, raise their chicks and wheel above the waves. It's perfect for the beginner birder, and highlighted by the RSPB as a family favourite.

Bempton Cliffs Nature Reserve *Cliff Lane, Bridlington, East Yorkshire YO15 1JD (01262 851179/www.rspb.org.uk).*

88 Do some potato printing

Take a potato and cut it in half. Draw a simple shape on the cut surface with a felt tip pen, then carefully cut round the shape so that it sticks out from the rest of the potato. Press the shape into a saucer of poster paint, then print on to paper or card. If you use fabric paint, this is a terrific way to customise a plain white T-shirt.

89 Make a peggy

A peg doll is easy if you have an old-fashioned peg, with a rounded 'head' and two 'legs', rather than the modern spring-loaded sort.

First, draw eyes, a nose and a mouth on the 'head' of the peg to create the face. Next, cut out a circular piece of fabric. The radius must be the height of the peg. Cut a small hole in the middle and pull the fabric over the head. Tie a small length of cotton around the middle of the peg to create a waist. Wrap half a pipe cleaner round the back of the doll to make the arms, glueing it in place at the back.

For the doll's hair you can use strands of yarn of equal length. Run a thin line of glue down the middle of the doll's head, from front to back (not ear to ear). Take the pieces of yarn and carefully line them up along the head. Finally, decorate the doll's clothing by glueing on lace, ribbon, beads or tiny buttons.

90 Grow a salad on your window sill

Salad always tastes better if you've grown it yourself. It'll have more vitamins too. If you have a sunny window sill (and lettuce needs about 12 hours of good light to germinate), you can try raising your own.

Buy a packet of mixed salad leaf seeds – lettuces of different colours and shapes look pretty as they grow – and a bag of sterile potting compost. Put some compost in a well-drained container (the sort of plastic tray tomatoes are sold in is fine; just make sure it has drainage holes), and place it on another tray. Give the compost a good watering, thinly sow some seeds on the top, then cover them with a light dusting of soil. Make sure the compost stays moist and, as the seeds germinate, spray them with water every now and again. As the leaves get big enough, snip them off and eat them in your sandwiches.

91 *Hunt a monster*

Loch Ness (located about 37 kilometres south-west of Inverness in the heart of the Scottish Highlands) is a monstrous body of water. It's more than 32 kilometres long, 1.6 kilometres wide and over 213 metres deep – you'd need to be a hardy soul to swim in it, as it's freezing, even during the summer. Then there's the small matter of a certain scaly monster said to lurk in its murky depths – the world-famous Nessie. Magnificent ruined Castle Urquhart (01456 450 551, www.historic-scotland.gov.uk), perched right on the banks of the loch, affords panoramic views over the water, making it an ideal monster-spotting locale. Those in the know say another good spot to look for the monster is from the A82, on the north side of the loch. For details of Nessie-themed visitor centres, see www.visitlochness.com.

92

Coo over a pink pigeon in Jersey

Dedicated to saving endangered species from extinction, the Durrell Wildlife Conservation is a zoo with a difference. Its colourful inhabitants range from Madagascan giant jumping rats and Mauritian pink pigeons to immense silver-back gorillas and wild-haired Sumatran orang-utans – sadly, now critically endangered, due to the destruction of their forest habitats. Hang out in the woods with the playful black lion tamarins and silvery marmosets, then attend one of the keeper talks, where, if you're feeling brave enough, you can stroke a snake or pick up a giant hissing cockroach. Joining the Dodo Club (£15 per year) entitles kids to free entry to the zoo and a twice-yearly newsletter, along with special activities, events and workshops.
Durrell Wildlife Conservation Trust *Les Augrès Manor, La Profonde Rue, Trinity, Jersey JE3 5BP (01534 860000/www.durrellwildlife.org).*

93 Blast off to infinity and beyond

Leicester is closer to outer space (100 kilometres, fact fans) than it is to the seaside (Skegness, 142 kilometres) – which might explain why the National Space Centre has become such a popular holiday-time destination in these parts. The attractions and hands-on galleries work to give you a real sensation of the vastness of the universe, and the gargantuan effort required to escape our earthly home. Big-story topics covered in the galleries include man's exploration of space, how the universe began and how it may end, as well as the ways in which space technology has improved life on this humble planet. Highlights include the the awesome Rocket Tower and the Soyuz capsule, the 3D specs-enhanced simulator ride and a superb hi-tech planetarium – with a voiceover by Luke Skywalker himself.
National Space Centre *Exploration Drive, Leicester LE4 5NS (0116 261 0261/ www.spacecentre.co.uk).*

94 Eat a cream tea designed by kids

At the Georgian Pump Room restaurant in Bath, the cream teas have been designed to appeal to under-11s – because the menu was created by them. It's the result of a bake-up with pupils at the St Martin's Garden primary school, organised by chefs Mark Pearson and Gary Trueman. Expect gingerbread men, pizzas, scones and fairy cakes. Yum.
Pump Room *Stall Street, Bath BA1 1LZ (01225 444477/www.searcys.co.uk).*

95 Create a glittery glow

Take a small jar, such as a baby food one, then paint it with PVC glue. Sprinkle the entire glued surface with glitter and let it dry. Next, take a tealight in its metal holder and pop it into the jar – it makes a lovely sparkle.

96-98 *Skateboard down a hill*

Mountainboarding involves launching yourself down a hillside at full tilt, perched on a giant skateboard with all-terrain tyres. Add a few ramps and lots of protective gear into the equation and you've got a fast and furious extreme sport. At Haredown ATB (Droke Farm, East Dean, Chichester, West Sussex PO18 0JQ, 0124 381 1976, www.haredown.com), first-timers are given an hour's tuition before being released on the slopes; a tractor takes you back to the top after the descent. Another good spot for beginners is Court Farm (Tillington, Herefordshire HR4 8LG, 01432 760271, www.courtfarmleisure.co.uk), with its broad, grassy nursery slope. The XBP Mountainboard Centre (Priory Farm, Nutfield, Redhill, Surrey, RH1 4EJ, 0845 0944 360, www.ridethehill.com) has a drag lift and a range of runs: novices can wobble down the gentle Orchard Slope while old hands shoot down the slalom or launch themselves off the four-metre quarterpipe.

99 *Go down a mine*

Killhope, The North of England Lead Mining Museum, may not sound like the most obvious place for a grand day out – but the enthusiastic staff will ensure children have fun. Dress up warm: the old mine is nearly 450 metres above sea level, so the temperature can be brisk. Kids are lent wellies and hard hats with cap-lamps for their trip/paddle down the dark tunnel to see the working waterwheel. They can also have a go at working as washerboys – separating lead ore from waste – to learn just how tough you had to be to survive 19th-century mining life. After that, helping with the washing-up will seem a breeze.

Killhope, The North of England Lead Mining Museum *New Cowshill, Upper Weardale, County Durham DL13 1AR (01388 537505/ www.durham.gov.uk/killhope).*

Haredown ATB

100-107

Lay siege to the country's most exciting castles

Choose your castle carefully; few children enjoy hours of filing past roped-off rooms stuffed with old furniture. They want keeps, ramparts and tales of boiling oil poured on marauders. Here are the most appealing.

Most ruined

This has to be Tintagel – it's barely there at all. Windswept and far from buggy-friendly (you approach it up a winding rocky path), Tintagel's crumbly glamour is best appreciated outside the summer season. Go on a stormy day and tell Arthurian legends (this is one of the king's fabled birthplaces) as you toil up the 100 steps to where the castle faces the Atlantic.

Tintagel Castle *Tintagel Head, Tintagel, Cornwall PL34 0HE (01840 770328/www. english-heritage.org.uk/www.tintagelcastle.co.uk).*

Most haunted (1)

Northumberland's Chillingham Castle claims to be rife with spooks, and has ghost trails to prove it. Peering into the dismal depths of the oubliette, a six-metre pit into which prisoners were mercilessly hurled then left to die, it's not hard to believe. The castle's most famous ghost is the blue boy, who appears dressed in blue and surrounded by light – and emits unearthly screams.

Chillingham Castle *Chillingham, Alnwick, Northumberland NE66 5NJ (01668 215359/ www.chillingham-castle.com).*

Most haunted (2)

Sitting like a giant granite dice in a bleak, remote Borders valley, Hermitage Castle is a forbidding sight even on a summer's day. Ask the guides about Bad Lord Soulis, black magic and the disappearance of local children, and you'll unleash a torrent of dark tales of strange atmospheres and spooky spectral figures.

Hermitage Castle *Hawick, Roxburghshire TD9 0LU (0131 668 8800).*

Bamburgh Castle

Most like a child's drawing

Bodiam Castle, located beside the River Rother in East Sussex, was built in the late 14th century. Its graceful symmetry and wide moat appeal to children, who love the fact that its fairytale exterior conceals a lovely ruin inside. They can explore the battlements and enjoy various activities during the school holidays. At the gate, you can also pick up a Bodiam Bat Pack with games and trails for a small fee.

Bodiam Castle *Bodiam, near Robertsbridge, East Sussex TN32 5UA (01580 830196/ www.nationaltrust.org.uk).*

Most completely medieval

Built on a rocky outcrop overlooking the Wye Valley in Herefordshire, Goodrich Castle has a 12th-century keep, a chapel and a maze of small rooms and passageways to explore. You can climb the ramparts, peer through defensive 'murder holes' and, with the help of the free audio tour, learn all about the famous Civil War Siege. 'Roaring Meg' – the gun that destroyed the castle – is also on display.

Goodrich Castle *Ross-on-Wye, Herefordshire HR9 6HY (01600 890 538/www.english-heritage.org.uk).*

Most handy for the beach

Set on the unspoilt Northumbrian coast, Bamburgh also wins our prize for the castle with the creepiest dungeons. The castle itself is in impressive condition, looming over undulating dunes and plenty of sandy beach and looking out to the Farne Islands. The dungeons are filled with realistic models of prisoners in extremis, while the big, echoey rooms feature plenty of exciting weaponry.
Bamburgh Castle *Bamburgh, Northumberland NE69 7DF (01668 214515/www.bamburgh castle.com).*

Most fortified

The dramatically positioned Harlech Castle has soaring walls and a tower, and frowns angrily over Tremadog Bay, with mighty Snowdon as its backdrop. One of the 'iron ring' of fortresses, it was built by Edward I to overawe Wales and considered impregnable. But it was captured in 1404 by the Welsh, led by Owain Glyndwr. It is in pretty good nick, and the displays give a telling Welsh history lesson. The views from the battlements and vertiginous wall-walks are astounding.
Harlech Castle *Castle Square, Harlech, Gwynedd LL46 2YH (01766 780552/ www.cadw.wales.gov.uk).*

Largest (ruined)

Kenilworth's spectacular ruins are all that's left of a fortification that was one of the strongest in the Midlands in the 12th century. It's most famously known as the place where Robert Dudley romanced Elizabeth I; though the pair never married, Elizabeth kept Dudley's last letter to her in a casket by her bed until she died. There's plenty to explore here, including the restored Elizabethan garden, and English Heritage lay on various holiday activities for children.
Kenilworth Castle *Castle Green, Kenilworth Green, Warwickshire CV8 1NE (01926 864152/ www.english-heritage.org.uk).*

108 *Practise your Poohsticks...*

The game of Poohsticks is a cracker, requiring nothing more than a likely-looking stick and a traffic-free bridge over a stream. Drop your sticks over the edge, then race to the other side to see which emerges first – a matter of luck, some say, but true aficionados know better. Pay your respects to the Bear of Little Brain who invented it (aka Winnie-the-Pooh) by having a game in Posington Wood in Sussex, where AA Milne and his son Christopher used to play. Pick up a map of sights from the Ashdown Forest Centre, then follow the signposts from the car park (just off the B2026) to Poohsticks Bridge. Collect your twigs en route – around the bridge, they're often in short supply.
Ashdown Forest Centre *Wych Cross, Forest Row, East Sussex RH18 5JP (01342 823583/ www.ashdownforest.org).*

109 *...then become World Champion*

The annual World Poohsticks Championship at Days Lock in Oxfordshire (www.pooh-sticks. com) is a hotly-contested affair. Strategies vary, but you can't go wrong following Eeyore's advice and 'letting your stick drop in a twitchy sort of way'.

110 *Stay on a farm*

There are few better ways of teaching children about this nation's proud agricultural heritage than staying on a farm. Country charm, self-catering freedom and animal encounters are all on the agenda at Pig Wig Cottages, set in the grounds of an 18th-century farm near Bradford on Avon. The rental cottages are surrounded by open pasture, where goats, ducks and chickens roam and children can help collect the eggs for breakfast. There's also a games room and play area for family use.
Pig Wig Cottages *Beeches Farmhouse, Holt Road, Bradford on Avon, Wiltshire BA15 1TS (01225 865170/www.beeches-farmhouse.co.uk).*

111-113 *Play like a pirate*

The pirate ship must be the most popular theme for adventure playgrounds in these isles. Long before chiselled Cap'n Jack took over from Pugwash as the child's favourite buccaneer, kids were shinning up ladders and ropes to reach safety-tested crow's nests in ship-shaped wooden play areas marooned on seas of sand.

The most famous pirate ship of all has to be the one in the Diana, Princess of Wales Memorial Playground in Kensington Gardens, London (020 7298 2117, www.royalparks.gov.uk), where the ship's wheel, pulleys and ropes keep young children amused for hours. The south-east's biggest adventure playground,

sitting pretty by the sea in Folkstone's Lower Leas Coastal Park (01303 853000, www.shepway.gov.uk), is, of course, a fine contender for pirate-ship play; you'll find the vessel half buried in the sand alongside a helter skelter, climbing wall and aerial runway.

The most impressive pirate ship, however, is more land-locked. It's located in one of the country's finest adventure playgrounds, at Bowood House in Wiltshire (01249 812102, www.bowood.org). The ship is life-size, with rigging and a crow's nest, while the playground's other assets include a space dive with giant slides, chutes, trampolines and high-level rope walks. Sadly, the best adventures in life aren't free, and in order to have fun here, you have to pay for entry to the stately home in whose grounds it sits (£25 family ticket).

Diana, Princess of Wales Memorial Playground

114 Make your own marshmallows

You need:
    1 tbsp icing sugar
    1 tbsp cornflour
    25g gelatine powder
    125ml boiling water
    500g granulated sugar
    red food colouring
    2 egg whites
    250ml water
    20cm square cake tin
    wooden spoon and oiled knife
    sugar thermometer

Sift the icing sugar and cornflour into a bowl, then lightly oil the cake tin and dust it with the mix. Dissolve the gelatine powder in boiling water, adding a couple of drops of red food colouring for pink marshmallows. Whip the egg whites into stiff peaks in a food processor.

Put the sugar into a saucepan with 250ml water, stirring it with a wooden spoon over a low heat until dissolved. Stand a sugar thermometer in the pan, bring the mixture to the boil, and boil fiercely until it reaches 122°C. Turn off the heat. Stir the dissolved gelatine into the syrup. Turn the food mixer with the beaten egg whites on low, slowly pour in the syrup mixture and when ribbons of marshmallow remain on the surface, pour into the prepared tin and leave to set for a couple of hours. Dust a chopping board with icing sugar and cornflour mix, turn the marshmallow on to the board and cut. Now all you need is a campfire to toast your marshmallow over.

115 Watch some bog snorkellers in action

Every August bank holiday, flipper-clad contenders waddle their way to the starting line of the World Bog Snorkelling Championships in Llanwrtyd Wells, Mid Wales (www.green-events.co.uk). The course is daunting: a 55-metre trench cut into the peat bog, filled with chilly, muddy water. Competitors must swim two lengths. To participate in the Junior event, you have to be 14 or above, and bring your own flippers and snorkel: wetsuits are a wise idea.

116-118 See some topping topiary

It may have fallen in and out of fashion over the centuries, but children love topiary – the art of clipping unsuspecting trees and shrubs into extravagant shapes. The beautiful garden at Great Dixter (Dixter Lane, Northiam, Rye, East Sussex TN31 6PH, 01797 252878, www.greatdixter.co.uk) has some superb geometric shapes carved into the yew trees; don't miss the flock of proud peacocks. See if you can find the pebble mosaic of two dachshunds, Dahlia and Canna. Their master was Dixter's late owner, gardening writer Christopher Lloyd.

Another garden famed for its tremendous topiary is the Lake District's Leven's Hall (Kendal, Cumbria LA8 0PD, 01539 560321, www.levenshall.co.uk); some trees here were planted way back in 1694. Kept shipshape by a team of gardeners, the designs are mostly off-the-wall abstract shapes, with blobs, cones and towering obelisks – though keep an eye out for the umbrella and the judge's wig.

Our favourite topiary feature is at Knighthayes Court (Bolham, Tiverton, Devon EX16 7RQ, 01884 254665, www.national trust.org.uk). Here, a pack of hounds chase a fleet-footed fox along the top of a magnificent square-edged yew hedge. Look out too for the pair of hounds standing guard at the side entrance to the garden. Tally-ho!

119 Be inspired by the Three Peaks Cyclo-Cross

Cyclo-cross involves racing round an obstacle-packed, often muddy course on a bike, and Yorkshire is its heartland. Every year at the end of September, the Three Peaks Cyclo-Cross race (www.3peakscyclocross.org.uk) is staged in the Yorkshire Dales National Park. The toughest cyclo-cross event in the UK, it's for adults only, but youngsters should find spectating exciting enough, and it might encourage them to get training. Especially when they realise the race was inspired by a 14-year-old Skipton boy, Kevin Watson, who in 1959 completed the Three Peaks running course on his bike.

120 Bungee into the abyss

The Big Melt is one of the hottest things at Rotherham's Magna Science Adventure Centre. It's a dramatic reconstruction of steelmaking, with lots of sparks, noise, flames and excitement. For a real adrenaline rush, the UK Bungee Club regularly organises death-defying plummets into its heart (07000 286433, www.ukbungee.com) – though it's over-13s only, and under-16s need parental consent.

Elsewhere, Magna's four pavilions are devoted to air, fire, earth and water, with hands-on experiments and activities to get kids going on the science front. Children say it's 'really cool', but prepare to be more chilled than you thought possible if you visit in winter. Housed in a former steelworks, it's impossible to heat. In summer, children splash through the jets and sprays of the Aqua-Tek play zone.

Magna Science Adventure Centre *Sheffield Road, Templeborough, Rotherham S60 1DX (01709 720002, www.visitmagna.co.uk).*

121 Get to know the Wuffings

The Wuffings were the royal family of East Anglia during the late sixth and early seventh century. Sutton Hoo is the Suffolk burial ground where a ship belonging to one of the Wuffing kings was interred, along with all its treasure. Visitors to the National Trust site, which is set in a 100-hectare estate, can walk around the mysterious burial mounds, learn more about the Anglo Saxons in the visitors' centre and take part in all sorts of special activities. The big one, held during the summer holidays, is a themed history event, with storytelling, tours and combat displays to celebrate Sutton Hoo down the ages, from the twilight of the Roman empire right through to the Norman Conquest, taking in Anglo Saxon and Viking rituals and ceremonies on the way. The Sutton Hoo Society's website (www.suttonhoo.org) is packed with information.

Sutton Hoo *near Woodbridge, Suffolk IP12 3DJ (01394 389700/www.nationaltrust.org.uk).*

Magna Science Adventure Centre

122-128 *Learn to surf*

When children are finding their sea legs, they need safe surfing beaches. The north coasts of Devon and Cornwall are good, if popular choices (so often crowded); you'll find more space (but a brisker wind) on the Gower Peninsula and in Saltburn in Yorkshire. Brush up on your surf lingo before setting out: for starters, a grommet is the surf-dude term for a young board rider.

Bude, North Cornwall
Bude's Big Blue Surf School (01288 331764, www.bigbluesurfschool.co.uk) offers half-day sessions for around £25; in most cases, budding surfers must be over eight and able to swim 50 metres.

Croyde Bay, North Devon
Croyde has allied itself firmly to surf culture, with numerous surf equipment shops and trendy cafés, restaurants and bars for après-surf posing. Croyde Bay Surfing (01271 891200, www.surfingcroydebay. co.uk) offers a two-and-a-half-hour group taster session for under-16s for £25.

Caswell Bay, Gower
Conditions are top-notch for beginners at Caswell Bay, with gently sloping sands, calm waves and a friendly vibe. GSD (01792 360370, www.gowersurfing.com) offers lessons for any would-be surfers over the age of five who can swim 50 metres – though under-eights must be accompanied by an adult. In summer, the Junior Surfing Academy's syllabus includes surfing, beach games and lifeguard skills – much more fun than an ordinary day at school.

Saltburn-by-the-Sea, North Yorkshire
With its broad sandy beach and dramatic cliffs, Saltburn-by-the-Sea is one of the best spots for safe surfing along the north-east coast, and Saltburn Surf School (01287 625321, www.saltburnsurf.co.uk) is one of the friendliest we know. It offers individual or group lessons, and in summer runs a week-long Junior Surf Academy for eight-to 16-year-olds. Not up for surfing? Drop in at the surf shack on the seafront and hire a wetsuit and bodyboard for the best hour of fun you can have for £6.

St Ouen's Bay, Jersey
The open, exposed waters of St Ouen's are perfect for catching a wave, with plenty of room for wobbly beginners and wave-carving pros. Jersey Surf School's (01534 484005, www.jerseysurfschool.co.uk) family lessons mean only your nearest and dearest will see you grubbing, mullering or wiping out – in short, falling off. There are also summer camps and weekend sessions for kids (eight and above) between June and September. Alternatively, you can hire a bodyboard for £4 an hour.

Watergate Bay, North Cornwall
Occupying a prime stretch of Cornish coastline, Watergate offers splendid surfing terrain, with its sandy seabed and rock-free shores. The Extreme Academy (01637 860543, www.watergatebay.co.uk) will teach anyone over eight the joys of carving and fading and how to avoid an almighty wipe-out. Accommodation abounds, though for sheer family friendliness, it's hard to beat the Watergate Hotel, with its Ofsted-registered childcare, holiday activities and Kids Zone area for rainy days.

Woolacombe & Sennen, North Devon
A key player in North Devon's Gold Coast renaissance, beautiful Woolacombe is home to the Nick Thorn Surf School (01271 871337, www.nickthorn.com). Down the coast, the Sennen Surfing Centre (01736 871227, www.sennensurfingcentre.com) runs family courses for groups of four or more, at a mere £20 per person for two hours.

129

Feed a seal

The National Seal Sanctuary on the banks of the River Helford in Cornwall (Gweek, near Helston, TR12 6UG, 01326 221361, www.sealsanctuary. co.uk) has six pools housing rescued seals, from grey seals to Californian sea lions. Some are long-term residents, others are just passing through. The main pool houses seal pups, and there are two underwater observation windows. At feeding time (11am, 2pm and 3.30pm) you'll hear each seal's story. Sahara, the Arctic hooded seal, has a pool with its own ice machine. You can pay to feed him sprats; the seriously smitten can adopt a seal or seal pup (from £20).

Sylvia Young
Theatre School

EASTER SCHOOL
THEATRE SKILLS: 8-18 YRS
Acting, Singing, Streetdance, Audition Technique,
Microphone Technique, Basic Circus Skills.
6th - 9th April

SUMMER SCHOOL

MUSICAL THEATRE WORKSHOP: 10-18 YRS
A choice of three sessions in which students
rehearse in preparation for a studio-style
workshop performance for parents.

Session 1: 27th July - 1st August
Session 2: 3rd - 8th August
Session 3: 10th - 15th August

THEATRE SKILLS: 8-18 YRS
Acting, Singing, Streetdance,
Audition Technique, Microphone Technique,
Basic Circus Skills.

Session 1: 17th - 21st August
Session 2: 24th - 28th August

PART TIME CLASSES
Thursday Evening and Saturday classes (4-18 yrs)
Acting, Singing, Tap, Jazz and Streetdance

ADULT CLASSES
Friday Evening classes for students aged 18 and over.
Singing, Acting, Jazz and Musical Theatre

FULL TIME SCHOOL
Education to GCSE. Full Vocational Training (10-16 yrs)

www.syts.co.uk
Rossmore Road, London NW1 6NJ   Tel: 020 7402 0673
Tube/National Rail: Marylebone or Baker Street

130 Make your own bath salts

Use a tea cup to measure out two cups of Epsom salts, one cup of coarse salt (sea salt or rock salt) and half a cup of baking soda. Mix them together in a bowl, then add about 20 drops of aromatherapy oil; lavender is soothing, lemon invigorating and rose good for the skin. If you want them to be an attractive colour, add some red or blue food colouring first – a few drops at a time to make sure each grain is covered. Mix thoroughly, then spread the salts in a thin layer on a tray lined with greaseproof paper and let them dry out. Store the finished salts in a wide-mouthed jar; about half a cup is needed for a sweet-smelling, relaxing bath. If you want to give them as a gift, make two bowls of salts in two different colours, then layer them in a pretty jar.

131 Visit the rector's eyrie

When RS Hawker was appointed rector of Morwenstow in 1834, it was a wild and lawless place. The most northerly parish in Cornwall, the area was full of smugglers, and dark rumours swirled about wrecking crews, who scavenged from ships caught on the treacherous rocks. Shocked to learn that the crews would let sailors die in the water while they searched for booty, Hawker took it upon himself to do what he could for the seamen, by giving their drowned bodies a Christian burial. He also built a little clifftop hut from driftwood, where he would sit, smoke opium and write poetry. The good rector is remembered for doing some much madder things, though. He dressed up as a mermaid, excommunicated his cat from the church for catching a mouse on a Sunday, and wore a pink hat, long sea boots and a poncho made from a yellow horse blanket, calling his outlandish garb the 'ancient habit of St Pardarn'. If you visit the cliffs above Morwenstow you can still sit in Hawker's Hut (the smallest building owned by the National Trust) and pen a verse in his honour.
Morwenstow is off the A39, about 5 miles north of Bude, Cornwall.

132 Cast off in the Mumbles

Set by Swansea Bay, the Mumbles is best known as the original stamping ground of actress Catherine Zeta Jones – and she's not too grand to introduce her children to the delights of her hometown. When she visits the area with her family, a trip to Singleton Boating Lake is often on the agenda, where they have been seen enjoying a swan-shaped paddleboat ride to the small island in the middle. What's good enough for the Douglases is good enough for us, and the boat rides are a bargain at £5 for half an hour.

133 Be a virtual trainspotter

Families that like to get out and about should invest in a Family Railcard. At £24 a year, it gives you a third off UK train travel when adults and children travel together, and is a genuine bargain. (You can recoup the inital outlay in just one day trip.) Children who love trains also get a big kick out of the Network Rail family website, Trakkies, which has loads of games, competitions and downloads to keep them occupied while they're on a train. Brainteasers and loads of techie information keep train buffs happy, while the artistically inclined can draw pictures of futuristic trains for the online gallery. Rail journeys will never have flown by so fast – go to www.trakkies. co.uk and you'll see what we mean.

134 Cross the causeway at Lindisfarne – but don't hang about

Twice a day, the North Sea cuts off the island of Lindisfarne (www.lindisfarne.org.uk) from mainland Northumberland. You can give children the heebie jeebies with dark tales of being stranded – show them the little refuge box on stilts where people can escape the rising water. Tell them there's no need to worry, however: visitors are made fully aware of the safe crossing times – they're on the website – and about 650,000 people cross the causeway without mishap every year.

135-137 *Find fabulous fossils*

This little island of ours is bristling with important geological sights. You can hunt for an ichthyosaur or a plesiosaur – enormous ones have been discovered in the rock and shale of north-east Yorkshire's Dinosaur Coast. If Jurassic crocodiles prove elusive, 160-million-year-old ammonites and belemnites are not, and none is better than the one you found yourself. Good hunting grounds are Runswick Bay, Boggle Hole and Brackenbury Wike, a remote bay north of the forgotten harbour of Port Mulgrave and only accessible at low tide.

Alternatively, join a fossil hunt led by an expert, one of a programme of events run by the Dinosaur Coast Project (www.dinocoast.org.uk) and put your hand in a dinosaur's footprint. The Whitby Museum (Pannett Park, Whitby, North Yorkshire YO21 1RE, 01947 602908, www.whitbymuseum.org.uk) and the Rotunda Museum (Vernon Road, Scarborough, North Yorkshire YO11 2TW, 01723 353665, www.rotundamuseum.co.uk) both hold world-class fossil collections.

Way down south, the Jurassic coast, which stretches from Exmouth in east Devon to Swanage in east Dorset, is the perfect place to embark on a fossil hunting expedition. Lyme Regis and Charmouth are particularly rich in finds – and are where paleontology, the science of fossils, took off in the 19th century. Fossils can still be found on the beaches, though it's illegal to hammer directly into the rock face. The best time to look is on a falling tide, when fossils can be found protruding through the slumping clays along the top of the beach or scattered on the foreshore. Worth a visit is the ammonite graveyard on Monmouth Beach, just west of Lyme Regis, which has hundreds of ammonites, though they cannot be collected. Regular guided fossil walks (adults £10, children £5) are organised by Discovering Fossils (www.discoveringfossils.co.uk).

If you're holidaying overseas – the Isle of Wight, to be precise – you can scarcely move for fossils, as the crumbly cliffs of the south-western coast keep dumping treasures on the beach; try searching at Hanover Point, near Compton Bay. Shaped like a giant pterosaur, Dinosaur Isle (Culver Parade, Sandown, PO36 8QA, 01983 404344, www.dinosaurisle.com) is stuffed full of bones from local digs and has lots of imaginative interactive exhibits.

Dinosaur Isle

138 *Be a yogi*

Not only is yoga fantastic for children's general fitness levels, but it can also really help asthma sufferers. The big stretches of some positions help unknot the chest muscles, and aid controlled breathing and relaxation. Yoga Bugs (www.yogabugs.com), created by Fenella Lindsell for three- to seven-year-olds, has done much to promote yoga for kids, and now has more than 200 trained Yoga Bugs teachers working in nursery, prep and primary schools. Postures are cleverly worked into stories, so classes might involve walking like a crab in an underwater adventure, or taking a space shuttle to the moon.

139

Visit a chilli jungle...

More than 100 different varieties of chillies are grown in South Devon Chilli Farm's polytunnel, ranging from the cool Hungarian Wax to the hottest chilli in the world, the Naja Jolokia. The tunnel is open to visitors from June to October, when the lush jungle is transformed into a riot of sizzling yellows, hot reds and luscious purples as the fruit starts to ripen. Look out for the dark purple Royal Black, with its rich red chillies, or the Hot Pixie's pixie-hat shaped fruit. Entry is free, while the on-site shop has a wealth of chilli sauces, jams and chocolates to sample. Young fans of the fiery capiscums can also buy chilli seeds or seedlings to start their own jungle on a sunny window sill at home.

South Devon Chilli Farm *Wigford Cross, Loddiswell, Kingsbridge, Devon TQ7 4DX (01548 550782/www.southdevonchillifarm.co.uk).*

140 *... or an enchanted glen*

Deep within a hidden Cornish valley near Tintagel lies St Nectan's Glen. In this ancient wooded dell, a waterfall plunges 18 metres into a kieve (basin). It's said to be one of the most important spiritual sites in the country, and its waters are reputed to have magical healing properties. It's not the only surprising thing about this place: people have claimed to see fairies, gnomes, orbs or balls of light and ghostly monks, as well as two ethereal grey women, said to be the sisters of St Nectan. All this supernatural activity prompted an investigation by the Paranormal Research Organisation, which reported that several sentient spirits are present in this beautiful place, which lies on a point where powerful ley lines cross.

The site has restricted opening times in winter, so check online at www.stnectan.currantbun.com before paying a visit.

141-144 *Go Roman along the Wall*

That's Hadrian's Wall – the one that took the noble emperor six years to build, handily separating the Roman Empire from the barbarians for 250 years. Running from Ravenglass in the north-west to South Shields in the north-east, it's 85 miles long. It would take about seven days to walk, by which time most children would be revolting; better, then, to concentrate on the fun bits.

Near South Shields, Arbeia Roman Fort & Museum (Baring Street, NE33 2BB, 0191 456 1369, www.twmuseums.org.uk) is one of 17 forts originally built to defend Roman interests, and there's enough of it left to interest small people. Today it consists of excavated ruins, with reconstructions of original buildings – though the best remains of a cavalry fort are at Chesters (Chollerford, Northumberland NE46 4EU, 01434 652220, www.english-heritage.org.uk). You can scamper round exploring the foundations of the fort's courtyard, hall and and commandant's house. Down by the river, the steam rooms and bath house have been nicely preserved, and there's also a museum with some entertaining displays.

Standing above the River Irthing in Cumbria, Birdoswald (Greenhead, CA8 7DD, 01697 747602, www.birdoswaldromanfort.org) is a treat to explore. Along with the remains of the fort and its gateways and the smaller 'milecastle' gate, the visitors' centre details what it was like to live there – it was a thriving settlement long after the Roman withdrawal.

If you're keen to fill the day with all things Roman, catch the 1240 or 1440 bus from Birdoswald to Vindolanda & the Roman Army Museum (Chesterholm Museum, Bardon Mill, Hexham, Northumberland NE47 7JN, 01434 344277, www.vindolanda.com), where there are more reconstructed interiors, stone altars, graves, jewels and weapons – plus a Roman toilet. Visitors can also listen to audio monologues from fictional inhabitants. At the museum, a recruitment film about joining the Roman army raises a smile, and during the school holidays actors dressed as Roman army officers run activities for children, which often involve drafting them into the ranks.

Westway – for sport, for fun, for everyone

From Perfect Parties to Training for Excellence plus open after-school and weekend sessions for all!

Book Online Now

Climbing age 5 up | Handball – learn Eton Fives – age 8 up
Football age 5 up | Tennis age 3 up (lessons, coaching, open sessions)
Term-time and holiday programmes in all sports

Westway Sports Centre:

England's largest indoor climbing centre, 12 tennis courts, 6 football pitches, 4 Eton fives handball courts, basketball, netball, gym and more.

Westway is an LTA High Performance Tennis Centre with London's leading junior development programme

020 8969 0992
www.westwaysportscentre.org.uk

Book Online Now at:
www.westwaysportscentre.org.uk

**Sport for health, fitness and wellbeing
Run as a social enterprise
by Westway Development Trust
Registered charity no. 1123127**

To find out more about participation, sponsorship or supporting young sportspeople from under-privileged backgrounds call **020 8962 5735**

145 See that freedom is a noble thing

Climb to the top of the National Wallace Monument and take in the views – on a good day, you can see for miles, from Ben Lomond in the west to the eastern Pentland Hills. On the long trek up, counting the stairs as you go, learn the truth about Wallace and check out his infamous broadsword. The jury is most definitely out about the statue at the visitors' pavilion at the base of the rock: Mel 'Braveheart' Gibson still has a lot to answer for.
The National Wallace Monument *Abbey Craig, Hillfoots Road, Causewayhead, Stirling FK9 5LF (01786 472140/www.nationalwallacemonument.com).*

146 Be tickled pink at Under the Pier

Ordinary amusement arcades aren't a patch on Southwold's Under the Pier, created by inventor Tim Hunkin. You can journey to the seabed in the Bathyscape, play ping pong on a bike, or experience an Instant Eclipse. Try out the Expressive Photobooth, which tickles and tilts its victims as it takes their picture.
Under the Pier *Southwold Pier, North Parade, Southwold, Suffolk IP18 6BN (01502 7221055/ www.underthepier.com).*

147 Pay your respects to a stuffed celebrity

Alfred arrived in Bristol Zoo from the Congo in the 1930s – and as one of the first gorillas to be successfully kept in captivity in the UK, soon became a star turn. Hordes of Bristolians came to goggle at the mighty primate, who was paraded around the zoo, dressed in woolly jumpers. During World War II Alfred's fame spread stateside too, after visiting GIs sent postcards of him to their families. Although Alfred died in 1948 after catching TB, it wasn't the end of the road: his stuffed remains are on show in Bristol's City Museum.
Bristol's City Museum & Art Gallery *Queen's Road, Bristol, Avon BS8 1RL (0117 922 3571/www.bristol.gov.uk/museums).*

148 Make a fat cake for the birds...

All you need is some fat such as suet or lard (unhealthy for us, great for our feathered mates) and sundry dry ingredients (scraps of cheese, porridge oats, muesli, bread and cake crumbs). Use one part fat to two parts dry stuff. Melt the fat in a saucepan, then thoroughly mix in the other ingredients. Take a yoghurt pot, make a hole in the base, then thread through some garden twine to make a hanger. Pack the mixture into the pot and allow it to set in the fridge. When it's hardened you can cut the pot away and hang up the fat cake from a tree in the garden. Watch the birds flock in to tuck in!

149 ...then deck a Christmas tree for garden wildlife

There are more altruistic ways of making the garden Christmassy than garish outdoor lights. String peanuts in their shells and unsalted popcorn to make edible 'tinsel' for squirrels. You can create little fat baubles from the bird cake recipe above by packing fat cake into each of the little sections of an egg box, knotting a string into the base of each and when it's set solid, cutting out the little fat-filled bell for the tree. You can also place raisins (blackbirds love them) under the grooves in pine cones and hang them on the tree. Put your edible decorations on a potted conifer on the balcony or patio, or a handy shrub in the garden, and watch the wildlife feast while you scoff Christmas pud.

150 Make a finger-puppet family

You need two matching pieces of felt; each piece represents half a finger puppet, so they need to be equal in size and shape. Place the pieces on top of each other and stitch around the edges, leaving an opening at the bottom for your finger to fit through. Turn the finished puppet inside out. Sew enough to make a family. Use fabric pens, paint or small pieces of felt or yarn to make facial features, and stitch or glue on fabric, buttons and yarn for outfits and hair.

151-152 Visit some miniature worlds

Children may yawn over the mezzotints and fine ceramics at Nunnington Hall near York (Nunnington, North Yorkshire YO62 5UY, 01439 748283, www.nationaltrust.org.uk), a 17th-century manor house on the River Rye, but they – or the girls at least – will be enchanted by the collection of miniature rooms in the attic. Sixteen wonderfully detailed re-creations of historic rooms are on display, packed with tiny treasures: a working walnut grandfather clock, say, or the exquisite Noah's ark in the nursery.

The most lavish doll's house of all, however, is the palatial residence once played with by Queen Mary. It was designed in 1921 by the most eminent architect of the day, Sir Edward Lutyens, and is now displayed in a great glass cabinet at Windsor Castle (Windsor, Berkshire SL4 1NJ, 020 7766 7304, www.royal.gov.uk). Be prepared to queue to have a good look at this showcase for British craftsmanship, with its fully functional miniaturised plumbing system, wine cellars, well-stocked library and painstakingly detailed kitchen. Children long to get their hands on it, but as with all such dolly showhomes, it's strictly look and don't touch.

153 Sleep in a fisherman's hut

Set along Whitstable's seafront, the Hotel Continental's black-and-green cockle-fisher's huts are a marvellously atmospheric place to stay. Wake up to the squalling of seagulls, then walk through the town's old-fashioned harbour for a slap-up breakfast at the main hotel. You can also book the Anderson Shed: a converted boat builder's shed with room for a family of six. **Hotel Continental** *29 Beach Walk, Whitstable, Kent CT5 2BP (01227 280280/www.hotel continental.co.uk).*

154 Hit the Thames running in a DUKW

A DUKW is a six-wheeled amphibious vehicle, originally designed for use in World War II. These days, many earn an honest crust ferrying tourists around cities. In London , canary-yellow DUKWs tour Westminster for 75 minutes, starting at the London Eye before plunging into the Thames at Vauxhall and powering down the river. Details on 020 7928 3132, www.londonducktours.co.uk.

London Duck Tours

A few of my favourite things

155-165

Pauline Quirke, actress

My son Charlie is 14 and obsessed with football, so most of my life is spent in a muddy field somewhere watching him play. Either that, or going to see our local team, Wycombe Wanderers (01494 472100, www.wycombewanderers.co.uk). No one can accuse me of not being a good 'soccer mom'.

I also try to be a good mum by taking the kids to museums, if there's something good on – I feel a bit guilty if I don't. We went to see the recent Tutankhamun exhibition, and we're always in the Natural History Museum (Cromwell Road, London SW7 5BD, 020 7942 5000, www.nhm.ac.uk). Museums have changed so much since I was a kid: my memories are of being dragged along by teachers, and not being allowed to touch anything. Nowadays it's all interactive and most places are free, so there's no excuse.

Being an actress, I felt it was my responsibility to take Charlie to Stratford-upon-Avon (0870 160 7930, www.stratford-upon-avon.co.uk). He was doing a school project on Shakespeare, but I don't think it meant anything to him until he spent the day wandering around and seeing where the Bard lived. It just seemed to bring the whole thing to life for him, and when he went back to school I reckon he paid a bit more attention.

We're bigger cinema-goers than theatregoers, really. I recently went to see *Mamma Mia!* (www.mamma-mia.com) with my daughter, Emily. My little boy would have hated every second of it, but she loved it. It's a really girly film and it was a good excuse to spend a couple of hours having a giggle together.

Whenever I have visitors to stay, I always take them to visit Bekonscot Model Village (Warwick Road, Beaconsfield, Buckinghamshire HP9 2PL, 01494 672919, www.bekonscot.com), so the kids have been there just about every year of their lives. It's an entire village in miniature and every year they add a little bit more. The kids are probably sick to death of it, but I think it's fab.

Another place I drag them to is the Roald Dahl Museum & Story Centre (81-83 High Street, Great Missenden, Buckinghamshire HP16 0AL, 01494 892192, www.roalddahlmuseum.org). If you're a fan of his books, which my children are, it's a great place to go. You get to see where Roald Dahl wrote and find out all about his life – and there's a tea shop.

Because I was always out working when the kids were little, I always tried to make an effort to do fun things with them whenever I was home. One thing I did was organise treasure hunts. I'd hide anything from the dustpan and brush to the alarm clock somewhere in the house, and give them a list of items to look for. If they found them, they'd get a prize – only a chocolate bar, mind, not a Rolex watch.

When Emily was little we didn't have a garden, so we used to make up a little picnic – she would help me – and go to the local park. We'd meet up with Linda Robson [Quirke's co-star in TV sitcom *Birds of a Feather*] and her daughter, who was about the same age, and go and feed the ducks. It's a lovely, cheap way to have fun and get out of the house for the day. When we lived in Hackney we also used to visit the city farm (1A Goldsmiths Row, London E2 8QA, 020 7729 6381, www.hackneycityfarm.co.uk). We've got Odd's Farm (Wooburn Common Road, Wooburn Common, High Wycombe, Buckinghamshire HP10 0LX, 01628 520188, www.oddsfarm.co.uk) near us now, which also has a petting zoo. You can buy a massive bag of grain and spend the day feeding various overweight animals.

I'm no great cake-baker, but I do love cooking, and I managed to get Charlie into it when he was younger. It started with little Rice Krispies cakes, but now his signature dish is chicken escalopes – not bad for a teenage boy, although I think he just likes the bit where you bash the chicken.

On the
road

Fiona McAuslan discovers the cycle-logical benefits of two wheels.

Time was when a brand spanking new bicycle was the glowing symbol of childhood: the ultimate in Christmas wishlist fulfilment, and the passport to unfettered freedom and newly tested responsibility. But for the last decade or so the humble bicycle has been relegated to the garden shed of childhood entertainment, outclassed by the rise of the Wii and Xbox.

However, with sedentary lifestyles expanding the waistbands of the country's youngsters, as well as the push bike's impeccable eco-friendly credentials, two wheels are slowly spinning back into popularity.

While many parents will enthusiastically strap mountain bikes to the back of the car and depart for a weekend offroading, the prospect of allowing children loose on their bicycles as an everyday form of transport can be daunting. A fifth of all pedal cycle casualties are children, according to the Department of Transport – so how do you make sure that your child stays safe once they cycle out of sight?

Sophie Stringer works for Cycling England's Bikeability (www.bikeability.org.uk), an initiative to get kids back in the saddle, and is adamant that it's just a question of training. For anyone who remembers slaloming in and out of traffic cones on their cycling proficiency test in the 1970s and '80s, Bikeability will strike a chord. The modern equivalent, however, puts the emphasis on fun and personal achievement for kids – it's about confidence as well as gaining safety skills. It's obviously successful: during the 2006 pilot scheme, 10,000 red, amber and green badges were awarded to kids, and Bikeability was rolled out across the country a year later. It seems that parents are keen to allow children the freedom of two wheels, so long as they are confident that they can conduct themselves safely.

Bikeability training falls into three levels. The first is a basic introduction suitable for kids of all ages – as long as they're stable on a bike – which teaches them where to put their feet when stopping and how to check for traffic behind them. Level two teaches nines to 11s what they need to know in order to tackle a daily ride to school along quiet roads, while

level three deals with challenges on busier roads, such as roundabouts and traffic lights.

According to research by Bike for All (a joint initiative between Bycycle and the Dept of Transport), the scheme couldn't come at a better time. Only two per cent of children currently ride to school, but kids are champing to give it a go; one in three would like cycle to school if they were allowed. Needless to say, the Bikeability scheme is popular with its target market. Ten-year-old Jane Jones has been riding to school since taking a five-week course. 'It was a great opportunity for me, and our tutor Sam was really tolerant and great fun,' she says. The fact that she got time off from classes to complete the course was a bonus that didn't go unnoticed.

Reports from the scheme even suggest that there's a knock-on effect within the classroom too, with kids who cycle to school settling down to lessons more readily. Bikeability also say that the course gives shy and retiring children a confidence boost that benefits other social interactions. Whether or not you take these claims with a pinch of salt, tangible benefits include increased physical activity for kids, the chance to learn new skills, and a welcome break for parents from the position of family cabbie.

Most Bikeability courses are arranged through schools for free, but families can arrange private tuition with an accredited trainer for a small charge. The website guides you through finding a personal Bikeability trainer in your region. Making it a family affair

'Tangible benefits include increased physical activity for kids… and a break for parents from the position of family cabbie.'

has the advantage of allowing you to brush up your road skills too – essential if you don't want inadvertently to pass on bad habits (swearing and rage-induced fist shaking are obvious no-nos). It's also the handy way to assess your child's progress. 'Parents are often the best judges for their own children, rather than us being really prescriptive,' says Stringer. 'A switched-on nine-year-old can ride alone on quiet roads with no traffic lights or roundabouts, but with other kids you might want to wait until they're ten or 11.'

There are far-reaching advantages of cycle training too. 'The more bicycles on the road, the safer the roads get for bike users. Other road users grow accustomed to dealing with bikes and there's more of an overall presence,' says Stringer. It means that the biggest bugbear that cyclists have to face is avoided too. Although cycling on the pavements is often a given for children, it's actually illegal – and the quicker kids can break the habit by being confident enough to use the roads, the better for cycling public relations all round.

Bicycles are a quick and efficient means of transport, and children who exercise their pedalling muscles daily are bound to feel benefits both in terms of fitness and general traffic confidence. Once car drivers get used to seeing child cyclists using the roads, rather than the pavements, they'll learn to be more vigilant and everyone will feel safer. A well-run course like Bikeability can improve children's road sense and give them a ticket to ride that lasts a lifetime. So dig out your bikes, get them serviced if needs be and reclaim the streets – you have nothing to lose but your spare tyres.

167 *Make their eyes shine*

Tiu de Haan is the woman behind Eye Shine: a Lottery-funded non-profit organisation that runs magical weekends on Dartmoor for families, reminding parents how to play with their children and get back to nature. Families enjoy simple pleasure such as singing round campfires, building dens, playing hide and seek and generally finding their family mojo again. Workshops are free for Devon families with children aged five to 11, and the plan is to extend Eye Shine weekends throughout the country. For more information and dates of upcoming workshops, check the website: www.eyeshine.co.uk.

168 *Try a bizarrely flavoured scone*

At Newbiggin by the Sea, in Northumberland, a little café called Nevin's Nibbles has cornered the scone market. You may think plain with jam and cream is best, but we urge you to try the rhubarb and custard, the mince and onion or the leek and garlic. They're all concocted by Jackie Nevin, who's aiming to get into the Guinness World Records with the 42 varieties – and counting – of scone currently available at her fragrant establishment.

Nevin's Nibbles *4 Bridge Street, Newbiggen by the Sea, Northumberland NE64 6EG (01670 816271).*

169 *Get a Cobb on*

Set on the stunning Jurassic coast, beautiful Lyme Regis is a delight at any time of the year. The historic Cobb (harbour) dates from the 13th century and has inspired writers from Jane Austen to John Fowles. For the younger visitor, though, it's a perfect place to drop a crab line, gaze out to sea or eat a leisurely ice-cream. The sheer delight of standing at the very end of the Cobb as gulls whirl and call, watching the fishing boats come in, is an experience to be savoured. For more information on the town, see www.lymeregis.com.

170 *Grow a beanstalk*

In spring, take a runner bean seed (you can buy a packet for about £1.50, or ask a gardener friend to give you a seed from their stash). Place the seed in a plastic container on some moistened kitchen towel. Keep the paper moist and the container covered, in a warm place, until the seed begins to germinate – about ten days. When a long, thin root has emerged, place the seed very carefully, root pointing downwards, in a nine-centimetre pot of moist compost. The compost should cover the seed; leave about two centimetres between the surface of the compost and the top of the pot. Put a slim stick in the pot for the emerging plant to clamber up.

Leave the pot on a sunny window sill, and don't let the compost dry out as first the shoot, then the first leaves unfurl. As the plant grows, ensure the stake is tall enough for the beanstalk to twirl around. Once the plant seems to have filled its pot, transfer it to a larger one with a taller stake. You can grow a very tall plant in a medium-sized pot outside, or transfer the beanstalk to open ground in the garden. Watch for bright red flowers, then bean pods – or stray giants attempting to climb down.

171 *Take a quick stroll around Britain's smallest city*

St David's in Wales may be of teeny-tiny proportions, but its magnificent 12th-century cathedral means it is officially Britain's smallest city. After scooting around town, follow the footsteps of centuries of pilgrims and head for the cathedral. Don't miss the marvellous carved ceiling, or the casket that's thought to hold the bones of St David and St Justinian. There are more earthly delights on offer too, in the shape of cakes or lunch in the refectory; alternatively, pick up a picnic in town and head for lovely Whitesands beach.

St David's Cathedral *The Close, St David's, Pembrokeshire SA62 6RH (01437 720199/ www.stdavidscathedral.org.uk).*

172 *Make papier mâché*

You can make fantastic sculptures simply by moulding glue-soaked strips of torn-up newspaper to wire or balloon forms. It's the perfect cheap, non-toxic moulding material. To create a round papier mâché shape that can be cut into bowls or made into masks, you need: a balloon; PVA glue (mix one part glue to two parts water); loads of old newspaper; a throwaway turkey basting tin or large aluminium tray; a pin and paintbrushes.

Step 1

Start by blowing up the balloon (a plastic bowl or colander is a useful resting place for it while you stick on the paper).

Step 2

Tear the newspaper into thin strips (about 3cm x 12cm). Take a few strips at a time and put them in the basting tin/aluminium tray with the glue mix. Then paste the strips one by one on to the balloon, using a brush.

Step 3

Smooth the saturated strips down as carefully as you can. Be sure to overlap the strips and apply several layers; the more layers there are, the sturdier your creation will be (though the longer it will take to dry). Leave a section the size of a 5p coin at the bottom for balloon-pricking purposes.

Step 4

Leave the balloon to dry overnight – or a couple of days, depending on how many layers you've had the patience to apply – in the airing cupboard. When the glued-paper strips are dry, take a pin and prick the balloon. Remove the deflated rubber from the hardened paper shell.

Step 5

Use a sharp knife to cut your finished shape in half if you want a bowl or a mask (for the latter, also cut out eye holes). Or leave it as a head shape, to be decorated as you please.

Step 6

When you've honed your basic papier mâché-making skills, you can practise covering wire shapes with the paper-and-glue, to make sculptures like the red dragon here.

173 Count the counties in Worcestershire

Perched on a wildflower-covered hilltop in the Cotswolds, Broadway Tower is a 20-metre Gothic folly that looks like a Lilliputian castle. Climb to the top and you're rewarded with views that stretch over 13 counties – all the way to the Welsh mountains on a clear day. Back at ground level, there are country walks aplenty.

Broadway Tower *Broadway, Worcestershire WR12 7LB (01386 852390/www.broadwaytower.co.uk).*

174 Be a panting Santa

A Liverpudlian Christmas means you might spot not one, but hundreds of Santas scurrying through the streets. The annual Liverpool Santa Dash (www.runliverpool.org.uk), usually held in the first week of December, is a 5km charity race. Entry costs £15 and you're given a Santa suit. Kids can join in – there's no lower age for entries – but they might prefer to do the shorter scarper that takes place after the main run.

175 Scoff some spicy gingerbread

Overlooking the grave of Grasmere's most famous resident (clue: he liked a stroll among the daffodils) in St Oswald's churchyard is Sarah Nelson's gingerbread shop – a fixture for over 150 years. The spicy recipe hasn't changed in centuries, and is just the ticket after charging up and down the hills and dales.

Grasmere Gingerbread Shop *Church Cottage, Grasmere, Ambleside, Cumbria LA22 9SW (01539 435428/www.grasmeregingerbread.co.uk).*

176 Watch a trailer

The Screen Machine is a 102-seater cinema based in an articulated truck. It tours the Scottish Highlands and Islands providing screen entertainment (mainly recent releases, with full digital surround sound) for communities where cinemas are scarce. To catch a movie before it moves on, check www.screenmachine.co.uk.

177 Go for a spin in a setout

A setout is the term for a carriage, horse, harness and attendants, and if you go along to Arlington Court, home of the National Trust's National Carriage Collection, you'll see plenty set up for action. Here Scrooge, Jacob, Tiny Tim and Magnus, the resident horses, obligingly take visitors for a turn round the grounds.
Arlington Court *Arlington, near Barnstaple, Devon EX31 4LP (01271 850296/ www.nationaltrust.org.uk/arlington).*

178 Admire the Pictish stones

Head to Aberlemno village on the B9134 in Perthshire (0131 668 8600, www.historic-scotland.gov.uk). Three intricately carved Pictish stones stand by the roadside; another is situated in the village kirkyard. The carvings include Christian and pre-Christian symbols, such as mounted warriors, Celtic crosses, a serpent, weeping figures, disks and rods.

179 Visit Arthur at Goonhilly

Once the world's largest satellite earth station, with more than 60 dishes pointing into space, Goonhilly Satellite Earth Station (located on Cornwall's Lizard peninsula) is home to 'Arthur', the oldest working antenna in the world. Now a Grade II listed building, Arthur is open for tours: hard hats and boots are provided (note that height restrictions apply and the tours are dependent on the weather). Goonhilly also offers the attractions of Future World. The visitors' centre has plenty of interactive exhibits to tell the history – and look at the future – of international communications; you can also have fun with the resident robot. Techie kids will love the Xbox 360 Play Zone, with its games and racing car simulator. Those over 135 centimetres tall and 38 kilos in weight can take a spin on the Segway, a gyroscope transporter; book ahead on 01872 325400. There's also a café, picnic spot and indoor and outdoor play areas.
Goonhilly *Helston, Cornwall TR12 6LQ (0800 679593/www.goonhilly.bt.com).*

Make the most of London life

**TIME OUT GUIDES
WRITTEN BY
LOCAL EXPERTS**
visit timeout.com/shop

180

Marvel at the bird-eating spider

At BUGS!, London Zoo's invertebrate (that's creepy crawlies) area, there are more than 140 species of animals with no backbones but lots of legs. Star of the show is the red-kneed bird-eating spider, who comes out to be admired at 3pm everyday. The zoo's resident community of Madagascar roaches force air out of their spiracles to have their famous hissy fits. Come along to watch their keepers wind them up as part of the daily Megabugs demo (11.15am).

BUGS! stands for Biodiversity Underpinning Global Survival, and this place is all about celebrating invertebrates. After all, they make up 98 per cent of all animal life and are vital to the earth's ecosystems – so while you're marvelling at the spider, roaches, stick insects and millipedes, you're communing with nature's unsung superheroes.

BUGS! at London Zoo *Regent's Park, London NW1 4RY (020 7722 3333/ www.zsl.org/zsl-london-zoo).*

181

See some lucky police horses

There are two big draws for children at the National Trust's Ormesby Hall near Middlesbrough. The first is an 18th-century stable block that houses nine well-turned out horses, which belong to the Cleveland Police Mounted Section. Many of the horses take their names from Middlesbrough FC legends, such as George Hardwick and Wilf Mannion. The second attraction is three incredibly detailed model railway layouts, including a Thomas the Tank display for very young fans. Volunteers keep the trains in perfect order; details on www.ormesbyhallmrg.co.uk.

Ormesby Hall *Church Lane, Ormesby, near Middlesbrough, Redcar & Cleveland TS7 9AS (01642 324188/www.nationaltrust.org.uk).*

182

Picnic in the past

Burrough Hill is a vast Iron Age hill fort overlooking Melton Mowbray in Leicestershire, and several surrounding counties from its vantage point 210 metres up. Nowadays it's a prime venue for picnics and long, circular walks around the high ramparts, but on high days and holidays until the 17th century it became a huge pagan playground, with shooting, running, wrestling and dancing into the night. In the 18th century, Grand National steeplechases were run here before Aintree was ever heard of. Expect wonderful views, palpable ancient vibrations and lots and lots of sheep.

Burrough Hill County Park *between Burrough and Somerby, Leicestershire.*

183

Make a garden obstacle course

Lawns and flower beds are boring: what children want is tunnels, streams, stepping stones and balancing planks. Here are our ideas. Line up four or five chairs for children to wriggle under, followed by a paddling pool to splash through. Place bricks at intervals for kids to use as stepping stones, balance a plank on two bricks to walk along, arrange a rope in a twirly shape to tip-toe through and set out bin bags to have a sack race in, bean bags or potatoes to throw into a wastepaper bin and a football to kick up or bounce ten times. Time each child as they work their way through the course and see who's the fastest.

184

Gorge on mountain biking at Cheddar

Broadway House at Cheddar Gorge is one of the best-equipped mountain bike race venues in the country, so the two-day Cheddar Bikefest in September is an ideal place to kickstart the racing careers of any would-be Hoys and Pendletons. Age categories are up to five, five to ten, and ten and over. Entry is free and you can register on the day. More information on 0117 9532698 or www.bike-fest.com.

London Fields Lido

185 Brave the water at London Fields Lido...

Derelict for decades, this lovely lido on the edge of leafy London Fields was resurrected by Hackney Council in 2006 after much campaigning by pool-starved locals. It's the capital's only 50-metre heated outdoor pool – the water's kept at a balmy 25°C – and is open year round (bar Boxing Day and New Year's Day). Come the summer holidays, swimming lessons are put on for kids, for all abilities from beginners to Michael Phelps wannabes. There are two poolside cafés and plenty of picnic space in London Fields itself.

London Fields Lido *London Fields Westside, London E8 3EU (020 7254 9038/www.hackney. gov.uk/c-londonfields-lido.htm).*

186-193

...then visit more open-air pools

Most of these lidos are open only in high summer, so call to check opening hours before you pack your swimming cossies.

Aldershot Lido, Hampshire

A water fountain, three enormous slides and a good-sized shallow end are among Aldershot's charms. Younger children get their own smaller pool. Toddlers can take a break from splashing to play in the sandpit, and there's a big grassy area for picnics, along with a cafeteria.
Guildford Road, Aldershot, Hampshire GU12 4BP (01252 323482/www.rushmoor.gov.uk).

Chagford Swimming Pool, Devon

Fed by the cool, clean waters of the River Teign, Chagford's pool is a summer-only affair, with solar pool covers to reduce the chill factor. There's a separate paddling pool for small fry, and a qualified lifeguard on duty at all times.
Rushford, Chagford, Devon TQ13 8BB (01647 432929/www.chagfordpool.co.uk).

Droitwich Spa Lido, Worcestershire

The heated pool at Droitwich tapers into a 'beach' at one end, where children can splash in the sun-warmed shallows. The wet play area is joyously awash with water cannons, jets and fountains.
Worcester Road, Worcestershire WR9 8AA (01905 799342/www.wychavonlesiure.co.uk).

Jubilee Pool, Cornwall

Seagulls wheel above this magnificent art deco tidal pool, which juts into the bay at Penzance. Lifeguards watch over the enormous (and very deep) main pool and the baby pool, and there are free inflatables and deckchairs. It's incredibly popular with families, who set up camp for the day with their picnics. There's also a lovely café, open all day for snacks and coffee or a full-blown evening meal.
Promenade, Penzance, Cornwall TR18 4HH (01736 369224/www.jubileepool.co.uk).

Pells Pool, East Sussex

Set on a tree-lined lawn, this spring-fed pool makes for an idyllic family day out in Sussex. There are rafts for the kids to scramble on, a paddling pool and a snack kiosk, serving slices of delectable home-made flapjack.
Brook Street, Lewes, East Sussex BN7 2PA (01273 472334/www.pellspool.org.uk).

Saltdean Lido, East Sussex

An inviting alternative to Brighton's pebbly beach, Saltdean is a vision of 1930s elegance. It's also a family-friendly spot, with a shallow children's pool, a sandpit and a picnic lawn.
Saltdean Park Road, Brighton, East Sussex BN2 8ST (01273 888308/www.saltdean.info).

Sandford Parks, Gloucestershire

A heated children's pool, paddling pool, slides, a playground and table tennis make Sandford a child's idea of paradise – and a treat for beleaguered parents. In addition to the café, there's plenty of room for picnics.
Keynsham Road, Cheltenham, Gloucestershire GL53 7PU (01242 524430/www.sandfordparks lido.org.uk).

Stonehaven Pool, Aberdeenshire

Painted in primary colours, this Olympic-sized pool (opened 1934) in Aberdeenshire is heated to a toasty 29°C. The main pool has a thrilling water shoot, and a brand-new paddling pool. Best of all are the midnight swims beneath the stars on Wednesday nights.
Queen Elizabeth Park, Stonehaven, Aberdeenshire AB39 2RD (01569 762134/www.stonehaven openairpool.co.uk).

194 *Discover Discover*

A step over the threshold at Discover in Stratford, east London, takes you into a world of stories, colour, fact and fantasy. This creative learning centre for 11-and-unders consists of a Story Trail full of adventures through secret caves, sparkling rivers and flying pages inhabited by baby space monsters, spoon puppets and big-footed giants. This is a venue where children can use up excess energy and exercise their imagination by playing in the water fountain, sliding down a monster's tongue, or flying to the moon in a spacerocket.

There are activities and story-building events year round, and the Story Den hosts interactive exhibitions based on stories from around the globe. From playing, observing and telling tales to simply listening or watching, each visit to Discover is indeed 'the start of a new story'.
Discover *1 Bridge Terrace, London E15 4BG (020 8536 5563/www.discover.org.uk).*

Discover

195

Celebrate Apple Day...
The first Apple Day was held on 21 October 1990, with 40 stalls in London's Covent Garden. A decade later, 600 Apple Days were held around the country, celebrating the apple with tree dressing, apple identification and apple bobbing for the kids.

In Borough Market – London's favourite food market – Apple Day is a big deal, with harvest parades, a special service in Southwark Cathedral, travelling players and the chance to taste and buy ciders, preserves and pastries. To find out about Apple Day events in your area, visit www.commonground.org.uk.

196-199

...then be an apple bobber and prepare an October feast

Who'd have thought that apples could be so much fun? Try bobbing for them and you'll see what we mean. Fill a large bucket or washing-up bowl with water, add some apples and then take turns to grab them using only your mouth. Keep those hands behind your back! Prepare for a drenching. Canny bobbers look for fruit with longish stalks to get their teeth into...

Once you've secured your apples, try the peeler challenge. Using a potato peeler, try to remove the apple skin in the longest single strand. The secret is to make the strand as narrow as possible, without it breaking. You might be able to manage a peel of 150 centimetres, but the longest ever piece was produced in the US in 1976, when Kathy Walfer kept a peel whole for 52.51 metres. We don't believe it.

Four peeled apples, stewed with a little water and sugar, topped with 25g butter mixed with 175g muesli, can be baked in a crumble.

Another option for unpeeled, washed apples is to press them for juice. Throughout the autumn, Orchard Link, a group of enthusiasts helping to save Devon's apple heritage, takes its traditional apple press to community events and farmers' markets (to find out when and where, go to www.orchardlink.org.uk). Just turn up with your apples and a container for the juice. Membership of Orchard Link is £18 a year and provides access to all sorts of apple-related info and happenings. Members can hire a smaller mobile press and hold their own apple-pressing parties.

200 *Laugh at slapstick silliness in Bristol*

The high-octane absurdity of silent comedy stars like Charlie Chaplin and Buster Keaton is irresistible to children. Bristol's Slapstick Silent Comedy Festival (www.slapstick.org.uk) brings the classics back to the silver screen for four days in January – often with live musical accompaniment, as well as much guffawing.

201 *See the Hand of Glory*

Don't leave Whitby Museum for a rainy day; it's brilliant whatever the weather. Glass cases display the town's maritime history in all its quirky, glorious splendour: narwhal tusks and Inuit canoes are among the trophies brought back from Arctic whaling expeditions and Captain Cook's exploration of the South Seas. There are fabulous model ships too: ships in bottles, ships in light bulbs, ships made by POWs from food scraps and bone. Weirder still is the gory Hand of Glory. The pickled hand of a hanged robber, it had the blood squeezed out before being steeped in saltpetre, then left to dry in the sun. With a candle between the fingers made from the fat of the robber, it was used as a gruesome lucky charm.

Whitby Museum *Pannett Park, Whitby, North Yorkshire YO21 1RE (01947 602908/ www.whitbymuseum.org.uk).*

202 *Take tea at the Tailor of Gloucester's place*

At the World of Beatrix Potter Attraction in Cumbria, tableaux from Ms Potter's best-loved tales feature carrot-snaffling Peter, bonnet-wearing Jemima and trout-bait Jeremy in an indoor Lakeland countryside set. The author is celebrated in a jolly virtual walk, but best of all is the tea room, with its outdoor terrace dotted with whimsical sculptures, children's menu, hot chocolate, cream teas and victoria sponges.

The World of Beatrix Potter Attraction
Bowness-on-Windermere, Cumbria LA23 3BX
(015394 88444/www.hop-skip-jump.com).

203 *Get an eyeful of the Battle of Hastings*

Every year, time rewinds to 1066 on Senlac Hill, scene of the famous clash between William the Conqueror and his invading troops, and King Harold's stalwart Saxons. Hundreds of archers, cavalry and footsoldiers gather to re-enact the bloodythirsty battle, before dusting themselves off and heading for the tea tent for a spot of light refreshment. Cheer them on from the sidelines – and watch out for King Harold meeting his grisly demise.

1066 Battle of Hastings, Abbey & Battlefield
High Street, Battle, East Sussex TN33 0AD
(01424 775705/www.english-heritage.org.uk/events).

Battle of Hastings

204-206
Try the Three Dome Challenge

For adventurous adults, the National Three Peaks Challenge involves climbing the three highest peaks of England, Scotland and Wales (Scafell Pike, Ben Nevis and Mount Snowdon) inside 24 hours. A child-friendly London variant is the Three Dome Challenge. The idea is to visit the domes of the principal places of worship of Islam, Hinduism and Christianity. (You can enter only one dome, St Paul's.)

Central London Mosque

Take the tube to Baker Street. All is quiet and peaceful in London's main mosque. Leave your shoes at the door. Boys this way, girls upstairs behind the lattice on the balcony. The dome above is impressive. Outside on the forecourt, a book stall sells pamphlets about healthy living, as the prophet Mohammed practised.
Central London Mosque *146 Park Road, London NW8 7RG (020 7725 2213/www.iccuk.org).*

Neasden Temple

Take the tube to Neasden, where the awesome Hindu temple, built from brilliant white Carrara marble, stands out against the sky. Aim to arrive between 4pm and 6pm, when the temple is open to the public. There are three main deities, Brahma, Shiva and Vishnu. Models of these, plus Hanuman the monkey god and Ganesha the elephant god, are sold in the souvenir shop.
Neasden Temple *105-119 Brentfield Road, London NW10 8LD (020 8965 2651/ www.mandir.org).*

St Paul's Cathedral

Take the tube to St Paul's. There is an entrance fee to Sir Christopher Wren's edifice, and a supplement to go up to the Whispering Gallery. If you put your ear against the wall, you can hear what people 30 metres away are whispering. From the dome, you can step out on to the roof to see what God sees of London from on high. Once he saw nothing but traffic jams, and so introduced the congestion charge.
St Paul's Cathedral *Ludgate Hill, London EC4M 8AD (020 7236 4128/www.stpauls.co.uk).*

207 Head into no-man's land

24 November 1917. Ypres. You are sent out on patrol with a squad of nervy new conscripts. You leave the safety of the trenches and breathe the chilly night air. It is dark. Suddenly you spot the enemy on the path you have been commanded to take. Do you a) take cover, b) launch an immediate attack, or c) change direction and find another route? Your answer to this question in the Soldiers of Gloucestershire Museum's popular computer game will either lead to a glorious outcome and the awarding of the Victoria Cross, or to a miserable death in the mud between the trenches. Afterwards you can try on World War II kit from a box in the reception and have your picture taken in the armoured car outside the entrance, a Ferret two-man reconnaissance vehicle used in Cyprus and in Germany by NATO peacekeepers.
Soldiers of Gloucestershire Museum *Custom House, Gloucester Docks, Gloucester GL1 2HE (01452 522682/www.glosters.org.uk).*

208 Check a snail's pace...

Each child must collect a stable of pesky molluscs from the garden, then mark their team's colours on their snails' shells. Lay out a race circuit, with a few obstacles along the way, and let 'em loose. This may take some time.

209 ...then see the champs race at Snailwell

The annual snail-racing championships have taken place at the appropriately named Snailwell in Suffolk (just north of Newmarket) for more than 16 years. Organised by St Peter's Church as part of the village's summer fete, the event involves painted snails 'racing' around a wooden track. Sadly, you can't bring your own champion snail-sprinter, as the organisers supply their own.

210-211
Float off to a balloon festival

Over 100 balloons take to the skies for the four-day Bristol International Balloon Fiesta in August (0117 953 5884, www.bristolfiesta. co.uk). Festivities begin with a mass lift-off of novelty balloons, which might range from a giant fire extinguisher to a bagpipe-playing Scotsman. Another highlight is the 'night glow', when 30 lit balloons flicker and pulse in sequence, followed by a dazzling firework display. Also held in August, the Northampton Balloon Festival (01604 838222, www. northamptonballoonfestival.com) combines balloon racing and parachute displays with masses of family-friendly activities on solid ground, including Wild West shows, an arts area and a circus.

212 Make stone monsters

Gather some smooth stones and paint them using acrylic or tester pots of household paint. Once dry, stick on goggly eyes (available from craft and stationery shops such as Paperchase) and paint on a teeth-baring mouth. You can give them away as paperweights.

213
Be a film critic

Launched in 2005, the London Children's Film Festival (www.londonchildrenfilm.org.uk) has proved that children aren't just suckers for big blockbusters. Held in November, the week-long event screens films from all over the world, including premieres, archive titles and movies made by young people. Children aged seven to 16 can be on a judging panel and take part in workshops – great experience for would-be critics and directors. It's based in the Barbican Centre, with screenings at venues across town.

214 Pedal the New Forest

Famed for its free-roaming ponies and deer, the New Forest has miles of car-free cycle paths threading through the trees. In summer it's glorious for family bike rides. There are plenty of bicycle hire shops: try Brockenhurst's Country Lanes (Railway Station, Brockenhurst, Hampshire SO42 7TW, 01590 622627, www.countrylanes.co.uk) or Burley's Forest Leisure Cycling (The Cross, Village Centre Burley, Hampshire BH24 4AB, 01425 403584, www.forestleisurecycling.co.uk), which has child seats, trailers and tag-alongs and 'muttmobiles' for lazy family pooches.

215 Have a wild time in Pembroke

Oriel y Parc is the supremely green (grass-roofed, solar-panelled, wool-insulated) home to the National Park Visitor Centre in St David's, as well as being a delightful first stop on the long National Trail that runs along this coastal swoop. The education officer oversees creative events throughout the year, from bird-box making in summer to taffi (treacle toffee) making over Christmas. Stay for lunch at the café, where the chef has produced her own cookbook and uses local produce to create a proper Welsh menu.

Oriel y Parc *High Street, St David's, Pembrokeshire SA62 6NW (01437 720392/ www.orielyparc.co.uk).*

216 Get jiggy with the diggers

For any child who's ever dreamed of driving a bulldozer or a dumper truck, Diggerland is heavy plant heaven. You can get behind the controls of a diggers to gouge out trenches or fill 'em in, take to the air in a giant JCB scoop, and watch diggers dance to music. There are Diggerland adventure parks in Kent, Devon, Durham and Yorkshire – check the website, www.diggerland.com, for information on opening times and admission prices.

217-224

Be a ghosthunter

Even a child with no appetite for history or strolling can be persuaded out on a walk if ghosts, ghouls and gore are on offer. Very young children, however, and those of a nervous disposition, should beware. Teens, though, love a haunted jaunt.

Most cities with a sense of history run ghost tours. In York, at 7.30pm every night, whatever the weather, a strange man in a frock coat and a Gladstone bag strides down the Shambles, the city's oldest medieval street. He's here to meet the brave souls who will accompany him into back alleys to hear dark tales of York's macabre history. The resulting Ghost Hunt (01904 608700, www.ghosthunt.co.uk) is a treat: funny, spooky and surprising. Meanwhile, the Original Ghost Walk of York (01759 373090, www.theoriginalghostwalkofyork.co.uk) offers more ghoulish stories and murky corners. No need to book for either walk; just turn up.

In Whitby, rich in Dracula connections, the Man in Black leads the Whitby Ghost Walk (01947 821734, www.whitbywalks.com), leaving from the Whalebone Arch at 8pm (days vary).

Another creepy corner of the world is Edinburgh. Mercat Tours (0131 225 5445, www.mercattours.com), Witchery Tours (0131 225 6745, www.witcherytours.com) and Black Hart Entertainments (0131 225 9044, www.blackhart.uk.com) all run creepy night-time ambulations around the old city's dark and murderous alleyways. Sometimes they employ 'jumper-ooters' to rack up the tension.

Equally hair-raising tactics are used on the walks organised by Ghost Tours (01983 520695 www.ghost-tours.co.uk) on the Isle of Wight. They're run by a spooktacular bunch of enthusiasts who love to scare the pants off their guests with many a tale of bloodthirsty smugglers and ruthless wreckers; they employ ghouls to drop down from the trees as you totter nervously around the Botanic Gardens.

For chills and thrills in the capital, London Walks (020 7624 3978, www.walks.com) runs a wonderful, often lighthearted Ghosts of the Old City walk – just ask about 'Scratching Fanny'.

Pins and needles

Consummate knitter **Buzz Stokes** *gets her pins out.*

It's 9am on a Thursday, and I am sardined on a Central line train between school run and work. Miraculously, at Tottenham Court Road station, the carriage empties. As the doors close once more and the train continues westwards, the few remaining passengers unfold themselves into the unaccustomed luxury of a seat. And – how glorious is this – the woman opposite me, immaculately tailored in a City suit, whips out her needles (a rather dinky looped pair) and starts knitting...

She doesn't know that I am gearing myself up to write about the stress-busting properties of knitting in these straitened times, or that I am heading to open up my knitting and craft shop, All the Fun of the Fair. But she couldn't have illustrated my point better. We exchange conspiratorial smiles of silent recognition as I shuffle off at the next stop with my overflowing bags stuffed with yarn: two members of the ever-growing band of knitters.

You only have to browse the burgeoning websites and blogs to realise that knitting is big these days. The choice ranges from the learned www.knitting-and-crochet-guild.org.uk, to the irreverant www.stitchnbitch.co.uk – my personal favourite. Outside cyberspace, knitting circles are rapidly stealing a march on the ubiquitous book club. They're even encroaching into the workplace: North East Derbyshire District Council has offered council employees knitting classes to combat stress, while North Wiltshire district councillor Ruth Coleman regularly knits during meetings. 'Political meetings can be quite stressful and I find knitting very relaxing,' she says. 'If find it keeps me calm and helps me to concentrate.'

It's not just adults who benefit from knitting therapy; many creatively inclined children also enjoy the soothing clicketty-clack of of the needles, and the

'Most six-year olds have the manual dexterity to knit; the only problem is how to start them off.'

satisfaction gained from seeing a scarf grow ever longer. It also helps that you can buy really hip haberdashery basics these days; blue needles and needles with funny faces for the boys, flowery needles and gigantic 20mm-knit-a-scarf-in-an-hour needles for the girls. Then there are yarns to satisfy every tweeny fad (self-striped wool for Harry Potter scarves, fluffy wool, eco-friendly wool, even non-wool wool for the no-sheep-for-me vegan knitter), plus buttons, beads, ribbons and trims galore.

To get started, all you need is 4mm needles and standard weight double knitting (DK) yarn – a fiver should do it. Standard DK is cheap and easy to work, though if you go shopping for yarn, children will inevitably be drawn towards 'novelty yarns'. Stay away from these, as they can be difficult to use and it's hard to see the stitches clearly. Also avoid very dark colours, as lighter-coloured wool will make it easier for children to see their stitches.

Most six-year-olds have the manual dexterity to knit: the only problem is how to start them off. In our workshops, we first teach them how to make a slip knot (explaining they have to make a pretzel-shaped loop might appeal). Then they learn to cast on and to knit and purl a square. I use a little rhyme that gets – and keeps – them going:
'In through the front door
Once around the back
Peek through the window
And off jumps Jack.'
They say necessity is the mother of invention: a square can become a hat, a bag or an iPod cover, and a rectangle turns into a snake for the boys or leg warmers and fingerless gloves for the girls. There is so much to keep precocious knitters motivated beyond the scarf, and then a whole world more if you look beyond knitting to crochet and sewing.

If you need more inspiration, check out such patterns as the Pudsey Bear outfit kit (www.kingcole.co.uk/pages/pudsey.html) or the Exterminknit, a knitted Dalek (www.entropy house.com/penwiper). There are also plenty of exciting things to make with yarn without knitting: think pompom trees, string belts, wool pictures, tassels and more.

All this fun has a serious point too. Now all our wallets are being squeezed, perhaps we should rediscover the beauty of a little more making do and mending. The benefits lie way beyond the territory of retail therapy, holiday activities or after-school clubs. When you give children organic Cornish wool or some other wonderful natural fibre such as hemp or banana to knit with, you're offering up a whole world of possibilities to learn about material science, farming and cultural history. The world in a skein of wool…

All the Fun of the Fair *Unit 2.8 Kingly Court, off Carnaby Street, London W1B 5PW (020 7287 2303/www.allthefunofthefair.biz). Check the website for the current schedule of knitting, crochet and sewing classes for adults and children.*

226 Make a tiny walnut boat

You have to crack the walnut very carefully for this, straight down the middle. It's difficult to do with a nutcracker, so try piercing the join in the middle of the nut with the blade of a sharp knife – adults only! Once you have your perfect halves, eat the nut, then put a small piece of Blu-Tack in the base of the boat and poke a cocktail stick flying a paper or cloth sail in it. You can even make some tiny paper people as sailors. Set them afloat in a bowl of water, or your bath.

227 Walk in Paddington's pawprints

There is part of west London that will be forever connected with the Bear with the Hard Stare. A little brass statue of him at Paddington Station reminds you of his celebrity status. The Paddington Waterside Partnership, a friendly organisation that organises all sorts of events to promote this newly regenerated part of central London, runs a programme of walks – the most child-friendly of which is the Paddington Bear Walk. To book a place, go to www.inpaddington.com.

228 Follow Lewis Hamilton round the track

Buckmore Park kart circuit has near-legendary status, thanks to a certain Master Hamilton, who trained here. During the school holidays, fledgling speed freaks should make tracks to the Arrive 'n' Drive sessions. Four to sevens can zip round their own track at six miles per hour, while eight to 11s can watch the speedometer climb to 20mph on the Club Circuit. Over-12s, meanwhile, can tackle the hairpin bends of the National Circuit, reaching speeds of up to 40mph. A helmet, suit and gloves are provided, and drivers are given a safety briefing before getting behind the wheel.
Buckmore Park Karting *Maidstone Road, Chatham, Kent ME5 9QG (0845 603 7964/ www.buckmore.co.uk).*

229 Enter Scruffts

Canine best friends only are eligible to enter the Kennel Club's famous crossbreed competition. If your mutt is of mixed blood, log on to www.thekennelclub.org.uk to find out where your nearest Scruffts heat is. Winners of each heat are invited to the Discover Dogs event, taking place in London's Earl's Court exhibition centre every November. There are prizes for most handsome, prettiest, golden oldie and child's best friend – any of which are guaranteed to put a wag in his tail.

230 Skim a perfect stone...

The perfect skimming stone is flat and round, and fits into the palm of the hand. Hold it between the crooked index finger and the thumb and fling it across open water as if it were a flying saucer. As long as it hits the water flat, it will bounce – several times, if you're lucky. (This was the principle of the bouncing bomb.) Keep practising until you score a personal best in stone bouncing. Make sure there is someone there to see it – there's nothing worse than breaking a world record without a witness.

231 ...then join the skimming champions

Anyone of any age can join the World Stone Skimming Championships, held at Easdale Island in the Inner Hebrides at the end of September. You can't select your own stones as the authorities do that for you. Points are awarded for the distance thrown, not the number of skims – though the stone must bounce at least three times for a skim to qualify.
World Stone Skimming Championships *Easdale Island, near Oban, Argyll PA34 4TB (www.stoneskimming.com).*

232
Tower over tiny beasts

No, not insects in the grass: these are proper mammals, wandering winsomely in their paddocks. There are teeny-tiny Shetland ponies, dinky donkeys, pint-sized pigs and pygmy goats. The farm occupies around 40 hectares on the edge of Dartmoor, so there's plenty of space to run around and play. Be warned that the animals, especially their impossibly tiddly offspring, are so sweet that children invariably want to take them home. They can't, but they can pet the little darlings and help feed them at certain times of day. There's also a play area called Sandy Farm, which has scaled-down buildings, tractors and an indoor assault course.

Miniature Pony & Animal Farm
Moretonhampstead, Devon TQ13 8RG
(01647 432400/www.miniatureponycentre.com).

233
Frolic with otters and flit with butterflies

Watch otters at play and walk through clouds of brilliantly coloured butterflies in a tropical glasshouse at the delightful Buckfast Butterflies & Dartmoor Otter Sanctuary in South Devon. Exotic butterflies feed on tropical plants in the steamy butterfly house, where you can also see owl butterflies tucking into rotting fruit. Outside you'll find the purpose-built otter sanctuary, where species include the shy native British or European otter, the playful and vocal Asian otter and the North American river otter, who are real show-offs. Children love watching their antics – they can be really dextrous with pebbles – and especially enjoy feeding times (11.30am and 2pm daily), when the otter keeper talks about the differences between the species. Glass enclosures also allow a glimpse of these usually secretive creatures in action in their element: underwater.

Buckfast Butterflies & Dartmoor Otter Sanctuary *The Station, Buckfastleigh, Devon TQ11 0DZ (01364 642916/ www.ottersandbutterflies.co.uk).*

234
Play ancient games

At Fishbourne Roman Palace near Chichester – unearthed in the 1960s, much to the surprise of workmen who were actually looking for a suitable place for a water main – children can immerse themselves in Roman culture. Admiring historic mosaics is all very well, but having a go at making them, or writing with a stylus on a wax tablet, or playing centuries-old games like knucklebones or counters is much more fun.

Fishbourne Roman Palace *Salthill Road, Fishbourne, Chichester, West Sussex PO19 3QR (01243 785859/www.sussexpast.co.uk).*

Fishbourne Roman Palace

235 Learn a very, very long name

Llanfairpwllgwyngyllgogerychwerwdrobwll llantysiliogogogoch. Got it? The town with the longest name in the world is in the island of Anglesey, off the north-west coast of Wales. The name plate at the station is almost as long as the platform, and a classic photo-opportunity. In fact, the name is really several words joined together: Llan Fair Pwll Gwyn Gyll Gogerych Werw Drobwll Llan Tysilio Gogogoch. Llan is a church. Fair is Mary. Tysilio is a famous Welsh saint. The whole thing means: the church of Mary on a hollow of white hazel and the church of St Tysilio near a red cave. Double 'l' in Welsh is pronounced like the 'ch' of loch. W is 'oo'. That's all you need to know. How many other words can you make from it?

236 Steam along by train and pedal power

Watch the heather moors and glacial gorges glide by from the comfort of an old steam train that runs for 29 kilometres between Pickering and Grosmont, then travel under your own steam by going on a family bike ride. The North Yorkshire Moors Railway (01751 472508, www.nymr.co.uk) sells a Pedal & Puff leaflet for 50p, which details the lovely bike trails around the railway line.

237 Make pasta jewellery

Pasta isn't just for dinner; you can adorn yourself with the stuff too. Select a shape that can be threaded through with a length of wool, string or ribbon; penne or pasta wheels are ideal. In a zip-lock plastic bag, mix one teaspoonful of rubbing alcohol with a few drops of food colouring. Use a different bag for each colour. Add the pasta, close the bag and shake it to colour the pasta, then spread the pieces on paper to dry. Necklaces and bracelets could be enhanced with beads and sequins. You'll look delicious!

238 Be a mudlark

In the 19th century, barefoot children could often be seen scavenging on the muddy shores of the tidal River Thames. It was a dangerous business – the children often drowned or contracted fatal diseases. These days, there's not much to stop curious would-be beachcombers on the South Bank from descending damp steps to the sandy beach that's revealed at low tide. The safest way to be a modern mudlark, though, is through the proper channels. Contact the Museum of London or Museum in Docklands (for both, go to www.museumoflondon.org.uk) to find when education officers are organising the next Thames foreshore dig. This happens in the holidays – no doubt the original barefoot mudlarks could have done with a few friendly education officers in their day.

239 Gongoozle at the renaissance of the Foxton Locks

Hidden away on the Grand Union Canal, amid rural Leicestershire, Foxton's steep 'staircase' of ten locks is the largest in the country – a masterful engineering feat for 1810. Even so, by 1900 heavy traffic was causing costly bottlenecks, which brought about a yet more spectacular scheme to bypass the locks.

The Inclined Plane Boat Lift was the answer – a 100-metre long, steam-driven pulley system that enabled barges to steer into vast tanks at the top and bottom of the hill and, once counterbalanced, to be winched up the long 45-degree slope. Though the lift fell into disrepair in the 20th century, work has begun on a Lottery-funded scheme to restore it.

There's a museum in the old Inclined Plane boiler house, but it's also fun to spectate ('gongoozlers' the old boatsmen call us!) as boaters lock horns with the locks, straining over winding gear and heavy watergates, releasing thousands of gallons of water into the side ponds. If watching all that hard work makes you peckish, visit the shop for picnic provisions and stale bread for the ducks. For details, visit www.foxtonlocks.com.

240 *Design a dinner*

What's your favourite meal? Ever tried lobster? What's wrong with eating your peas with honey? Children's food fantasies can be played out on paper plates with this game. Get some magazines with photos of food, a pair of scissors, some glue, and cut out pictures of edibles and arrange them deliciously on the plate. Food, glorious food, and not a bite to eat. Decide who's made the tastiest meal, play cafés with the plates or go all educational and make this an opportunity to talk about a balanced diet.

241 *Visit an empty village*

In 1943 the seaside village of Tyneham, between Kimmeridge and West Lulworth in Dorset, was requisitioned by the army. About 250 villagers were evacuated, but told they would be allowed to return to Tyneham when hostilities ceased. That never happened, and the land is now used for military training. You can still nose round, however, as the Ministry of Defence allows in ramblers: Lulworth Range walks and Tyneham village are accessible most weekends and school holidays throughout the year. Ring the range officer (01929 404819) to check access before you set out, keep to the waymarked paths and watch out for red flags, which indicate live firing. The church and school remain intact and are open from 10am to 4pm.

242 *See a real shipwreck*

Over the centuries, the rocky coastline of the Gower has proved to be treacherous terrain for passing ships, and sent many a sailor down to Davy Jones' locker. Stroll along lovely Rhosilli Bay (01792 361302, www.enjoygower. com) at low tide and you can still see the bare bones of the *Helvetia* sticking out of the sand. A Norwegian cargo ship, she met her end here on a stormy night in 1887, and is a slowly eroding reminder of the sea's fearsome power.

243 *Meet an Antarctic explorer*

Now safely berthed in Dundee's docks, the *RRS Discovery* has a thrilling past. For a start, she carried Captain Robert Falcon Scott and his intrepid team to the icy, uncharted wastes of Antarctica in 1901. Kids can roam above and below deck, exploring the mess deck, where the sailors slept, and the cramped galley, where the cook did his best to rustle up grub from the tinned, bottled and dried rations on board. Later, the *Discovery* ran munitions to Russia during World War I and became a cargo vessel, before returning to her home port in 1986.
RRS Discovery Point *Discovery Quay, Dundee DD1 4XA (01382 309060/www.rrsdiscovery.com).*

244 *Step inside a mountain*

The mighty summit of Ben Cruachan conceals an unexpected secret: a massive man-made cavern, home to an underground hydro-electric power station. From the viewing gallery, you can look down on the soaring central turbine hall, which is high enough to house the Tower of London – and has the unmistakeable air of a James Bond villain's lair. After whisking round the visitor centre, look out for ospreys, eagles and red kites above Loch Awe.
Cruachan Visitor Centre *Dalmally, Argyll PA33 1AN (01866 822618/www.visitcruachan.co.uk).*

245 *Have a brilliant budget holiday*

The mighty Youth Hostel Association (www. yha.org.uk) has really raised its game for families in recent years. Members are spoiled for choice for unusual places to stay in England and Wales. Private family rooms with kitchens and entertainment on the doorstep come as standard in the 200-strong hostel collection. Banish all thoughts of draughty bunkhouses in the middle of nowhere – you can stay in the City of London, a mansion by the sea in Dorset or an all-mod-cons eco-friendly complex near a theme park in Derbyshire.

246-249

Grab a pencil for the Big Draw

Every October, galleries, museums, church halls, schools, community centres, libraries and art clubs across the land become venues for the Big Draw (www.thebigdraw.org.uk), organised by the Campaign for Drawing. The aim is to explore all types of drawing, from fine art to architectural blueprints, and events are open to people of any age. The following venues always run a packed programme of activities.

Chislehurst Big Draw

The residents of Chislehurst in Kent have won a national prize for their imaginative use of the local common in this event. It has become something of a fair, with stalls and animals in a convenient triangle of land between the school, the church and two pubs. For details, see www.thebigdraw.co.uk/aboutus.html.

Edinburgh Big Draw

In 2008 the Scots sat on the battlements of Edinburgh Castle and created a panoramic skyline of their city. Every year a new theme is announced through a newsletter, which participants are invited to sign up to.
National War Museum of Scotland *Edinburgh Castle, Edinburgh EH1 2NG (0131 247 4413/ www.nms.ac.uk).*

Harrogate Big Draw

Professional artists descend on Harlow Carr, a lovely Royal Horticultural Society garden, to inspire and help with drawings and paintings made using horticultural materials.
RHS Harlow Carr *Crag Lane, Harrogate, North Yorkshire HG3 1QB (01423 724680/ www.rhs.org.uk).*

The Hub Big Draw

The Hub National Centre for Craft & Design likes to push the boat out for the Big Draw. In 2008 'A Lincolnshire Sketchbook' was the theme of three days of drawing workshops.
The Hub National Centre for Craft & Design *Navigation Wharf, Carre Street, Sleaford, Lincolnshire NG34 7TW (01529 308710/ www.thehubcentre.info).*

250

Keep your balance on Honister's Via Ferrata

Going deep underground into Honister's old slate mine is scary enough, but you'll need nerves of steel to tackle its Via Ferrata. A perilous-looking system of iron rungs and cables that picks its way across the summit of wind-scoured Fleetwith Pike, it follows the precarious route taken by miners in Victorian times. You're given a harness and attached to a fixed cable, but the ledges, tunnels and bridges still make for an adrenaline-fuelled scramble. Kids need to be over 1m 30cm tall.
Honister Slate Mine *Honister Pass, Borrowdale, Keswick, Cumbria CA12 5XN (01768 777714/ www.honister-slate-mine.co.uk).*

Big Draw

251 *Take an orange and create a scentsation*

A cloved orange looks pretty and scents the house delightfully at any time of year, but is especially lovely as a Christmas decoration. Make holes in an orange with a cocktail stick and then fill each hole with a clove. If you want to hang the orange from the tree, fasten ribbon around it.

During Advent Christians create Christingles – a traditional gift for children – in which the orange represents the world God made. Some churches also hold special Christingle services for children. A red ribbon wrapped round the orange represents forgiveness. Sweets and dried fruits such as apricots and dates, skewered on to four cocktail sticks and poking out of the orange, represent the good things provided by the world, as well as the compass points. A candle placed in the top of the fruit, in the centre, represents Jesus, the light of the world.

To make a Christingle, wrap double-sided sticky tape around the middle of an orange to hold your ribbon in place. Tie the ribbon with a small knot or bow. Use an apple corer to make a hole in the top of the orange, big enough to stick a candle into. Then wrap foil around the base of the candle and push it firmly into place. Take your sweets and dried fruits and skewer them on the cocktail sticks, kebab-style, then press the sticks into the orange as a final tasty flourish.

252 Start your own worm ranch

You can can buy a ready-made wormery, or simply set one up in an old bin or wooden box – though you must have an outlet at the bottom to drain excess liquid. Start with a bedding mix (leaf mould, compost and newspaper are all good) and water it well. Then add around 500g of composting worms, such as tiger worms, red worms and brandlings – but not garden worms. You can buy the right sort at fishing shops or order from specialists such as Wiggly Wigglers (01981 500391, www.wigglywigglers.co.uk).

Worms need to be fed little and often. A quarter of everything you put in should be cut-up cardboard or shredded paper; the rest should be kitchen scraps. Avoid cheese, meat, fats, oil and other proteins; worms don't like citrus, garlic or onion either. Within 18 months your worm ranch will be busting at the seams, with happy worms going about their business, turning waste into wonderfully rich compost.

253 Make bread rolls

You will need:
  750g strong white bread flour
  2 tsp salt
  25g butter or tablespoon olive oil
  1 sachet or 1 tsp easy-blend dried yeast
  1 level tsp caster sugar
  430ml hand-hot water

Put the dry ingredients in a bowl and make a well in the centre, then add the water. Mix until you have a dough, then knead on a work surface for ten minutes. If the mixture is really sticky, add a little extra flour. Shape into about ten rolls; the number depends on how big you want them to be. Place the rolls on a floured baking tray and cover with a tea towel, then leave them somewhere warm to rise. An airing cupboard is ideal. When the rolls have doubled in size, they can be baked in an oven (preheated to 210°C). They'll take about 15 minutes. Tap the base of the rolls: if they sound hollow, they're ready. Cool them on a wire rack, then slather with butter and scoff.

254 Personalise a pot

Is there a gardener in the family? A delightful – and cheap – way to make them a present is to paint a terracotta pot (from about 99p in garden and DIY superstores). Wash and dry the pot, then use ordinary poster paint or special ceramic felt tips for your designs. Let each layer of paint dry before adding another. If you want to extend the life of your artwork, you can brush the pot with clear varnish once the paint has dried. Fill the pot with packets of seeds, sundry horticultural accessories (plant tags, twine), sweets or home-made cakes for an extra-special present.

255 Be fit for life at Rutland Water

You can explore Rutland Water in the Midlands (www.rutlandwater.org.uk) from the reservoir or make like a landlubber on the 40-kilometre shoreline path – either way, there's a fabulous range of activities to enjoy, from boats and birds to bikes and butterflies. You can join holiday schemes or go freestyle. Whatever you choose, it's bound to involve something healthy, sporty and/or eco-aware.

Even a boat trip on the luxury cruiser *Rutland Belle* is guaranteed to put some colour in your cheeks – although probably not as much as that on offer at Rutland Sailing Club (www.rutlandsc.co.uk), on the south shore near Edith Weston. It's the largest inland sailing club in the country; we're talking RYA Laser-class sailing days or four/five-day courses for ages seven and up. On the north shore at Whitwell, there's reasonably priced windsurfing, powerboating and canoeing (see www.anglianwaterleisure.co.uk), as well as a cycling centre and climbing wall. Normanton on the south shore also has bikes for hire.

The entire western end of the reservoir is a nature reserve, with two centres for nature detectives to visit. Ospreys, red kites, buzzards and all manner of waterbirds can be spotted, but for tropical butterflies head for the Butterfly Farm (www.rutlandwaterbutterflyfarm.co.uk) in nearby Empingham.

256

Meet the giants

The Great Hall of the National Railway Museum in York (01904 621261, www.nrm.org.uk) contains 22 monsters of steam displayed in all their painted and polished glory. Wonder at the futuristic-looking Mallard, which in 1936 steamed its way into the record books at 126mph. Gawp at the biggest loco ever built in Britain – a black monster, 4.5 metres tall and 28 metres long, made for the Chinese National Railway in 1935 – or board the Japanese shinkansen (bullet train). At the other end of the gauge is an enchanting model railway, where steam trains chug past goods yards and sidings, villages and rural halts: perfect escapism.

257-258
Follow the otter

Following its hero from birth to heroic death (how we cried!), Henry Williamson's *Tarka the Otter* is a classic. The story was set in North Devon – and you can still spot many of the locations. The best way to follow Tarka's pawprints is to walk a stretch of the Tarka Trail (www.devon.gov.uk/tarkatrail), a 290-kilometre path that loops round Barnstaple, with the fringes of Dartmoor to the south and Exmoor to the north. You can download an audio tour from the website. Alternatively, hire bikes in Barnstaple at Bike Trail Cycle Hire (Stone Barn, Fremington Quay, 01271 372586) and ride to Braunton on a traffic-free path that meanders beside the River Taw and the Torridge Estuary. It's just over eight kilometres of flat terrain and lovely scenery.

259 *Run free*

Parkour is the art of free running – using the street as your playground. You can find classes across London that show you how to skedaddle up walls and jump off railings in a loose-limbed, freeflow style via Parkour Generations (07789 742919, www.parkourgenerations.com). Many of the classes run term-time only, but there are events in the holidays too – for example, the sportif types at the Youth Academy organise monthly jams for all-comers in Vauxhall and Waterloo; check the website for details.

260 *Do put your daughter (or son) on the stage*

Find out how at the two-week July Project (www.thejulyproject.co.uk), which takes place in Calderdale. It's a children's festival that celebrates young people's achievements in sport, drama, music and dance and, what's more, holds audition masterclasses for those desperate to get into the limelight.

261 *Skewer a fruit or two*

We know that an apple a day keeps the doctor away, but a more exciting healthy pud can be yours by gathering a few exotics and skewering them into fresh, fruity kebabs.

Take a couple of different types of melon (galia and honeydew, say), red and white grapes, strawberries and a fresh pineapple (or tinned pineapple chunks in juice). Chop the melon flesh (and the pineapple, if you're using fresh) into bite-sized wedges, wash the grapes and strawberries and drain the pineapple chunks. Thread the pieces of fruit on wooden skewers, then chill your fruit kebabs until you're ready to eat.

Too healthy for you? Melt some good-quality chocolate (dark, 70 per cent cocoa) to dip your kebab into, for a more luxurious pud.

262 *Get arty in a wigwam*

Here's a jolly place to stay or play in beauteous Northumberland. Pot-A-Doodle Do is an arts centre and a collection of 12 wooden wigwams (heated, with mattresses) for people who can't bear to leave. The arty bit has creative workshops in ceramic painting, making mosaics and sand art.

Pot-A-Doodle Do *Borewell, Scremerston, Berwick-upon-Tweed, Northumberland TD15 2RJ (01289 307107/www.potadoodledo.com).*

263 *Keep a kayak under control*

Kayaking in open water is a difficult skill to master, but you'll have fun trying during a session with Anglesey Adventures (01407 761777, www.angleseyadventures.co.uk). Kayaking sessions take place year round (most people prefer summer) on the bracing beaches of Holyhead. Children aged eight and above are loaned a wetsuit and all the gear, plus expert tuition from chief adventurer Grant Mitchell and his team of instructors. At £25 for a kid's half-day taster session, it's great value.

A few of my favourite things

264-278

Bob Flowerdew, gardener and broadcaster

My twins are only three, so we haven't really started taking them out yet. One thing I'm really keen for them to learn about, however, is scent. These days, we're bombarded with sight and sound from films and media, but smell is a sense that is neglected. I encourage my children to sniff plants and flowers when they're out with me in the garden. It was funny when they went to nursery; they saw some flowers and rushed over to smell them, then turned to me in dismay when they discovered the blooms were made of plastic!

The children spend a lot of time in the garden. They enjoy digging and are particularly fond of my chickens and geese, although some birds can become quite aggressive. That's good, I think: children have to learn to respect animals. Mine get such pleasure from collecting eggs. The most popular activity in the garden is fruit-picking – raspberries and strawberries are the best crops. I'm often asked which crops are best for a school garden, and I always say strawberries. There are so many varieties: an interesting activity for children is a strawberry tasting. Set out fruits from a number of different types and do a blind-tasting to see which ones each child finds the tastiest. It's good for children to describe the contrasts in smell and taste.

Growing things in the garden is a great way to introduce children to wildlife and gardening basics, such as companion gardening: for example, while you're growing strawberries, you can put a few onion in the plot as strawberries and onions make good growing mates. Also have a go with miniature fruit trees. You can grow them in pots and they'll crop very well. Herbs are great too; put a variety in a big container and encourage children to rub the leaves and discover the distinctive scent of each herb. Parents tend to be paranoid about laburnum and other supposedly toxic plants, but do you know how many children are recorded as having been killed by plant poisoning in this country? Precisely none. True, a few things in the garden may cause a skin rash or tummy upset, but they'll do no more harm than that.

When we're not in the garden, we also like cooking. I feel there should be a lot more communal cooking and eating. People think nothing of eating a substandard pub meal, when for the same money they could produce a banquet at home. We love experimenting with food: I once grew wheat and ground it myself to make bread, just for the fun of it. It was very labour intensive, but a good exercise – the taste of freshly ground flour is far superior to the stored stuff. Although we eat healthily most of the time, we don't refuse the children any type of food; if we're at a fair they'll have candy floss and other treats. Nothing should be forbidden, because forbidden fruits are the most attractive. The twins help to juice our apples in the crush – they're strong enough to turn the handle now.

Another healthy snack I like to make is fruit leather. Simmer soft fruits such as strawberries and blackcurrants (preferably homegrown) until you make a thick purée, and pour the mixture into a lined baking tray to about the thickness of your finger. Leave it to dry in a warm, dry place such as an airing cupboard or by an Aga, then cut it into strips and hang it up – it lasts forever, and is a sweet fruity treat.

If we do go out and about, it's locally – to see the steam trains at Bressingham (www.bressingham.co.uk), say, or visit a local beauty spot at Waveney, North-east Suffolk, where there's an old bridge and picnic area. We also go to seaside resorts such as Great Yarmouth, (www.great-yarmouth.co.uk) where the children try out the arcade attractions and have ghastly (I mean, delicious) fish and chips.

At home, we're happy to let the children watch the television sometimes. I've looked at the available children's programmes and found some of them quite sensible, actually...

279

See inside a duck egg

The London Wetland Centre is a stretch of managed habitat in the lovely suburb of Barnes, and a stopping-off point for a huge collection of wildfowl, which migrate here from all over the world. Watch the birds arrive at the 'bird airport' (a glass-walled observatory) or sit tight in one of the centre's six hides and spy on them unobserved. The children's Discovery Centre is full of amazing stuff to play with, but things really get going in the Easter holidays, when the sap is rising and chicks are hatching and children can watch some 'egg candling'. They're taken to the art gallery to see eggs in incubation (during days seven to 26), then shown the development of the duckling inside by means of the bright light shone on it.
WWT London Wetland Centre *Queen Elizabeth's Walk, London SW13 9WT (020 8409 4400/ www.wwt.org.uk/london).*

280
Hear ghostly bells from under the sea

On 14 January 1286, England's shores were hit by a mighty storm, which howled and raged for five long days. When the fury abated, the inhabitants of the Sussex town of Dunwich discovered tonnes of displaced shingle blocking their harbour, spelling ruin for the prosperous port. In the 14th century, two further storms hit the unlucky town, swallowing 400 houses and several churches – and the beleaguered townspeople left en masse.

The coast continued to erode over the centuries, and more and more of Dunwich's buildings vanished under the relentless waves, until virtually nothing was left of the powerful medieval town. Once in a while, or so the local fishermen say, you can still catch the distant ringing of church bells under the sea. Take a stroll on the deserted beach one fine evening, then sit on the shingle and listen hard – maybe you'll hear the church bells amid the sounds of the waves breaking and the gulls calling. *www.visit-dunwich.co.uk.*

WWT London Wetland Centre

281 *Make sugared almonds*

Take about 225g of ready-made roll-out icing and a bag of almonds (blanched or brown – the skins add a little extra fibre). Colour half the icing with a few drops of red food colouring, so it turns pink. To make each sugared almond, tear off a small section of icing and carefully knead it around a nut. Repeat until all the almonds and icing are used up, then lay the sugared nuts on a baking tray lined with greaseproof paper. When the icing is firm, pack the sweets into little gift bags or boxes. If pink and white hues seem too tame, use any colouring you can lay your hands on for a rainbow assortment of sugary snacks.

282 *Lift a Mini Cooper*

Through an impressive array of interactive exhibits, indoors and out, Snibston Discovery Park explores the impact of technology on our everyday lives. You can go on an underground tour of a colliery with a former miner, or enjoy above-ground nature trails and the thought-provoking Science and Water playgrounds; there are also displays on body-forming fashion, vintage buses and jet engines, and a 1920s chip shop. Yet somehow, in the minds of most kids, all this pales into insignificance compared with the chance to lift a half-ton Mini Cooper with one hand.
Snibston Discovery Park *Ashby Road, Coalville, Leicestershire LE67 3LN (01530 278444/ www.leics.gov.uk/museums/snibston).*

283 *Take the little pink ferry across the Hamble*

Where do you wait for the little pink ferry on the Hamble in Hampshire (023 8045 4512, www.hamble-warsashferry.co.uk)? At the little pink ferry shelter! Walk along the river on the Warsash side or drop in to explore the crooked, Noddyland backstreets of Hamble-le-Rice – any excuse to chug out among the bigger boats in the busy estuary marina.

284 *Walk with lemurs in Somerset*

Creeping through Cricket St Thomas's four acres of woodland is a thrilling experience – because round every corner, lemurs lurk. On ground level, watch for the family of ringtailed lemurs – a laid-back bunch who love basking in the sun on hot days. The white-fronted brown lemurs are trickier to spot: look for the male of the group, Juan, who has a white fluffy head.

In the other half of the wood lives Club, born with just three legs. She's the wildlife park's only red-fronted brown lemur, but, luckily, the red-bellied lemurs have adopted her as one of their tribe. Last but not least are the black ˙ and white ruffed lemurs.

'They live higher up in the trees, but come down at feeding time,' says primate keeper Tracey Mason. 'They're bigger than the other lemurs, and gorgeously fluffy.'

For the best sightings, arrive at noon and join a guided tour through the woods, or turn up at 3.30pm for feeding time, when these attractive little beasts emerge from the foliage to get their grub.
Wildlife Park at Cricket St Thomas
Chard, Somerset TA20 4DD (01460 30111/ www.cstwp.co.uk).

285

Head for Deep waters

There are sea life centres all over Britain, but only one Submarium. This is the fancy name given to the Sir Terry Farrell-designed aquarium called the Deep, located on the Humber estuary. As well as all the sharks, manta rays, seahorses, jellyfish and other sea creatures you'd expect to find at such a place, this landmark aquarium has Europe's deepest viewing tunnel (seeing sharks gliding over your head is always an unsettling experience), an underwater lift and, at the other end of the building, a lofty viewing platform and top-floor café with stunning vistas across the Humber.
The Deep *Tower Street, Hull, Yorkshire, HU1 4DP (01482 381000/www.thedeep.co.uk).*

286-294
Keep looking out of the window

Travel sickness is usually caused by reading books in the back seat – so stop reading, children. Better to look out of the window and play intelligent games. I Spy is the obvious one, but when that palls, try these diversions.

The Atlas Game
The driver starts by naming a country. The next person says the name of another country beginning with the last letter of the previous one. Afghanistan. Nicaragua. Azerbaijan. Netherlands. Somalia. Armenia. Australia. Amazing how they keep coming back to A. Widen it to include any place name. Antwerp. Pomerania. Arkansas. Wales. Bong! You're out – Arkansas ends in S, you numb-nut!

Guess the Tune
Switch between music radio stations. Listen to what's playing, can you identify the tune? Name the composer or pop group? When someone succeeds, switch stations. Try Capital or BBC Radio 1 for the low-brow, Classic FM and BBC Radio 3 for the high. Really well-rounded families should be able do all five.

One Song to the Tune of Another (with apologies to popular radio show I'm Sorry I Haven't a Clue)
The driver suggests lyrics that should be fitted to tunes usually associated with other lines, containing an equal number of syllables. 'Don't You Wish Your Girlfriend Was' to the tune of 'Good King Wenceslas', would be an example.

Pub Cricket
This diversion is dying as fast as the pubs are closing. The basic rules, published in the Automobile Association's *Book of the Road* in 1970, state that a player scores 'runs' according to how many legs there are in any passing pub name. Thus the Red Lion scores four and the Lord Nelson scores two. A player is out if the pub name contains the words 'head' or 'arms' – so the King's Arms, while scoring two for the king, sees that player depart for the pavilion.

Registration Plates
Passengers suggest words that contain the letters on the registration plate of any overtaking or overtaken vehicle. The letters must remain in the order in which they occur on the registration. For example TDS could be 'tedious', BNG, 'boring' and NAD 'nauseated'.

Silly sentences
Each person in the car supplies a word. Don't think too hard; the faster the sentence goes, the more fun will be had. See if you can grow your sentences into whole stories, maybe one that will last the whole journey.

Snooker
The colours of the cars are the colours of the snooker balls. A red car is one point, yellow is two, green three, brown four, blue five, pink six and black seven. You must pass or be passed by one to score. A red is followed by a 'colour' until you have seen 15 reds. If a white car passes or is passed you've potted the cue ball, you idiot, and that's the end of your turn.

Tunnels
Passengers must hold their breath for as long as any tunnel lasts or until they pass out, whichever is the sooner. See how red your face can get. The driver should not participate in this amusing, quiet game.

Twenty Questions
The traditional cry, 'I've got one' indicates the beginning of this old favourite. The starter identifies his or her item as animal (living things, excluding plant life), vegetable (plant life) or mineral (anything else). It could, of course, be a mixture of all three. Farmers' markets, for instance, would qualify for each category. Everyone else poses questions to try to work out what the starter, who may answer only with 'yes' or 'no', is thinking of. The person who starts keeps the score, giving frequent updates as to how many questions have been asked to up the tension.

A natural
break

Kate Fuscoe and assorted children become creative conservators.

The caterpillar that was the Conservation Corps, born in the 1950s, has transformed into the astonishing BTCV (British Trust for Conservation Volunteers) and now runs a vast range of activities. With its 50th birthday in 2009, BTCV offers thousands of placements for young people, running from school activities to UK breaks (over-16s only for these) where participants learn hands-on skills, such as hedge-laying and tree-planting. Other initiatives reach out to new volunteers, such as the funky Green Gym scheme: outdoor gardening and conservation sessions that function as a fun (and free) alternative to boring workouts on the treadmill. Taking 'Inspiring People, Improving Places' as its watchword, the BTCV aims is to inspire people to engage with their environment.

According to Susan Le, Wildlife Project Officer for Buckingham, events can cater for all ages, with the activities adapted according to who turns up on the day. As a primary school teacher, artist and conservationist, she was particularly well placed to put us through our paces in 'Wild Art'. Any initial shyness was dispelled as we all stood in a circle, welly to welly, and got our instructions. Forewarned with visual aids as to what nettles and brambles look like, and how to get out of them (the trick is to go backwards), we're given a ball of clay and set off, grabbing anything from the woodland to decorate it with. The children loved this and, as a family event, adults participated equally – no café to skulk off to for a latte... and anyway, this was part of the Family Learning Festival.

The lack of distraction was a real boon, and inspired by some pics of fabulous natural art by Andy Goldsworthy, soon we were all busily working at our personal oeuvre without a care in the world. Well, apart from the weather, which was indeed bracing. Mercifully, there was a break for hot chocolate – provided by the magical Susan, who even stumped up soya milk and gluten free biscuit for those in need. That's what I call service.

Events are as diverse as those participating. Observational ability is developed through bat or badger watching, while building mansions for minibeasts encourages home-making and architectural prowess. Developing such bushman skills as tree identification or fungi foray could be especially handy in these lean times, and there might be a chance to hunt for wild food, uncovering what the hedgerow has to offer rather than relying on Waitrose for snacks. Another session on identifying mammal prints and poo ranks high on the must-do list for most children of a certain age.

You can supplement your learning with the BBC Breathing Spaces site at www.bbc.co.uk/breathingplaces, which works in partnership with BTCV. Here you can download various pocket guides – 'Have Fun with Fungi', for example – as well as learning how to make a home for a hedgehog or a cake for the birds.

Activities can take place in a surprisingly small space (walking in circles is Susan's tip); a thorough exploration of an urban environment can reap rewards – little patches of woodland and wildlife made all the more exciting because of their unpromising surroundings.

'Just remember the wellies and wrap up warm… you're not necessarily moving about as much as when playing sport. As one child noted after an hour in the woodland, "I could live in an oven".'

I, for one, was pleasantly surprised by my foray into conservation volunteering. In my family, the great outdoors mostly means parks. For the children, urban parks are all about endless football, frisbee and rushing about in the playground, while I usually stand about watching, shiver on a park bench, chat to other mums, or if it all gets too much, retire to the café for refreshments. Our day out with the BTCV forced me to engage with the woodland – not to mention my kids – and it cost us nothing. Many of the other parents were regulars, and their children clearly loved what they were doing, and the freedom it entailed.

Going back to nature for our family day out also meant we didn't have to stump up hideous theme park admission charges, spend inordinate amounts of time waiting in queues, or run the gauntlet of the dreaded museum shop, buying tat or dispensing wads of cash for fripperies. Whats more, the mini testers proved that their BTCV experience was a successful one by insisting on going back into the woodland for more exploration and fun after their reviving hot chocolate and biscuits. Just remember the wellies, and wrap up warm, as you're not necessarily moving around as much as when playing sport or walking. As one child noted, after a chilly hour in the woodland, 'I could live in an oven'. *www.btcv.org.uk.*

296-300
Pedal in the slow lane

Camel Trail
Named after the River Camel, this 27 km Cornish cycle path follows an old railway line from Wenfordbridge to Padstow, via Bodmin. Hire cycles at Bridge Bike Hire in Wadebridge (01208 813050) and take an 8km spin down to Padstow harbour. Avoid the summer holiday crowd, by cycing from Wadebridge to Bodmin instead. For a map, call 01872 327310.

Crab & Winkle Way
Just over 11km long, this short but sweet route meanders through Kent from Canterbury to Whitstable following the disused railway track of the Crab & Winkle line. The path threads through Clowes and Blean Woods, before eventually emerging in Whitstable.

Kennet & Avon Cycle Route
This 135km trail runs from Bath to Reading and is Britain's most popular waterside cycle route. The first section passes through Bristol and Bath on the traffic-free Avon Valley cycle path. Trail walk leaflets are available from British Waterways (01380 722859, www.british waterways.co.uk). You can hire bikes from the riverside Lock Inn Café (48 Frome Road, Bradford-on-Avon, Wiltshire BA15 1LE, 01225 868068, www.thelockinn.co.uk).

Moor to Sea Cycle Route
The disused railway line that runs for 28km along the Yorkshire coast from Whitby to Scarborough (www.moortoseacycle.net) is never too steep, and almost car-free. Trailways Cycle Hire (The Old Railway Station, Hawsker, Whitby, Yorkshire YO22 4LB, 01947 820207, www.trailways.info) provides steeds and offers unusual accommodation in the shape of a 1950s railway carriage.

Speyside Way
The 12-kilometre Speyside Way is a boon for families. It's flat, with no motor traffic and panoramic views over the River Spey – plus enough twists, tunnels and woodland to sustain interest levels. Adults, note: it's studded with famous malt whisky distilleries.
www.cycling.visitscotland.com.

301
Celebrate Samhain and Beltain

Butser is a re-creation of an Iron Age farm, where ancient breeds such as Soay and Manx Loaghan sheep wander and bygone farming practices are demonstrated. Visitors are welcome all year, but the two big shindigs are Beltain (the traditional welcoming of summer) and Samhain (the Celtic New Year). They usually take place on the first Saturday in May and the last Friday in October respectively, and both involve eating, drinking and leaping over flames. For Beltain, the revellers set a wicker man alight, then repair to the farm for much feasting. Samhain sees a bonfire, apple bobbing, the baking of spuds and much making of noise. Children who've developed a taste for this Celtic caper can also sign up for the summer holiday workshops, where they can learn to cook like a Roman or knap flint like a flint-knapper.

Butser Ancient Farm Chalton Lane
Chalton, Waterlooville, Hampshire PO8 0BG (02392 598838/www.butserancientfarm.co.uk).

302
Man the lifeboats

A quirky weekend of seaside activities draws the crowds to the Royal National Lifeboat Institution's annual fundraiser in the little fishing village of Staithes, north of Whitby (www.staithes-lifeboat.co.uk). The fun begins on Friday evening with a nightgown parade through the old cobbled streets. Saturday takes off with RNLI displays, stalls and games. There are canoeing classes, boat trips, various fancy dress competitions and a totally irregular raft race across the harbour – with cheating, sabotage and water bombing all permitted. Evening brings a barbecue, disco and fireworks. Sunday's 'famous' duck race sees 1,000 yellow plastic ducks bobbing down Roxby Beck; the winning number gets a prize. An open-air service closes the weekend, when the villagers pray 'for those in peril on the sea' and a bugler plays the last post as the station flag is lowered. It would take a hard heart not to be moved.

303 *Hug a snake in the tropics*

Kids are desperate to get their hands on the snakes, millipedes and giant snails at the Meet the Keeper sessions in the Palms Tropical Oasis at Stapeley Water Gardens. Even though you're in chilly Cheshire, it's pretty hot in this re-creation of a rainforest, and you'll be sweating buckets once that millipede is working its way down your vest. Sadly, the resident crocodiles aren't up for handling.
Stapeley Water Gardens *London Road, Nantwich, Cheshire CW5 7LH (01270 623868/ www.stapeleywg.com).*

304 *Grow a bloomin' enormous sunflower*

If you want a really big bloom, select Russian Giant, a variety that can grow over three metres. You can choose whether to sow the seeds directly into the soil in your garden from May, or start them off in pots of compost earlier in the spring, then transfer them to the garden. If you're sowing in a pot, fill it with compost to about two centimetres from the top, moisten the soil and pop in your sunflower seed, about a centimetre below the surface. Place the pot on a sunny window sill and wait for the shoots to appear (it may take ten to 14 days). Once the plant has two true leaves, you can transfer it to the garden. Hold the seedling very gently by the leaf while transplanting, to avoid damage to stalk and roots.

Plant your sunflower in full sun, against a fence – or place a tall stake in the hole. Make sure the earth has plenty of organic matter, as giant sunflowers are hungry and need fertile soil. You can also grow your giant in a very large pot or bucket with holes drilled in the base, filled with good-quality compost. Place the pot by a house drainpipe so that you may use this as a stake, otherwise the pot can blow over. Sunflowers need plenty of water and feeding to grow huge – be prepared to protect the tender little seedlings from slugs and birds. Once the sunflower's big face has developed, note how it always turns to face the light: it's a true sun-worshipper.

305-307
See a House in the Clouds

The House in the Clouds in Thorpeness, Suffolk, is a fairy tale clapboard cottage, perched on a 21-metre tower. Even discovering that it was built to hide a water tank can't dispel the magic. With five bedrooms and a games room on the uppermost floor, it's a magical holiday let (020 7224 3615, www.houseintheclouds.co.uk) – if you've got enough puff to tackle the 67 stairs to the top. The village is also home to the Meare (01728 832523), a Peter Pan-themed boating lake that opened in 1913. Comandeer a rowing boat, punt, kayak or canoe to explore its many islands – looking out for the alarm clock-swallowing crocodile, Wendy's house and the pirates' lair, guarded by cannons. It's open for adventures from Easter to the end of October half-term. After your exertions, retire to the lovely tea room (01728 452156), with tables down to the water's edge.

308
Do the twist around a campfire

Make a soft dough by mixing flour, water and a pinch of salt. Find a sturdy stick and whittle the bark from it. Knead your dough into a sausage shape and wrap it around the stick, then toast it over a campfire. Serve with butter and jam.

309
Bury a beetle's breeding bucket

Stag beetles have a hard time surviving in these tidy times. Their larvae need rotting wood to eat during their four years underground, before they can emerge as the glossy horned beauties we all should love. Help the larvae by taking a plastic bucket, making some holes in it, then filling it with three-parts woodchip and one-part soil. Bury the bucket in the garden, with the top at ground level, and hope that a female beetle with some eggs to lay happens by and likes the look of it.

310
See squirmy worms at work

Ask nicely at Holywell Mead's volunteer-run environment centre and you'll be allowed to peek in the wormery, and have a poke around the compost heap. Inside, get a buzz from watching the honey bees at work in their glass-sided observation hive – and buy a jar of their honey to take home for your toast. Special themed activities and exhibitions run in the school holidays – so you might learn to make a kite on Wind Power day, or weave a festive wreath for Christmas.

The Environment Centre *Holywell Mead, Bassetsbury Lane, High Wycombe, Buckinghamshire HP11 1QX (01494 511585/www.ecobuzz.org.uk).*

311
Survive the Iron Age at Castell Henllys

Site of the BBC series in which modern folk roughed it Iron Age-style, Castell Henllys in Wales is a partially reconstructed Iron Age fort, which was occupied from around 600 BC to the first century AD. Visitors can tour the roundhouses, kitted out with looms, bread ovens, beds and hanging clothes – done up to look as if their inhabitants have just stepped out. Guided tours take place twice a day, and there's storytelling, crafts and activities for those aged six to 12 in the school holidays, from bread-making to woad face-painting.

Castell Helleys *Pembroke National Park, Lianion Park, Pembroke Dock, Pembrokeshire SA72 6DY (01239 891319/www.pcnpa.org.uk).*

312
Get wordy

As part of Wimbledon's Book Festival, which runs in October, Polka Children's Theatre hosts an event called The Word, usually on a Sunday. 2008's shindig involved Michael Rosen, Charlie Higson and Jamila Gavin, and all manner of writing and book workshops. Contact www.polkatheatre.com.

313 Guide an ocean liner into dock

Would-be sea captains should set sail for the National Maritime Museum in Greenwich, south-east London, if they want to immerse themselves in life on the ocean wave without leaving dry land. The best interactives are up on level three, where there's a quite addictive ship's bridge simulator, based on the software used to train masters of P&O ferries and lifeboats. Five screens show tricky harbour situations in New York, Dover and Sydney. All you have to do is use navigational equipment, electronic charts and radars to steer the vessel safely to shore. Easy, peasy? See how many points you score.
National Maritime Museum *Romney Road, Greenwich, London SE10 9NF (8858 4422/ www.nmm.ac.uk).*

Felix School of Rock

314 Enrol in Felix School of Rock

Felix Glenn takes on the Jack Black role in this highly regarded rock music school, based in Lewisham, London, for young musicians aged nine to 16. The school has been running for five years and provides an intensive four-day experience, with kids writing music and performing in a rock gig. The band works towards the big show on the final day, to which friends and family are invited. The school is equipped with a full PA, lights and a smoke machine – essential kit for raucous rock 'n' roll performances. For details of fees and bursaries, check www.fsor.org.uk.

315 Be king of the castle

Take a cardboard shoebox and cut a wide rectangle out of the front and back to create four corner turrets. Next, cut crenellations along the top edge and on each of the turrets. In the front cut an arch, leaving the bottom edge attached to the base of the box as a portcullis. Paint it and make paper flags to fly from the turrets. Install toy knights and guards.

316 Join the gold rush

Fortune-hunters have been panning for gold in the rivers and burns around Wanlockhead and Lockhills for centuries. At the Museum of Lead Mining you can buy a gold pan to try your luck, or take part in a summer holiday taster session to maximise your chances of turning up something other than iron pyrite (fool's gold).
Museum of Lead Mining *Wanlockhead, Buiggar, Lanarkshire ML12 6UT (01659 74387/ www.leadminingmuseum.co.uk).*

317 Have a swell time at the movies

The old Wesleyan Chapel in the former smugglers' village of Robin Hood's Bay on the north-east coast of Yorkshire is now a tea shop, with glorious views from its terrace overlooking the bay. Upstairs, the wonderful old concert hall with box pews operates as the Swell Cinema, open for family films during school holidays.
Swell Cinema *Chapel Street, Robin Hood's Bay, Whitby, North Yorkshire YO21 4SQ (01947 880180).*

318

Join the jet set in Wales

Riddled with caves, secret coves and soaring cliffs, the rugged Pembrokeshire coast is home to all sorts of wildlife. There's no better – or faster – way to zip around its nooks and crannies than on a RIB (Rigid Inflatable Boat) trip. Venture Jet (01348 837764, www.venture jet.co.uk) has been speeding round these parts for over 20 years, and knows all the best spots to peep at a puffin colony or see baby seals. If you go on the 90-minute Wet & Wild trip, expect to get soaked as the skipper shows off the boat's awesome 360-degree steering and thrilling power braking.

319

Make a piñata

Mexican gatherings traditionally centre round a piñata, now a stalwart at children's parties. It consists of a colourful papier mâché shape, full of goodies that are released when you hit it with a big stick. Blindfolded.

Small children aren't bothered about how perfect your piñata is, as long as there are plenty of sweets inside. The good thing about making your own is that it's a fairly imprecise art, and there are lots of jobs for kids of various ages. But allow a few days for the process, so the papier mâché can dry.

Blow up a big balloon and follow the papier mâché method as outlined on p68, leaving a hole at the top that's big enough tto insert the sweets. Use white paper for the final outer layer: it will make it easier to decorate. When the piñata is completely dry, pop the balloon and remove. Make a couple of small holes for string to hang it up, then paint and decorate with crepe paper, glitter and streamers. A round balloon is ideal for a face, but could equally become a flower, a fish, a sun or whatever takes your fancy. Fill with plenty of sweets, and let the fun begin.

320
Cruise the River Tyne

If you'd like to find out how it feels to be a celebrity (no special skills required), there's no better way than taking a cruise down the Tyne, taking in views of the old shipyards, the Tyne Gorge and Tynemouth Priory at the rivermouth. Time it right on a Saturday afternoon, and the crowds thronging Quayside and the South Shore as far as the Baltic Centre all stop and watch and wave as the Millennium Bridge does its 'winking' party-piece especially to let your boat through. Make believe you're James Bond, or try a regal wave.
01670 785666/www.riverescapes.co.uk.

321
Tour a chocolate factory...

Learn about the Aztecs' love of chocolate, write your name in chocolate, or be drenched in a deluge of chocolate rain – a virtual-reality downpour, sadly. That said, there's plenty of real chocolate to enjoy as you explore Cadbury World, with all its big vats of melted chocolate, free samples en route and a shop at the end. To work off the calories, get the kids chasing computer-generated Creme Eggs in the interactive zone, or try out the playground.
Cadbury World *Linden Road, Bourneville, Birmingham B30 2LU (0845 4503599/ www.cadburyworld.co.uk).*

322
...or make your own

West London chocolate shop Melt is a hotbed of confectionery creativity, stirring up daily batches of truffles, chocolate nut slabs and delicious chocolate dippers in its open kitchen. Visitors are welcome to watch the chocolatiers at work – but more of a treat are the Wednesday and Saturday Children's Hour sessions. Here, over-sixes can pour chocolate into animal moulds and make their own lollipops. The cost is £25-£35 a session.
Melt *59 Ledbury Road, London W11 2AA (020 7727 5030/www.meltchocolates.com).*

323 Feed the penguins at Birdworld

Cackling, vibrant macaws, secretary birds and green jays are among the feathered residents at Birdworld in Surrey. The highlight of the day, though, is when the penguins snaffle fresh fish at feeding times (11am and 3.30pm). Visitors can pay to dole out the fish (it costs £29.95) – over-sevens only. Book in advance.
Birdworld *Holt Pound, Farnham, Surrey GU10 4LD (01420 22838/www.birdworld.co.uk).*

324 Be a Cleversticks

Don't be afraid of chopsticks. Why not set yourself the challenge of eating every meal with them until you're a champ? Grip one stick between thumb and fourth finger, the other between forefinger and middle finger. Pick up food morsels by pinching them together. When you can bring a pea neatly to your mouth, you're a Cleversticks – just like the boy in Bernard Ashley's book of the same name.

325 Join King Henry VIII for Christmas

Festive frolics abound at Hampton Court as King Henry VIII and his courtiers celebrate a Tudor Christmas, and the opulent apartments come alive with music and entertainment. Your senses will be filled with the sounds, smells and tastes of life 500 years ago: play Tudor games, dance the farandole and exchange jibes with the resident jester, then slip below stairs where the Master Cook and his chefs are bringing the palace's kitchens to life once more, preparing a sumptuous Christmas feast. Warm yourself by roaring fires where chickens and lambs turn on the spit and watch Hampton Court's famous team of food historians produce a meal fit for a king. With foolery, guzzling and fire-juggling, King Henry VIII's Christmas party makes for some right royal revelry. The event runs from around 27 December to 1 January, with admission included in the price of a standard ticket; a daily programme of what's on is available online from early December.
Hampton Court Palace *East Molesey, Surrey KT8 9AU (0844 482 7777/www.hrp.org.uk).*

Hampton Court Palace

326-328 *Go out after dark*

To see natural illuminations

There are some insects that you might just miss in the daylight. Take glow-worms, for example. They are in fact beetles, and the flightless female's bright bottom is her bling to attract night-time suitors. Some wildlife centres organise glow-worm hunts. One of the best places to hunt for the somewhat rare glimmering grubs is Hambledon Hill Reserve, at the heart of an Iron Age earthwork near Blandford Forum in Dorset. In summer, Natural England (www.naturalengland.org.uk) runs glow-worm walks; to join in, call 0845 600 3078.

To marvel at moths

National Moth Night takes place annually, usually towards the end of summer, and is run by *Atropos* (the journal for butterfly, moth and dragonfly enthusiasts) and Butterfly Conservation. Participants throughout the British Isles record the moths in their chosen location and the results are pooled into Britain's largest survey. For more on mothing, moth traps and moth events, and to find out what your local lepidopterists are doing, log on to www.nationalmothnight.info.

To visit an enchanted forest

Each November and December, a swath of trees at the beautiful National Arboretum in Gloucestershire (Westonbirt, near Tetbury, GL8 8QS, 01666 880220, www.forestry.gov.uk) are lit up to become the Enchanted Wood. A kaleidoscope of colours illuminates the 1.6km trail through the dark woods. Near Pitlochrie in Perthshire, Faskally Wood (www.enchanted forest.org.uk) is another forest with surprises in store, if you visit in autumn. Its spectacular night-time light and sound show is based around a changing theme: one year, intrepid visitors blasted off on a voyage into space, beginning with a rocket lift-off.

Enchanted Forest

329

Play with your food

Art is such sweet pleasure if you raid the larder for materials. Rifle inside the jam cupboard for runny honey, chocolate spread or smooth peanut butter to use as glue on your sheet of paper: press on strawberry laces, hundreds-and-thousands, silver balls, Jelly Tots and rainbow drops for a colourful confection. Stick your designs on sheets of rice paper and you can eat the lot when you've finished.

1000 songs, films and books to change your life

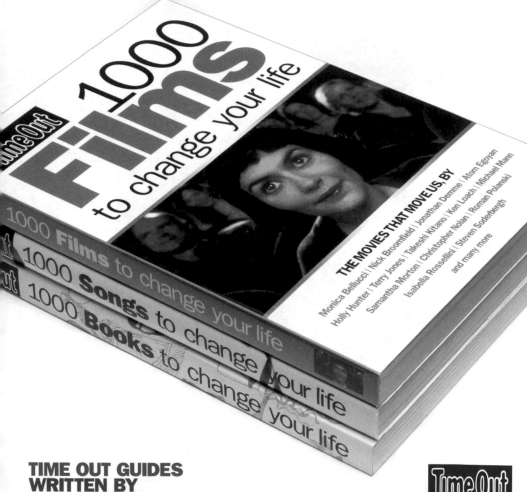

1000 Films 1000

Films to change your life

TimeOut

THE MOVIES THAT MOVE US, BY

Monica Bellucci / Nick Broomfield / Jonathan Demme / Atom Egoyan
Holly Hunter / Terry Jones / Takeshi Kitano / Ken Loach / Michael Mann
Samantha Morton / Christopher Nolan / Roman Polanski
Isabella Rossellini / Steven Soderbergh
and many more

1000 **Films** to change your life

1000 **Songs** to change your life

1000 **Books** to change your life

**TIME OUT GUIDES
WRITTEN BY
LOCAL EXPERTS**
visit timeout.com/shop

TimeOut
Guides

330 *Make the world a better place*

Teach Your Granny to Text & Other Ways to Change the World contains 30 small things to make the world a better place. It's the brainchild of an organisation called We Are What We Do (www.wearewhatwedo.org) – and of 4,386 children, who suggested the ideas. It's full of gems, such as always asking 'why?', growing something and eating it, or testing your teacher. The book costs £10, and might just change your life.

331
Be spooked by skulls in Kent

Hythe, in Kent, looks like an unassuming seaside town – but it has a dark secret. Below the 11th-century St Leonard's church is Britain's largest ossuary (a resting place for human bones), home to around 2,000 ancient skulls and some 8,000 thigh bones, neatly piled along one wall. Venture down, if you dare, and stand eyeball to eye socket with a skull – it'll send a delicious shiver down your spine.
St Leonard's *Oak Walk, Hythe, Kent CT21 5DN (01303 263739/www.stleonardschurchhythe kent.org).*

332 *Create a colourful carnation*

Step one: take a pure white carnation with a long stem. With a sharp knife (and the help of a willing grown-up), split the carnation's stem lengthwise, from the bottom to about halfway up. Step two: fill two glasses with water. Use food colouring to turn the water in one glass dark red, and the other blue. Step three: place the glasses next to each other, with one half of the carnation's stem in each glass. Step four: check the carnation a day later, then two days later. Can you tell that the carnation has been drinking the water? You'll be able to see – in glorious technicolour – how water travels up the tubes in the stem to reach the other parts of the plant.

333 *Flock to the Big Sheep*

The lambs at this sheep farm may be sweet, but it's the fleet-footed sheep who get the attention in the races held from Easter to October. Place your bet on Red Ram, Woolly Jumper or Sheargar as they jostle at the starting line, ridden by fearless knitted jockeys. Dog and duck trials and horse-whispering demonstrations are enthralling. Wet weather activities include pottery making and enjoying cream teas in the café; there's an indoor play area too. Activities are seasonal, so call to check what's on before paying a visit.
Big Sheep *Abbotsham, Bideford, Devon EX39 5AP (01237 472366/www.thebigsheep.co.uk).*

334 *Sit on Arthur's Seat*

Not many cities can rival the craggy splendour of Edinburgh (www.edinburgh.org), where Holyrood Park is dominated by a cluster of lofty hills. The main peak is known as Arthur's Seat – though there's no throne to relax on once you've clambered 251 metres to the top to survey the city. Many people think that the hill is nothing to do with the king, and that its name comes from 'Archer's Seat': in Gaelic, 'ard-na-said' means 'height of arrows', and the hill provided a vantage point from which to repel marauders in the Middle Ages.

335 *Descend into the Pit*

Once you've been kitted out with a hard hat and lamp, you're ready to take a trip down the 91-metre mineshaft at the colliery at Blaenafon, near Abergavenny, locked in a steel cage. After an hour exploring the cramped and chilly tunnels, you'll be relieved to re-emerge into the fresh air – though spare a thought for the boys who worked in the darkness in the early 19th century, some as young as eight.
Big Pit National Coal Museum *Blaenafon, Torfaen NP4 9XP (01495 790311/ www.museumwales.ac.uk).*

A few of my favourite things

336-345

Gail Porter, television presenter

My daughter Honey and I have an annual pass for London Zoo (Outer Circle, Regent's Park, London NW1 4RY, 020 7722 3333, www.zsl.org), so we tend to go there a couple of times a month. They have all sorts of activities, like drawing the animals or having your face painted, and we get involved in everything. Honey loves the monkeys – she just stands and laughs at them for ages and ages – and she likes hanging out with the gorillas too. We know many of the staff by name because we're in there so much.

One of our favourite days out in London is to visit the Trocadero (12 Coventry Street, W1D 7DH, 020 7439 1791, www.london trocadero.com) for bowling. It has the only bowling alley in central London. It's great to eat out together too. After bowling, Honey and I often visit the nearest branch of Yo! Sushi (19 Rupert Street, W1D 7DH, 020 7434 2724, www.yosushi.com). Honey loves watching the moving plates going round, and choosing what she wants. She has become a big fan of sashimi. I've always said to her, 'Don't knock anything until you've tried it,' so she'll try anything once. She tried sashimi and fell in love with it. I'm very proud of her for that.

We also visit Regent's Park (020 7298 2000, www.royalparks.org.uk), a beautiful open space. Our favourite activity in the park is to go rowing on the lake there. It's especially good when it's rather cold in the winter – we put on our hats and get a boat (the shallow boating lake hires out boats by the hour for £6.50, or pedalos for smaller children for £3/20min). Honey always wants to row, which results in us going round and round in circles, but it's great fun.

I took Honey to the Slow Food Market on the South Bank (Southbank Centre, Belvedere Road, London SE1 8XX, 0871 663 2501, www.southbankcentre.co.uk), and she really adored it, tasting the produce and admiring the various displays. In fact we spend a lot of time hanging out on the South Bank: it's a terrific place to take a walk as there's so much to see. Honey loves riding on the carousel, and there are always all sorts of street performers to watch.

Another thing Honey enjoys is taking one of the half-hour boat trips on the Thames (www.citycruises.com), where they tell you all about the architecture. It's like going out with a mini-adult for the day. She also loves the open-topped tourist buses – the ones that fill you in on the history of London (020 8877 1722, www.theoriginaltour.com). She's quite the little historian.

Honey's getting to the age where she wants to try out rollercoasters, but she is only six so quite often she'll freak out and change her mind halfway down the queue. I took her to Chessington World of Adventures (Leatherhead Road, Chessington, Surrey KT9 2NE, 0870 999 0045, www.chessington.com) and she was fine, but when we went on the 'Finding Nemo' ride at Euro Disney, she cried because it was in the dark. She really wants to go to Thorpe Park (Staines Road, Chertsey, Surrey KT16 8PN, 0870 444 4466, www.thorpepark.com), but we'll have to see.

When we were at Euro Disney, Honey was trying out her French. She's been learning it since she was three, and we've got a board game in French at home so she's teaching me too. She tried to say 'bonjour' to everyone, but they all kept speaking to her in English and she couldn't understand why. She kept saying, 'Mummy, why won't they talk to me? I'm really trying!' I had to explain to her that they're not used to English people speaking French.

Honey's a tomboy, just like I was. She doesn't want to do ballet. I offered, but she said, 'It's boring, Mummy, that's what everyone does.' We went to Pineapple Dance Studios in Covent Garden (7 Langley Street, London WC2H 9JA, 020 7836 4004, www.pineapple.uk.com) and watched the classes, and she decided street dance was what she wanted to do. She's got her little street dance outfit and her leggings, so she's all set.

Festivals and families can be a match made in heaven – if you pick the right one. Under-fives are always free, but at some places you don't pay until you're over 12. Extra charges may apply if you bring more than two children for each paying adult.

Camp Bestival, Dorset
Lulworth Castle is the backdrop for this offshoot of the Isle of Wight's Bestival. Past delights in the Kids' Garden have included space hoppers, clown shows, a bouncy castle and dressing-up. The Breastival Baby Temple area is for breastfeeding and nappy-changing. *020 7379 3133/www.campbestival.co.uk.*

Glastonbury, Somerset
A happy chaos reigns on the Kidz Field at Glastonbury, with wacky children's theatre companies, teetering stiltwalkers, juggling clowns and music and craft workshops. In the Green Kids Field, children can climb, paint, make pottery or curl up to listen to a story. *www.glastonburyfestivals.co.uk.*

Larmer Tree Festival, Wiltshire/Dorset
With just 4,000 tickets on sale, this fun-sized festival is ideal for families. The setting is leafy, the line-up varied, and the eco policies spot-on; even the loos are award-winning. For teens, there might be drumming, T-shirt design and graffiti art workshops; for tinies, a carnival parade, baby yoga or a teddy bears' picnic. *023 8071 1820/www.larmertreefestival.co.uk.*

Latitude, Sussex
Southwold's Henham Park is the setting for Latitude's mix of music, art, literature, comedy and theatre. Kids can make flags, hats and costumes to sport on Sunday's big parade, be wildlife detectives in the woodland or perfect their unicycling. *Information 020 7009 3001/tickets 0871 231 0821/www.latitudefestival.co.uk.*

Secret Garden Party, Cambridgeshire
This four-day festival embraces the offbeat, with hula Olympics, blazing pirate ships, Secret Adventure walks and dressing-up. Kids' Camp is in the family camping zone. *www.secretgardenparty.com.*

Shambala, Northamptonshire
'Plenty of surprises' are promised at Shambala, which prides itself on its green approach and cuddly, community feel. Early-bird cartoon sessions get the day off to a cracking start, after which the trampolines, puppet shows, swing boats and cookery sessions beckon. Music-wise, expect a mix of folk, reggae and world music. *www.shambalafestival.org.*

Solfest, Cumbria
Held on the Cumbrian coast, Solfest is a delightful alternative to bigger festivals. Yoga, t'ai chi and laughter workshops add to the vibe, while crafts range from making bird masks to fashioning fairy skirts. Grown-ups quaff Solfest ale and enjoy the music: Roisin Murphy, the Bees and Alabama 3 have graced the stage in the past. Ticket numbers are limited. *www.solwayfestival.co.uk.*

Wychwood, Gloucestershire
Held at Cheltenham Racecourse, Wychwood is a compact, well-organised shindig, with plenty on for kids. More than 100 free workshops take in all sorts of crafts and activities, from making balloon animals to learning the trapeze: the children's literary festival is a recent addition. At Sunday's family parade, kids can show off their home-made costumes and masks. *01993 772580/www.wychwoodfestival.com.*

Bestival

Get the local experience

Over 50 of the world's top destinations available.

354 Hug a giant redwood

You'll never get your arms around the trunky Californian beauty known as *Sequoiadendron giganteum*, located outside the Elizabethan mansion at beautiful Wakehurst Place. It's 35 metres tall and at Christmas becomes even more alluring, when 2,000 fairy lights are draped on its branches. It's so luminescent that pilots flying into Gatwick look out for it. **Royal Botanic Gardens Wakehurst Place** *Ardingly, West Sussex RH17 6TN (www.kew.org).*

355 Dress up as a monk

The World Heritage site of Fountains Abbey makes for a full day of exploring among the mighty abbey ruins and the glorious grounds, watercourses and follies of the adjoining Studley Royal Water Garden – which also encompasses a medieval deer park. Activities run throughout the year: try on a habit and learn how the monks lived; get medieval with re-enactors at their encampment; or join Regency dancers in the Georgian water garden. In summer bring a picnic and watch some outdoor theatre: *Peter Pan*, perhaps, or *The Hound of the Baskervilles*.
Fountains Abbey & Studley Royal Water Garden *Ripon, near Harrogate, North Yorkshire HG4 3DY (01765 608888/www.fountains abbey.org.uk).*

356 Get pedalling on the cheap

When buying a child's bike, says Nick Fish of the Cycling Tourists' Club, be sure it fits and is light to handle. A cheap machine can be a false economy, but you can save money with the Bikeman, whose supply of second-hand mounts includes BMXs and mountain bikes, which have come from police auctions or been rescued from old sheds. For an overhauled model, guaranteed for six months, expect to pay around £89.
Bikeman *9 Abbey Street, Cambridge CB1 2QP (07850 814186/www.thebikeman.co.uk).*

357 Build a better sandwich

Children love a bit of hands-on sandwich designing. Get them involved by starting a discussion about favourite fillings. Encourage them to write a list of their ingredients; creative spelling and fillings are both allowed! Younger ones could draw or dictate their ideas. The next step is assembling the required ingredients. You could either challenge the children to do this from fridge and store cupboard, or take them shopping with their lists. Next, the children make their own sandwiches, spreading, sprinkling, grating and cutting (depending on age). If the sandwiches are for a picnic, the children can wrap and label them. Try a sandwich swap: who has made a super sandwich?

358 Go dolphin-spotting in Scotland

The north-east shoreline of Scotland is awash with marine wildlife, with pods of bottle-nosed dolphins living in the Moray Firth, alongside harbour porpoises, minke whales and other cetaceans. You can see the animals from cliffs and headlands: good spots include Chanonry Point on the Black Isle, Spey Bay, near Fochabers on the Moray coast, and the Sutors, two headlands that sit at the mouth of the Cromarty Firth. All you need is warm clothing, binoculars, something to eat and drink, and plenty of patience (that might be in short supply among younger children). The dolphins often come quite close to land, and are easy to see on a calm day.

If you want to get closer, all kinds of boat trips are available, from high-speed RIBs (Rigid Inflatable Boats) to more sedate cruisers. Prices (from around £20 for adults, £18 for children) and time on the water vary, so it's best to book ahead. Trips usually run from March/April to September/October; they are weather- and tide-dependent, and none can guarantee dolphin sightings. For guidelines on watching from the shore, and a list of approved boat operators, consult www.dolphinspace.org.

Dogs have their disadvantages – all that stick-chasing and poo-scooping. Instead, why not take a llama for a walk? There are centres across the country where you can amble with the gentle South American beast of burden; here are some ideas to get you started.

Anyone over eight can explore the softly rolling Surrey Hills with one of the eight-strong flock at Surrey Hills Llamas (01428 682883, www.surrey-hills-llamas.co.uk). Look out for super-friendly Surya, who likes snuggling up to unsuspecting visitors, or see if fuzzy-coated Fidel Castro will give you a kiss.

The Forest of Dean is also fine llama strolling terrain, and home to Severnwye Llama Trekking (01594 528482, www.severn wyellamatrekking.co.uk). Children can lead one of the centre's 12 llamas, or ride in Geoffrey the donkey's trap. There are three resident camels – though, because of their size, they're more suited to strolls with adults and teenagers.

Northamptonshire's Catanger Llamas (01295 768676, www.llamatrekking.co.uk) offer an hour-long trek through the woods, planned with shorter legs in mind – though you have to be eight or older.

For a really wild llama walk, try Lochend Llamas (07887 828756, www.highlandllama treks.com) in the glorious Scottish Highlands. Walks are tailored to visitors' requirements: an hour's amble round the shores of Loch Duich would be perfect for families, though kids also love the thrill of getting up early for a sunrise wildlife-spotting walk.

Surrey Hills Llamas

363 Mill around at Avoncroft

Avoncroft's six-hectare site is a wonderful jumble of history. A beamed Tudor pile, a cheap and cheerful 1940s prefab and a tiny octagonal counting-house are among the motley gathering; if you like your history hands-on, pop into the working 19th-century windmill to try your hand at milling some grain. The museum is also home to the National Telephone Kiosk Collection: check out the 1960s Police Box, which found fame as Dr Who's TARDIS.

Avoncroft Museum of Historic Buildings
Stoke Heath, Bromsgrove, Worcestershire B60 4JR (01527 831363/www.avoncroft.org.uk).

364 Explore outer space (but be back in time for tea)

Ready to face the final frontier? Then take a seat in Intech Science Centre's digital planetarium and prepare for lift-off. Experience a rocket launch from inside an astronaut's body, speed around the solar system or watch galaxies collide on the 17-metre dome, right above your head. With surround sound and a shuddering floor, it's edge-of-the-seat stuff. Once you've come back down to earth, there are 100 hands-on exhibits and experiments, from bending light to creating your own tornado. You can also hold birthday parties here – fuelled by sausages, ice-cream and pizza, mind, rather than sachets of space food.

Intech Science Centre & Planetarium
Telegraph Way, Morn Hill, Winchester, Hampshire SO21 1HX (01962 863791/www.intech-uk.com).

365 Clown around in Bognor

Every March, clowns across the country polish up their red noses for the Clown Convention, held in the seaside town of Bognor Regis (www.bognorregistc.org.uk). The three-day event brings a feast of tomfoolery and tricks. It culminates in a street parade on Sunday – watch out for squirting flowers in buttonholes and low-flying custard pies.

366-368 Construct a cunning disguise

Unleash your children's creativity with an afternoon of mask making, then watch as they're transformed into robots, superheroes, monsters and monkeys.

Paper bag masks

Use large brown paper bags, big enough to pop over your child's head. Children will need help making holes in the correct places for their eyes; once this is accomplished, decorate the bag with felt pens, paint, scraps of material, wool and glitter. The bag's corners can also be twisted to make rather nifty ears.

Paper plate masks

With cut-out eye holes, the addition of ears and a few judicious ornaments, a paper plate makes a cheery animal mask. Colour the plate with paints or crayon, or stick on furry fabric, sheeps wool or feathers. Pipe cleaners make whiskers, yarn is an effective mane. For a three-dimensional pig mask, fold a piece of card concertina-style, then glue it to the plate and fix a circle on it. Your mask can either be attached to a stick and held in front of the face, or attached around the head with elastic, threaded through side holes .

Traditional masks

Draw a mask shape on a piece of card, making sure it's the right size for your child's face. Once it's cut out, decorate it as a superhero mask in black or spider's web patterns, or create a colourful carnival mask: glitter, sequins and colour-clashing feathers look fantastic. Add elastic to the sides, or hold it mysteriously in front of your face on a slim stick.

369 Have a slug-collecting competition

Don't be sluggish – pick up the slimy pests in your garden, take them far away – to the park, perhaps – and do your seedlings a favour. For the richest pickings, head out after a rainfall, as that's when they crawl out to feed.

370 Ski in any season...

Take a short but sweet ski break to one of the UK's indoor snow slopes – pricey, but less ruinous than a family jaunt to the Alps. Xscape (020 7932 8000, www.xscape.co.uk) has centres dotted across the country, while the SnowDome at Tamworth (River Drive, Tamworth, Staffordshire B79 7ND, 08448 000011, www. snowdome.co.uk) offers an all-year winter wonderland, with tubing and ice-skating, plus a play area for snowball-toting tinies.

371 ...or hone your toboggan technique

Swadlincote Ski & Snowboard Centre may not have real snow, but it does have a thrilling toboggan run. Instead of a snowy slope, you race down a slick, 650-metre steel slipway, with plenty of twists and turns; four to sevens must be accompanied by an adult, but over-eights can go it alone. Ready, steady – slide!
Swadlincote Ski & Snowboard Centre
John Nike Leisuresport Complex, Sir Herbert Wragg Way, Swadlincote, Derbyshire DE11 8LP (01283 217200/www.swadlincoteskislope.co.uk).

372
Make fabric bows

Take some pretty fabric, then cut into two rectangles of equal size, 9cm long x 4cm wide. Lay one rectangle on the other with the outside surface (the one you want to display) facing each other. Sew around the edge, leaving a gap (so that you can turn the fabric right side out). Turn it right side out and stitch the small gap. Lay a small piece of ribbon across the narrow part of the rectangle, in the centre, and tie it tight until it scrunches into a bow. It should look a bit like a bowtie. Slip a hair pin or safety pin on the ribbon, so that you can wear the bow in your hair or pin it on to clothes or bags.

373-377
Go on a bug safari

Have a family adventure in your back garden. Ingredients: inquisitive kids, magnifying glass, clear container. Net optional. The easy method: send the children into the garden. Put the kettle on. Once they've found a bug, they must pop it into the insect-viewing chamber (aka a jam jar with a few holes in the lid). Then it's time for a bit of observing: count their legs and eyes, and note how they move – is it fast or slow? Can they jump? Sketch them in a notebook, give them a few leaves to munch – do release the bugs after your observations, though.

If you want some help with your studies, visit a wildlife centre. The Washington Wetland Centre in Tyne & Wear (Pattinson, Washington NE38 8LE, 0191 416 5454, www.wwt.org.uk) has a new insect garden, with plants and features that attract the creatures. Kids can observe or build their own 'insect hotel'. They might also be interested in Insect Week, usually in June (www.nationalinsectweek.co.uk). The Wildfowl & Wetlands Trust reserve in Cambridgeshire (Welney Wetland Centre, Hundred Foot Bank, Welney, near Wisbech, PE14 9TN, 01353 860711, www.wwt.org.uk) likes to mark this special week with insect trails, pond dipping and mask making.

The Rye Harbour Nature Reserve (Harbour Road, Rye, East Sussex TN31 7TT, 01797 227784, www.wildrye.info) is a salty wetland area with reedbeds, lagoons and an incredible quantity of wildlife. The wardens organise activities throughout the year. Devil's Dyke in West Sussex also offers an Ugly Bug Safari, during which families can search for different creatures that live on the South Downs (0844 800 1895, www.nationaltrust.org.uk).

Real keenies may want to join the Amateur Entomologists Society (PO Box 8774, London SW7 5ZG, www.amentsoc.org), which offers junior membership for £12 (five to 15 years). It includes a Bug Club magazine six times a year, fun things to make, articles and experiments to stoke interest in the world of bugs (such as building a maze to determine whether we can influence the turning behaviour of a woodlouse). Fascinating stuff.

378 *Watch a lobster undress*

At Padstow's National Lobster Hatchery, there are thousands of marine crustaceans in various states of development. It's a lobster restocking project, so local fishermen bring in 'berried' (ie heavy with eggs) female lobsters, whose larvae can hatch and swim about without fear of predators. The young are transferred to tanks and on plankton to grow up big and strong.

Visitors to the hatchery can see the growing babies and stroppy adolescents, as well as full-grown celebrity giants such as Dai the Claw. The undressing bit is when a semi-mature lobster goes through a moult. Sometimes the soft moulted lobster is bright blue, sometimes creamy grey. Once they're mature, the lobsters are released into the wild. There's an 'adopt a lobster' programme for £1.50.

National Lobster Hatchery *South Quay, Padstow, Cornwall PL28 8BL (01841 533877/ www.nationallobsterhatchery.co.uk).*

379 *Search for s-s-snakes*

Spotting ponies and deer in the New Forest is as easy as falling off a log – for more of a challenge, make snake sightings your mission. The forest is home to number of species. Grass snakes (green and black) are at home on land or water as they search for frogs, bird's eggs and mice. Grey-brown smooth snakes are secretive, living in burrows on the heath. Venomous adders are easy to spot, thanks to their zig-zag markings. They love basking in the sun. If you see one, admire it from a distance. Sunny days are best for observing snakes at the New Forest Reptile Centre.

New Forest Reptile Centre *Bournemouth Road, Lyndhurst, Hampshire SO43 (023 8028 3141/ www.thenewforest.co.uk).*

380 *Set up the perfect making station*

What do children need to get creative? A well-equipped making station: an accessible, wipe-clean table on which to work, ideally with a unit of plastic drawers that your child can pull out easily, nearby; IKEA does a good one. Be sure your collection of making materials contains items that are appropriate for your child's age. Here are some ideas:

● Paper in a range of colours, size and textures. Envelopes.

● Card. A4 and A5 sheets are ideal for cutting and folding into cards, bookmarks and boxes.

● Paint. Put ready-mix paint in sturdy spill-proof tubs with lids that have holes for brushes. Stick to a few colours and encourage colour mixing, and provide a selection of brush sizes as well as paint rollers and sponges.

● Glue sticks are great, but stronger PVA glue is better for collage work using heavier materials. Include a spreader or two, as well as a plastic pot with a lid to store leftover glue, which will save you money.

● Collage materials – beads, sequins, plastic shapes, shells and buttons – organised into boxes with separate lidded compartments. Encourage children to keep the compartments in order.

● Glitter in shaker pots.

● Scissors that are sharp enough to cut paper; plastic scissors are just frustrating. Train your child in good scissor habits and no one will get hurt; pointed ends are more versatile.

● Tape, string, ribbon in all colours and textures , elastic, paper clips and fasteners, a hole punch and a stapler.

● Doilies, felt, wool, net and scraps of material. The shiny stuff is particularly popular.

● Felt-tip pens, wax, crayons, oil pastels and pencils in good condition, with lids in place and tips sharpened.

A song in their heart

*Rick Jones **joins the kids in singing an ode to Laura Joy.***

In the city of chocolate, children sing in the holidays. It's not because of the dark brown confection that youngsters suddenly become melodious, though, nor is it even for joy at the break-up of school. Instead, it's thanks to the popular holiday singing workshops set up and led by one of the residents of Bournville, the Birmingham suburb that was built by Cadbury's for its esteemed employees.

Laura Joy Godwin, a mezzo-soprano and graduate of the Birmingham Conservatoire of Music, started the Bournville holiday singing courses in 2008. Though she has been involved in singing all her life, she is also possessed of an instinct for enterprise and, on leaving the conservatoire, decided to go out and create her own opportunities. The church of St Francis in Bournville had already had reason to be grateful for Godwin's marketing skills as she had started a choir there, recruiting by visiting local schools and addressing assemblies. The children came forward and were kitted out with cassocks, which made them feel important.

Parents soon began to report an excellent effect. 'The kids weren't just learning singing,' says Godwin. 'Their reading skills improved too, as a result of following the hymns and the song-sheets.'

Godwin's Holiday Singing Courses, which fill the Easter and summer vacations, take place in St Francis' church hall. There is no audition. The children, usually is groups of about 15, aged six to 16, work from 10am until 3pm daily for five days. The focus is on the singing, but they also learn other aspects of stagecraft, such as dancing, acting and costume- and prop-making. At the end of the week, they show off these skillls by putting on a show. Parents pay £100 per child for the whole week – a mere £4 an hour for 25 hours' tuition. Godwin is aided by a specialist drama teacher and her pianist friend Natalie, a fellow student from the conservatoire, who accompanies her in concerts outside the singing workshops. 'The first concert we put on together was a charity event for Action Aid.

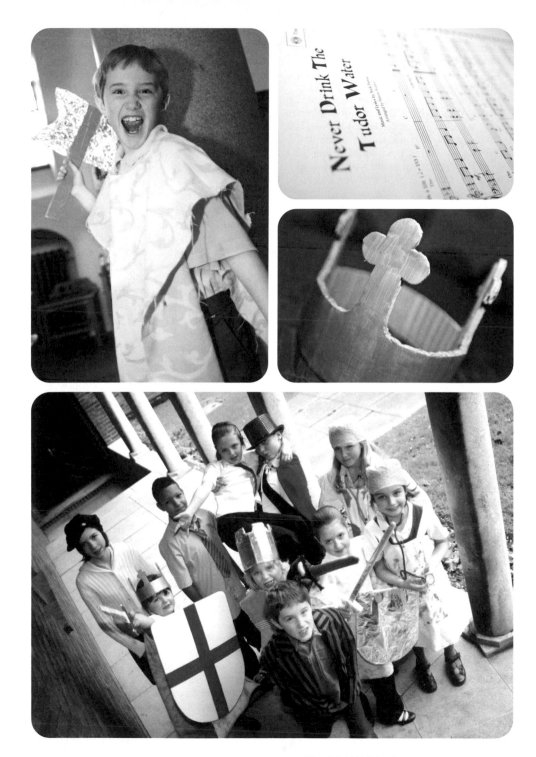

Text within image: Never Drink The Tudor Water

It was all our own idea and we raised £508,' says Godwin proudly, ever the entrepreneur.

The workshop teaching day is broken into five slots. The first contains welcome songs, vocal exercises, rounds, canons, a silly dance or two, and breaking-the-ice games such as 'the fishy song', which has gaps for children to insert their own names. In Bell-under-the-Chair a child is blindfolded and sits on a chair in the centre of a circle of other children. One of these then attempts, without making any noise, to retrieve the bell. If it rings, the blindfoldee points in the direction of the sound. 'It hones their listening skills, because they have to be really, really quiet,' explains Godwin.

'In schools they call me the crazy singing lady.'

After a short break, the group listens to, discusses and rehearses the music for the forthcoming show. Young children pick up music very effectively by ear, says Godwin, while reading music is a skill acquired with more experience and maturity. Of the two daily afternoon sessions, the first is a music

rehearsal and the second a prop and costume workshop. During the midday break, the children eat their packed lunches and let off steam in Bournville Park beside the church unless the weather is bad, when they play games in the church hall. 'You always know if it's going to rain here because they open all the vents in the factory, and you can smell the chocolate throughout Bournville,' says Godwin.

In 2008 the work chosen was Nick Perrin's *The Keymaster*, about a supply teacher confronted by a history class who express their boredom in a song. To liven up proceedings, the teacher produces a key which can turn a clock back to different dates in history. Of the 12 scenes written for the original show, Godwin chose four for production: The Battle of Hastings, Tudor Medicine, Victorian Child Labour and World War II Evacuee. Godwin believes her workshops are effective not only at bringing out children's basic musical abilities, but also at creating awareness of the need for co-operation when working with others, instilling confidence and improving the participants' social skills. 'Because the workshops happen during the holidays, the kids have to get on with those from other schools, and end up making new friends. The friends I've made through music have lasted me all my life.'

Nor can you underestimate the confidence-building that singing in a choir and staging a show provides. Inevitably, some children take the lead more willingly than others, but everyone soon becomes aware of the contribution even the youngest chorus member or lowliest props-provider makes to the ensemble. Godwin distributes solo opportunities equally, but doesn't pressurise children who feel they're not ready; simply being part of the team is experience enough.

'In schools they call me the crazy singing lady,' Godwin laughs. She currently busy running choirs and teaching singing in four different schools in Berkshire. 'I always wanted to be a primary school teacher,' she confides. 'Now my singing training has given me that opportunity and I love it.' The kids and parents seem to love it too: her courses fill up six months ahead, before she even starts advertising.
0781 761 7923/www.laurajoygodwin.com.

382 Create a spinning snake

You need tin foil, scissors, a tea light, an elastic band and a knitting needle. Take some tin foil and cut out a spiral snake shape. Attach the knitting needle to the tea light using an elastic band, then bend the snake's head over the top of the knitting needle. Light the tea light, and watch the snake spin as the heat rises.

383 Have a family poetry slam

Among the ancient Greeks, poetry was always spoken. It was accompanied by a lyre – which is where the word 'lyric' comes from. Prizes were awarded, in the form of crowns made from laurel leaves. Revive the practice with family and friends. Tell everyone to write a limerick, agree whose is the funniest and award them the laurel crown.

384 Spy on the hives

Established in 1949, Quince Honey Farm (North Road, South Molton, Devon EX36 3AZ (01769 572401/www. quincehoneyfarm.co.uk).has 1,500 hives scattered across Devon. In its exhibition hall are 18 colonies, whose quarters range from a hollow tree to a dolls' house. Each colony is safely contained behind glass, its inner workings revealed by the touch of a button that opens up the hive. There are interactive displays about the honey-making process from flower to table, and lots of samples to taste.

385 Meet long-extinct animals in Tring

Walter Rothschild started his first museum at the age of ten, and as a grown-up, filled the grounds at Tring Park in Hertfordshire with giant tortoises, zebras and cassowaries – huge, flightless birds, with long, dagger-like claws. He also founded Tring's Natural History Museum: a Noah's Ark of stuffed species from around the globe. Polar bears, pangolins and crocodiles are on display, along with a handful of now-extinct species: this could be your one-and-only chance to see a South African quagga. In gallery three, most visitors stop to gawp at the enormous elephant, but we'd suggest investigating the creepy-crawlies cabinet. It's here that you'll find the oddest exhibit of all: a pair of fleas, dressed in Mexican dancer's costumes.

Natural History Museum at Tring
Walter Rothschild Building, Akeman Street, Tring, Hertfordshire HP23 6AP (020 7942 6171/www.nhm.ac.uk/tring).

386 Eat a proper pasty on the toe-tip of the country

The pasty, that meat-and-two-veg pastry packet and piece of Cornish culinary history, dates all the way from the 13th century. The best spot in the world to crunch through a Cornish's crust is on the Lizard peninsula, the wild southernmost point of the British mainland – and the best place to purchase your pasty is Anne Muller's shop. In her expert hands, the humble pasty becomes a feast fit for a king – and should keep you stuffed until teatime.

The Lizard Pasty Shop
Beacon Terrace, The Lizard, Helston, Cornwall TR12 7PB (01326 290889).

387-396
Go down to the sea

Being beside the seaside is a timeless pleasure – whether you're basking in the sunshine or huddled round a thermos and a bag of hot, salty chips. Here are the best beaches to…

Pretend you're in the Sahara
Stagger off into the towering sand dunes at Camber Sands (www.visitrye.co.uk) and you could on a desert mission – so bring a picnic and plenty of water. So convincing are the dunes that this corner of East Sussex stood in for the Sahara in *Carry On… Follow that Camel*. A blowy, sandy beach lies beyond the dunes: bring a windbreak.

Sit in solitary splendour
Sinclair's Bay is a deserted stretch of sand, hidden well off the beaten track, off the A99 near Wick in Caithness (for map see www.welcometoscotland.com/beaches). On sunny days the white sands and bright blue sea look more Caribbean than Scottish, but don't be fooled – the North Sea has an icy edge,with summer surface temperatures peaking at 13ºC. There are no lifeguards or family-friendly facilities: if you want an ice-cream or drinks, you'll have to bring your own.

Paddle safely
Reach the golden sands of Barrafundle Bay, on the Pembrokeshire coast in Wales (www.visitpembrokeshire.com) via a beach path through the fields, beneath a stone archway and then down a flight of steps. Backed by dunes, it's a lovely, sheltered spot: the tranquil turquoise water and sandy, bare feet-friendly seabed make it perfect for a paddle.

Picnic in 'God's pocket'
The sandy beach at West Wittering (www.westwitteringbeach.co.uk) in West Sussex has its own balmy microclimate.

Bedruthan Steps beach, Cornwall

In place of rocks and crashing waves there are gently shelving sands and shallow pools of sun-warmed water – no wonder the locals have nicknamed it 'God's pocket'. It's prime picnic terrain, and barbecues are allowed too.

Go rockpooling
Rockpooling forays are most successful on a falling tide, as the sea recedes and leaves treasures exposed. Prime rockpooling spots are along the coasts of North Cornwall (www.north-cornwall.com) and of East Yorkshire (www.yorkshire.com), notably Runswick Bay, Robin Hood's Bay, Staithes and Scarborough.

Ride a donkey
Donkey rides are a Blackpool institution (www.visitblackpool.com), the animals ambling amiably up and down the sands in summer. Donkeys have rights too, you know: under the town's Donkey Charter (established 1942), they get a proper lunch break and Fridays off.

Build the ultimate sandcastle

Boffins say the best beach in Britain for sandcastle building is Torquay in Devon (www.torquay.com): its fine sand locks together beautifully, and hits just the right sand-to-water consistency (eight parts sand to one part water).

Be a shell-seeker

Lovely Barricane Bay in Devon (www.devonguide.com/beaches) is a sliver of North Devon renowned for tropical seashells – over 40 different types. They have hitched a lift on the Gulf Stream that sweeps in from Caribbean, picking up the shells and carrying them across the Atlantic before dropping them on this shore. Alongside British scallops, periwinkles and limpets are miniature sand dollars, sunset shells and tusk shells, but Barricane is most famous for the exquisite cowries, no bigger than a fingernail.

Spot seabirds

With its treacherous tides, vast expanse of shingle and nuclear power station, Dungeness (www.dungeness.org.uk) can seem like a hostile place to holidaying humans. For birds, it's heavenly: fish and sea life flourish in the power station's warm waste waters. At Dungenness RSPB reserve (01797 320588, www.rspb.org.uk)you can spot warblers and waders and widgeons; to see fluffy cygnets and goslings, visit in June.

Take the dog along too

Pooches are welcome to stretch their legs at Bamburgh, on the Northumberland coast (www.visitnorthumberland.com). There's plenty of room to chase sticks and snap at waves on the five-kilometre-long beach, overlooked by Bamburgh Castle (01668 214515, www.bamburghcastle.com). Bins are provided, so clean up after your canine.

397 Meet giant bunnies in the forest

Once the grown-ups have finished swooning over the 17th-century formal gardens at Groombridge Place, make a beeline for the Enchanted Forest. In place of prim and proper flower beds and perfectly manicured lawns, there are giant swings, scrambling nets and brilliant aerial boardwalks – not to mention some mysterious footprints, which look suspiciously like dinosaur tracks… Deep in the woods, small children can enjoy the sandpit and swings in the Groms' Village – and fall head over heels for the gorgeous giant rabbits. Another unusual inhabitant is the zeedonk, a zebra-donkey hybrid with glorious stripey legs who lives near the Chime Walk.

Groombridge Place Gardens & Enchanted Forest *Groombridge, Tunbridge Wells, Kent TN3 9QG (01892 861444/www.groombridge.co.uk).*

398-400
Grab a raptor

Nothing matches the thrill of a bird of prey gracefully swooping down to your wrist – just think of Harry and Hedwig. At Cheshire Falconry (Blakemere Craft Centre, Chester Road, Sandiway, Northwich CW8 2EB, 01606 882223, www.cheshirefalconry.com), Junior Owl Experiences are open to anyone aged over four, wizard or not, with black-eyed barn owls flying to and from children's gloved hands; if the eagle owls are in a good mood, they might make an appearance as well.

If you're more of a falcon-fancier, the Hawk Conservancy Trust (Sarson Lane, Weyhill, Andover, Hampshire SP11 8DY, 01264 773850, www.hawk-conservancy.org) runs a Junior Falconer's Experience for 12 to 15s, during which you help to feed the birds, learn to swing a lure and fly both falcons and barn owls. School holiday courses, suitable for seven to 16s, are also offered at the English School of Falconry & Bird of Prey Centre (Old Warden Park, near Biggleswade, Bedfordshire SG18 9EA, 01767 627527, www.birdsofpreycentre.co.uk).

401

Pedal up hill, down dale...
Mountain Bike Rider *magazine says that Dalby Forest on the southern edge of the North York Moors has some of the best mountain biking trails in England. There are 55 kilometres of tracks weaving through the trees, graded from green (nice and easy) to black (experts only). Purple Mountain Bike Centre (01751 460011, www.purplemountain.co.uk) hires out bikes, including trailers, tag-alongs and child seats. During the school holidays, the centre's mountain bike skills days help riders brush up their technique.*

402 ...and in the forest

The first forest in the country to be developed for mountain biking was Coed y Brenin in Snowdonia (01341 440742, www.mbwales.com). It's a legend among mountain bike parks, and any biker worth their spokes has launched themselves down its vertiginous descents. The relatively low-level Yr Afon trail is designed specifically for families, taking you on a ten-kilometre pedal past the gold mines of Gwynfynedd and along the length of the Mawddach river valley. Trails are free to ride, and you can hire bikes from the Coed y Brenin shop at the visitors' centre.

403 Walk the 'Street' at Whitstable

At low tide in Whitstable, Kent (www.see whitstable.com), the sea divides to reveal the 'Street' – a narrow strip of shingle, stretching out to sea for about a kilometre. From a distance, you'll look as if you're walking on water: keep an eye on the rising tide, though, if you want to avoid a hasty sprint back.

404-405

See cantering panto horses

Horses and jockeys train hard for the annual Panto Horse Grand National in the centre of Birmingham during panto season. Enter yourself or go along to watch people make asses of themselves. Spin-off events include a children's fancy dress party. In Cumbria, meanwhile, junior and senior panto horse races take place in May. They also have Shetland pony races, non-competitive donkey rides and fun fairs. Pantomime equestrianism hopes to become an Olympic sport. Oh no, it doesn't.
Panto Horse Grand National
Birmingham Town Centre (0121 303 3008/ www.birmingham.gov.uk).
Shetland Pony & Panto Horse Grand National
Ford Park, Ulverston, Cumbria LA12 7JP (01229 585542).

406 See light at the end of the Tunnels

The Tunnels Beaches of Ilfracombe, on Devon's north coast, are an extraordinary seaside experience. Hand-carved in the 1820s, the four tunnels allowed separate access to the men's and women's beaches, leading to sheltered coves and a large tidal swimming pool. The pool is ideal for snorkelling and inflatables, appearing for three hours before and after low tide – check tide times on the website. The grey sand and shingle beaches, cleaned daily in peak season, have a prestigious Blue Flag award and there's a lifeguard on duty in the summer. The 19th-century naturalist William Henry Gosse, founder of the world's first aquarium, discovered half a dozen new species in the rock pools here, and it's still prime rock pooling territory: the Devon Wildlife Trust (www.devonwildlifetrust.org) organises guided rock pool rambles for budding naturalists. Other activities include kayaking, and a play hut for under-tens.
Tunnels Beaches *Bath Place, Ilfracombe, Devon EX34 8AN (01271 879882/ www.tunnelsbeaches.co.uk).*

407 Join the mela

Held on the last weekend in July, Manchester Mega Mela is a joyous, free jamboree of Asian culture, fusing music, dance, sports, crafts and food. Children can jig to the beat of the dhol drums, have their hands adorned with intricate mehndis, or spend some time in the crafts tent, where experts are on hand to explain how to sprinkle coloured sands to create elaborate rangoli patterns. The bazaar sells gorgeous bejewelled slippers, sparkly saris and all manner of spices, while food stalls groan under the weight of golden-brown bhajis, crisp samosas and deliciously sticky Indian sweets – along with less adventurous hotdogs and fish and chips.
Manchester Mega Mela *Platts Fields Park, Fallowfields, Manchester M14 5LL (0161 256 4518/www.manchestermela.co.uk).*

408-413 *Run away to join the circus*

Learning circus skills, such as trapeze, unicycling, juggling and tightrope-walking is a hilarious way of keeping active, improving co-ordination and balance – and having fun. Circus schools across the country run after-school, weekend and half-term skills workshops and summer schools for children aged from about eight. For information on other courses, visit the Circus Development Agency's website, www.circusarts.org.uk.

In London, Circus Space (Coronet Street, N1 6HD, 020 7729 9522, www.thecircusspace.co.uk) has a Sunday morning 'Little Top' workshop, which is extremely popular, as is its summer school week. Also in the capital, Albert and Friends Instant Circus (Riverside Studios, Crisp Road, W6 9RL, 020 8237 1030, www.albertandfriendsinstantcircus.co.uk) runs day-long workshops and holiday activities, with skills such as diabolo and stilt- and wire-walking to master. This steep learning curve often leads to a performance for fond parents to marvel at.

In Bristol, Circomedia (St Paul's Church, Portland Square, BS2 8SJ, 0117 924 7615, www.circomedia.com) runs a week-long summer school for children to learn juggling, acrobatics, stilt-walking, diabolo-spinning and daredevil aerial trapeze skills, working towards a show at the end of the week.

The Circus Project in Hove (Hangleton Community Centre, Harmsworth Crescent, BN3 8BW, 01273 884 732, www.thecircusproject.co.uk) is a charity that specialises in aerial circus; weekly classes for all ages throughout the year may lead to a place in the highly skilled Brighton & Hove Youth Circus and– who knows? Play your trapeze right and a glittering career in international theatres and big tops beckons.

Teaching adults and children the life-enhancing fundamentals of circus skills, Rochdale's Skylight Circus Arts (Broadwater Centre, Smith Street, OL16 1HE (01706 650676, www.skylightcircusarts.com) also focuses on fun. As well as after-school classes in circus and aerial skills, Skylights runs weekend courses in specialised skills such as German wheel and Chinese pole, with intensive aerial training. Their Family Circus Adventure Days provide a challenging, often hilarious workout for parents and children together.

Sheffield Youth Circus (Greentop Circus Centre, Saint Thomas Building, 74 Holywell Road, S4 8AS, 0114 244 8828, www.greentop.org) is mostly an after-school project for eight- to 16-year-olds, but there are plans to run family fun days and workshops in the school holidays, so swing by their website to see when these are scheduled.

Circus Space

Discover the city from your back pocket

Essential for your weekend break, 25 top cities available.

POCKET SIZED
from £6.99

A few of my favourite things

414-418

Bryn Terfel,
opera and
concert singer

A favourite place to take the children is Caernarfon Castle (Castle Ditch, Caernarfon, Gwynedd LL5 2AY, 01286 677617), scene of the investiture of the Prince of Wales all those years ago. I love it because of the historic implications of the place. It amuses me, the idea of King Edward I building this huge monument and actually sitting in it in all his splendour, enjoying the wines from his vineyards in France and starting a family there. He lived in it for quite a while. It's one of the best castles in North Wales. They've really done it well for visitors, with the kitchen exhibitions and so on. The Holder of the Key is a very nice gentleman and a neighbour. Tony Snowdon, actually.

The summit of Mount Snowdon has to be on the list. My kids are definitely about ready to go up there now. They're aged 14, ten and eight. You can walk up, of course, but you can also take the train to the top (0871 720 0033, www.snowdonrailway.co.uk). It runs alongside the easy route from Llanberis, and is a lot safer now than it was on its maiden journey at the end of the 19th century, when it came off the tracks. From the house I can see the brand-new visitor centre at the top – it glistens when the sun hits the side of it. When there's snow up there, the whole summit sparkles.

Greenwood Forest Park (Y Felinheli, Gwynedd LL56 4QN, 01248 671493, www.greenwoodforestpark.co.uk) is a relatively new venture – it's been going for two or three years. It's what we've been missing in North Wales: an attraction that's open in all weathers. The kids love it. It has rides and slides and an archery centre. You can climb trees, take a boat trip and feed animals. There are cafés and picnic areas. There's a stilt pit, a tractor go-kart course and even a little outdoor theatre (I've not performed there, no). There's also a rollercoaster that works entirely by gravity, one full train descending and pulling up an empty one as it does so. You can cut pieces of wood and carve names into them. It's all good outdoor action.

How could I describe everything that Portmeirion (01766 770000, www. portmeirion-village. com) is in one sentence? It's a magical place. Buying this plot of land and then building a fantasy town, on either side of World War II, was a stroke of genius on Clough Williams-Ellis' part. It's a complete fantasy (and was where cult TV series *The Prisoner* was shot, of course). There are Arts and Crafts rustic-style buildings as well as more classical houses. Some were brought wholesale, as it were – complete houses that were due for demolition. Then you've got the parkland with 700 different types of trees and shrubs – fabulous for walks. You can even stay in two hotels, one of which, Castell Deudraeth (01766 770000), I opened. What was Clough Williams-Ellis' motto? 'Cherish the past, embrace the present, build the future.' Something like that. Very positive.

419 *Save the Bombus terrestris*

The plight of the bumblebee was brought to the nation's attention by the busy campaigning work of the Bumblebee Conservaion Trust (www.bumblebeeconservationtrust.co.uk). Three species are extinct, and populations in general are in decline. You can help by joining their beewatch survey and looking for bumbles in your area. Take a digital photo if you can, email it to the survey, and they'll let you know what species of *Bombus* you've discovered – 14 are commonly found in gardens and the countryside. Fascinated? Join the Trust and you'll receive a handsome bumblebee species poster, among other goodies.

420-421
Make like Tarzan in the treetops

Treetop walks are a bit like buses – you wait forever on the boring old forest floor, and then two turn up together, eager to ramp you up into the dizzy heights of the woodland canopy. Entered through an apparent crack in the ground, and named after the Greek for 'root', the 200-metre long Rhizotron & Xstrata Walkway at Kew Gardens (Richmond, Surrey TW9 3AB, 020 8332 5655, www.kew.org) begins by revealing the subterranean life of trees and the complex ecosystems beneath the soil. It stands 18 metres in the air, allowing visitors to peruse the canopy of sweet chestnuts, limes and deciduous oaks – while also looking out for man-made landmarks such as the Gherkin. The Canopy Walk in Salcey Forest, near Hartwell, Northants (01780 444920, www.forestry.gov.uk), meanwhile, is longer and loftier than its London counterpart: unknown by many even in the Midlands, it's a real gem.

422
See the ghastly licking stones

Carlisle Castle, a formidable 12th-century fortress, has seen its fair share of human suffering. During the English Civil War, Royalists were besieged for eight months by Scots sympathetic to the Parliamentarians and survived by eating rats and dogs before surrendering in 1645. A century later it again became a prison when Bonnie Prince Charlie's Jacobites tried to hold off the Duke of Cumberland's army. They became desperate for water and were reduced to licking the stones of their prison for moisture.
Carlisle Castle *Carlisle, Cumbria CA3 8UR (01228 591922/www. english-heritage.org.uk).*

423
Watch the dairymaid

At Acton Scott Farm in Shropshire they still milk the cows by hand and work the fields with horse-drawn ploughs. They can't compete with their modern neighbours, but they do attract a lot of visitors who admire their ancient ways. The farm, which is open March to October only, has Longhorn cattle, Tamworth pigs, Shropshire sheep, and poultry running free in the farmyard. A farrier turns up to shoe the horses. Butter and cream made in the dairy is sold in the shop.
Acton Scott Farm *Church Stretton, Shropshire SY6 6QN (01694 781306/ www.shropshire.gov.uk).*

424
Draw a cartoon

Come on, admit it: the most enjoyable read is a comic. Children can learn the techniques of drawing cartoons in holiday workshops at the Cartoon Museum in London. One-day courses (£22) are split by age group: eight- to ten-year-olds on Wednesdays, 11 to 14s on Thursdays. Participants bring examples of their favourite characters, which professional cartoonists then teach them to draw. Animation workshops on Fridays for nine to 13s cost £26, including a DVD of their efforts to take home. The museum's permanent exhibition of cartoons, caricatures and comic art from the 18th century to the present tends to be more political than funny. There are not many laughs in Hogarth's 'Gin Lane', its most famous exhibit.
Cartoon Museum *35 Little Russell Street, London WC1A 2HH (020 7580 8155/ www.cartoonmuseum.org).*

425

See ostriches hatch

At Eden Ostrich World, an animal-packed farm visitors' centre in Cumbria's Eden Valley, you can witness new long-legged life emerging from giant eggs. The ova are collected and placed in incubators between May and October, where they slowly start to hatch. Visitors would have to be very patient to watch the whole process, from beak emergence to the wobbly hatchling stage, because it takes all day. The miracle of comparing cracking egg to ruddy great sprinting giant (check out the African black ostriches running around the paddocks), however, is a delight for all-comers. And no one needs to know that ostrich meat is very nutritious, if they don't want to.
Eden Ostrich World *Langwathby Hall Farm, Langwathby, Penrith, Cumbria CA10 1LW (01768 881771/www.ostrich-world.com).*

426 *Play sevensies*

Take a tennis ball, find a good wall without windows, and try these skills:
● Throw the ball against the wall and catch it, seven times.
● Throw the ball against the wall, let it bounce, and catch it, seven times.
● Throw the ball against the base of the wall and catch it as it bounces off higher up, seven times.
● Throw the ball under your right leg against the wall and catch it with your right hand, seven times.
● Throw the ball under your left leg against the wall and catch it with your left hand, seven times.
● Throw the ball against the wall, twirl round and catch it, seven times.
● Throw the ball against the wall, clap once, and catch it, seven times.

427 *Step inside Concorde*

The glorious, droop-nosed, supersonic superstar plane that only the wealthy and lucky competition winner ever managed to fly on was taken out of service in 2003. Concorde was such a celebrity that her fans would dash out to spot her when they heard that distinctive rumble – the sonic boom! – that so riled her detractors. One top model, however, is enjoying a happy retirement in Somerset. The first British Concorde (built 1969) takes pride of place as one of a multitude of aeronautically inspired attractions at the the Fleet Air Arm Museum, the country's largest naval aircraft collection. Visitors can step inside to wonder at her sleek lines and plush interior, then tour the rest of the site where aircraft carriers, submarine detectors and helicopter simulators await their pleasure.
Fleet Air Arm Museum *RNAS Yeovilton, Ilchester, Somerset BA22 8HT (01935 840565/ www.fleetairarm.com)*

428

Take to the air in a boat

A highlight of any trip down the Trent & Mersey Canal in Cheshire is taking flight on the magnificent Anderton Boat Lift. Built to connect the River Weaver with the canal, 15 metres above, the lift was restored in 2001 to full working order – not bad for a contraption that was erected in 1875. To see the mammoth structure for yourself, take a 30-minute trip aboard the *Edwin Clark* (named after the designer of the original lift), then learn about the restoration at the interactive exhibition in the visitor centre. There's also a maze, a children's playground, a café and picnic area. Boat trips take place from the end of March to early October, and the whole operation is closed in January and December.
Anderton Boat Lift *Lift Lane, Anderton, Northwich, Cheshire CW9 6FW (01606 786777/ www.andertonboatlift.co.uk).*

Dramatic start

Leicester's £61m state-of-the-art theatre has opened its doors at last, and Derek Hammond *is first in the queue.*

I'm sitting halfway back in Curve's empty 750-seat auditorium – the larger of the two spaces here, which can either look down on a shared central stage, or put on two different productions simultaneously. It's still hard to fathom exactly what's going to happen where, and what effect this revolutionary open-plan theatre will have on performance as we know it. One thing's immediately apparent: it's going to turn everything inside out.

Indeed, that was the aim of Uruguayan architect Rafael Viñoly: to make the process of staging theatre more transparent, and to strip it naked. But there's no feeling of the emperor's new clothes either about the landmark glass arc of the Curve building, or the bravura experiment it embodies.

For now, the stage below is bare, separated from the surrounding foyer by twin sets of 32-tonne steel walls. When these acoustic curtains are hoisted up into the cavernous free space above, the stage will be visible not only from the open-plan foyer around the two inner auditorium 'drums', but from the street outside. The backstage area – for centuries the ultra-private lair of the players, prop builders, dressers and costumiers – will also be visible from the auditorium and the foyer bars. In order to make their grand entrance, actors will have to come down in a lift and cross the foyer space beneath the great glass façade. Backstage is now front of house. Inside is out.

There are no boundaries, no barriers, no musty old curtains here. There isn't even a stage door. Actors turn up for work and leave through the foyer along with the rest of us, rubbing shoulders with staff and punters.

Still, I can't help wondering what Laurence Olivier would have made of having to adjust his tights and wig in full view of passing shopgirls… And what unseemly out-of-sight delights Leicester playwright Joe Orton would have conjured, given this brave new world of rules to play with. With a space like this, writers, actors, set designers and lighting and sound technicians will be able to rewrite the

rules to fit a whole new set of possibilities. It isn't just the physical theatre space where the inside-out, back-to-front approach is applied.

Participation and learning lie at the heart of everything, from the window on to the set builders' workshop and offices open to view from the back of the circle, to after-show discussions at which members of the public can meet and talk to the director and players. Even the final dress rehearsals, traditionally a big secret hidden away behind locked doors, are to be thrown open to the public, the admission fee just a quid.

Children, especially, are encouraged to join in, removing some of the mystique and secrecy of performance as well as much of the awkwardness traditionally involved in putting yourself forward as a wannabe hoofer or technician, as a start-up scene-painter or scene-stealer.

'Imagine a young person coming to the theatre for the first time,' says Curve's artistic director Paul Kerryson, 'and finding the whole creative infrastructure revealed, so that you might be able to see the props being painted, the actors rehearsing, the lighting bars being raised – it could inspire any number of potential career options.'

Me, I'm already thinking of running away and joining the theatre; but, first, there is the

'Anyone can get involved, whether by performing, being an apprentice stage manager, working with costumes or technical aspects.'

media circus that greets the official opening of Curve [in November 2008].

Together with my kids, I'm taken on a tour of the building – a very different place now it's populated with actual punters rather than being a series of theoretical spaces. Here are human slinkies, stilt-walkers, dancers, singers, busy bars and cafés, face-painters and their many small jaguar/space-alien victims spilling out of auditoria into the crowded, airy foyer, and then outside into Orton Square. Some meat, at last, on the bare bones of hopeful theory.

A theatre company of actors with disabilities pulls in an enthusiastic audience as they perform in one of the studio theatres/rehearsal spaces. We're invited into workshops where props and walls are being painted with such enthusiasm it isn't clear where one ends and the other begins. Up in the space above the stages, a sound technician usually hidden from view assures us that the 20 computer systems in operation here are well beyond state of the art; that nowhere else in the world do they all co-exist in a single theatre; that it's possible for a computer-driven hoist to drop a grand piano on a sixpence, in synch with an opening beat. Meanwhile, audiences follow promenading performers around the unique spaces of the theatre, and the age-old Do Not Cross The Line between stage and front row really begins to blur.

The grand theatrical opening was starry: a seasonal production of *Simply Cinderella*, followed by kids going feral in *Lord of the Flies* and Juliette Binoche dancing with Akram Khan in *In-I*. After these treats, there continues a steady rollout of 1,000 opportunities for children to get involved: to learn, to perform, to experience, and to immerse themselves in creating theatre.

'The whole theatre-making engine is what we're interested in here,' says assistant artistic director Adel Al-Salloum. 'The very design is to expose the internal workings of theatre, so you can look into the engine room and see how it all works. But then, when your imagination is all fired up, you can actually come in and make demands of this place.'

The first culmination of this open-to-all approach will be a production of *His Dark Materials* – a piece of epic theatre in the 750-seater space, with a non-professional cast of

12-pluses at the centre. 'It's all about high-quality participation, matched by high-quality production values,' Adel enthuses, 'so people get the buzz of working or creating on that main stage, working with the best technical expertise we can offer them.

'Anyone can get involved, not just through performing, but by coming and being an apprentice stage manager or working in our wardrobe department with our costume designers, designing or making props, or getting into the technical aspects such as sound and light.'

What's more, all ages are welcome. 'We want children and young people to be able to explore their creative talents' insists Adel. 'I'm even planning drop-in classes for parents and toddlers.'
Curve Theatre *Rutland Street, Leicester LE1 1SB (0116 2423560/www.curveonline.co.uk).*

www.treesforcities.org
Trees for Cities
Charity registration number 1032154
Travelling creates so many lasting memories.
Make your trip mean something for years to come - not just for you but for the environment and for people living in deprived urban areas.
Anyone can offset their flights, but when you plant trees with Trees for Cities, you'll help create a green space for an urban community that really needs it.
Leave Your Mark
Create a green future for cities.

Arsenal FC

Tours of the swanky new Emirates Stadium include the changing rooms, players' tunnel, dug-outs and directors' box. The museum revisits Arsenal's 120-year-history in pictures, videos and exhibits, including Charlie George's FC Cup Final shirt from 1971. Photos of the Edwardian crowd show not a man without a hat or moustache.

Emirates Stadium *Drayton Park, London N5 1BU (020 7704 4504/www.arsenal.com).*

Chelsea FC

The museum traces the Blues' history from modest wasteground origins to present success on the profits of the Russian oil industry. Visitors can tour the trophy room, changing rooms, dug-outs and 'Chelsea Shed', which is not for tools unless one describes the fans in such terms.

Stamford Bridge *Fulham Road, London SW6 1HS (020 7385 5545/www.chelseafc.com).*

Liverpool FC

The romance of the club's history looms large at Anfield. The highs are the multiple trophies, the lows Hillsborough and Heysel. The tour visits changing rooms, dug-outs, the tunnel, directors' boxes and 'the Kop' where fans sing 'You'll never walk alone' – if you can call it singing.

Anfield Stadium *Anfield Road, Liverpool L4 0TH (0844 499 3000/ www.liverpoolfc.tv).*

Manchester United FC

The museum soberingly recalls the 1958 Munich air disaster in which half a team were lost. There are tributes to great players: Charlton, Best, Law and Ooh Aah Cantona, who once kicked a spectator. The trophy room is packed with gleaming hardware. On the tour you see the changing rooms, the tunnel and the manager's dug-out. What are those hardened white blobs on the ground? Why, Fergie's chewing gum, of course.

Manchester United Museum & Tour Centre *Sir Matt Busby Way, Old Trafford, Manchester M16 0RA (161 868 8000/www.manutd.com).*

National Football Museum

The honour of housing the nation's sporting mementos goes to humble Preston North End FC, one of the founding clubs of the Football Association in the 19th century. The 'First Half' of the gallery houses exhibits such as a replica World Cup and Maradona's shirt. The 'Second Half' is interactive and involves a lot of touch-screens testing football knowledge. One of them makes you a pundit on *Match of the Day*.

Preston North End FC *Sir Tom Finney Way, Preston, Lancashire PR1 6PA (01772 908442/ www.nationalfootballmuseum.com).*

Scottish Football Museum

Although the fixture was abandoned for some years because the fans could not be trusted to behave themselves, Scotland vs England 1872 was the first soccer international. A tour of the Glasgow Rangers' ground takes in the changing rooms, players' tunnel and royal box.

Hampden Park *Glasgow G42 9AY (0141 616 6139/www.scottishfootballmuseum.org.uk).*

Wembley Stadium

The national football ground offers a 90-minute tour of the stadium including dug-outs, changing rooms, tunnel and executive suites. Is that Prince Charles standing there? No, it's a replica of the FA Cup. You may lift it up and in your imagination hear the cheers.

Olympic Way *Wembley, Middlesex HA9 0WS (0844 800 2755/www.thestadiumtour.com)*

Emirates Stadium

437-447 *Own a pony...*

It may be every little girl's dream to have a pony, but if you're worried it could eat you out of house and home, an Own a Pony Day could be the solution. Many riding schools offer the chance to learn how to catch, tack up, brush, feed and muck out horses as well as ride them and play gymkhana games. The following are approved by the British Horse Society (www.bhs.org.uk), which lists accredited riding schools around the country.

Borlum Riding Centre
Set in 400 acres on the shores of Loch Ness, Borlum combines a riding school with self-catering apartments and a campsite. Own a Pony Days take place year round and cost £35, which includes a trek around the loch.
Borlum Farm, Drumnadrochit, Inverness-shire IV63 6XN (01456 450220/www.borlum.co.uk).

Foxes Riding School
Own a Pony Days at Foxes start at £45. To take part, children must be able to walk and trot off the lead rein.
Badgers Rake Lake, Ledsham, Cheshire CH66 8PF (0151 339 6797/www.foxesridingschool.co.uk).

Hyde Park Stables
Pony Camp mornings or afternoons at these central London stables include two hours of riding in the park, and an hour's pony care demonstration – though they cost a hefty £144.
63 Bathurst Mews, London W2 2SB (020 7723 2813/www.hydeparkstables.com).

Kentish Town City Farm
Own a Pony mornings during the Easter and summer holidays cost £20.
1 Cressfield Close, London NW5 4BN (020 7916 5421/www.ktcityfarm.org.uk).

Kingsbarn Equestrian Centre
A large riding school in Scotland with more than 70 horses, Kingsbarn runs one-, two- and four-day Own a Pony sessions at £55 per day, including lunch and two riding lessons.
Westershieldhill, Falkirk FK1 3AT (01324 630404/www.kingsbarnequestrian.com).

Kingston Riding Centre
Children already learning to ride at the centre can look after their favourite pony for the morning for £80. The price includes one lesson.
38 Crescent Road, Kingston-upon-Thames, Surrey KT2 7RG (020 8546 6361/www.kingstonridingcentre.com).

Newquay Riding Stables
Own a Pony mornings are available for £15, including a ride on the beach.
Trenance Leisure Centre, Newquay, Cornwall TR7 2HU (01637 872 699/www.newquay ridingstables.co.uk).

Owl House Stables
Fun Days at Owl House cost £25, and include at least one ride, along with lessons in how to catch, brush and tack up your horse.
Station Road, St Margarets-at-Cliff, Kent CT15 6HN (01304 852 035/www.theowl housestables.co.uk).

Swinhoe Farm Riding Centre
Set on a family-run working farm, Swinhoe offers Own a Pony Days for £45 during the school holidays.
Swinhoe Farm House, Belford, Northumberland NE70 7LJ (01668 213 370/www.swinhoe cottages.co.uk).

Valley Farm Riding Centre
Valley Farm boasts 80 secluded acres next to the River Deben in Suffolk, 50 horses and ponies and a camel called Camelot. Own a Pony Days cost £50 and culminate in an in-hand horse show.
Wickham Market, Woodbridge, Suffolk IP13 0ND (01728 746916/www.valleyfarmonline.co.uk).

Willowtree Riding Establishment
This sweet little stables in Lewisham, south-east London, has been in business for 50 years. It's got some beautiful ponies to own for a day, at a cost of £30 with two hours' riding and mounted games thrown in.
The Stables, Ronver Road, London SE12 0NL (8857 6438/www.willowtree ridinglondon.co.uk).

448 *...and take it for a ride on the beach*

On the glorious North Wales coast, with a private bridle path leading to the beach, Bridlewood Riding Centre must be the loveliest place in Britain to indulge your need to own a pony. If you're a good enough rider, you can take your new-found friend for an exhilarating canter along the usually deserted Ty'n-y-Morfa beach. Own a Pony days during school holidays cost a modest £30. Children can work towards nationally recognised badges and certificates.
Bridlewood Riding Centre *Ty'n-y-Morfa, near Prestatyn, North Wales CH8 9JN (01745 888922/ www.bridlewood.co.uk).*

449 *Go BMX mad*

If horses aren't your thing, then how about bikes? BMX riders start as young as four, making it probably the most popular cycling sport among kids – even more so these days thanks to female World Champion and GB Olympics contender Shanaze Reade. British BMX Championships take place annually, but most tracks have club nights from April to September with practice sessions and races. Anyone can join in, all you need is a bike, some safety equipment and parental consent. Find details of your nearest club at British Cycling (www.britishcycling.org.uk). Next stop the Olympics!

Bridlewood Riding Centre

450 *See the penguin parade*

Edinburgh Zoo's most celebrated residents are its king, gentoo and rockhopper penguins. They get their own Penguin Awareness Day every January, as well as a daily penguin parade, when the birds come out of their enclosure for a photocall. The tradition started in 1951 after a keeper accidentally left the door open and a posse of escapees started waddling after him. The zoo's special relationship with the seabird began in 1913, when the Norwegian family of Christian Salvesen presented the newly opened zoo with its first king penguins. The Norwegian connection continues, thanks to one Very Important Penguin, named Nils Olav, who is the mascot of the Norwegian Royal Guard. The Guardsmen visit every few years and he does his duty by walking past the troops for inspection.

Edinburgh Zoo *Corstorphine Road, Edinburgh EH12 6TS (0131 334 9171/www.edinburghzoo.org.uk).*

451 *Mess about at Mudeford*

Lying at the entrance to Christchurch harbour, Mudeford in Dorset was once a smuggling hotbed. In 1784, it was the scene of the 'Battle of Mudeford', a bloody clash between smugglers and customs men; one of the miscreants, George Coombes, was hanged at Haven Quay. The ferry (07968 334441, www.mudeford ferry.co.uk) takes you to Mudeford sandbank, a spit of land adjoining Hengistbury Head. Walk along Mudeford beach, paddle, collect shells and covet the stunning beach huts.

452 *Dust off a museum*

Do you know a museum that could be a little more family-friendly? Whatever you want from a museum, you've a chance to voice it via Kids in Museums (www.kidsinmuseums.org.uk). Go online and sign up to the latest manifesto, compiled from visitors' ideas and comments.

453 *Make a yarn dolly*

This is a good way of using up any leftover wool you may have lying around. Wrap the yarn about 100 times around the long sides of a postcard, forming a coil. Tie the final loop to the previous one, to prevent it all unravelling. Ease the coil off the card, then section off enough to make a head shape and tie it with a small piece of yarn. Make arms by separating off about ten strands at each side of the coil of yarn, then putting small elastic bands near the ends to make wrists (or tie them with small lengths of yarn) . Cut the loops to make hands. Wrap an elastic band around the middle to make the dolly's waist. Split the remaining yarn in half for legs (or leave as is to form a 'dress') and attach elastic bands at the ankles. Trim the ends. To make hair, wrap some yarn around four fingers about ten times, then slip it off. Use another piece of yarn to tie the coil in the middle, then cut open the loop. Glue it to the doll's head, spreading the strands out.

454-456 *Brush up your Shakespeare*

There's nothing to beat watching a production of *A Midsummer Night's Dream* on a balmy July evening, picnic at your side, a natural soundtrack to the iambic pentameter provided by the breeze ruffling the trees. We can but dream: *The Tempest* accompanied by summer downpours is usually the reality. Still, Shakespeare in the open air is a delightful way to familiarise yourself to the works of the Bard.

The New Shakespeare Company is based at the open-air theatre in London's Regent's Park (0844 8264242, www.openairtheatre.org). The theatre and the stuccoed terraces around it were planned but unfinished by John Nash, the best friend and confidant of the Prince Regent, son of mad King George III. Non-Shakespearean productions are sometimes allowed.

Also in London, Shakespeare's Globe in Southwark (020 7401 9919, www.shakespeares-globe.org) is an authentic reconstruction of Shakespeare's 'wooden O'. It was fun to be a groundling in the 16th century and heckle the actors at appropriate moments. The original site is round the corner in Park Street; all that is left are the cobbles in their tell-tale circles. The reconstruction was the project of Sam Wanamaker, an American actor who could not believe there was no memorial to Shakespeare in his place of work.

The miniature sceptred isle of Brownsea Island in Poole Harbour, Hampshire (01202 251987, www.brownsea-theatre.co.uk) has staged Shakespeare every summer since the Bard's 400th anniversary in 1964. The ticket price includes the ferry from the mainland. An amphitheatre-style stage is set up, surrounded by raked seating, and the show goes on every evening, regardless of the weather.

457-460

Be a canny cake-maker

Use this simple sponge cake recipe for fairy cakes or a victoria sponge.

Take 175g self-raising flour, add one rounded teaspooon of baking powder, then mix in three large eggs, 175g soft margarine, 175g caster sugar and a dash of vanilla essence. You can either divide the mixture between two 20cm-diameter circular tins for a victoria sponge (jam in the middle) or little paper cases for fairy cakes. Bake at 170°C for 30 minutes for the large cake, about 20 minutes for the fairies.

Or you could try creative cake containers. Bake a cake for a gardener friend in terracotta flower pots, greased and lined with baking paper. Leave the cake in the pot, tie ribbon around and over the cake and tuck a packet of seeds into the pot to use once the cake is eaten. Tin cans well scrubbed, greased and lined can be used to bake a sponge. The resulting cakes are candle-shaped and can be iced to look like candles (make a paper 'flame' for the top).

Wartime cake is a great idea for people who are allergic to eggs. During World War II, eggs were scarce, so bakers created cakes without them. Mix 140g of brown sugar, 118ml water, 70g raisins, 20g margarine, ½ teaspoon cinnamon and ¼ teaspoon each of nutmeg and ground cloves in a saucepan and heat to a boil, then let it simmer for five minutes. Combine 200g flour, ¼ teaspoon salt and ½ teaspoon each of baking soda and powder in a bowl, then add the cooled sugar mixture and fold it together until the batter is smooth. Then add 50g chopped walnuts. Pour into a lined 20cm x 10cm loaf tin and bake for 45 minutes at 140°C.

461

Read all you can

Roald Dahl was right. Reading 'is the slowly growing joy/that fills [children's] hearts'. So turn off the telly and open a book during the hols. Bookstart (www.bookstart.co.uk), a scheme to encourage young people to read, sends infant literature free. They recommend parents read aloud to their children.

462

Go bodyboarding in Devon

A sea change in British beach behaviour has occurred over the last few years, and the key to it all has to be the wetsuit. Buy a 'shortie' for £20 or so, grab a bodyboard and the water is yours to enjoy, whatever the British summer throws at you. It's great when your kids have passed the bucket-and-spade stage and move on to something more challenging – and higher in the cool stakes. Plus it's free. A take-away cream tea and flask of hot coffee makes watching much more enjoyable.

Family beaches in North Devon include Woollacombe (www.woolacombetourism.co.uk) and Croyde Bay (www.croydedevon.co.uk). Note the flags indicating where bodyboarders and surfers should go. Park at the top of the dunes and take it from there. If you want to test the waters before investing in wetsuits and boards, equipment can be hired by the day.

463

Enter a witch's hovel

Do you dare? Will she cast a spell? Is she boiling up a brew? Her abode is one of 13 period buildings that have been restored as part of the open-air Ryedale Folk Museum. If the witch is too spooky, visit the 17th-century thatched cottage, which has a rare 'witches' post' to protect you from her evil ways. Someone there may be baking bread or boiling broth on the big black Yorkshire range. As well as a 1950s villlage shop, Edwardian photographer's studio, Victorian cottage and Elizabethan manor house, there's a gypsy caravan, a Merryweather fire engine and a reconstructed Iron Age settlement. Children's activities run throughout the year.
Ryedale Folk Museum *Hutton-le-Hole, North Yorkshire YO62 6UA (01751 417367/ www.ryedalefolkmuseum.co.uk).*

National Marine Aquarium

464 *Sleep with sharks*

Do you dare sleep with the sharks at the National Marine Aquarium in Plymouth? Those brave enough will be rewarded with an extraordinary night with some of the centre's 70 sharks, including the stars of the show: sand tiger sharks Emily, Enzo and Howardine. They hang out in the huge Mediterranean Sea exhibit, flashing their needle-sharp gnashers – though Enzo, who is the smallest, is afraid of the dark. Luckily, soft-hearted staff leave a night-light on for him. During the sleepover you'll be given an exclusive twilight tour; next, after some fishy games and a movie in front of the Atlantic reef tank, it's time for the midnight feast. Finally, snuggle into your sleeping bag. Sleepovers cost £40 for one child, though prices are reduced for bigger groups and families.

National Marine Aquarium
*Rope Walk, Coxside, Plymouth PL4 0LF
(01752 600301/www.national-aquarium.co.uk).*

465 *Admire the Northern Lights*

The Northern Lights are an awesome display of greens, reds and violets that sweep and shimmer across the night sky, and are guaranteed to send a shiver down your spine. They occur when streams of plasma emitted by the sun crash into the earth's magnetic field; though most are deflected, some particles make it through at the poles and collide with atmospheric gases, emitting intense pulses of colour. They're also called the Aurora Borealis, after Aurora, the Roman goddess of dawn, and Boreas, the Greek name for the north wind.

The further north you go in the UK, the better your chances of a sighting; they can appear from autumn to spring, though the peak season is late September to October. Minimal light pollution means that the best place to see the show is the Hebrides (www.visithebrides.com); even if you don't see the Lights, you can gaze at a magnificent night sky, scattered with impossibly bright stars.

466

Grow an avocado plant

First, eat your avocado. Then wash the stone and take three toothpicks, inserting each around one-third of the way from the stone's widest end. Balance the stone by its toothpick spikes in a narrow-rimmed glass of water, making sure that the lower two-thirds of the stone are in water at all times. Place the glass on a window sill, and top up the water as necessary. After three weeks or so, the stone's brown skin will break and a root will extend into the water. A shoot will appear near the top. When both are a couple of inches long, plant your avocado in a pot of compost. A broad-leaved plant will develop – but probably won't fruit as avocados prefer warmer climes.

467 *Gather round the campfire at La Rosa*

Hidden away in the woods of the North Yorkshire Moors National Park, La Rosa is the coolest caravan site we've ever seen. Delve deep in the circus tent's dressing-up box or take a candlelit shower in the old hay byre – accompanied by a wind-up gramophone, if you like singing in the shower. With just 16 visitors on site at any one time, it's wonderfully friendly, and you're bound to end up exchanging ghost stories round the campfire at some point during your stay. The preponderance of candles and lack of heating (the site is run on low-impact environmental lines) means it's best suited to older kids; the kitsch clutter of ornaments and vintage memorabilia in the retro caravans is also horribly tempting to curious toddlers, making for a stressful stay for parents.

La Rosa *Murk Esk Cottage, Goathland, Whitby, North Yorkshire YO22 5AS (07786 072866/ www.larosa.co.uk).*

La Rosa

468

Meet the wickerman
Meandering through the millennia doesn't require the use of a time machine. Simply get yourself to Archaeolink (01464 851500, www.archaeolink.co.uk) in Aberdeenshire. Start at the park's Mesolithic huts and wander until you arrive at the super-organised Roman marching camp. Everything is based on either archaeological remains found at digs or contemporary depictions, so this isn't history Hollywood-style. The biggest event of the year is the Wickerman weekend, with arts, crafts, story telling and a torchlit procession, which culminates in the dramatic burning of the wickerman (empty, of course...). Bear in mind that night falls a lot quicker the further north you go, so if you don't want to face a long dark drive after leaving the park, visit in summer.

469 Cave under Exeter High Street

Below Exeter's perfectly ordinary-looking High Street a thrilling subterranean world awaits. Built in the 14th century to carry fresh water to the city, a network of dark, vaulted passageways stretches for over 400 metres beneath the streets. The tunnels are a tight squeeze and not for the claustrophobic, but there's no shortage of visitors clamouring to be taken on the 90-minute guided tours: in the school holidays, arrive early to secure places.

Exeter Underground Passages *2 Paris Street, Exeter EX1 1GA (01392 265887/www.exeter. gov.uk/passages).*

470 Make a rag rug

There are lots of different ways of making a rag rug, but the easiest technique for children is braiding fabric. First, take lots of fabric offcuts of different colours and patterns. Then cut the fabric into strips of equal width, and sew the strips end to end to make three long strips. Next, get braiding: it'll be easier if the fabric is held as securely as possible to a non-moving base. To make your rug, sew the finished braids together into a rectangle shape with heavy string along their long edges.

471 Meet Brum

Win lots of Brownie points by taking your youngsters to the home of Brum, the four-wheeled star of his own CBeebies show. The Cotswold Motoring Museum & Toy Collection is an award-winning attraction in Bourton-on-the-Water that will satisfy any tiny (or overgrown) tot hooked on all things automobile. Exhibits include Austins, MGs, Rileys and Rovers from the 1920s and '30s, plus a covetable collection of pedal cars.

Cotswold Motoring Museum & Toy Collection *The Old Mill, Bourton-on-the-Water, Gloucestershire, GL54 2BY (01451 821255/ www.cotswold-motor-museum.com).*

472 Get that sinking feeling

Caswell Bay, just 15 minutes drive from Swansea, is a huge sandy beach, popular with families and surfers. It look harmless enough, with its souvenir, sweet and surf shops, but beware the scary sinking sand! Just a few hundred metres in front of the GSD surf centre (www.surfgsd.com) is a metre-wide spot where, if you step on it, you get sucked down to shin-level and freezing spring water bubbles up. Unsuspecting children find it pretty scary.

473 Be a bolder folder

Join the British Origami Society (www.british origami.info) and you'll find that paper has limitless possibilities in skilled hands. Junior membership gives you six magazines a year, access to the library and to meetings and conventions, and all the tricks and skills available on the website. To find an origami group near you, check the website.

474 Learn some Cockney rhyming slang

To be a true Cockney, you have to be born within earshot of the bells of St Mary-le-Bow church in Cheapside, London EC2. Otherwise, you can pretend to be one by imitating the actors on *EastEnders*, and learning some rhyming slang – the coded language that, historically, Cockneys used among themselves. Instead of saying 'hair', for instance, say 'Barnet Fair'. 'Harry Lime' means time, feet are 'plates of meat', mate becomes 'Dutch plate', phone is 'dog and bone', mental is 'Radio Rental', and so on. Interestingly, once the rhyme had become generally recognised it was often shortened by dropping the rhyming word. Thus hair became just 'barnet', while 'having a butcher's' means having a look ('butcher's hook') and 'me old dutch' means my old mate. We could start talking about merchant bankers, but this is a book for children.

475-481 *Slurp a sundae*

We're as partial as the next ice-cream lover to the organic, farm-fresh variety, but the sundae still holds a special place in our hearts – and the best place to tuck in is a 1940s-style ice-cream parlour: a nostalgia trip for adults and pudding heaven for kids.

Brucciani's

Grown-ups can admire the pink etched mirrors and Bakelite fittings at this Grade II-listed seaside Lancashire café, but kids won't be able to take their eyes off the ices: simple but superb peach melbas and chocolate nut sundaes.

217 Marine Parade, Morecambe, Lancashire LA4 4BU (01524 421386).

Harbour Bar

Opened in 1945, Scarborough's Harbour Bar is a vision of bright yellow Formica and cherry red banquettes. At the chrome-edged counter, neatly uniformed staff serve stupendous knickerbocker glories and ice-cream sodas.

1-3 Sandside, Scarborough, Yorkshire YO11 1PE (01723 373662).

Marine Ices

There's proper Italian pasta and pizza on the menu at this north London institution, but more of interest to small fry is the ices menu. Simple scoops of vanilla or chocolate suit fussy eaters, while more adventurous offspring can delve into a bespoke-blend sundae or a chocolate sauce-slathered banana split.

8 Haverstock Hill, London NW3 2BL (020 7482 9003/www.marineices.co.uk).

Marine Ices

Minchella & Co

Grown-ups can quaff excellent espressos at this 1940s Italian-owned gelataria in South Shields, while their offspring feast on ice-cream. Biggest and best is the knickerbocker glory, but there are also various fruity and chocolately offerings.

11 Ocean Road, South Shields NE33 2HT (01914 561905/www.minchella.co.uk).

Morelli's

Sundaes at the legendary Morelli's in Broadstairs are resplendant, wafer- and cherry-studded affairs, while cornets come in a dazzling array of flavours – from classic coconut or vanilla to bubblegum and turkish delight.

14 Victoria Parade, Broadstairs, Kent CT10 1QS (01843 862500/ www.morellis.com).

Notarianni's

The 1930s ice-cream parlour at Notarianni's in Blackpool offers all manner of sundaes. The house special is the Notarianni, an almost-healthy blend of kiwis, ice-cream and strawberries: bonus points for kids who notice it's the colours of the Italian flag.

9-11 Waterloo Road, South Shore, Blackpool, Lancashire FY4 1AF (01253 342510/ www.notarianniicecreamblackpool.co.uk).

S Luca

Frothy milkshakes and towering sundaes are standard at this Edinburgh institution. You won't find any fancy-pants flavours on the menu, but a scoop of Luca's creamy strawberry ice-cream takes some beating.

32-38 High Street, Musselburgh, Edinburgh EH21 7AG (01316 652237/www.s-luca.co.uk).

Just the cricket

Howzat! Cricket is making a comeback, says Andrew Shields – and not a moment too soon.

Ella Willmoth absolutely loves cricket. Every week from January on, she's a regular at indoor coaching sessions run by South Loughton Cricket Club in Essex. When the outdoor season gets under way in late April, right through to the summer holidays, she continues to practise and play in a FUNdamentals League contested by other local clubs and a handful of school teams. Ella, by the way, is nine years old.

Cricket has changed hugely over the last two decades. Just as the game played by international stars like Kevin Pietersen and Andrew Flintoff has embraced coloured clothing, floodlights and all the razzmatazz more usually seen in football, so the sport has worked hard to broaden its appeal to children. Some of the rather starchy formalities have been dispensed with, such as the insistence on pristine white kit (which is invariably grubby after a single wearing), while girls are as welcome to get involved as boys.

Another major change is the realisation that a hard ball can be a serious turn-off. How many kids have shunned cricket for life after suffering a thwack on the shins from that red leather sphere? Instead, the introductory versions of the game now employ more child-friendly equipment. Kwik Cricket uses plastic bats and stumps, and a soft, bouncy orange ball. The next step up is to play with an 'Incrediball', which behaves like a proper cricket ball but won't send you wincing to the pavilion if you misjudge a catch. You can buy Kwik Cricket kit and balls at any good sports shop, Alternatively, call the Kwik Cricket Action Line on 0800 214314, or visit the England & Wales Cricket Board's website at www.ecb.co.uk/development/kids.

The name of the competition organised by South Loughton Cricket Club (www.south loughton.org.uk) is significant: the emphasis is on FUN. Four years ago, the club was among 51 from across the country chosen by the ECB

to pilot a FUNdamentals programme for kids aged six to nine. In this, the traditional virtues of a classical cover drive or leg-spin bowling action are downplayed in favour of developing ABCS. No, nothing to do with spelling tests, but Agility, Balance, Co-ordination and Speed – qualities common to every sport or physical activity.

As head coach at South Loughton, I've been involved with FUNdamentals since its inception. In my experience, many kids nowadays need this multi-skill approach before our coaching team can even think about teaching them the specifics of cricket. When I was a child and played games in the street or in the park, the skills of catching, throwing, hitting or aiming at a target developed naturally. Now, in this more sedentary age, we must devise activities to cover the same ground. That's why you'll find Ella and her friends jumping over low hurdles, playing hopscotch and running relays long before the bats, balls and stumps emerge from the kitbag.

Another key element in cricket's bright, fresh image is Chance to Shine (www.chance toshine.org). In 2007, this national scheme,

which is run by the Cricket Foundation and creates partnerships between cricket clubs and a cluster of local schools, saw 99,000 boys and girls playing almost 10,000 matches and benefiting from more than 44,000 hours of coaching.

In addition to coaching and matches during school time, holiday camps are also firmly on the Chance to Shine agenda. Last year, for

> *'Test your skills against a bowling machine, cranked up to hurl the ball like an England quickie or set to deliver wicked spin like Shane Warne.'*

example, Abingdon Vale Cricket Club in Oxfordshire (www.abingdonvalecc.co.uk) ran three weeks of cricket for kids of all ages and abilities, while former England fast-bowling hero Devon Malcolm pitched up to lend a hand at the camp run by Welbeck Colliery Cricket Club in Nottinghamshire (www.welbeck ccc.co.uk). When Leeds & Broomfield Cricket Club in Kent (http://lbhcricket.net) held their first holiday camp in May 2007, 20 of the 33 kids taking part had never set foot in a cricket club before. Just as good for the club as a whole (and their bar takings), 13 parents asked about getting involved.

You'll also find plenty of holiday activities going on at the many purpose-built cricket centres around the UK. In Birmingham, the Edgbaston Cricket Centre (www.edgbaston. com) caters for 'the absolute beginner through to the stars of tomorrow' with group coaching for all ages, plus specialist sessions for kids who show promise. You can even test your

skills against a bowling machine, cranked up to hurl the ball down like an England quickie or set to deliver wicked spin like Shane Warne.

In Manchester, the indoor cricket centre at Old Trafford (www.lccc.co.uk) hosts a Saturday Club for children under 11, plus one- and two-day holiday courses covering every aspect of the game including batting, bowling, wicket-keeping and fielding. And at the Ashwell Graham Gooch Cricket Centre in Chelmsford (www.essexcricket.org.uk), day courses, indoor leagues, birthday parties, masterclasses, skill days and individual coaching for all ages and levels are on the schedule.

However, it's hard to beat the sheer range of activities available at the Glamorgan Cricket Centre in Cardiff (www.glamorgancricket.com). A packed summer programme features taster days for six- to 13-year-olds, Kwik Cricket sessions, masterclasses, one-to-one coaching, two-day camps, FUNdamentals courses and, best of all, Glamorgan Experience days. These include four hours of tuition, a chance to watch the professionals play a county match and even an opportunity to meet the players. Not much likelihood of that on a typical football coaching course…

Useful websites

www.play-cricket.com
Use the search facility to find registered clubs in your area, then identify which ones have junior sections and what they offer.

www.ecb.co.uk/development/ get-into-cricket
Lists the 39 county cricket boards, which can be contacted for details about kids' cricket. Also offers plenty of information about starting out in the game.

483 Get up very early indeed

Human beings may be slouches when it comes to getting up early, but dawn is one of the busiest times of day for birds – especially in spring. As the sun rises there's a glorious burst of song, with robins, thrushes, blackbirds and great tits vying for attention from female birds, and establishing their patches of territory. Held in early May, the annual International Dawn Chorus Day brings all sorts of early morning events to birdwatching centres, nature reserves and forests across the country; for details, visit www.idcd.info. Start times can be as early as 4am, and most events are suitable for children; while you're still clinging to the duvet, they'll be raring to set off in the misty, pre-dawn hush.

484 Embark on a colour safari

All you need for this is access to an outside space and keen eyesight. Each participant on the safari decides on the colour they wish to hunt for, and is given a small oblong of white card and a little bag. Once outside, they must look carefully for natural treasures of that colour. Tiny bits and pieces will do: a flame-red autumn leaf; a fragment of geranium petal; a smooth, colour-flecked pebble. Encourage children to get down on the ground and really look; they will be amazed at what they find. Once they have filled their bags, take out the contents and lay them carefully on the card. Challenge each child to arrange their objects from lightest to darkest, and marvel at the many shades within a single colour.

International Dawn Chorus Day

485-490 *Pick your own*

Supermarket produce that's been flown halfway around the world is no match for seasonal fruit and veg picked fresh from the field. Here are a few of our favourite PYOs; visit www.pick-your-own.org.uk to find your nearest. Most are open from June to September, but check before visiting.

Brocksbushes Farm, Northumberland

Plump strawberries and raspberries are the real crowd pleasers here, but there are also tart gooseberries or tayberries: a blackberry and raspberry hybrid that makes scrumptious jam. After your exertions, head to the tea room for a cream tea, with own-made strawberry jam.
Corbridge, Northumberland NE43 7UB (01434 633100/ www.brocksbushes.co.uk).

Cairnie Fruit Farm, Fife

Once you've wandered the strawberry fields or ventured into the brambles, there's plenty to keep children enthralled – not least the maize maze. With straw bale fortresses, go-karts, trampolines and a giant sandpit with diggers, Cairnie makes for a full day out: there's also an excellent tea room.
Cairnie, Cupar, Fife KY15 4QD (01334 655610/www.cairniefruitfarm.co.uk).

Clives Fruit Farm, Worcestershire

The season begins in June with strawberries, followed by raspberries, cherries and plums – but late summer's apple crop is the main event. Traditional varieties galore are grown, and you can watch the fruit being pressed and then buy a bottle to take home. There's also an adventure playground, mini tractors, and chickens and peacocks to feed.
Upper Hook Road, Upton upon Severn, Worcestershire WR8 0SA (01684 592664/ www.clivesfruitfarm.co.uk).

Garson's Fruit Farm, Surrey

With over 40 crops and five sorts of flowers, Garson's has something to tempt even the most steadfast of fruit and veg refuseniks. Connoisseurs can choose between four kinds of cauliflower and eight types of eccentric-sounding squash varieties.
Winterdown Road, Esher, Surrey KT10 8LS (01372 464389/ www.garsons.co.uk).

Garson's Fruit Farm

Millets Farm Centre, Oxfordshire

Over 30 PYO crops are grown at Millets, including tulameen raspberries. In September you can wander through the orchards picking apples and pears. Resident animals include goats, curly-haired mangalitza pigs and alpacas, while summer brings the maize maze.
Kingston Road, Frilford, Oxfordshire OX13 5HB (01865 391555/www.milletsfarmcentre.com).

Parkside Farm, Middlesex

FARMA's PYO of the year for 2009 is a family-run establishment, whose fruit and veg are fertilised with manure from its own cows. There are strawberries and broad beans from June, while high summer's feast of produce includes plums from the orchard and plump, sun-ripened tomatoes.
Hadley Road, Enfield, Middlesex EN2 8LA (020 8367 2035/www.parksidefarmpyo.co.uk).

491 *Meet the kids*

This farm in Bucks is home to around 40 goats, as well as wallabies, donkeys and llamas. Buy a £1 bag of feed and they'll all want to be your friend. From Easter, there are (goats') kids to coo over and, if you're lucky, you may be allowed to take a boisterous calf for a walk. On sunny days, hitch a ride on Trevor the tractor or investigate the giant trampolines. There's also an indoor play area.

Bucks Goat Centre *Layby Farm, Stoke Mandeville, Buckinghamshire HP22 5XJ (01296 612983/www.bucksgoatcentre.co.uk).*

492 *Get swapping*

Rather like eBay for children, Jumbleword (www.jumbleworld.com) is an online trading site where young entrepreneurs can buy, sell and swap unwanted toys and games. From unloved Tamagotchi in search of a new home to nifty night-vision goggles, there's all sorts of stuff to trawl through. Accounts can be set up so that parental approval is required for each transaction, so your kids can't barter away the family car or sell their sibling's favourite teddy.

493 *Swim with minnows*

At the ancient clapper bridge of Tarr Steps in Exmoor National Park, you can pit your wits against the resident minnows that live in the shallows of the River Barle. The bridge is steeped in legend: it's said that the Devil built the bridge, and still sunbathes on its stones. The shallows around the Tarr Steps are popular with young naturalists, who can potter with a fishing net in pursuit of minnows or ride the gentle rapids on rubber rings. Further upstream, through the woods, are deeper swimming holes for older children. The main car park and toilets (400 metres from the bridge) are reached from the B3223 between Withypool and Dulverton. Parking and refreshments are available nearer the bridge.

494 *Help a toad cross the road*

Toads are particular about where they spawn, and like to return to a favourite, deep pond to breed. Often, the migration of toad colonies to a breeding ground involves crossing roads, with sometimes fatal consequences. The excellent amphibian rescue group Froglife are hopping mad about this, and so coordinate a nationwide Toads on the Roads campaign. Log on to www.froglife.org to find a toad patrol near you, and between February and April volunteer to save a toad's life. You know it makes sense.

495 *Be a designer at the Burrell*

Purpose-built to house Sir William Burrell's art collection, which he bequeathed to the city of Glasgow in 1944, the Burrell Collection is a treasure trove of art, artefacts and ephemera from many centuries and many cultures. There should be something to satisfy every visitor, old or young, among this lot – whether it's the size of the adults' gloves from the Middle Ages, the gorgeous Greek war helmet, or the fact that all the medieval combs look like nit combs. On a more edifying note, paintings and sculptures on show usually include works by Degas, Cézanne, Rodin and Boudin.

Weekends bring family-oriented events, including dressing up as knights or serfs, fabric design and seasonal gift making. Some activities are probably best for older kids, but the good thing is that you'll come away with something to show for your efforts. Set aside a good couple of hours for the collection, as there are literally thousands of things to take your interest; if younger children tire of the culture, there's plenty of parkland to run free in.

The Burrell Collection *Pollok Country Park, 2060 Pollokshaws Road, Glasgow G43 1AT (0141 287 2550/www.glasgowmuseums.com).*

496 *Get heavy in Leeds*

Blood, gore, nasty medical instruments, amputations without anaesthetic…it's all good gory fun at the Thackray Medical Museum in Leeds. Mothers who want to show their progeny just what they went through to bring them into the world might like to escort the family to the Having a Baby exhibition on the first floor, where there's an empathy belly visitors can strap on – it weighs four and a half kilos and makes bending down to do up your shoelaces a challenge, let alone walking around all day. Welcome to mother's world, boys.
Thackray Medical Museum *Beckett Street, Leeds LS9 7LN (01132 444343/ www.thackraymuseum.org).*

Thackray Medical Museum

497 *Meet John McEnroe*

The young tousle-haired firebrand turned telly tennis pundit cuts a ghostly figure in the excellent Wimbledon Lawn Tennis Museum. He is, in fact, a hologram that stands and chews the fat about a memorable career in tennis while guests look on. McEnroe's image appears as if by magic in a 1980s gentlemen's dressing room, taking listeners on a tour of the area, while reminiscing about meeting Jimmy Connors and the ways he'd psyche himself up for matches.

Elsewhere in the museum, there's a history of tennis and real tennis, which was a favourite game of Henry VIII – we bet he was a volatile player too – exhibitions of the original trophies and equipment boxes and a mock-up of a 1901 changing room. You can try on old-fashioned sports kit, test your reflexes on the 'reaction station' and prove your knowledge on the game's laws in a 'you are the umpire' display.
Wimbledon Lawn Tennis Museum
All England Lawn Tennis Club, Church Road, London SW19 5AE (020 8946 6131/ www.wimbledon.org/museum).

498 *Charm a worm or two*

Whether they're short, fat slimy ones or long, thin, skinny ones, every worm counts at the International Worm Charming Championships (01803 712149, www.wormcharming.co.uk) in Blackawton, Devon. At this annual charity event, held on the first Sunday in May, teams consisting of a Charmer, a Catcher and a Counter work their magic on a one-metre square turf plot. The Worm Master ensures fair play, and digging is not allowed, although you can pour liquid on to your plot during the 'worming up' period to draw the wrigglers to the surface; there's a Charming substance tasting to prove it won't harm the worms. Stamping, singing and dancing are other popular charming tactics. Teams have 15 minutes to catch the greatest number of worms, and there's a prize for the best fancy dress. At the end of the event the worms are returned to the ground, and everyone goes to celebrate in the village hall.

Mystical Fairies

499 *Sing a sea shanty*

Every salty seadog knows the words to a shanty or two: there's nothing like a good singalong when you're heave-hoing on a rope or winding a windlass. Every year in mid June, the Falmouth International Sea Shanty Festival (www.falmouthshout.com) brings three glorious days of shanty-singing, with plenty of audience participation and dressing up in nautical stripes or piratical attire. Invest £4 in a copy of the official songbook (all proceeds go to the RNLI) and sing your heart out. Kids will love the raucous, rollicking dittics and catchy choruses, while the songs' sometimes fruity subtext mercifully passes over their heads.

500 *Enrol in Fairy School*

Fledgling fairies love the Mystical Fairies shop in north London – a glittering, predominantly pink paradise of tutus, toys and tiaras. Book for a Fairy Makeover or enrol in one of the regular Fairy School days. Here, four- to eight-year-old sprites can play games, participate in arts and crafts and learn the fundamentals of being a fairy – including fairy cake decorating, naturally.

Mystical Fairies *12 Flask Walk, London NW3 1HE (020 7431 1888/www.mysticalfairies.co.uk).*

Ponds conceal all manner of intriguing insects, ripe for investigation. Armed with nets and clear-sided containers, you can stage your own (supervised) pond-dipping sessions; after observing and identifying your catch, always return your spoils to the pond. For expert guidance, head to an organised pond-dipping session, held at parks and nature reserves across the country.

Camley Street Natural Park

Tucked away behind the bustle of St Pancras Station, Camley Street is a wildlife oasis of ponds, meadows and woodland. In the holidays, weekday drop-in activities include pond-dipping sessions. Sit on the boardwalk and see what delights the pond's depths yield: sturdy-legged water boatmen, antennae-waving water fleas or wriggling red bloodworms. Parents must be present at all times to supervise.
Camley Street Natural Park *12 Camley Street, London NW1 0PW (020 7833 2311/ www.wildlondon.org.uk).*

Flag Fen

Flag Fen reconstructs the Cambridgeshire countryside before the Romans arrived, with roundhouses, placidly grazing Soay sheep and various ancient plant species. Pond-dipping sessions take place on a platform set amid the reeds, with all equipment provided; although parental supervision isn't required, 'they can

rarely resist joining in', according to the centre's learning officer. Look out for dragonfly nymphs, freshwater shrimps and mayfly larvae.
Flag Fen *The Droveway, Northey Road, Peterborough, Cambridgeshire PE6 7QJ (01733 313414/www.flagfen.com).*

Pensthorpe

Pensthorpe Nature Reserve and gardens is a stunning natural attraction and plays host to the BBC's *Springwatch* series. The specially designed pond-dipping facilities provide children with nets, identification sheets and buckets. The experts here also lead bird- and bug- watching activities and quizzes.
Pensthorpe *Fakenham, Norfolk NR21 0LN (01328 851465/www.pensthorpe.com).*

Rainham Marshes

One of the RSPB's newest reserves, Rainham Marshes is a waterlogged wonderland of bird species – though there are plenty of smaller critters lurking in the ponds. The reserve has a purpose-built platform for pond dippers, and regular family fun days; children are provided with nets, containers and a species sheet, with friendly education officers at hand to explain what's what.
Rainham Marshes Nature Reserve *New Tank Hill Road, Purfleet, Essex RM19 1SZ (01708 899840/www.rspb.org.uk).*

Rainham Marshes

505 *See the giant catapult in action*

There's much to entertain the troops at Warwick Castle, one of the country's best-kept medieval strongholds and the repository of all kinds of chilling ghost stories. The bit that fascinates weaponry-obsessed children the most, however, is the giant trebuchet, which is, in essence, a massive catapult. Warwick's replica trebuchet is the world's largest working siege machine; it weighs 22 tonnes and stands 18 metres tall. The machine is fired daily, so make a date to watch it in action.

Warwick Castle *Warwick, Warwickshire, CV34 4QU (0870 442 2000/www.warwick-castle.co.uk).*

506 *Make breadsticks*

Take a packet of instant breadmix and make up the dough according to the instructions. Once you've kneaded the dough, break off small pieces from the main lump to roll out sticks, about 15cm long and as thick as your index finger. Place the sticks on a greased baking tray, cover with clingfilm and leave in a warm place to rise. Once they've doubled in size, brush with water and sprinkle poppy and sesame seeds on them. Bake in a hot oven (about 220°C) until they're crisp and golden.

507 *Get behind the wheel at Gleneagles*

Set in 344 hectares of Perthshire countryside, Gleneagles Hotel has room to run all sorts of outdoor activities – and you don't have to be staying there to sign up. One of the more unusual offerings is off-road driving instruction, with four- to nine-year-olds steering specially commissioned quarter-sized Land Rovers across the rugged terrain. For ten-and-overs, there's the thrill of taking an amphibious, eight-wheel-drive Argo Cat along a purpose-built track, with water splashes and hair-raising descents.

Gleneagles Hotel *Auchterarder, Perthshire PH3 1NF (01764 694347/www.gleneagles.com).*

508-511 *Take in some heavenly views*

Durham Cathedral

A wonder of 11th-century Norman architecture it might be, but just as jawdropping as its celebrated interiors is the view from the clifftop cathedral's tower, overlooking wooded gorges and the whole city nestling around a meander in the River Wear. Entrance is £3 and a 1.3 metre height restriction applies.

The Chapter Office, Durham DH1 3EH (01913 864266/www.durhamcathedral.co.uk).

Monument

Some say the fabulous views are reward enough, but children might think they deserve a medal for climbing 311 steps. That's how many you have to toil up to see London from this colossal Doric column, erected as a memorial to the Great Fire of London in 1666 and to celebrate the city's rebuilding afterwards. Still, the commemorative certificate will look impressive on your bedroom wall – and is worth the £3 admission fee. The Monument is 61 metres high, by the way, the exact distance from it to the site in Pudding Lane where the fire began.

Monument Street, London EC3R 8AH (020 7626 2717/www.themonument.info).

Westminster Cathedral

The spectacular views over the capital as seen from the bell tower of the red and white striped Westminster Cathedral can be enjoyed by paying £5 to go up in a lift – so you don't even have to break a sweat. The campanile is 83 metres high.

42 Francis Street, London SW1P 1QW (020 7798 9055/www.westminstercathedral.org.uk).

York Minster

This is the biggest Gothic cathedral in northern Europe, with the largest area of medieval stained glass in the world. For most children, however, the biggest thrill is scampering up 275 steps to admire the city views from the top. Kids have to be aged eight or above.

Church House, Ogleforth, York YO1 7JN (01904 557200/www.yorkminster.org).

Farne Islands

512-515 *Spot seals...*

Blakeney National Nature Reserve, Norfolk

The sandbanks at Blakeney Point are covered with basking grey and common seals. Boat trips have been coming here for years, so the seals aren't afraid of humans and don't mind posing for pictures. Blakeney is now a National Trust-run nature reserve (01263 740241, www.nationaltrust.org.uk); for details of boat trips from Morston Quay, check the website.

Donna Nook, Lincolnshire

In November and December, hundreds of grey seals haul themselves out of the sea at Donna Nook and head for the sand dunes to give birth to their pups (www.lincstrust.org.uk). If the mothers feel threatened, they may abandon their young – so leave the family dog at home, and don't come too close to the seals.

Farne Islands, Northumberland

Seals can be spotted year-round on these lonely, rocky islands – though to see some sloe-eyed seal cubs, you'll need to visit between late September and January. Several different boats run from the harbour at Seahouses village; try *MV Glad Tidings* (01665 720308, www.farne-islands.com), run by the Shiel family.

Ramsey Island, Pembrokeshire

Run by the RSPB, Ramsey Island is best known for its flourishing seabird colonies. In autumn, as the peregrines and choughs wheel overhead, grey seals swim here to breed, and you can spot big-eyed, white-furred pups on the beach. Voyages of Discovery (01437 720285, www.ramseyisland.co.uk) runs boat tours around the reserve's spectacular sea caves and shoreline.

516 ...or take a swim with them

The seals at Lundy Island sometimes join visitors for a dip. Sailing from Clovelly harbour on the North Devon coast, the *Jessica Hetty* (01237 431405, www.clovelly-charters.ukf.net) offers seal-swimming trips; participants should be competent swimmers, with children allowed at their parents' discretion. Bring a snorkel or goggles to watch the seals playing underwater. If you have a wetsuit, wear it; waiting for the seals to make their star turn can be chilly.

517 Be a knight in cardboard armour

Take a big cardboard box (large enough to step into and to cover your torso). Remove the ends and attach two lengths of ribbon to the top edges with split pins – these will act as shoulder straps. That's the breastplate done. Next, take two tissue boxes and cut them open to fit over your shoulders as spaulders (armoured plates), then place them under the shoulder straps. Take four longish, thin boxes and open them out to cover your thighs and shins, using ribbons or elastic to keep them in place. Your helmet can be a shoebox: create an oval shape for your head, and cut off one end so it will fit your neck. The whole lot can be painted silver and, presto! You're invincible.

518 Celebrate city life

Just arriving at Urbis, the arresting glass building in Manchester dedicated to city living, is a treat – children love the ride to the top floor in the smooth Skyglide elevator. Come at weekends or in the school holidays and you can join in one of the regular creative workshops. Children are guaranteed to come away with a unique, hand-made souvenir of their visit to this unusual cultural centre.
Urbis *Cathedral Gardens, Manchester M4 3BG (01616 058200/www.urbis.org.uk).*

519 Watch the Royal Highland Show

Held near Edinburgh Airport over four days in the third week in June, the Royal Highland Show is a celebration of all things agricultural. As well as hundreds of animals, including enormous Clydesdale horses and miniature Shetland ponies, there are usually Highland Games, so you can see how big a caber really is. Listen to a pipe band, watch as sheepdogs round up a flock of quacking ducks, or try your hand at the arts and crafts workshops in the Children's Discovery Centre: you could come away with your own birdhouse or bug hotel, or a lovingly hand-crafted beeswax candle.
Royal Highland Show
Royal Highland Centre, Ingliston, Edinburgh EH28 8NB (0131 335 6200/www. royalhighland show.org).

Urbis

520 *Scare the crows*

For one week in August, more than 100 scarecrows – happy, sad, silly and funny – are dotted around the classic Yorkshire Dales village of Kettlewell. It's a great way to introduce kids to the glories of the Dales without threatening them with a wet and windy walk. Take the trail, solve the riddles and spot the drunks and vicars, fishermen and strippers, babies and even scarecrows of scarecrows. Then retreat to the village hall for tea and cakes. For more information, see www.kettlewell.info.

521 See the oldest living thing in Europe

The Fortingall Yew, in the Kirkyard in Fortingall (16 kilometres west of Aberfeldy in Perthshire) is dated at between 3,000 and 9,000 years old. The tree has a protective wall and fence. It is fragmented, but still impressive: it's incredible to touch something that has survived millennia and is still alive. For more information, visit www.forestry.gov.uk.

522

Be prepared on Brownsea

Picnics can be wild affairs on Brownsea Island in Dorset, thanks to its hungry chickens, who think nothing of helping themselves to the odd tasty sandwich. Don't let this put you off, though, as Brownsea (run by the National Trust) is a top place for alfresco eating. Robert Baden-Powell ran his first scouting camp here, and your inner scout will be awakened on this car-free green and wooded island. Comb the beach for treasures, dabble your toes in the sea and keep your eyes open for the island's famous red squirrels. Children are lent tracker packs from the visitor centre to use on themed trails, and take part in arty, crafty activities.
Brownsea Island *Poole Harbour, Dorset BH13 7EE (01202 707744/www.nationaltrust.org.uk).*

523 Be a giant at Bekonscot

Grown-ups have to squint to appreciate the finer details of Bekonscot Model Village, but children are the perfect height to appreciate its Lilliputian charms. Its realms encompass everything from cricket games on the green to rows of tiny terraces. Look out for the line of knotted sheets dangling from a window at the prison, and the smoke above a burning house as firemen tackle the blaze. As for Borrowers, we've never seen any – but we wouldn't be surprised.
Bekonscot Model Village *Warwick Road, Beaconsfield, Buckinghamshire HP9 2PL (01494 672919/www.bekonscot.com).*

524 Wander with birds and butterflies

You'll feel a long way from Lincolnshire in the tropical gardens at Long Sutton's Butterfly & Wildlife Park. It's a lush indoor jungle, where hundreds of butterflies flit between brightly hued hibiscus and bougainvillea. To admire the insects' beautiful markings, creep close to one of the feeding stations, where the butterflies feast on rotting fruit – bananas are a favourite. If creepy-crawlies are more your thing, watch the leaf-cutting ants skilfully slicing the leaves with their jaws, or brave one of the 'meet the invertebrates' sessions, where you can handle some fearsome-looking spiders. Outside, the new adventure play area has an awesome 40-metre zip wire.
Butterfly & Wildlife Park *Long Sutton, Spalding, Lincolnshire PE12 9LE (01406 363833/ www.butterflyandwildlifepark.co.uk).*

525 Meet the thoroughbreds

There would be little point in visiting the West Berkshire village of Lambourn (www.lambourn.info) unless you're interested in racehorses. The valley is full of them – 2,000 at last count, stamping and snorting in more than 50 racing yards. In the ordinary scheme of things, only stable lads, trainers and owners can get close to these fabulously valuable equine athletes – except on Good Friday. This is when the home of horseracing flings open the stable door to welcome visitors. You can pay for a day pass (under-12s are free) to tour the yards and see the pampered horses working out in their hydrotherapy pools, having massages and reading *Hello!* (the last two details might not be true), then browse the trade stands and take some refreshments. In the afternoon, watch the jockeys and stable lads compete in fast and furious mounted games; there are also dog skill displays, a tug of war, motorcycle stunts and a glossily groomed parade of the animals. It's a top day out for horse-mad kids, and a chance to find out how fit you have to be for a career in racing – ask the stable workers about their daily routine and be impressed.

526

Admire the Illuminations
What a spectacle! See Blackpool's Prom, Tower, piers and Pleasure Beach awash with shimmering electric light, neon, LED, lasers and fibre optics. There's no better way to view the town's famed autumn Illuminations (01253 478222, www.visitblackpool.com) than from the top deck of a tram, wending its way down the glittering Golden Mile.

A few of my favourite things

527-536

Frank Furedi, Professor of Sociology, University of Kent

Obviously what kids enjoy doing during the holidays changes as they grow older. Still, one thing that we have found over the years is that although children aren't always terribly interested in what their parents like to do, and vice versa, it's crucial that you learn to meet halfway.

We like to go for walks in the ancient woodland near our home, King's Wood (King's Wood, off White Hill, Challock, Ashford, Kent, www.forestry.gov.uk). Now that he's 13, our son prefers to disappear for protracted lengths of time, exploring and building dens. Last summer he went off cycling with his friends, taking some lunch and making camps in the forest. It's very important for children to be able to do things like this. They can learn to be self-sufficient and use their imaginations, unsupported by digital technology.

It's important for us to create a sense of family identity, through conversations about who we are and our common interests. In our family, much of this shared experience revolves around food. My son loves going out to restaurants – the more sophisticated, the better. He was in Madrid last year on a school exchange trip, and when he rang us up his only complaint was that the family seemed to think he wanted to eat children's food. He loves to eat out in Italian and French restaurants and enjoys working out what to choose from the menu. A particular favourite when we go into London is the Gay Hussar (2 Greek Street, London W1D 4NB,

020 7437 0973, www.gayhussar.co.uk). I'm Hungarian, so through enjoying the food there we learn more about our background and culture.

Another activity we do as a family is going to art galleries. This probably wouldn't be my son's first choice for a day's outing, but if you combine the visit with other things he remains interested. There's an implicit negotiation involved. Don't try to do too much, either; like all of us, children can only take in so much art at any one time. My son likes the Wallace Collection (Hertford House, Manchester Square, London W1U 3BN, 020 7563 9500, www.wallacecollection.org), as much for the magnificent armoury and sword displays as for the artworks. The Wallace has a very good restaurant too. Down by the river, Tate Modern (Bankside, London SE1 9TG, 020 7887 8888, www.tate.org.uk) is also a wonderful space with a lively atmosphere.

Places close to where we live that we all still enjoy include Leeds Castle (Maidstone, Kent ME17 1PL, 01622 765400, www.leeds-castle.com), for which we have a season ticket, and the gardens at Mount Ephraim (Hernhill, near Faversham, Kent ME13 9TX, 01227 751496, www.mountephraimgardens.co.uk). The gardens are full of unexpected treasures. We've enjoyed seeing various Shakespeare productions in the open air here – much better than sitting in a stuffy theatre.

At the age of 13, my son is in the final interlude before adulthood, and he's indulging in moments of rebellion against family outings. He's an only child too, so it's only right that he spend more time with his friends now. One activity that he does still enjoy is bumming around in central London – going to the Science Museum (Exhibition Road, London SW7 2DD, 0870 870 4868, www.sciencemuseum.org.uk), or maybe for a walk around Regent's Park (www.royalparks.org.uk/regents), perhaps taking a boat out on the boating lake. Then it's up to Primrose Hill (www.primrosehill.com) and on to Swiss Cottage for a drink and something to eat at the wonderful Louis Pâtisserie (32 Heath Street, London NW3 6TE, 020 7435 9908). Hampstead is the perfect urban village, and there's the wide open expanse of the Heath for running around on.

537 Toddle along for charity

The Big Toddle is an annual short walk for short people (under-fives) to raise money for the charity Barnardos. Children can join in with one of the official toddles going on all over the country, or organise their own event with their family, local nurseries, playgroups or crèche. If you register and pledge money, you qualify for an event pack goody bag to help you get started. Visit www.bigtoddle.co.uk and put your best foot forward this summer.

538 Wrap greenly

If you want to save money, and trees, experiment with different coverings for presents, other than bog-standard gift wrap. We've had good results from the following:
● A big roll of plain brown paper from a stationery shop, stamped with sponge shapes or potato prints and poster paint.
● Offcuts of soft material from dressmaking, tied with ribbon.
● Large maps that are no longer needed, or colourful pages from magazines – especially if they have some relevance to the recipient.
● Redundant wallpaper rolls, or wall-lining paper decorated with glitter and paint.

539 Make a date in the dairy

All the old agricultural skills are given due respect in the Yorkshire Museum of Farming. Family events include baking bread, weaving, wood-turning and apple pressing in season, while dairy days are particularly popular. Try your hand at churning butter (it won't set if there's a cream witch about, apparently), milking a (wooden) cow or discovering what goes on inside a cow's many stomachs. You can also watch the blessed cheesemakers at work and enjoy a dairy-based tasting session.
Yorkshire Museum of Farming *Murton Park, Murton Lane, Murton, York, YO19 5UF (01904 489966/www.murtonpark.co.uk).*

540 Roll your own sushi...

You can tuck all sorts of goodies into sushi maki (rice and seaweed) rolls: pieces of avocado, cucumber, sections of tinned mini corn cobs, tuna, smoked salmon, bits of hard-boiled egg or even beetroot (which makes the rice a lovely shade of pink).
You need:
  square sheets of nori (seaweed)
  bamboo sushi mat (optional)
  sushi rice
  rice vinegar
  sugar
  salt
  soy sauce
  your chosen fillings
All of the above can be bought in Japanese food stores or good supermarkets.

First, cook the sushi rice as instructed, then leave it to cool. Make sushi vinegar (sushi-zu): mix six tablespoons of rice vinegar with two tablespoons of sugar and one teaspoon of salt, then cook over a low heat until the sugar and salt have dissolved.

Put the cooled rice in a bowl and mix in the sushi vinegar. Fold a piece of paper and fan the rice to make it glossy.

Take a sheet of nori and cover two-thirds with a layer of rice, then place three or four pieces of vegetable or fish at equal intervals in the centre of the rice. Roll up the nori and its contents into a neat swiss-roll shape. Seal the edge with a little vinegar or water, then cut the roll into three equal parts. Tuck a little more vegetables or fish into the rice at the top of each roll for decoration, then serve your sushi, with a bowl of sweet soy sauce for dipping.

541 ...or practise your maths while eating someone else's

Children love nationwide chain Yo! Sushi, where the sushi parades around on a conveyor belt and diners help themselves. Dishes cost £1.70-£5 each. If you have £10, how many dishes can you try? Find your nearest branch at www.yosushi.com.

542 *Build a kite*

Watching a kite that you've made with your own hands dipping and swooping through the sky is a magical experience. The making part is wonderfully simple, if you follow our guide.

Step 1

First, take two garden canes, one 45cm long and the other 75cm.

Step 2

Tie the shorter cane across the longer cane, about one third of the way down, using a piece of string.

Step 3

Stretch a piece of string around the outside edge. It helps if you make little grooves in each end of the sticks, in order to keep the string frame in place. Four hands are better than two here. Keep the string as taut as possible, while taking care not to bend the frame out of shape.

Step 4

Cover your frame with an opened-out carrier bag, using masking tape to secure it in place.

Step 5

Tie a piece of thin nylon twine or fishing line, decorated with small scraps of material or plastic from a carrier bag, to the bottom point of the frame to make a colourful tail.

Step 6

Tie a loop of fishing line from one end of the horizontal stick to the other, and attach to it the end of your roll of fishing line – that's the string you hold while flying your kite. As the kite climbs higher in the air, let the line unravel so the kite can soar ever higher.

543 *Join the quad squad*

The petrolheads at Glasfryn kit out children in safety helmets, overalls and gloves, give a ten-minute safety induction, pop them on a quad bike and accompany them over the green, green grass of Gwynedd. Children must be at least 12 years old to experience the 50-minute quad bike safari. Younger children, aged from six, are only allowed out on the track on the quads. Safaris cost from £25 for 50 minutes, while quadding for tinies is from £3 per minute.

Glasfryn Parc *Pwllheli, Gwynedd LL53 6PG (01766 810202/www.glasfryn.co.uk).*

544 *Take the plunge in Paignton*

Open from May to September, Quaywest is a watery wonderland of slides and tube rides, heated to a balmy 27°C. The more adventurous slides, like the Wild Kamikaze, snake overhead, while thrill seekers can plummet almost 20 metres in the Devil's Drop, take an enclosed speed slide in the aptly named Screamer or ride the Raging Rapids. Children who measure in at under 1.07m aren't allowed on the bigger slides.

Quaywest *Goodrington Sands, Paignton, Devon TQ4 6LN (01803 550034/www.quaywest.co.uk).*

545 *Swan about in Wells*

When the swans who live in the moat at Wells' magnificent Bishop's Palace get peckish, they have an unusual way of demanding their dinner – by bossily ringing on a bell that hangs by the water. It's been a tradition here since the 19th century, with wise elder birds teaching the next generation the art of bell-ringing.

Bishop's Palace *Wells, Somerset BA5 2PD (01749 678691/www.bishopspalace.org.uk).*

546 *Visit a leafy, living cathedral*

Children learn enough about World War I in Key Stage 2 history lessons to appreciate the significance of this beauty spot. Trees, hedges and shrubs set out in the form of a medieval cathedral create a green nave, chancel and chapels. It was planted between 1931 and 1939 by Mr EK Blyth, in the spirit of 'faith, hope and reconciliation' following the deaths of two of his friends in the Great War. He also fought in World War II, but returned to complete his work, which you can wander through today.

Whipsnade Tree Cathedral *Chapel Farm, Whipsnade, Dunstable, Bedfordshire LU6 2LL (01582 872406/www.nationaltrust.org.uk).*

Bishop's Palace, Wells

547 *Go stargazey crazy*

The spectacular Christmas lights in the Cornish fishing village of Mousehole extend along its harbour, boats and streets. The decorations, which use more than 7,000 bulbs, include rather fetching illuminations based on local legends – notably that of Tom Bawcock, who braved stormy winter seas to catch enough fish to feed the starving villagers. The catch was made into a stargazey pie – a pastry-topped pie with protruding fish heads peeping out. On Tom Bawcock's Eve, 23 December, children lead a lantern procession to the water's edge, and a stargazey pie is baked at the quayside Ship Inn (South Cliff, Mousehole, Cornwall TR19 6QX, 01736 731234). You can also spot a fish-filled pie picked out in lights on the harbour wall, alongside one of Mowze, the Mousehole cat. The lights are on from 5pm to 11pm until the first week of January.

548 *See how kids used to learn*

In the 19th century, few people imagined that the poor even wanted to be educated, until one or two earnest philanthopists proved otherwise by offering to teach working-class urchins for free and discovering enormous demand. Then, of course, the pupils found out how much they hated school and changed their minds – but by then it was too late, and the Ragged Schools had come into being.

The Ragged School Museum in London's East End is the original school where Dr Barnardo worked, fresh from Dublin and full of idealism. The museum has free children's activities on Wednesdays and Thursdays in the school holidays, from 10am to 5pm, involving art workshops, detective trails and treasure hunts. Otherwise, the star attractions are the classroom with its antique desks, slates, blackboards and dunce's hats, and the kitchen with its mangle, stove, tin mugs, carpet beaters and toasting forks.

Ragged School Museum *46-50 Copperfield Road, London E3 4RR (020 8980 6405/ www.raggedschoolmuseum.org.uk).*

549 *Meet scary Hairy Jack*

You might not find out all you need to know about this nation's rollicking smuggling history, but embarking on a Smugglers Adventure in Hastings is exciting all the same. At the entrance you'll meet one Hairy Jack, via the miracles of modern science, then you're on your own in deep, dark tunnels to find out how the dastardly ne'er-do-wells escaped the might of the customs men and hid their booty. Be aware that the adventure might not be ideal for the very young or easily spooked.

Smugglers Adventure *St Clement's Caves, West Hill, Hastings, East Sussex TN34 3HY (01424 422964/www.smugglersadventure.co.uk).*

550 *Do some leaf printing*

This is a lovely autumn activity. Go on a walk and collect leaves of all sizes and shapes. Bring them home, lay them out and mix up some poster paint. Carefully brush the leaves with it, then press them, wet side down, on to some plain paper. Remove the leaves to see the accuracy of the print. Make it into a greetings card, or cut out the leaves to make a tree mural.

551

Visit Britain's last battlefield

The windswept moor at Culloden is an eerie spot. It was here, on a bitter day in April 1746, that Jacobite forces led by Charles Edward Stuart faced government troops, in a last attempt to reclaim the throne for a Stuart king. The Jacobites were defeated in the brief, bloody clash, the last hand-to-hand battle fought on British soil. In its aftermath, the British crushed any further rebellion among the Scottish clans, and even the kilt and tartan were banned. Walk among the headstones, then go to the visitors' centre, where a 360° 'battle immersion film' plunges you into the thick of the action.

Culloden Moor *Inverness IV1 2ED (0844 493 2159/www.nts.org.uk).*

552-554
Keep your head in the clouds

If you think clouds are heavenly, and enjoy watching them make pictures in the sky, you are not alone. The Cloud Appreciation Society shares your passion. Drift over to their website (www.cloudappreciationsociety.org) to discover more. The membership fee is a wispy £4 (plus 52p postage).

You don't need the CAS's help, however, to keep a cloud diary. Make a habit of checking the cloud shapes daily at the same time, drawing what you see and then identifying the various types. Are they cirrus, cumulus, altostratus or cumulonimbus? Check www.bbc.co.uk/weather to find out.

Once you've become a cloud expert, try making a cloud in a bottle. Take a clear plastic water bottle and cover the bottom with a little warm water. Then light a match, blow it out and put the smoking head of the match into the bottle, letting all the smoke go in. Very quickly screw on the bottle cap. Once the cap is tightly fastened, rapidly squeeze the sides of the bottle seven times. Then squeeze once, slowly, holding it for a few seconds before suddenly releasing it. You should see a perfect cloud in your bottle.

555
Accessorise!

Northampton Museum & Art Gallery has a fine collection of Italian art, but for us its real treasures lie in the shoe department. The footwear on display includes a tiny boot that once belonged to the 19th-century midget Tom Thumb, dainty pumps worn by Queen Victoria on her wedding day and gallumphing great cherry red Doc Martens worn by Elton John in the 1975 film *Tommy*. The education staff run accessory-based workshops for children over eight. You can design a shoe, create a bag or take part in some brilliant costume design workshops. Do book ahead, as these activities are very popular.

Northampton Museum & Art Gallery
Guildhall Road, Northampton NN1 1DP
(01604 838111/www.northampton.gov.uk).

556
Create a time capsule

A time capsule is a special cache of items that has been buried or hidden for people to find in the future. The idea is that it gives the people who discover it clues as to what life was like in the old days. It's similar to sending a message in a bottle to the future. Some people make a pact to open the container in, say, 20 years, while others prefer to leave it to a chance finding generations hence.

Take a suitable container (preferably waterproof and rustproof) and fill it with significant treasures, such as photographs of yourself or your pets, school reports, theatre or sports fixture tickets, a newspaper or magazine front page, sweet wrappers, letters to your penfriend in the future, hairclips, badges and fridge magnets, pressed flowers or seeds… the possibilities are endless. Clearly label your box with the date it should be opened, before hiding it up the chimney, in the attic, or buried in the garden. Then forget about it.

557
Experience wartime life

A parked Hurricane bomber signals the entrance to Eden Camp, a former POW camp that's now a museum of Britain at war. Original huts house reconstructed scenes from World War II, with moving figures, sounds and smells, while another display covers more recent conflicts. Clamber into a U-boat mock-up, experience the simulated smoke, fire and dust of the Blitz, or see how the Italian and German POWs lived here, with 64 men to a hut. After a round on the junior assault course, head for hut 16, the NAAFI (Navy, Army & Air Force) canteen for 'soup of D-Day' or steak-filled Churchill's pie, or go upmarket in the Officers' Mess. All, inevitably, to the soundtrack of George Formby and Vera Lynn.

Eden Camp *Malton, North Yorkshire YO17 6RT*
(01653 697777/www.edencamp.co.uk).

558 Pay homage to two Cornish giants

The bewitchingly beautiful beach at Bedruthan Steps, between Padstow and Newquay, was once a giant's playground, so locals say. Legend has it that its massive volcanic rock stacks were stepping stones used by the giant Bedruthan to cross the bay between Park Head and Berryl's Point in the south. (In fact they were created by the cliffs' erosion over the centuries, but most children prefer the giant story.)

Another Cornish giant said to have made his mark on this coastline is Bolster – so big he could stand with one foot on St Agnes Head (west of Newquay) and the other on Carn Brea, six miles inland. He was in love with the beautiful Agnes, who craftily told him that to prove his love, he should fill a hole in the cliff at Chapel Porth with his blood. Little did Bolster know that the hole led into the sea, and his blood poured away until he lost consciousness and died. A trail of red still marks the place where the lovestruck giant's blood flowed.

559 Clamber aboard the SS Great Britain

In her 19th-century glory days, the *SS Great Britain* was one of the finest passenger liners in the world. A propeller-driven, iron-hulled beauty, she completed her maiden voyage to New York in a record-breaking 14 days. After a long and illustrious career, she ended up ingloriously rusting in the Falkland Islands, before being rescued and returned to Bristol's dry dock in 1970. After having a go at steering the ship on a giant interactive exhibit in the Dockyard Museum, children can search for Sinbad the ship's cat amid the decks, cramped sailor's quarters and more salubrious first-class passenger cabins, or visit the talking toilet. There are all sort of smells to sniff out, from fresh-baked bread in the galley to dirty socks in steerage; watch out for the seasick passenger. Tickets allow unlimited return visits for a year.

SS Great Britain *Western Dockyard, Gas Ferry Road, Bristol BS1 6TY (0117 926 0680/ www.ssgreatbritain.org).*

560-567 *Be a junior keeper for the day*

Chessington Zoo

This is four hours of animal magic for seven to 16s, who spend their allotted time in the Children's Zoo and Creature Features sections (£95). The experience is reserved for one child at a time, although a keeper will accept two siblings. Children are expected to do everything the keeper does – feeding, grooming, mucking out and exercising the farm animals, as well as the more exotic meerkats, capybaras (like pig-sized guinea pigs), wallabies, ferrets and skunks.

Leatherhead Road, Chessington, Surrey KT9 2NE (0870 444 7777/www.chessington.com).

Colchester Zoo

A two-hour Junior Keeper experience takes in the farm area and bug and reptile house – so you might get to meet the bearded dragons, feed the llamas or groom a horse. It costs £75 and is suitable for eight to 14s. Twelve-and-overs can opt for shorter Shadow a Keeper sessions (£50), which focus on one species: tigers or komodo dragons, for the brave.

Maldon Road, Stanway, Colchester, Essex CO3 0SL (01206 331292/www.colchester-zoo.co.uk).

Drusillas Park

Any animal-lover above the age of five can spend an entire day shadowing a keeper at Drusillas (£130-£140) – though under-tens must be accompanied by an adult. Preparing lunch for the prairie dogs, ring-tailed lemurs and lizards might be on the agenda, along with the terrific job of feeding sprats to the hungry penguins and cleaning out the porcupine's den.

Alfriston Road, Alfriston, East Sussex BN26 5QS (01323 874100/www.drusillas.co.uk).

Dudley Zoo

As a Little Zoo Keeper at Dudley, you'll spend the morning at the farm, helping to clean, feed and care for its friendly kune-kune pigs, giant rabbits and pygmy goats. In the afternoon, it's time to meet some of the zoo's more exotic inmates, including giraffes, Brazilian tapirs, lemurs and red pandas. The experience is suitable for children aged eight to 13 and costs £105 for one child or £170 for two.

2 The Broadway, Dudley, West Midlands DY1 4QB (01384 215313/www.dudleyzoo.org.uk).

Chessington Zoo

ZOO KEEPER

Exmoor Zoo

Depending on their age, childen can be a keeper for a morning (£65) or a whole day (£110) at this friendly zoo. Handling wallabies, meeting meerkats and grooming the alpacas' beautifully soft coats are among the activities; in the afternoon, you might hang out with lemurs, polish up the tortoises and visit the zoo's baby animals. Participants must be eight or above.

South Stowford, Bratton Fleming, near Barnstaple, North Devon EX31 4SG (01598 763352/www.exmoorzoo.co.uk).

Lakeland Wildlife Oasis

Wear your wellies and be ready to get hands-on during your two-hour stint at Lakeland (£40). Keepers tailor the experience to participants' interests, so if you're crazy for snakes or dying to touch a tarantula, just say so. Feeding the spider monkeys is a highlight – though be warned, their favourite grub is live mealworms. It's aimed at seven to 11s, with whole-day sessions (£90) for older kids.

Hale, Milnthorpe, Cumbria LA7 7BW (01539 563027/www.wildlifeoasis.co.uk).

Newquay Zoo

Spend two busy hours with Newquay's keepers (£55) helping to feed the otters, preparing a snack for the monkeys and meeting the penguins. All that hard work will leave you pretty peckish; luckily, the morning concludes with lunch. Sessions are aimed at adult-accompanied eight to 14s, who are given a Junior Keeper's badge, certificate and T-shirt as mementos of the day.

Trenance Gardens, Newquay, Cornwall TR7 2LZ (01637 873342/www.newquayzoo.org.uk).

Port Lympne Wild Animal Park

The keeper scheme here is more of a VIP tour than a hands-on experience – though you might get to touch a snake. The day involves taking a safari around the park, with big cat and rhino talks and an introduction to the tapirs; at 3pm, it's time to visit the gorillas to see if they fancy a monkey nut or two. Kids must be over five, and accompanied by an adult; each person pays £50.

Lympne, near Hythe, Kent CT21 4PD (01303 264647/www.totallywild.net).

Newquay Zoo

568 *Film with the fairies*

During the summer holidays, the woods and meadows around the town of Chagford, on the north-east edge of Dartmoor, come alive with fairies and ogres as the Chagford Filmmaking Group (www.fairytalefilms.co.uk) shoots its latest movie. The group is dedicated to creating films of British fairy tales for children, with mums, dads, grandparents and kids pitching in alongside industry professionals to create extraordinary tales of enchantment, which are then screened locally. Membership is free and open to everyone, and the directors try to fit in as many kids as they can. 'It's just amazing how the children transform when you get them out into nature – it's as if these stories run in their blood,' says founder and local mother Elizabeth-Jane Baldry. The group makes a film a year, with the principal shooting dates in the school summer holidays.

569

Work on holiday

Shake away those cobwebs with a National Trust working holiday in one of their gorgeous rural or historic locations (0845 470 7558, www.nationaltrust.org.uk). There are around 450 working holidays a year to choose from, in locations throughout the UK. Youth Discovery holidays, during which 16-18s can learn such skills as coppicing or dry stonewalling, count towards Duke of Edinburgh awards (or are good to mention on the dreaded UCAS form). Working holidays can also be arranged for families with up to three children aged eight to 16. Expect baked potatoes around the bonfire, hostel-style accommodation and plenty of energetic outdoor fun.

Chagford Filmmaking Group

570

Enter an Elizabethan timewarp

With its roofless frame and empty windows backlit by the sky, the mansion at Lyveden New Bield in Northamptonshire looks like a ruin. In fact, it was never completed – like the moated gardens that surround it. In 1605, when debt-ridden gentleman farmer Sir Thomas Tresham died after a lifetime of being hounded for his Catholic beliefs, the craftsmen working on the grand summer house and pleasure gardens promptly downed tools and left, knowing they would never be paid.

Time has stood still here for over 400 years – though since the 1990s, the National Trust has worked to rescue the gardens from brambles and scrub. Only now are the originally planned orchards being planted and the different gardens and terraces slowly uncovered. It's great fun to wander about the remote, hugely photogenic estate, unravelling the Biblical architectural code and centuries-old graffiti. Walk through the basement kitchens and parlours, and wonder at what might have been.

Lyveden New Bield *near Oundle, Peterborough, Northamptonshire PE8 5AT (01832 205358/ www.nationaltrust.org.uk).*

571

Be a prisoner at Beaumaris

Imagine you have been convicted of sheep stealing and sentenced to a stretch in this ancient, dark prison on the isle of Anglesey. After a breakfast of slop, you divide your day between breaking rocks in an empty room and powering the treadmill (still in working order). You were chained to the treadmill for an hour at a time and couldn't get off without breaking your leg. In an upper cell, actors recreate the final miserable hours of the second to last man to be hanged at the prison, a bigamist. He had to walk to a second-floor door high in the wall of the prison, outside which was the gallows and a crowd from the town who had come to watch.

Beaumaris Gaol *Steeple Lane, Beaumaris, Anglesey LL58 8EP (01248 810921/ www.beaumaris.org.uk).*

572-575

Seek out a secret bunker

Your mission, should you accept, is to brave four of the UK's secret subterranean bunkers – built during the Cold War to protect the top brass, and allow the army to launch a retaliatory rocket or two against the enemy.

First up is Kelvedon Hatch in Essex (Crown Buildings, Kelvedon Hall Lane, Brentwood, Essex CM14 5TL, 01277 364883, www.secret nuclearbunker.com). Built on farmland, the bunker looks for all the world like an ordinary bungalow, but don't be fooled by appearances. Below the decoy building, a 120-metre tunnel leads to a vast subterranean complex. It had enough room to shelter 600 people, along with its own air-purifying plant and BBC studio for emergency broadcasts.

Its guardhouse disguised as a farmhouse, Scotland's Secret Bunker (Crown Buildings, Troywood, Fife KY16 8QH, 01333 310301, www.secretbunker.co.uk) remained a closely guarded secret for over 40 years. Only in 1994 was the labyrinthine complex opened to the public. It's a bit chilly and creepy for small kids, but older childen will be enthralled, especially by the tales of privation that staff would have endured in the bunker had nuclear war been declared. The dormitories could sleep up to 300 personnel; each person was allowed to rest for six hours, then had to vacate their bed for the person coming off shift. They wouldn't see daylight or even shower for up to three months – by which time the authorities hoped the radiation outside would be slightly less potent.

Hack Green Nuclear Bunker (off the A530, Whitchurch Road, Nantwich, Cheshire CW5 8AQ, 01270 629219, www.hackgreen.co.uk) is another hidey-hole on a grand scale, with its own generating plant, emergency water supply and nuclear fallout filter rooms. Children can look out for dastardly 'spy mice', with sharp eyes rewarded by a certificate.

The York Cold War Bunker (Monument Close, York, North Yorkshire YO24 4HT, 01904 646940, www.english-heritage.org.uk), meanwhile, had room for just 60 lucky souls. Book a place on the tour to explore the secrets behind its heavy steel doors.

576 Learn the art of glass

Here's one you've probably never tried before: sandcasting a paperweight with molten glass and colourful sparkly bits. Don't worry: it's well supervised, and under-15s must be accompanied by an adult. You come away with a real sense of achievement and your own unique piece of art. A fabulous, glass-roofed contemporary building, great exhibits and a good restaurant add to the appeal.

National Glass Centre *Liberty Way, Sunderland SR6 0GL (0191 515 5555/ www.nationalglasscentre.com).*

National Glass Centre

577 Cook and eat a Victorian lunch

Ickworth is a marvellous Italianate property, owned by the National Trust, with masses of parkland. Younger visitors (seven to 13) can snoop around the kitchens and learn what was eaten both upstairs and down, then try their hand at cooking and eating Victorian dishes. Then it's time for fun and games in the orchard. After lunch, follow the cycle route to counteract all that homemade lemonade and cake.

Ickworth House, Park & Gardens *The Rotunda, Horringer, Bury St Edmunds, Suffolk IP29 5QE (01284 735270/www.nationaltrust.org.uk).*

578 Dive into the lakes... virtually

This freshwater aquarium in the Lake District is a delightfully unshowy watery journey from mountainside spring to lake bottom. Along the way various habitats are well explained, with guest appearances from riverside mammals such as otters and voles. It may not have all the exotic tropicals and scary sharks of saltwater aquariums, but there are some quirky underwater sights to be seen, thanks to the recently acquired virtual diving bell. This interactive exhibit is a set of three huge screens, in whose murky depths you can come face to face with all sorts of diving delights. Thanks to the miracle of computer-generated graphics, you can watch crocodile eggs hatch or hippos being born, and learn a great deal about the creatures as you play.

Lakes Aquarium *Newby Bridge, Cumbria LA12 8AS (015395 30153/www.lakesaquarium.co.uk).*

579 Live in a Landmark

All sorts of peculiar properties can be rented out for your holidays from the Landmark Trust (01628 825925, www.landmarktrust.org.uk), which rescues quirky old buildings and turns them into holiday lets. A pineapple-shaped pavilion, a cowshed or a lighthouse keeper's cottage are just a few of the eccentric options.

Discover the wild ponies

How lovely it is to see ponies enjoying pure, unbridled freedom in the wild! There are still a few places where you can glimpse them, although some breeds are easier to spot than others and none are really wild these days – many are owned by farmers and all are carefully monitored.

Dartmoor

Ponies have roamed Dartmoor in Devonshire since prehistoric times, but the ones you see wandering across the moorland today are probably not pure-breeds but natives. That's because they've been running with mixed breed ponies. (The pure-bred, registered Dartmoor is now jealously guarded – too valuable to be left out to do its own thing.) Dartmoor ponies are owned by farmers, who let them graze free but identify them with brands, ear cuts and tags. To find out more about the 1,500-odd ponies living on the moor, download the fact sheet from the Dartmoor National Park Authority (www.dartmoor-npa.gov.uk).

Eriskay

The Eriskay Pony is a native of the remote island of the same name in the Outer Hebridean archipelago, and the last surviving breed of Scottish native horse. It's a good-looking creature, like a smaller, daintier version of the Highland pony, with a placid nature. Nearly all are born black but gradually turn grey as they mature. Its numbers have dwindled alarmingly over the years and it is now officially classed as a rare breed. The body that looks afters its interests is www.eriskaypony.org.uk.

Exmoor

This is the oldest British pony, which you may spot during a walk on North Devon and Cornwall's moorland region. The ponies are a brown or bay colour, and have a distinctive pale or 'mealy' muzzle. Exmoor ponies are an endangered breed, so the Exmoor National Park Authority has established two herds on the moor and looks after them carefully. For more information, visit www.exmoor ponysociety.org.uk.

New Forest ponies

New Forest

The most prolific native breed is the least wild of all. Each animal is owned by a practising commoner, who is exercising his ancient right of common pasture. Twice a year the ponies are rounded up by a team of Agisters, who look after the stock and ensure their hooves, teeth and coats are all in order. These ponies sometimes take an interest in day trippers' picnics, but don't be tempted to feed them – let's maintain the wild illusion at least.

Welsh Mountain

According to the society that protects them, the wildest and rarest ponies in Britain are the Welsh mountain breed that graze the Carneddau mountain range in Snowdonia. The Romans were keen on these hardy little creatures, and even shipped back some to the old country. Henry VIII wasn't a fan, however, as the ponies were too small to carry a knight in shining armour. He wanted to exterminate them, but thankfully failed in his mission. In the 19th century the Carneddau ponies pulled carts in the coal mines, but these days they're well looked after the hill farmers, who set up www.carneddauponies.co.uk.

Free play

Ronnie Haydon **picks up a few bruises at an adventure playground.**

What's your local playground like? Does it have vertiginous zip wires, tyre swings and a fireman's pole built into rickety treehouse platforms? Does it have a firepit, or a high slide that throws you squawking into the dirt? Probably not. The average park playground, with its rubberised safety surface, meek plastic slides, neat primary colours or aesthetically pleasing wooden climbing frame (usually in the shape of a pirate ship) holds little challenge for anyone over five. There's precious little scope for children to test their mettle – and with parents and carers lingering oppressively at the foot of the slide, little real opportunity for play.

Adventure playgrounds, however, are a very different beast. Many were built in the 1970s, in the halcyon days before public play areas became too safe for real fun, and can still be found in urban centres – though they're always under threat. Some are in areas where the land is valuable and developers want to use the space. Others feel the heavy presence of Health & Safety regulators at their backs.

London is good for adventure playgrounds, thanks to the work of playscape creatives such as Grant Lambie of Free Play Playscape Consultancy & Construction, whose mission is to 'involve young people, parents, staff and local communities in implementing the design and build of their playscapes using sustainable materials.' In short, Grant wants kids to have some fun.

Grant led a bicycle tour of a few of his favourite adventures one rainy day in August. It was part of the South London Gallery's Games and Theory season, and involved visiting local playgrounds and trying out some of London's largest swings, death slides and other play structures. We played falling over football on a huge see-saw trailer in the Charlie Chaplin in Kennington, dangled off high ropes in the Whitehorse and shinned down a fireman's pole in the Glamis.

The best adventure, however, was the Rockingham. This spectacular playground caters for the Rockingham Estate in Borough,

and has been keeping its children limber since the 1970s. Grant was brought in to design and build a new tower to replace the one that burned down in 2007. It's very high. The way down is via a wide silver slide with a big bump in the middle. Children are encouraged to throw water down the slide to make it even faster, and to go down in pairs, launching themselves at speed and crashing on to the ground below in a tangle of limbs. Even higher is the zip wire, and you travel pretty fast on that too. There's also a tango swing and plenty of trees and secret places in which to hide.

As we played, explored, and got extremely wet, Grant Lambie told me a little bit more about his playful life. 'I've always worked on summer play schemes, combining it with my day job as a nurse for people with learning disabilities. Indeed, designing play equipment for children with disabilities is a big part of my job. I went on to study fine art at Goldsmiths college, but never stopped working in the community, designing stuff for playgrounds. I moved into consultation work, being employed by councils to create and refurbish playscapes.'

The work never stops. Lambie describes himself as the playground equivalent of the Slow Food Movement. He designs a playscape,

stands back from it for a few weeks to see how the children are playing on it (this is of particular value when it comes to children with special needs, such as those who play daily on his design in the Stephen Hawking school in Tower Hamlets, east London), then comes back to make adjustments, or act on a new idea. And this he does with the children's input.

'When I'm designing a new space – and these playscapes are never complete, they're organic, always developing – I'm working with the children. In one place they used axes to clear the undergrowth. Others can be trusted with the power tools to help with construction. I found I could give them breakers to make holes for posts in the ground. They enjoy working with the tools, and are aware that you have to be sensible with them.'

Adventure playgrounds like the Rockingham offer a contained playscape, with an open-door policy that allows children (usually from the age of five to early teens) to use the space unaccompanied by parents and carers, but supervised by qualified play leaders. Their job it is to be around, but not interfere. Such playgrounds are an urban phenomenon – it was assumed that country children had all the access to wide open spaces and natural

materials they could possibly need – and the highest concentration of the old-style spaces seems to be in London. There are a few in Manchester, Nottingham and Bristol, but the trend in recent years has been to smarten them up and run them along the lines of more conventional play areas.

The most famous adventure playground of all, though, is the Venture in North Wales (Garner Road, Wrexham, Clywd LL13 8SF, 01978 355761), created in 1978. Based at a notably disadvantaged housing estate (as they often are), the Venture is the largest self-build adventure playground in the country, and holder of the 'Best Playground in Britain' gong.

'Self-build' is the key here. The original adventure playgrounds were conceived as places where children could forage for old bits of wood, tyres and greenery to make dens and wobbly climbing frames that would have given today's Health & Safety officers a cardiac arrest. They started as 'junk playgrounds', a term coined by Danish landscape architect Carl Theodor Sorensøn in the 1930s. He watched children playing on disused building sites, and saw how they gathered all kinds of scrap to make their own little kingdom. Inspired, he decided to include this idea in his plans for new housing estates and parks; despite recognising that a playground created by kids out of junk 'would look terrible', he was forward-thinking enough to realise that its beauty would be in the eye of the user.

Certainly many of the urban adventures we toured had more than a little of the ramshackle about them, but, Grant assures us, they are checked daily by play leaders and have annual full-scale Health & Safety checks. Rockingham is one of the more aesthetically pleasing spaces on his watch. He gave it a facelift and introduced a firepit and barbecue – a bit of a contentious issue these days.

The original adventure playgrounds were supposed to have access to fire and water alongside the high ropes, mud and junk that were considered essential to adventure play. Free play should be just that; unhindered and risky. Grant agrees. 'Children are attracted to the idea of risk, and that's what's built into the structure of a good playscape.'

The riskier elements of the playground could include things like high platforms and fireman's poles to zip down. You might see a young child

> **'Kids could forage for bits of wood, tyres and greenery to make dens and wobbly climbing frames that would give today's Health & Safety officers a cardiac arrest.'**

teetering on the edge, wondering if she can risk it. In a normal playground, a wobbling child is generally enough to have parents rushing in and distracting kids with their 'be carefuls' – and that's how accidents happen. Leaving the child to assess the dangers is a safer way to play.

Fortunately, the tide is turning against excessively risk-averse playground planning. The Play Pathfinder scheme, published in autumn 2008, talks convincingly about the need for children to get out and play properly. It remains to be seen, however, whether the £235m funding will go into the sort of places where children will be able to take risks on lofty zip wires high above muddy swamps, or the uniform play areas that look like they've been designed by Ikea.

Grant's opinion on the matter is evident, and its echoed by friends in high places. The Commission for Architecture and the Built Environment (CABE) has also stuck its neck out and highlighted the need for children to have more risky adventures. 'We must stop obsessing about risk and trying to wrap our children in cotton wool, and instead create spaces that allow them to use their imagination in a stimulating environment,' said a CABE spokesperson. It looks as if Grant and his young helpers are going to be busy with the axes and drills for a while yet.

Rockingham Estate Play Association
Dickens Square, off Harper Road, London SE1 4JL (020 7403 8337).

586

Take pride in pumpkins...

Autumn squashfests are increasingly popular on these shores, but we'll never match the North Americans in their veneration of the hefty orange gourds. Nonetheless, Willow Farm's annual Pumpkin Festival, held during October half-term and with jack o' lantern carving on the menu for Hallowe'en, is a perfect way to celebrate autumn's fruitfulness as the nights draw in. For more information, call 0870 129 9718 or visit www.willowsfarmvillage.com.

587

...then try growing your own

Want to have your own grinning jack o' lantern for Hallowe'en? To grow a decent sized pumpkin, you should start in April. Sow seeds in small pots in some general-purpose compost and leave on a sunny window sill. Varieties range from the huge Atlantic Giant to the petite Jack-Be-Little, and the attractive Ghostrider is a medium-sized variety.

Transplant your seedlings after four to six weeks (when there's no danger of frost) into well-drained soil in a sunny spot in your garden. Leave at least two metres between plants, and make sure you water them every morning; try not to splash the leaves, as this encourages mildew. Feed the plants regularly with a liquid plant food. To ensure big pumpkins reduce the number of fruit to two per plant. As the pumpkins mature, slip a brick or straw under each fruit to stop it touching the ground and rotting. A pumpkin is ripe when it sounds hollow when tapped. If your pumpkin hasn't turned orange by the autumn and frost is coming, pick it and lug it indoors, where you can let it gently ripen on a window sill.

588

Go Neolithic on Orkney

Long centuries have passed since Neolithic man lived at Skara Brae on Orkney, but his traces remain – discovered by accident in 1850 after a storm. Set by the sea is a cluster of stone-walled dwellings, connected by a network of cramped, covered passageways – our forebears clearly didn't relish the island's bone-chilling winds. Though roofless, the huts are beautifully preserved, with the original walls still standing and some sweet domestic details; each has a shelved dresser, built from *Flintstones*-style slabs of stone, plus watertight tanks used to store limpets. After exploring the site, head to the visitors' centre, where a replica hut suggests what life was like here some 5,000 years ago. More information on 01856 841815, www.historic-scotland.gov.uk.

589 *See stand-up*

Take in a show by James Campbell, the world's only dedicated children's stand-up comedian. He says there are advantages – children put their hand up to heckle and remain sober during the entire performance. For listings, visit www.jamescampbell.info.

590 *Steam along to Hollycombe*

We're as fond of steam trains as the next person – and Hollycombe has a fine fleet, from shiny narrow-gauge beauties to nifty miniature locomotives. All this pales to insignificance, though, when you see the collection's glorious centrepiece: steam-driven Edwardian fairground rides, all in tip-top working order. Enjoy the giddy whirl of the Chair-o-Planes, trot on the Golden Gallopers or close your eyes on the tilting Razzle Dazzle – built in 1908, and one of the world's first white-knuckle rides. Once you've paid the entrance fee, all rides are free; opening times are restricted, so check online before visiting.

Hollycombe Steam Fair *Iron Hill, Liphook, Hampshire GU30 7LP (01428 724900/ www.hollycombe.co.uk).*

591 *Make a matchbox treasure chest*

Find an empty matchbox and cover it with pretty paper – you can use glitter and stickers to make it look extra special. Then arrange some pieces inside: you could glue in tiny shells, sand and green-blue tissue paper to make a beach scene. Another idea is to cut out fragments of pictures from magazines and greetings cards, or stick in tiny pieces of ribbon or fabric, seeds, petals and pieces of butterfly wing you might have found in the garden, along with shiny buttons and sparkly beads. Let your imagination run riot. Put messages inside the gorgeously decorated boxes and give them to your friends and family as an alternative to greetings cards.

A few of my favourite things

592-603

Iris Harrison, co-founder, Education Otherwise

Listening to children is the most important thing you can do with them. When my children were growing up, we would spend a lot of time in conversation. Cooking together was another activity that we all enjoyed. Soups were their favourite. We grew all our own vegetables, and still do. Planting and harvesting your own food is a source of fascination for children. Preparing the vegetables and using the whizzer to blend them into soup is a most enjoyable activity for the children. You can use any vegetables in season, and spring nettles are an unusal ingredient. We have always loved making drinks from fruits from the garden too – blackcurrants, raspberries and apples. My great grandfather was a well-known baker (his surname was Baker, too) so we all have a love of breadmaking in our genes. We'd buy organic wholemeal flour from the wholesaler's.

I hate shopping, but my children were always happy going out on errands to Tenbury Wells [Worcestershire], our nearest town. Part of their education was to find out about prices in the local shops, and come back with the correct items. Food was very important in their education; we studied the qualities of different foods and what constituted a balanced diet. Life is very different for children in the countryside, so my kids had the freedom to wander all over the place. If I had young children now, I would still let them cycle off and go exploring. The walks around this area of Worcestershire are beautiful.

There are public footpaths everywhere, so having walks is a great pleasure. **You can build a history lesson around ancient objects you come across in everyday life. We found a cannonball in the stream and it inspired us to learn about all sorts of things. Worcestershire was the scene of several battles during the Wars of the Roses.** In Tenbury Wells we have the historic Pump Rooms on Teme Street (for information on visiting call the tourist office on 01584 810136, www.tenburywells.info), which were built in 1862 and have now been restored. The beautiful curved bridge over the River Teme in Tenbury is another lovely place. **The mobile library played a significant role in my children's lives. They would push a wheelbarrow full of books to return to the library every week, then load up with new ones. They liked to study all kinds of things. My son became very interested in clocks and taught himself how to mend them. He is now an expert clockmaker. At one time, his room seemed to chime all through the night.** Many of my children's activities stemmed from items picked up in auction houses. My daughter bought a lathe and the children would spend hours making doorknobs and other pieces. We also bought a pony trap and harness, which we restored and trained our pony to pull. Then there was spinning and the weaving, and attending pottery classes – these are all wonderful activities to improve a child's co-ordination. **Three of my children were extremely dyslexic, which was a reason they were educated at home (for more on this, visit www.educationotherwise.org). Dyslexics, it is said, have a different view of the world; a profound insight into the ways of solving problems. Mine were certainly inspired to mend things and learn how they worked. Sometimes we would be learning basic mechanics with a car engine on the kitchen table. It's all interesting; you just have to be willing to give the time.** Learning to play musical instruments was an important element in three of my children's lives. They still play now – guitar, piano and violin.

Iris Harrison is also chair of charity Speaks Volumes (www.speaksvolumes.org.uk), which helps children with dyslexia who can be assisted by technology to read and write.

604
Meet Manchester's bobbies

On Tuesdays, visitors are welcome to explore Manchester's old police station, packed with paraphernalia. The highlight for kids is the dark, windowless Victorian cell, whose cramped confines were shared by up to 12 prisoners. Let your imagination run riot as you lie on one of the two hard beds and try to get comfortable on the wooden pillows, then peek out of the door's tiny hatch – your only window to the outside world. Enthusiastic ex-officers are at hand to explain the exhibits, and have plenty of tales to tell. If your party includes any under-nines, the Crime Room is best avoided: exhibits include lengths of piping wielded during the Strangeways riot and other unwholesome homemade weapons.

Greater Manchester Police Museum & Archive
57A Newton Street, Manchester M1 1ET
(0161 856 3287/www.gmp.police.uk).

605
Make pot pourri

Raid the garden or the spice rack to make a mixture of sweet-smelling leaves, seeds and petals to scent the air. Experiment with quantities and fragrances. A spicy idea is to take some cinnamon sticks, cloves, dried bay leaves, cardamom pods and dried chillies. Dry out some pieces of orange and lemon peel in a very low oven, the airing cupboard or on the radiator until it goes brown. Chop up the bigger items and add a few drops of cinnamon or clove oil, available from health food shops and herbalists. These shops also sell dried flowers, such as chamomile, which also look really good in pot pourri.

If you have a garden, seek out rose petals, scented pelargonium leaves and eucalyptus leaves. Pick a few lavender heads of different colours and some sprigs of rosemary, germander, lemon balm or flowering thyme if you have a herb garden. Dry them all carefully, as before, and mix with a few drops of rose oil. Put your pot pourri in a suitably sized attractive pot or a sealed jar if it's a gift.

606-609
Have fun on a funicular

Designed to save your legs from precipitous cliffs and exhausting inclines, a funicular is a cable- and pulley-drawn railway. Travelling up and down the steepest of slopes, it's like a cross between a tram and a lift – and nail-biting stuff if you don't have a head for heights.

Britain's shores are dotted with cliff-climbing funiculars, open in summer – including the plunging rails of Saltburn-by-the-Sea's water-balanced lift (www.saltburnbysea.com). A fixture in this North Yorkshire seaside resort since 1884, it's a clanky ride for a mere 65p. Opened in 1890, the Lynton and Lynmouth Cliff Railway (01598 753908, www.cliffrailway lynton.co.uk) is a gem, plummeting 150 metres and with gorgeous views of the coast.

In the Shrophire town of Bridgnorth, the funicular (01746 762052, www.bridgnorth cliffrailway.co.uk) is used daily by locals. Before it was built in 1892, people had toil up 200 steps to reach the High Town from the Low Town; now it's a short but steep jaunt on the rails.

For a modern take on the funicular, hitch a ride on the eco-friendly, water-balancing lift at the Centre for Alternative Technology in Powys, Wales (01654 705950, www.cat.org.uk) – a lofty ascent up the mountainside to the centre's HQ.

610
Spy on a seabird

The problem with bird-spotting boat trips is you can get wet, cold or seasick (or a mixture of all three). Overlooking the islands of the Firth of Forth, the Scottish Seabird Centre is a perfect alternative. Inside there are high-tech cameras with live streaming, allowing visitors to view birds close up on the Bass Rock, Fidra and the Isle of May. Bird populations include gannets, guillemots and puffins, and you can watch grey seals and their pups on the Beach Cam in winter. For those with sea legs, boat trips are also available.

Scottish Seabird Centre *The Harbour, North Berwick, East Lothian EH39 4SS (01620 890202/www.seabird.org).*

Explore-at-Bristol

611
Walk inside a tornado

Dare you step through the mysterious doorway as the tornado descends? Can you freeze your own shadow? Housed in a massive former railway goods shed, the harbourside Explore-at-Bristol science centre makes for brilliant family days out. The tornado holds endless fascination for young children, who stand transfixed as it whirls into action. They also enjoy spinning the giant sphere to see how planetary atmospheres shift, zooming in on the tiny blood cells found in the human eye or trying to twirl rings on the giant rotating turntable. Clearly written panels accompany each exhibit to explain the science behind the phenomena, although we're still think there's magic at work somewhere.

Explore-at-Bristol *Harbourside, Bristol, Avon BS1 5DB (0845 345 1235/www.at-bristol.org.uk).*

612 *Celebrate spring with Jack-in-the-Green*

Covered head to foot in foliage, with just his green-painted face peeping out, Jack-in-the-Green was once an integral character in rural May Day celebrations. Disapproving of his pagan connections and rollicking ways (Jack always liked a drink or three), the straitlaced Victorians tried to replace him with the flouncy-frocked, well-behaved May Queen. Jack's back, though, with several towns reviving the ancient tradition. In Hastings (www.hastingsjack.co.uk), he's very much in evidence in the procession that parades though the Old Town and along the seafront, alongside ag-costumed 'bogie' attendants; there's also morris dancing, music and storytelling to enjoy . Other places around the country where you can spot Jack include Bristol, Whitstable, Rochester and Knutsford; dig out some green face paint and you'll fit right in.

Gift of the gab

Kaye MacAlpine **sits comfortably and lets the Scottish storytellers begin their tales.**

Storytelling is big news. Not the kind where people get together to try and tell the biggest lies they can, but the kind where people meet and listen to one individual at a time tell a tale, contemporary or traditional. It may have musical accompaniment, or it may require some audience interaction – but often it doesn't, and the onus is on the teller to engage the listeners until the end of the tale. Sharing stories is something humans have been doing for thousands of years, and it's a great way of bringing people together. Everyone is welcome; after all, it's as important to have someone listening as it is to be able to tell a tale in the first place.

The Scottish Storytelling Centre in Edinburgh is a hub for this cross-cultural form. Having undergone a massive renovation, the centre re-opened in 2006 and is one of the city's more successful blends of the traditional and the contemporary. Its glass facade merges with the Old Town architecture of the 15th-century John Knox House. On the wall you can see the last remnants of the Netherbow Port, which used to divide the parish of Edinburgh from that of the Canongate; the bell from the port, cast in 1621, is housed in a new tower at the top of the building.

John Knox House is one of the oldest buildings on the High Street: check out the insignia and initials celebrating past owners of the building, goldsmith John Mossman and his wife Marrietta Arres (IM and MA), the carved exhortation 'Luf God abufe al, and yi nychtbur as yi self', and the more modern addition of Knox preaching. Despite the house's name, no one is sure if John Knox – firebrand preacher and champion of protestantism in Scotland – ever actually lived in it. Nonetheless, you can learn about him here, along with the house's other past inhabitants.

It's pretty engaging stuff, with dressing-up opportunities and a wonderfully macabre puzzle, called the Tower of Destiny. (Put it together correctly and you can watch some of the city's more notable executions, including Mary Queen

'An intimate story-telling corner, the Bothy, is put to great effect during school holidays and festivals.'

of Scots parting company with her head.) Mind out for the trip stair and the false locks on some of the doors, which acted as security measures in the days before burglar alarms.

Next, it's on to the new Storytelling Centre; unlike John Knox House, it's free to enter. The first area you'll come to is the Storytelling Court, at the café end. It's a sleekly modern vision of pale wood and glass, with a glorious sense of space. Changing art exhibitions

hang on the walls, while permanent displays celebrate Scottish tales and literature. Robert Louis Stevenson, author of *Treasure Island* and *Doctor Jekyll and Mr Hyde*, has a nook more or less to himself – but kids will make a beeline for the Storytelling Wall.

This hinged wall, which can be swung out into the main space, is a four-level treasure trove, full of interactive information about tales and stories from Scotland. At the lowest level there are feely boxes, best for the under-fours, which contain fluffy Gruffalos and other pointers to books written by Scottish authors or well-loved rhymes. Next up on the wall are 3D models or pictures, hidden behind different doors. The top level is for older children and adults, covering everything from bardic tales of Columba to modern bestsellers such as Ian Rankin's series about hard-bitten Edinburgh detective Rebus.

The story wall performs a second function, creating an intimate storytelling corner, known as the Bothy, at the far end of the Court. It's put to great effect during school holidays and festival time, when there are daily story sessions. Each storyteller has their own style and repertoire, ranging from traditional tales to off-the-wall stories of their own invention; there are usually plenty of props to keep younger listeners occupied.

The centre is also the main focus of October's International Storytelling Festival, which has a different theme every year. Attracting storytellers from around the world, it offers a varied programme of workshops, drop-in events, ticketed performances and open-sessions, some of which are free. It's a great introduction to the art of storytelling, with a buzzing atmosphere and packed list of events.

If you look out of the windows at the north end of the Storytelling Court, you'll see some of the hidden gems of Edinburgh. The eerie-looking Trunk's Close, on the west side of John Knox House, leads you to Sandeman's House, headquarters of the Scottish Book Trust. Its peaceful gardens provide welcome respite from the High Street and offer a place for a moment of quiet reflection after a storytelling session, before you brave the city's bustle once more.

Scottish Storytelling Centre
43-45 High Street, Edinburgh EH1 1SR
(0131 556 9579/www.scottishstorytelling
centre.co.uk).

Go Ape

614

Swing through the treetops at Go Ape

Monkeying around in the treetops is the name of the game at Go Ape's centres, which offer adrenaline-packed aerial adventure trails. Families can swing, scramble, climb and slide to their heart's content amid the rope bridges, trapezes and zip slides, letting out the odd Tarzan whoop as they go. Luckily, ape-like gripping and climbing skills aren't required, as you're fitted with sturdy safety harnesses before heading into the treetops. Children must be ten years and over to tackle the courses, and height and weight restrictions apply; under-18s must be accompanied by an adult. Go Ape's 21 centres are set in forests across the country. Full details of your nearest centre can be found at www.goape.co.uk.

615

Say farewell to Nether Hambleton

Take a walk around lovely Rutland Water (www.rutlandwater.org.uk) on the way to what was once St Matthew's – the deconsecrated Italianate church saved from a watery grave when the reservoir valley was flooded in the 1970s. Down between dark trees dips a single-track country lane, only for the metalled surface to be shorn roughly off by lapping shallows. You can see where the road resurfaces a kilometre away, on the other side of the lake on the peninsula where Upper Hambleton still stands – surrounded on three sides by water – its prefix now sadly redundant. On the road beneath 30 metres of water, doomed Nether Hambleton lies shivering.

For more on the county's churches, contact Rutland County Museum & Visitor Centre, Catmose Street, Oakham, Rutland LE15 6HW, 01572 758440, www.rutnet.co.uk.

616 *Bake biscuits*

With the right shaped cookie-cutters, this basic recipe will do for Easter (bunny-shaped biscuits), Christmas (stars, fir trees), Valentine's Day (hearts) or general tea-time treats. You need:

- 100g butter, cut into small pieces
- 75g plain flour and 75g self-raising flour, mixed together
- 75g caster sugar
- 2tsp vanilla essence
- 1 egg yolk

Rub the butter into the flour mix until it resembles breadcrumbs, then add the sugar, vanilla essence and egg yolk. Add a tablespoon of cold water to make a dough, and chill in the fridge for about an hour. Heat the oven to 170°C and grease a couple of baking trays. Roll out the dough about one centimetre thick and cut your biscuit shapes. If you want to hang them on a tree, make a hole in the top of each biscuit for ribbon. Bake the biscuits for about 15 minutes. When they're cool you can decorate them with melted chocolate, silver balls and hundreds and thousands.

617

Learn some magic...

In school holidays (but not during the summer), members of the Young Magicians' Club (www.theyoungmagiciansclub.com), an offshoot of the Magic Circle, attend Saturday workshops in London. Run by the club's chair and 'Diva of Deception', Mandy Davis, they cost a mere £5 for a whole day (11am-4pm). Participants learn new tricks, magic theory and stagecraft, and may compete at prestidigitation in front of adult magicians, who will select a Member of the Month. Aspiring conjurors aged ten to 18 can join the club for £30 a year; on joining, you'll receive a membership badge and card, a copy of *Secrets* magazine, a free gift and a certificate signed by the president of the Magic Circle himself, the esteemed Ali Bongo.

618-622

...and then learn some more

Stand-up Hanky
Sew a drinking straw into the hem of a hanky. Grip the end of the hidden straw and make it stand upright. The handkerchief appears to rise. Practise showing the hanky in its limp position with the other hand.

The Four Robbers
Find the four Jacks in a pack of cards. Hold them in a fan with four other cards behind the last one. Put all eight face down on top of the deck. Tell the story of the four robbers, all called Jack, who escape from prison. Describe the first robber's flight while removing the top card (which is not a Jack, though the audience think it is) and placing it somewhere in the lower pack. Do the same with the others. Finally say '...but on this occasion, the police were lucky. The first door they knocked at, they caught them all in the same room.' Knock on the pack, and turn over the four Jacks.

Find their Cards
Divide a pack of cards so that all the flat-topped numbers and letters – A, 1, 4, 5, 7, J, K – are in one half, and all the round tops – 2, 3, 6, 8, 9, 10, Q – are in the other. (Note that 3 can be either flat or round.) Ask two people to take a card from one half and insert it anywhere in the other. The two cards will be easy to identify by their flat tops among the round, and vice versa.

Vanishing Toothpick
Wear a ring, if you don't already. Wave a toothpick before your audience. As cunningly as you can, slip it under the ring behind your hand. Show your palms. No toothpick! It's all in the prestidigitation, of course. Practise hard.

Loose Thumb
Cut a piece of carrot to look like your thumb. Hide it in your hand. Cover this hand with a hanky. Move the carrot up so it looks like your thumb is protruding. Tell someone your thumb feels a bit loose and ask them tighten it up. As soon as they are holding it, remove your hand from the hanky with the thumb tucked inside your fist. Act surprised.

623-629 *Muck in at a city farm*

Bath City Farm, Bath

The farm's seven friendly goats and two Tamworth pigs, Molly and Maggie, enjoy having visitors – though you're not allowed to feed them, as they'd soon get far too porky. There are regular volunteer days and special events too, from bonfire-lit wassailing sessions (to toast the apple trees' health) to Pancake Day wacky races.
Kelston View, Whiteway, Bath BA2 1NW (01225 481269/www.bathcityfarm.org.uk).

Gorgie City Farm, Edinburgh

Opened in 1982, Gorgie does a roaring trade in vegetables, freshly laid eggs and whiffy but wonderful manure. As well as farm stock (horses, pigs, sheep and hens) it has a pet lodge, where tortoises, chinchillas, guinea pigs and other small fry reside. Eight to 12s can enlist as farmers' helpers in the holidays, collecting eggs, cleaning out the cowshed and getting gloriously mucky; wellies are a must.

51 Gorgie Road, Edinburgh EH11 2LA (0131 337 4202/www.gorgiecityfarm.org.uk).

Heeley City Farm, Sheffield

A mile from the centre of Sheffield, Heeley has Soay sheep, large black pigs and goats, plus a packed small-animal house. Guinea pigs, rabbits, degus (Chilean rodents that look a bit like giant gerbils) and chipmunks are among its inhabitants, along with less cuddly lizards, stick insects and cockroaches. Before heading to the café to refuel on vegetarian grub, check out the newly built roundhouse, made from woven willow and mud to an Iron Age design.
Richards Road, Sheffield S2 3DT (0114 258 0482/ www.heeleyfarm.org.uk).

Mudchute Park & Farm, London

Meadows of sheep graze against a backdrop of skyscrapers at this farm in the middle of the Isle of Dogs, set on land saved from developers in the 1970s. Look out for the llamas,

then lunch at the marvellous Mudchute Kitchen, a family-friendly spot renowned for its weekend brunches and homemade daily specials. There's also an equestrian centre, offering riding lessons for children and adults, from beginners to advanced.

Pier Street, London E14 3HP (020 7515 5901/ www.mudchute.org).

St Werburghs City Farm, Bristol

Children love the adventure playground and farmyard favourites – Gloucestershire Old Spot piglets, if you're lucky, or a brood of fluffy ducklings. At the award-winning café, local ingredients are turned into all sorts of delicious dishes, from simple welsh rarebit and homemade burgers to more adventurous dishes – feta and sweet chilli muffins, perhaps, or farm terrine made from pigs' trotters.

Watercress Road, St Werburghs, Bristol BS2 9YJ (0117 942 8241/www.stwerburghs.org).

Surrey Docks Farm, London

This is part farm, part sculpture park. Sheep, goats and chickens mooch around a central farmyard, tolerating and providing endless entertainment. Out in the pens, there are organically reared cows, pigs, donkeys and horses too, many fenced in by wrought metal railings provided by the farm's other tenant, creative blacksmith Kevin Boys, who teaches classes in his forge. It's all part of a vision set in motion by city farm pioneer Hilary Peters in 1975, who wanted all schoolchildren to have an appreciation of food production and agricultural skills. You can stay for a hearty lunch at Café Nabo.

Rotherhithe Street, London SE16 5EY (020 7231 1010/www.surreydocksfarm.org).

Tam O'Shanter Urban Farm, Bidston

This pocket of paddocks and fields on the outskirts of Birkenhead is home to rare-breed sheep, goats, pigs and poultry, along with Arnie the black Shetland pony and some eminently strokable rabbits. There's also a couple of nature trails to follow. In the farmyard, meanwhile, childen have a go at milking Molly the fibreglass Friesian – much safer than sidling up to the real thing.

Boundary Road, Bidston, Wirral CH43 7PD (0151 653 9332/www.tamoshanterfarm.org.uk).

Mudchute Farm

630 Grow your own mistletoe

Mistletoe seeds penetrate the growth tissue of a tree, fooling it into thinking the invader is part of the tree. It usually gets 'planted' by the mistle thrush, but you can do this yourself.

Seeds germinate best between February and April, so take a few berries before bringing a branch into the house at Christmas (store them on a tray of sand in a shed), or get fresh berries from a grow-your-own kit (try www.teme-mistletoe.co.uk or www.mistle.co.uk). Plant the seeds by squishing them on to the smooth, thin healthy bark of a young branch; mistletoe thrives on apple trees (so best to avoid prize specimens). Label the planted branches, as mistletoe is slow to establish itself; you'll get the first pair of leaves after three years, and won't know if you have the berried female plants for about five years. Once established, the plant doubles in size every year. Harvest when it's a reasonable size, removing around a third of the plant. Berryless male specimens should be pruned, to stop them overwhelming the host tree.

631

Beat time with a flip-flop

FJ Horniman Esquire was a Victorian tea trader who collected strange souvenirs and artifacts on his business trips. He displayed everything at his home until he ran out of space – so he built a museum in spacious grounds in south-east London. When he died, he bequeathed it to the people of London. One of Horniman's chief fascinations was music and the means by which it is produced all over the world. Musical instruments occupy a whole gallery at the Horniman Museum, with computers in front of the display cases to reproduce the sounds. There are also large percussion instruments, such as Thai croaking toads and an Irish bodhrán, which visitors can play. One of them involves hitting the end of a tube with a flip-flop – you may have to queue for a go.

Horniman Museum *100 London Road, London SE23 3PQ (020 8699 1872/www.horniman.ac.uk).*

632 Venture inside King Arthur's Labyrinth

In the abandoned slate mines of Briach Goch something stirs – it's a monk in a boat and he's taking visitors to a magic waterfall, behind which subterranean tableaux tell the the legend of King Arthur. As you sail through the dimly lit caverns on the tour, the chilly surroundings and exciting light show really ratchet up the drama; it's a lovely way to learn the old stories wreathed around this most enchanting part of the country. The labyrinth is open from March to November.

King Arthur's Labyrinth *Corris Craft Centre, Corris, Machynlleth, Powys SY20 9RF (01654 761584/www.kingarthurslabyrinth.com).*

633 Make bean bags

Cut out a rectangle of fabric, measuring 20cm by 30cm. Fold it in half, then sew around the edges, using quite small stitches; leave an unsewn gap in one corner. Turn the resultant bag shape inside out, fill it with dried beans or peas, then sew up the hole. You can make bean bags of all sizes, for juggling games, target practice or races.

634 Stage a shadow show

Playing with shadows using your hands and a bright light is a timeless pleasure. Shine the light on your hand so that the shadow falls on a smooth surface like a wall or table, then throw some shapes with your hands. You can make a snail by placing your left fist on the flat back of your right hand, whose fingers are separated slightly, or the old favourite, a rabbit, by placing your hands upright and in clenched position, one in front of the other. On one hand, hold up your index and middle finger for the front paws, with your other fingers loosely bunched below to make haunches. Two fingers of your other hand become the rabbit's ears, the others its face. For inspiration, have a look at Raymond Crowe's fantastic show on YouTube.

635 Chase an orange down an Elizabethan high street

Enjoy some fruity Elizabethan fun at the annual Orange Race in Totnes, South Devon, organised by the town's Elizabethan Society to celebrate a visit by Sir Francis Drake in the 1580s. There are two stories about the race's origins. One is that Sir Francis, a regular visitor to Totnes, bumped into a delivery boy at the top of the steep High Street. The lad's basket of oranges fell to the ground and the fruit rolled down the hill, hotly pursued by hungry locals. The alternative version is that the famed sailor presented a 'fair red orange' to a boy– Robert Hayman, who later became the first governor of Newfoundland.

Despite having forgotten which story is true, townspeople commemorate their citrussy heritage by chasing oranges down the steep cobbled High Street on a Tuesday in mid August (01803 863168, www.totnes information.co.uk). The race has various categories, from youngsters to over-60s, so anyone can enter this Elizabethan madness.

David Beckham Academy

636

Bend it like Beckham

Spend the holidays like young David did – kicking a ball. His academy will make sure you get it right. With training pitches inside two aircraft hangars on the Greenwich Peninsula, just along from the O2 Centre, the David Beckham Academy hosts top-flight school holiday football courses. Children aged from eight to 15 can enrol for wall-to-wall football training lasting one to five days, from 9am-4pm. The fee (from £85 per day up to £270 for a five-day stint) covers kit, water bottles, a hot lunch, tuition by top players and coaches, and games. Our football-crazy tester who attended a five-day course declared it 'five star' and now requests we spend it on Beckham every holiday.

David Beckham Academy UK *East Parkside, London SE10 0JF (020 8269 4620/ www.davidbeckhamacademy.co.uk).*

637 *Meet Nina and the Neurons*

Best known throughout the world of the under-fives as the base of Nina and the Neurons, Glasgow Science Centre has three floors of hands-on scientific goodies. There's also the Climate Change Theatre, a planetarium, Scotland's only only IMAX cinema and the Glasgow Tower. The tower, which is 127 metres high, is the tallest free-standing building in Scotland, and has the unique capability of being able to turn 360° into the prevailing wind. You can travel up 100 metres in the viewing cabin and enjoy the vistas across the city – though not if the weather's too blowy. **Glasgow Science Centre** *50 Pacific Quay, Glasgow G51 1EA (0871 540 1000/ www.glasgowsciencecentre.org).*

638-639 *Rub it in*

A peculiarly British past-time, brass rubbing involves laying a sheet of paper over an engraved or embossed surface (traditionally an ornate church brass) and carefully rubbing the surface with wax crayons to create a copy. Try it with coins, tree bark or a nice knobbly manhole cover, or make some rubbings at your local church – ask the vicar's permission first, though, as antique brasses can be more delicate than they look. Alternatively, head to a dedicated brass rubbing centre, which will supply you with paper, wax and some expert assistance.

In central London, the crypt at St-Martin-in-the-Fields (Trafalgar Square, WC2N 4JJ, 020 7766 1122, www.stmartin-in-the-fields.org) contains the London Brass Rubbing Centre, whose brasses include unicorns, lions, medieval knights and a very fine dragon. It shares the vaulted space with a café.

Stratford Brass Rubbing Centre (Royal Shakespeare Theatre Summer House, Avon Bank Gardens, Southern Lane, Stratford-upon-Avon, Warwickshire CV37 6XP, 01789 297671, www.stratfordbrassrubbing.co.uk) also has a magnificent collection of replica medieval and Tudor brasses – including, of course, one of the Bard.

640 *Weigh up a gold bar...*

At the Bank of England Museum in London you can lift a gold bar (which is safely secured in a cabinet) and work out how far you could run with it, should you manage to free it from its moorings. It's one of the alluring entertainments laid on for your delectation at this quirky paean to mammon. **Bank of England Museum**, *Threadneedle Street, EC2R 8AH (020 7601 5545/www.bankofengland. co.uk/education/museum).*

641 *...then estimate your worth*

Too many people say 'you are worth your weight in gold' without really knowing how much that works out at. Any high-street pawnbroker (www.thenpa.co.uk) will give you a quote. The price of gold fluctuates, but usually hovers around £8 a gram or £470 an ounce for 18-carat gold depending on the condition and whether it's hallmarked. The average ten-stone child (if the obesity scare stories are to be believed) thus works out at just over £1 million melted down, which isn't a bad rate considering the way some of them behave.

Bank of England Museum

642

Make a perfect pompom...

On a piece of card, draw two identical large circles, each with a smaller circle inside – about a third the size of the big circle. The size of the outer circle depends on how big you want the pompom to be, but 6cm x 6cm is a good start. Cut out the circles, so you have two doughnut-shaped cards, and place together.

Then wind yarn around the shape, looping it through the hole in the centre and over the edge until the doughnut is fully covered. Keep going, so the wool layers over and over itself, and the hole in the centre gets smaller and smaller. The more wool you wrap round, the fuller the pompom will be.

Step three is the trickiest part. Using sharp scissors, cut the loops of yarn between the edges of the two circles. Be careful not to pull any of the cut strands. Gently ease the card circles apart a little, then pass a strand of yarn between the card circles and tie it tightly, so it holds all the strands of wool together. Knot it twice more, then remove the card.

Fluff up your pompom; if some strands are uneven, give it a trim. You could sew it to a woolly hat, make some big ones for the ends of a plain woollen scarf, or tie one on a piece of string for the cat to chase. Use different colours for multicoloured pompoms, or different textures for interesting effects.

643 ...or a tassel

Tassels are even easier to make than pompoms. Take a single strand of yarn, and a rectangular piece of firm cardboard, 4cm wide and long as you want your tassels to be. Wrap the yarn around the long sides of the card 25 times or more, then take a short piece of wool and thread it through the top end of the wrapped yarn, tying it securely. Cut the end off at the opposite end of the tassel. Wind another strand of yarn around the tassel several times, about an inch down from the top, to secure it. Finally, sew on a loop to hang your tassel by, and trim the ends so they look neat and even.

644-648

See the world turned upside down

A camera obscura (from the Latin, meaning 'dark room') is a forerunner of the camera we know today. It's a dark, enclosed space with a small hole in one side, through which an inverted image of the view outside is projected on to the opposite wall or screen. Nosy Victorians loved them, and spying on tiny panoramas was a fashionable leisure activity a century or so ago.

A few have survived to this day, the most famous of being in Edinburgh (0131 226 3709, www.camera-obscura.co.uk). Perched on Castle Hill, it was the city's first purpose-built visitor attraction. There are five floors of optical illusions and interactive experiments, which demand hands-on exploration – though young children may find the distorting mirrors on the building's exterior entertainment enough. The camera obscura is right at the top, providing a sneaky way to spy on the good people of Edinburgh down below. There are great views from around the parapet of the building too, and free telescopes with which to survey the city.

Bristol's camera obscura 0117 975 0687, www.english-heritage.org.uk), housed in the Clifton Observatory, a former windmill, offers splendid views of Clifton Suspension Bridge.

On the Isle of Man, the camera on Douglas Head (01624 686 7666), near the lighthouse, can be used to survey the surrounding headlands, or peek at unsuspecting bathers.

The nicely restored original Victorian beauty on the Grand Parade at Eastbourne pier (01323 410466) is another appealing spyhole, which gives a smashing view of activities on the seafront.

The Royal Observatory in Greenwich (020 8858 4422, www.nmm.ac.uk) has London's only public camera obscura. You'll find it in a small summer house on the Observatory courtyard, next to Flamsteed House. Open to the public during museum opening hours, it projects a close-up, real-time, moving panorama of Greenwich and the River Thames, the National Maritime Museum and the Royal Naval College on to a circular table.

It's all done with mirrors, you know.

649-656 *Muddle through a maze*

Blenheim Palace, Oxfordshire
The Marlborough maze at Blenheim covers half a hectare, with two raised bridges from which to plot your route and wave at all the other lost people. There are all sorts of unexpected delights hidden behind its hedges, including a putting green and giant draughts set.
Woodstock, Oxfordshire OX20 1PX (08700 602080/www.blenheimpalace.com).

Chatsworth, Derbyshire
It may be relatively small, but the maze at Chatsworth is trickier than it appears. It's made up of high, dense yew hedges, so there's no way of cheating your way to the centre – and not a lot to orienteer by either.
Bakewell, Derbyshire DE45 1PP (01246 565300/www.chatsworth.org).

Glendurgan Garden, Cornwall
The subtropical blooms at this warm, sheltered Cornish garden are a delight – but kids bypass the camelias and swamp cypresses and make a beeline for the undulating laurel maze, planted in 1833. There's also a brilliant swing, known as the Giant's Stride.
Mawnan Smith, near Falmouth, Cornwall TR11 5JZ (01326 250906/www.nationaltrust.org.uk).

Hampton Court Palace, Surrey
Designed in the late 17th century, the splendid maze at Hampton Court is one of the most famous labyrinths in the world. It's baffled thousands of visitors over the centuries, including kings and courtiers – but isn't too hard for kids to solve.
West Molesley, Surrey KT8 9AU (0844 482 7777/www.hrp.org.uk).

Hever Castle, Kent
With its high hedges and series of dead ends, Hever's yew maze is brilliantly baffling. Still more thrilling is the water maze, consisting of a series of walkways across the lake; step on the wrong stone and you're in for a soaking from hidden water jets.
Hever, Edenbridge, Kent TN8 7NG (01732 865224/www.hever-castle.co.uk).

Jubilee Maze, Herefordshire
With hedges over a metre thick, there are no illicit short cuts in the Jubilee. The shortest of the 12 routes to the centre is just 180 metres, but we'd be amazed if you found it first time.
Symonds Yat West, Ross-on-Wye, Herefordshire HR9 6DA (01600 890360/www.mazes.co.uk).

Leeds Castle, Kent
Planted in 1988, the maze at Leeds Castle is a corker. Those who find the centre make their escape via a dramatic underground grotto, adorned with eerie carvings of mythical beasts.
Maidstone, Kent ME17 1PL (01622 765400/www.leeds-castle.com).

Longleat, Wiltshire
More than 16,000 English yews line the paths at Longleat's magnificent maze – and while you may be able to see the observation tower at the centre, finding it is quite another matter.
Warminster, Wiltshire BA12 7NW (01985 844400/www.longleat.co.uk).

Glendurgan Garden

657

Every half hour, Archimedes is lowered from the ceiling into his bath to illustrate his principle of displacement. It's a must-see event at Eureka, the Museum for Children in Halifax (01422 330069, www.eureka.org.uk). Under-fives enjoy the Sound Garden, where the ladybirds giggle and a tree trunk hides a stash of dressing-up gear, while older kids can learn what it's like to be blind, become a postman or work the checkouts in the mini-supermarket. The most popular gallery is Me & My Body, which shows how our blood flows and what our skeletons look like; stepping inside a giant mouth to find the wobbly tooth is another splendidly surreal experience.

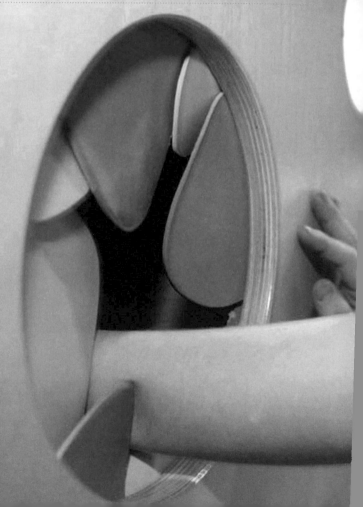

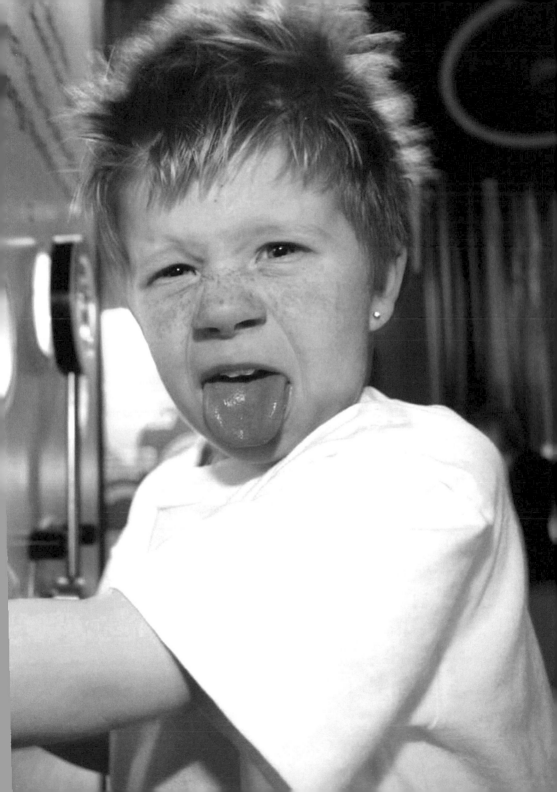

658 Make your own museum

Instead of boring your friends with holiday photos, create a museum of unusual items collected on your travels. Our display contains a lump of lava from Mount Etna, the jawbone of a Welsh sheep, some sand from the Sahara Desert and an ancient Egyptian figurine (probably fake). Each item must be labelled and numbered. The numbers refer the visitor to your catalogue. In it, you will have written about individual exhibits in great detail, having consulted a number of sources – including not just Google but also the *Encyclopaedia Britannica*. The research is the fun part, and is what a museum curator does for a living; the mighty British Museum started this way.

659 Enrol at knight school

Gallant heroes are few and far between in these benighted times – so English Heritage has decided to train a new generation of chivalrous champions. Summer holiday knight schools have sprung up faster than dragon's teeth at its castles: try Warwick, Kenilworth, Bolsover, Framlingham or Scarborough for starters. Activities include trying on armour, learning the finer points of chivalry and indulging in a spot of swordplay and jousting. For details, visit www.english-heritage.org.uk.

660 Be a rookie jockey

Portraits of haughty thoroughbreds adorn the walls at this temple to all things equine, while the Practical Gallery has some choice hands-on exhibits. Under the expert eye of a retired jockey or trainer, try tacking up a model horse; next, don racing silks and go for a good gallop on the simulator. Real jockeys sometimes use these things for training in winter, so there's no need to feel daft.
The National Horseracing Museum
99 High Street, Newmarket, Suffolk CB8 8JH (01638 667333/www.nhrm.co.uk).

661 Go bonkers for conkers

Held on the second Sunday in October in the village of Ashton in Northamptonshire, the World Conker Championship (01832 272735, www.worldconkerchampionships.com) is a fiercely fought affair. International competitors gather on the village green to discuss the merits of overarm swings and side strikes, before stepping up for combat. Competition conkers are supplied, so there's no danger of illicit nut tampering (soaking your conker in vinegar or part-baking are classic strategies). Here, good sportsmanship prevails: there's a lengthy set of Official Rules, not to mention two stewards officiating at each game. While adult competitors must register in advance, juniors can turn up and play on the day. Do you have the mettle to be an all-conkering champ?

662 Pencil it in

All sorts of free, artist-led drawing workshops and demonstrations are held at this museum, which honours the humble colouring pencil. The world's longest pencil (measuring just under eight metres) also resides here, in case any visiting giant fancies joining in.
Cumberland Pencil Museum *Southey Works, Greta Bridge, Keswick, Cumbria CA12 5NG (01768 773626/www.pencilmuseum.co.uk).*

663 See a rubbish dump reborn

Once an unlovely rubbish tip, this ten-hectare site in York is now a leafy nature reserve, with woodlands, wildflower meadows and a pond. The Environment Centre is now as green as its surrounds, with rainwater harvesting, compost loos and a living roof. A programme of activities runs through the summer – mini beast and treasure hunts are always popular.
St Nicholas Fields *York Environment Centre, Rawdon Avenue, York, North Yorkshire YO10 3ST (01904 411821/www.stnicksfields.org.uk).*

664-667

Do the Tates

First up, the Thames-side Tate Modern (Bankside, London SE1 9TG, 020 7887 8888). After marvelling at the latest super-sized art installation in the immense Turbine Hall, pick up Tate Teaser worksheets at the information desks and head up to Level 3 and the Family Zone. At weekends and during the summer holidays, you'll find the Start team in residence, with games to play and clue trails to follow through the various galleries.

Downriver from its younger sister, Tate Britain (Millbank, London SW1P 4RG, 020 7887 8888) also throws its doors open to younger visitors. The venerable art trolley trundles out on Saturdays and Sundays, laden with make-and-do activities, while eight to 12s can tune into a free audio tour of the collections, narrated by Tony Robinson.

More opportunities to get arty await at Tate Liverpool (Albert Dock, Liverpool L3 4BB, 0151 702 7400). On the first Saturday of the month, poet and storyteller John Hughes drops in to compose odes to the artwork in Tales at the Tate sessions. Sundays' Tate Explorers get-togethers, meanwhile, equip kids with maps and activity bags, then send them on a mission around the gallery.

Last but not least of the four Tates is the St Ives' outpost (Porthmeor Beach, St Ives, Cornwall TR26 1TG, 01736 796226). This one's perfect for children, being right on the beach. As it has no permanent collection the family trails and activities are linked to the current exhibition, but there's always something delightful to do. A typical family trail might involve handing over a small fee in exchange for an activity beach bucket, containing art materials, modelling putty and a sketchbook as well as laminated instuctions on how to follow the exhibition and create works of art as you look around.

A five-minute walk away is the leafy Barbara Hepworth Gallery and Sculpture Garden, which is also part of Tate St Ives. The garden has its own activity bag (£2) containing pencils, a sketchbook, clay to make your own sculptures and a postcard to Barbara, which you fill in and leave at the main gallery for vistors. Note that there are steps into the Barbara Hepworth Gallery, so buggies have to be left in the foyer.

For more information on all four Tates, have a look at www.tate.org.uk.

668

See some top tanks

Keep your eyes peeled: lurking somewhere, perhaps in the oldest tank in the world, or the Sherman Crab from World War II, is Reggie the Rat. The shy rodent can be tracked down among the dazzling display of tanks at the Bovington Tank Museum – a treat for those who like big machines and plenty of them.

As well as the Reggie hunt, children can draw, design or colour in tanks and enjoy a large outside play area. They're also allowed to climb on some of the tanks and experience standing in a cut-in-half Centurion for a simulated ride. The shop is bursting with tank-related souvenirs, toys and books, and there is a café and a picnic area. Special activities for children are offered during school holidays, so it's worth checking online if you're planning a visit.

Tank Museum *Bovington, Dorset BH20 6LJ (01929 405096/www.tankmuseum.org).*

669
Create your own floating garden

Flowers and candles floating in water make an appealing centrepiece for the tea table. You can use simple flowers such as gerbera (big faced, daisy-like flowers), or, if you prefer to use garden flowers, try lots of lawn daisies and buttercups, roses and rose petals, spring blossom or asters.

Take a large, wide-brimmed glass bowl (a fruit or salad bowl will do very nicely) and fill it almost to the top with cold water. Remove the stalks from your flowers, and place their heads (with a tiny bit of stalk left) on the surface of the water. If you have some floating candles, pop those in too.

You can colour the water with a few drops of food colouring; this looks particularly good against a mass of plain white flowers, as the blooms will eventually change hue as they suck up the colour.

670-672
Play French...

...bowls

The French version of bowls is called boule or *pétanque*. The game is usually played on gravel in city squares in Paris and, in particular, Marseille, where it was invented. Players aim to lob the silver balls as close to the jack, or *cochinot*, as possible. In France, adults drink Pernod and talk about existentialism during the game, which is never taken too seriously. In this country, families just squabble about the rules. (You can easily discover them at www.petanque.org.) Buy your boule sets at a motorway service station or any good toyshop.

...cricket

The French version of the British national summer game is relatively simple. The batsman's legs are the wicket, defended with the bat. Whoever has the ball bowls it, trying either to hit the batsman's legs or make him give up a catch. If the batsman hits the ball he may turn his whole body to face the next. If he misses it, he may not. There are no teams, no runs and no umpires. The winner is the player who has hogged the bat for longest, been too competitive and bored everyone to disinterest. Needless to say it is not played in France, where they have never heard of it. The name reflects the British confidence that if the French had taken up cricket, this is how it would be.

...skipping

French skipping is the playground sport of jumping in and out of a loop of elastic. You need three players. Two stand with their legs about shoulder width apart, with the elastic loop held taut around their ankles. The third player does the skipping and jumping. Rhiannon Cappa (aged ten) taught us this accompanying rhyme: 'England, Ireland, Scotland, Wales/Inside, outside, donkeys' tails'. The country names signal you to jump to the side of each elastic; at 'inside, outside' you land first with both feet inside the loop, then with a foot to either side of it. 'Donkeys' tails' means you land with both feet on top of the elastic.

A few of my favourite things

673-687

Janey Louise Jones, writer

We never get bored of visiting Edinburgh Castle (Castlehill, EH1 2NG, 0131 668 8800, www.edinburghcastle. gov.uk). For me, the loveliest part of the castle is the tiny chapel of St Margarets, which is a lovely intimate space within the huge fortress. My boys Ben (14), Oliver (12) and Louis (nine) prefer the weaponry, of course.

Holyrood Palace (Canongate, The Royal Mile, Edinburgh EH8 8DX, 0131 556 5100, www.royal.gov.uk) is another favourite spot, as is Our Dynamic Earth (112 Holyrood Road, Edinburgh EH8 8AS, 0131 550 7800, www.dynamicearth.co.uk). It explores the past and future of the planet, and has some amazing interactive exhibits.

The battlefield and visitors' centre at Bannockburn (Glasgow Road, Stirling FK7 8LJ, 0844 493 2139, www.nts.org.uk) is a very child-friendly place. It's full of topical history about William Wallace, and offers a refreshingly un-Hollywood vision of the Braveheart story. Another important Scottish battlefield is Culloden Moor (Inverness IV2 5EU, 0844 493 2159, www.nts.org.uk), where the Jacobites were defeated by the British.

It's always fascinating to attend the Edinburgh Book Festival (www.edbookfest. co.uk). Burns Suppers are another Scottish literary institution, taking place around the birth of Robert Burns. There's always lots of traditional music, poetry-reciting and toasting, and the children love the sense of occasion.

I really enjoy working on scrap and mood books with the boys, as well as memory boxes. We collect things like tickets to first rugby matches and theatre shows, report cards, judo certificates, letters and photos to go in their memory boxes, while the mood books focus on their current obsessions such as Daleks, cheetahs or racing cars.

We often take the dog for long walks on Gullane beach in East Lothian (www. edinburgh.org/beaches); being a labrador, he can't resist a swim. As well as drawing sand pictures, we pick up pebbles on our beach walks to decorate at home. Stones can be painted like sea creatures, fruits or lion faces, then varnished.

The Spey Valley and Perthshire are fairy tale places in the north of Scotland, where the running water of all the falls and rivers is very refreshing (go to www. perthshire.co.uk for a list of wild waterfalls and salmon leaps). We also love skiing at Aviemore, Glenshee and the Lecht. There's an excellent outdoor centre just outside Aviemore (Glenmore Lodge, Aviemore, Invernessshire PH22 1QU, www.glenmore lodge.org.uk). Scottish Islands like Skye (www.skye.co.uk) are incredible too, with their soft sandy beaches and breathtaking views, while Iona (www.isle-of-iona.com) and Findhorn (www.findhorn.org) are very spiritual places to be.

The boys bake bread and make endless smoothies and shakes in the blender. Rocky Road tray bake is a classic, with all the marshmallow and melted chocolate involved. They also adore concocting savoury wraps, piled with cheese, chicken, sour cream, salsa and guacamole.

The cycling is wonderful at Glentress Forest (about one-and-a-half kilometres north-east of Peebles on the A72 towards Innerleithen; see www.scottishsport.co.uk or www.thehubintheforest.co.uk for more information). Glentress has black, red and blue routes, graded according to their difficulty. Ben is very daring, and something of a stunt man.

We all love Bond movies and find going to the cinema a real treat. One of the nicest places to watch a film in Edinburgh is the privately owned Dominion Cinema in Morningside (18 Newbattle Terrace, EH10 4RT, 0131 447 4771, www.dominioncinemas.net), with its sofas and delicious snacks.

We try to indulge every stage the boys go through, but thank heavens WWE Wrestling (www.wwe.com) is over! My signature move in a big rumble is the 'frogsplash', but my back isn't really up to it these days.

688 *Make a sound collage*

Sticking items from the larder and recycling bin on to paper makes a pretty collage, but use the right stuff and you can create a useful percussion instrument as well.

Step 1

First, find a stiff piece of card and gather your collage materials together. These might include bits of corrugated cardboard, sandpaper, bubble wrap, scrunched-up tinfoil, pasta shapes, small shells, beads and buttons.

Step 2

Squeeze some glue on to the card.

Step 3

Then spread it all over.

Step 4

Stick your materials on to the glue, making sure there is enough of each material for you to scrape a drumstick along.

Step 5

Once the glue is dry, play your sound collage. Use a chopstick or a pencil to tap and scrape it, and a paintbrush for a quieter effect – or simply beat, brush and scrape it with your fingers. What else can you find to stick on and play?

689-692

Have a frog day afternoon

Spring is the season to celebrate frogs, and March the month when wildlife centres across the land hold their frog days.

The London Wildlife Trust (www.wildlondon. org.uk) has been celebrating Frog Day for over 20 years on its various sites across town. It's a chance for Londoners to celebrate our favourite and increasingly beleaguered amphibian – just think of it as a slippery facts of life lesson, with ample froggy fun thrown in. Reproductive life is tough for these guys: did you know that entire populations of toads will up sticks and travel to a certain pond to breed, many getting run over en route? That of 2,000 eggs, on average only five adults will survive to breed? Would humans be so dedicated?

Frog Day is also big news on the Greenwich peninsula, where the Ecology Park (Mudlarks Way, Greenwich, London SE10 0QZ, 020 8293 1904, www.urbanecology.org.uk) holds its amphibian shindig on the first Sunday in March, with a treasure hunt and various frog-related crafts and quizzes.

Outside London, at the headquarters of the Wildfowl & Wetlands Trust (Slimbridge, Gloucestershire GL2 7BT, 01453 891900, www.wwt.org.uk) every day is Frog Day (and Toad Day, and Newt Day…). All amphibians get special billing year round at its very own Toad Hall, which is in the wonderful, all-weather visitor centre. You don't have to stand around chilly ponds to meet the native British species of frog and toad, as well as species introduced to these shores. The toad keeper is on hand to discuss frogs, toads, newts and salamanders. The celebrity here is one Mr Custard, an American bullfrog, but we'd advise against getting too close to the pretty but deadly poisonous arrow frogs.

Milton Keynes likes to put on its Froggy Fiesta a little later in the year, at local beauty spot Walton Lake, off Newport Road (for more details, see www.theparkstrust.com). April is the time when the rangers bring out the tadpoles and frogs for inspection, and answer all your amphibious questions.

693-697 *Cook up a storm (in someone else's kitchen)*

Cooking with kids: it's the same story as painting sessions. You thought it was all going to be lovely and earth motherish, but in fact it's hell because you're a control freak and your home is getting wrecked. Sounds like you're ready for a spot of organised kids' cookery, a safe distance from the family kitchen and with minimal parental involvement; your sole task is getting them there. Most children's cookery courses are aimed at seven and overs, though there may be some flexibility.

One of the best-known course providers is Divertimenti, which offers sessions for adults and kids in London and Cambridge (020 7486 8020, www.divertimenti.co.uk). Growing Gourmet classes, held on one Saturday a month, are aimed at two age groups: five to nines and ten to 16s. Some events are themed; baking Valentine's cupcakes, say, or Easter birds' nests. Terrific pasta classes involve producing own-made pasta and sauce from scratch and creating a batch of authentic biscotti, all in two hours.

The Kids' Cookery School (107 Gunnersbury Lane, London W3 8HQ, 020 8992 8882, www.thekidscookeryschool.co.uk) offers year-round after-school courses for five to 11s, as well as short workshops during the holidays. As a registered charity it has a health agenda (not too worthy), and offers assisted places for families on benefits. Classes don't just focus on the pudding end of things, covering both savoury and sweet dishes. Kids are given recipes of the items made to take home, as well as some 'food ed'; hands up who knew the banana was a herb?

Carola Weymouth's Cookie Crumbles (0845 601 4173, www.cookiecrumbles.net) is best known for its tasty cookery parties, but the workshops, held in various venues across London during the school holidays, are gaining ground. They're popular, so check the website for the workshop dates before term ends. Cookie Crumbles has taught more than 10,000 children to cook and offers a range of menus – from fairy cakes and pizzas for the pre-school set, right up to more sophisticated fodder for teens keen to dip their wooden spoons into the dinner party circuit.

In Bristol, Bordeaux Quay (V-Shed, Canons Way, BS1 5UH, 0117 904 6679, www.bordeaux-quay.co.uk) offers a range of courses and workshops for youngsters aged seven up to teens, moving through introductory stages ('Look, Learn, Cook and Eat') to a Young Chefs' Course as their skills progress. The emphasis is on seasonality and organic produce, and the operation is run on a not-for-profit basis. Salmon goujons or homemade burgers with barbecue sauce are typical dishes the kids might learn to produce.

Betty's, the famous chain of Yorkshire tea rooms, obviously know how to bake a cake, but offer far more at their state-of-the-art Cookery School (Hookstone Park, Hookstone Chase, Harrogate, North Yorkshire HG2 7LD, 01423 814016, www.bettycookeryschool.co.uk). One-day workshops in the school holidays have titles such as 'One Pot Wonders' – to include scrumptious pork and apple crumble and lemon and sultana butterscotch pudding. Aimed at eight to 11s and 12 to 16s, they are quite costly at £80 to £90 per head, depending on the age group, but what price for having a highly accomplished chef in the family?

698

Be in fashion

There's plenty to delight children at the Bath Fashion Museum, from a pair of surreal heel-less shoes to gravity defying hats, courtesy of master milliner Philip Treacy. While you can't get your mitts on the museum's priceless haute couture and antique dresses, there are plenty of opportunities for dressing-up.

For primary-school age children, the replica Victorian sporting costumes are a hoot: stripey football jerseys and caps for boys, and elaborate archery attire for the girls. Visitors can also be laced into corsets and don crinoline petticoats to experience how fashionable women once suffered for their tiny waists. If you're hoping to rival Scarlett O'Hara's famous hand-span waist, it's probably something best attempted before tucking into your lunch.

Bath Fashion Museum *Assembly Rooms, Bennett Street, Bath BA1 2QH (01225 477173/www.museumofcostume.co.uk).*

699 *Say 'en garde' at the Royal Armouries*

It helps to be nimble on your feet if you fancy yourself as a fencer, according to Louise Walton of the Royal Armouries' Fencing Club. 'People think it's a lot of waving a sword around, but footwork's the integral part; learning to fence is all about balance, flexibility and co-ordination.' Think you've got what it takes? Then it's time to test your mettle.

Once you've mastered the en garde stance and basic footwork, you'll be taught how to thrust and parry with proper fencing foils – fully kitted out with protective clobber, naturally. During school holidays, the Armouries sometimes runs special introductory fencing sessions; for details, check the website. If you're interested in signing up for the club itself, there are six-week beginners' course for kids (£30), with meetings on Friday evenings. For more information, or to arrange dropping by for an informal taster session, email Louise at ffwarrior@hotmail.co.uk.

The Royal Armouries Leeds *Armouries Drive, Leeds LS10 1LT (08700 344344/www.royal armouries.org).*

Bath Fashion Museum

The dark side

Jill Turton **goes back to black at the ultimate goth get-together.**

Twice a year, the North Yorkshire seaside town of Whitby, better known for its abbey and kippers, fills with thousands of black-booted, pale-faced goths of every age and hue, out to party.

Whitby Goth Weekend (WGW) is the Glastonbury of goth. The streets are thronged with goths in corsets, goths in velvet, baby goths in prams and granddad goths in top hat and tails. There are sweet Victorian mistresses and wild-haired, biker-booted blokes; prim little girls and kohl-eyed teens. The streets and ginnels, the beach and the Whalebone Arch become the hub for one enormous, good-natured fashion parade – and Saturday night's shindig at the Spa Pavilion is an opportunity for outrageous excess.

It wasn't always like this. Thirteen years ago, Jo Hampshire was the only goth in her small mining town in the north of England. Fed up with being considered a freak, she decided to organise a weekend away with her like-minded goth friends, and told them to bring more friends. She chose Whitby for its seaside setting and its link with Bram Stoker's *Dracula*. When no less than 200 fellow goths turned up at the Elsinore Hotel on the first night, she knew she was on to something.

Now Jo is feted in the local paper, and her Top Mum Promotions (www.wgw.topmum.co.uk) brings in headline acts like the Mission, the Christian Dead and Voltaire. Besides the music, she puts together a programme that's designed to appeal to goths and 'normals' alike. There's a burlesque show, the Dead Funny Comedy Club, Cabaret Macabre, a goth dog walk and, on Sunday afternoon, an irreverent soccer match hosted by Whitby Town FC between Real Gothic and Athletico Gazette (aka the *Whitby Gazette*), with proceeds going to charities such as the Yorkshire Air Ambulance or the Bats Protection League.

Children and families have always been warmly welcomed at WGW. The organisers ask only that parents use their common sense in choosing events, and remember that the

Teenage goth for the day

Eleanor McKee, aged 14

As you turn into Whitby car park everything seems as it should – until you pull up next to a shiny black hearse. Mum goes to buy a parking ticket and a man with a long dark leather coat, white face and black lipstick asks politely if we have change for a fiver. It must be Goth Weekend.

As we enter Whitby we start goth-counting. Me and my friend Bonny once got up to 200 just entering Whitby. We go down the 199 steps but quickly lose count, distracted by whole families in amazing outfits. Frock coats and Victorian dresses trail on the floor; surrounded by black, a woman in a pure white wedding dress pushes a classic Silver Cross pram with a goth baby in it.

I am an ordinary teen girl. At home I'm very far from 'goth girl', but at Whitby Goth Weekend me and my friends dress up for a bit of a laugh and become goths for the day.

In the town centre, we look round the goth markets and pay £1.50 to go through the Dracula Experience. It's probably the most unscary experience ever, but we still run through it screaming, and are outside in the street again in about five minutes flat.

Then we might go for lunch at a restaurant looking out over Whitby beach. We watch the goths walking along the sand and point out the most outrageously dressed. Goths are divided into two categories: first, the hardcore, full-time goths, who come twice a year without fail in full goth costume. Then there are the part-time goths, like me, who dress up for fun just for Goth Weekend, but live a double life. Once home they go back to being an accountant or a schoolgirl and their goth side is forgotten… until next year.

Goths may look spooky, or even a bit scary, but after a while you realise they are just normal people. They are on the next table eating fish and chips, paddling in the sea, or stocking up at the Co-op.

Saturday night gig is aimed at late teens and adults. Still, there's plenty of fun to be had in the daytime, 'goth spotting' along West Cliff and Marine Parade and in the clifftop St Mary's churchyard. With its crumbling, ancient gravestones, it's darkly atmospheric; as *Dracula* fans will know, it was here that the unfortunate Lucy Westenra had her fateful encounter with Count Dracula.

But WGW isn't just about watching from the sidelines. Anyone can join in with the strange and glamorous, the wonderful and weird by gothing-up for the day, just for the hell of it. Not equipped for the occasion? There is no shortage of gear to buy at the four massive markets that take place across town, at the festival's chaotic Bizarre Bazaar: fluorescent dreadlocks, chunky biker boots, sparkly platforms, pink eyelashes and black lipstick, leather greatcoats, Victorian ballgowns, fur and velvet, leather and PVC and basques galore. For £80 you can even order a set of made-to-measure vampire teeth.

Dressed to kill and sporting plenty of black eyeliner, you can take part in one the countries most outlandish fashion shows – and all for free. Snappers are out in force, so expect to be photographed in what has become a very British Venetian carnival.

It was in Britain that the goth subculture first emerged back in the 1980s; a spin-off from punk, with bands like the Mission, Sisters of Mercy and Siouxsie and the Banshees. The distinctive look (black jeans, black boots, pale skin and dark lips) was as much part of goth culture as the music. Now the gothic movement embraces all sorts, from buttoned-up Victoriana fans with no interest in music, to body-pierced, rubber-wearing goths. Despite taking their name from the violent Eastern Germanic Goth tribe from the third and fourth century, goths are essentially non-violent, with affiliations to no particular political party, sexual orientation or religion.

The Whitby townsfolk probably knew nothing of this when the first goths began arriving in 1995. Understandably, they were wary of this invasion of the weird and wacky to begin with, and some were far from welcoming; a local church even organised their own 'Rave against Satan'. But the goths kept on coming and behaved well – and today they are warmly embraced.

> *'There are sweet Victorian mistresses and wild-haired, biker-booted blokes; prim little girls and kohl-eyed teens.'*

Now on goth weekends, when Bats and Broomsticks (the country's only goth B&B) posts 'No vacancies' and every other guest house is full, locals are happy to rent out their spare bedroom to a vampire. Shops, meanwhile, put on black window displays and sell goth ice-cream and vampire fudge. The 'black pound', some £750,000, has helped to smooth the way.

A new and sad tradition also takes place. High on West Cliff, close to the Whalebone Arch and the statue of Captain Cook, a crowd stand solemnly round a black-cloaked figure reading a eulogy. It is a tribute to the young goth Sophie Lancaster, who was kicked to death in 2007 by two youths in a park in Bacup, Lancashire, merely for being a goth. At the trial, judge Anthony Russell QC described the goth community as 'perfectly peaceful, law-abiding people who pose no threat to anybody'. He went on: 'This was a hate crime against these completely harmless people, targeted because their appearance was different to yours.' A bench dedicated to Sophie, who used to come to Whitby, has been positioned overlooking the harbour and a short service is held in her memory.

It's heartening, then, that Whitby has embraced the bi-annual gothic invasion – that goths like Jo Hampshire, who feel like freaks and odd-balls in their hometown, can come here and be accepted. There's a tangible atmosphere of friendliness and inclusivity about Goth Weekend, starting on Friday afternoon with the 'Whitby Virgins' welcome, and a carnival atmosphere that infects the whole town.

So ignore the car sticker that reads 'Goths are for life, not just for Whitby'. Nobody really minds if you enter into the spirit and become a goth, just for the day.

701

Bake a pizza base...

You will need:
1 level tbsp salt
1 tbsp caster sugar
1kg strong white bread flour
4 tbsp olive oil
2 x 7g sachets dried yeast
650ml lukewarm water

Place the flour in a large bowl. In a second smaller bowl, stir together the yeast, sugar, olive oil and water. Make a hollow in the flour and pour in the yeast mixture. Take a fork and mix everything together, slowly incorporating all the flour, then dip your hands into some flour and knead.

Dust a clean bowl with flour and put your ball of dough into it. Cover the bowl with a damp cloth and place in a warm room for about an hour until the dough has doubled in size. After this, knock back the dough (knead all the air out). The amount of dough you have will make about five medium pizzas, so roll out as many as you need into rough circles, each about half a centimetre thick. This is the point at which you can try throwing your pizza discs in the air and landing them on your fingertips.

Pop your rolled-out pizzas in a hot oven (about 200ºC) for a few minutes, then remove and prick to remove any baking bubbles.

702 ...then make a pizza face

Cover your base with a layer of tomato sauce and some grated mozzarella, then assemble the facial features. To make hair, use grated cheese, steamed broccoli tops or spinach. The eyes can be tomato or olive slices, with pineapple rings for glasses and eyebrows of sliced green beans. For the nose, try a baby corn or an asparagus spear. Make the mouth from a red pepper ring, with chopped white onion teeth. Bake for ten to 15 minutes, until crispy and brown on top.

703 Study bubbleology

Blowing bubbles is good for the soul, but you can do better than the insignificant suds created by mass-produced bubble solutions. Think big: Sam Sam the Bubble Man (www.bubble inc.co.uk), aka Sam Heath, can show you how. This is a man who once encased 19 girls and boys inside a giant bubble – we presume he asked their permission first. Heath is the country's leading bubbleologist, and his website is full of hints and tips, along with bubble solutions to buy. Alternatively, make your own. All you need is a thin piece of wire, some slivers of leftover soap and one teaspoonful of glycerine. Dissolve the soap in half a cup of water overnight, then add the glycerine. Carefully bend your wire around the handles of a wooden spoon, turning the end round on itself to create a closed loop. Dip the loop in the gloop and blow the soapy film gently until your giant bubble is fully formed.

704-709

Walk with bats

Taking place at twilight on summer evenings, bat walks are tremendous fun. Your guide will be equipped with a bat detector (*pictured*), which converts the bats' high-frequency calls into sounds that humans can hear, and it's a rare opprtunity to get close to these secretive creatures and learn a little more about them.

Dates are often few and far between, so call to book well in advance. Below are a few good places to start: for more events across the country, visit the Bat Conservation Trust's website at www.bats.org.uk.

David Marshall Lodge

Bats abound in the Queen Elizabeth Forest Park, making for thrilling bat-stalking; midges live here too, so don't forget the insect repellent. There's no charge for under-14s, making this walk a bit of a bargain.
Queen Elizabeth Forest Park, Aberfoyle, Stirling FK8 3UX (01877 382258/www.forestry.gov.uk).

Dunster Castle

Once a Norman stronghold, this turret-topped fortress has become a stronghold for lesser horseshoe bats, which roost in its ruined spiral staircase. An infra-red camera affords close-up views of the roosting bats and their pups, while guided walks take you into the wooded gardens to see tiny pipistrelles and agile, lightning-quick daubenton's bats.
Dunster, near Minehead, Somerset TA24 6SL (01643 821314/www.nationaltrust.org.uk).

Highgate Wood

Natterer's bats and pipistrelles flit between the oaks and hornbeams of this ancient patch of woodland, living in hollow trees or one of the carefully placed bat boxes. You might spy a fox or two as well.
Muswell Hill Road, London N10 3JN (020 8444 6129).

Ilam Park

Ilam's annual 'bangers and bats' night is a cracking event, kicking off with an audiovisual presentation on bats. After a fortifying supper of sausages and mash, the group heads across the formal gardens and into the parkland to search for bats amid the ancient trees and outbuildings. There's just one bat walk a year, generally in late summer, so book ahead.
Ilam, Ashbourne, Derbyshire DE6 2AZ (01335 350503/www.nationaltrust.org.uk).

London Wetland Centre

Birds may be the big daytime draw, but on summer evenings bats are the stars, with a programme of moonlit bat talks and walks between May and September. The lakefront bird hides provide a great vantage point as white-bellied daubenton's bats swoop low over the water, looking for unwary insects; other species spotted here include leisler's bats, serotines and noctules.
Queen Elizabeth's Walk, London SW13 9WT (020 8409 4400/www.wwt.org.uk).

Renishaw Hall

As dusk falls, you can roam around the lovely Italianate gardens of this imposing stately pile, in search of its bat inhabitants. Resident species include natterer's, daubenton's, pipistrelles, noctules and brown-long-eared bats. After the walk, there's supper in the café to warm you up.
Renishaw, Sheffield S21 3WB (01246 432310/ www.sitwell.co.uk).

London Wetland Centre

710 *See science come alive*

If you think physics is fearsome and biology a bore, prepare to be amazed by the Edinburgh International Science Festival (0131 558 7666, www.sciencefestival.co.uk). Held every year in the Easter holidays, its talks, demonstrations and workshops are far from dull and dusty; in previous years, unwrapping mummies, digging up dinosaurs and competing in the robot football champion's league have all featured on the agenda. Certain attractions have to be booked in advance, but there are loads of drop-in events on offer too.

711-716 *Pay tribute to the fallen*

In London, the human cost of war is marked every November at an immense, understated monument known as the Cenotaph (Whitehall, Westminster, London SW1A 2BX), designed by Sir Edwin Lutyens. Its inscription reads 'The Glorious Dead'. In this animal-loving land of ours, however, the beasts of burden are not forgotten. David Backhouse's sculpture *Animals in War* (www.animalsinwar.org.uk), inspired by Jilly Cooper's book of the same name, stands on Park Lane, just east of Hyde Park's Speakers' Corner. Eight million horses, as well as countless pack mules, donkeys, carrier pigeons, dolphins and even glow worms, died in the service of their country in World War I. They were not, as Backhouse notes in his inscription, volunteers.

Another little memorial to look out for, this time while walking on the Thames Path at Greenwich, stands in the little riverside garden on Ballast Quay, just past the Cutty Sark Tavern (4-7 Ballast Quay, London SE10, 0871 917 0007). It's a little goat kid, made from material salvaged from the river, rearing up as if to nibble some leaves from a tree. A plaque beside it reads: 'In memory of the millions of animals who died not from foot and mouth but from the cure for foot and mouth.'

In the lovely grounds of Newstead Abbey, once the home of Lord Byron (Newstead Abbey Park, Nottingham NG15 8NA, 01623 455900, www.newsteadabbey.org.uk), you'll find a marble monument to Boatswain, the poet's favourite dog. It's a grandiose affair, bearing a lengthy inscription to 'one who possessed beauty without vanity/Strength without insolence/Courage without ferocity...'

Such stellar canine qualities can turn dogs into national celebrities, although no one can verify the stories behind them. The town of Beddgelert (01766 890 312, www.beddgelert tourism.com), just south of Snowdon in North Wales, takes its name from the story of a faithful dog that saved a baby prince from a wolf, then was killed for its troubles when his owner got the wrong end of the stick. Some say this legend is a cynical attempt by village authorities to attract tourism.

Scotland, meanwhile, has the celebrated story of Greyfriars Bobby, a little Skye terrier who kept constant watch over the grave of his dead master, John Gray, in the kirkyard (Greyfriars Kirk, 2 Greyfriars Place, Candlemaker Row, Edinburgh EH1 2QQ, 0131 226 5429, www. greyfriarskirk.com) for 14 years until his own death in 1872. The Greyfriars Bobby statue at the top of Candlemaker Row is so touching that some visitors kiss it.

The most moving collection of animal memorials, however, has to be the sensitively restored animal cemetery of the PDSA (People's Dispensary for Sick Animals) in Ilford (Woodford Bridge Road, Essex IG4 5PS, www.pdsa.org.uk). This is the resting place of more than 3,000 animals, a number of whom are war heroes. A select few received the Dickin medal for bravery. Look out for the stones honouring Ricky the mine-detecting dog, given the medal in 1947, or Simon, the ship's cat, who was the only feline to be awarded the honour (in 1949). Mary the Pigeon, from Exeter, whose grave is also here, is another Dickin medal recipient. Their stories strike a chord with so many – young and old – that the PDSA is embarking on a programme of guided tours and talks for those who want to find out more about these feisty animals. Check the website for tour times and dates.

IN MEMORY OF
RICKY DM
SERVED AS
A MINE DETECTING DOG IN HOLLAND
AWARDED PDSA DICKIN MEDAL
MARCH 1947
FOR DEVOTION TO DUTY IN CONTINUING
TO CLEAR MINES THOUGH WOUNDED
DIED 20 JULY 1953

717

Get chocolatey and eat like a Twit

If it's sunny, story sessions at the Roald Dahl Museum & Story Centre take place out in the Wundercrump courtyard; if it's rainy, head for Miss Honey's classroom, where Matilda terrorised Mrs Trunchball with a stick of chalk. The centre also runs some inspired hands-on activities. Certain events must be booked in advance, such as the 'Make your own revolting recipe' sessions, which might involve making gloriumptious James's Peach Punch or Lickable Wallpaper. Others, like the ever-popular chocolate decorating sessions, are run on a drop-in basis.

There are more treats in store at Café Twit. Kids love the Dahl-inspired menu and gobble down delicious Bogtrotter chocolate cake or Whizzpoppers – swirls of hot chocolate with raspberry coulis, topped with Maltesers and marshmallows. It's not all Wonka though: healthy options include baked potato with Snozzcumber, or a Boggis chicken sandwich.

Roald Dahl Museum & Story Centre *81-83 High Street, Great Missenden, Buckinghamshire HP16 0AL (01494 892192/www.roalddahlmuseum.org).*

718 Venerate the venerable Bede

Known as 'the father of English history', Bede was a Benedictine monk, born in AD 673. His weighty, five-volume *Historia Ecclesiastica* may be of little interest to kids, but the centre dedicated to his life and times is unexpectedly family friendly. Pick up a 50p bag of feed and meet the rare breeds at the Anglo-Saxon farm, or head for the main exhibition. Here, the whole family can dress up in monastic habits, then raid the art cart for activity sheets. The holidays bring all sorts of events, from bead-making to warrior mask-designing, or tales from *Beowulf*.

Bede's World *Church Bank, Jarrow, Tyne & Wear NE32 3DY (0191 489 2106/www.bedesworld.co.uk)*

719 Take a turn on the Falkirk Wheel

It may look like a whopping piece of sculpture, but the Falkirk Wheel has a far more practical purpose. It's an immense, rotating boat lift that links the old Union Canal with the Forth & Clyde Canal, enabling boats to 'fly' the 35-metre drop between the two. See for yourself with an hour-long boat trip from the visitor's centre.

Falkirk Wheel *Lime Road, Tamfourhill, Falkirk FK1 4RS (0870 050 0208/www.thefalkirk wheel.co.uk).*

Falkirk Wheel

720 Visit Ratty's Refuge

Kenneth Grahame, who created the wise little water vole Ratty, would thoroughly approve of the campaign to introduce these snub-nosed creatures back into the waters around the Thames. Ratty's Refuge is the medal-winning garden created by English Eden in conjunction with the Wildlife Trust, set up at the delightful River & Rowing Museum, overlooking the meadows of Henley.

The garden is filled with the sorts of river-loving plants that shy water voles can hide in. Once you've found out about all the little creatures dependent on unspoilt wetland habitats like this, spend some time with Ratty, Mole, Mr Toad, Badger and friends in the highly amusing *Wind in the Willows* exhibition, which follows the original storyline, with some dramatic flourishes – children particularly love the excitement of the weasels being evicted from Toad Hall. After being inspired by the museum, a leg-stretcher along the Thames Path between Henley and Marlow is most definitely in order. Look out for little ratties as you go.

River & Rowing Museum *Henley, Mill Meadows, Henley on Thames, Oxfordshire RG9 1BF (01491 415600/www.rrm.co.uk).*

721 Delight in damsons

When April arrives and the blossom billows in the orchards at Low Farm, the fruity folk of the Westmorland Damson Association organise their annual special day. Farmers, cooks, craftspeople and the town cryer come out in force to make Damson Day a big occasion in the diaries of Kendal folk. Children love the party, helping themselves to goodies and balloons, petting alpacas and watching Highland dancing, candle-making and wood-whittling. It's all in honour of the diminutive dark purple plum, whose presence can be detected in the cakes, pies, preserves, crumbles and chutneys on the food stalls. (Uncooked, the fruit's flavour is too tart for most tastes.)

Low Farm *Lyth Valley, near Kendal, Cumbria LA8 9DG (01539 568479/www.lythdamsons.org.uk).*

722 Brew a batch of ginger ale

Fizzy ginger ale is great fun to make – and ideal for picnics and parties. The ingredients are:

1 cup of sugar
¼ tsp of granular, active baker's yeast
fresh ginger root, peeled
1 lemon

You also need a two-litre plastic bottle, which must be dry inside, a grater and a funnel. Start by funnelling the sugar into the bottle, then add the yeast. It's a quarter of a teaspoon, not a tablespoon; get this wrong and your ginger beer might explode. (This is why you should never brew ginger ale in a glass bottle.) Finely grate your ginger; you need about 1.5 tablespoons. Squeeze the juice from the lemon into the ginger, and stir. Funnel the mixture into the bottle then add cold water, leaving an inch or so of space at the top of the bottle. Screw the lid on tight, and give it a shake.

Leave the bottle in a dark cupboard for 20 to 30 hours, checking it at after 18 hours, then at regular intervals. You can tell if it's ready by squeezing it; as soon as the bottle feels hard and your thumb doesn't leave a dent, put in in the fridge and leave it to chill for 24 hours. It's crucial you get in it the fridge in time; otherwise it might explode and taste very nasty indeed.

Ease the bottle open to release the pressure slowly, strain the ginger pieces out and enjoy a glass of cloudy, fresh-brewed ginger ale.

723
Set off on a rocky ramble

Rockpools are at their best an hour before and after low tide, when they become natural miniature aquariums, filled with tiny fish, anemones, starfish and crabs. Local coastal wildlife groups organise guided rockpool rambles throughout the summer. Devon is one of the finest rockpooling areas in the country; Devon Wildlife Trust (www.devonwildlife trust.org) will take you on a tour of some for around £2 per person. The UK Rock Pooling Club (www.uk-rpc.org) has tips on other rockpooling hotspots around the UK.

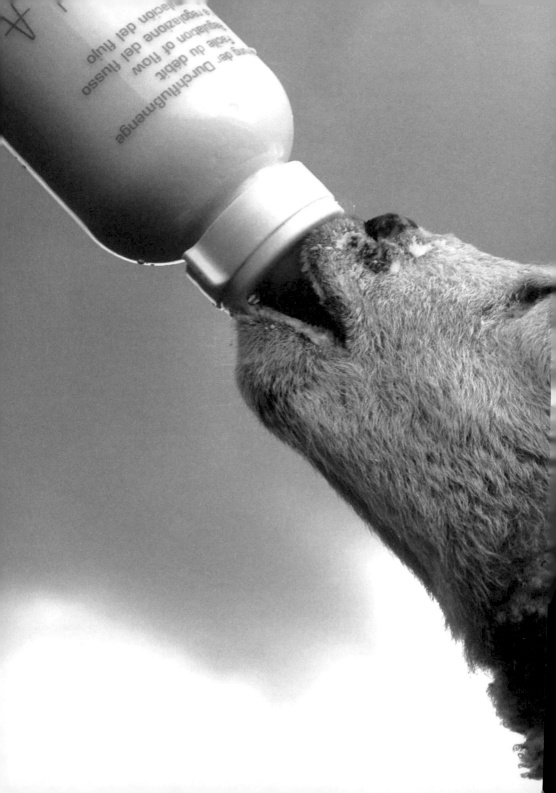

724

Dotted across the country, Feather Down Farms (01420 80804, www.featherdown.co.uk) let urban families get back to nature in an eco-friendly way. You stay in cosy 'tented cottages' on farms – under canvas but with wooden floors, proper beds and flushing loos. Children can run about on the farm, helping the farmers with their daily work, such as feeding the lambs, or just getting familiar with the countryside. Camping for softies? Definitely – but with our climate, it's camping for realists.

725 Wake up to a wildebeest

Once the gates of Port Lympne Wild Animal Park in Kent have clanged shut for the night, overnight safari guests can stay behind with the black rhinos, blue wildebeests, zebra and other animals. They have dinner with the wardens in the Livingstone Safari Lodge. After kipping in luxury tents, they wake up to a dawn safari, and have a hearty breakfast before joining the hoi polloi in the main park.
Port Lympne Wild Animal Park *Lympne, near Hythe, Kent CT21 4PD (01303 264647/ www.totallywild.net).*

726 See a dark, satanic mill

Quarry Bank Mill in Cheshire inspires the entire family. The gorgeous grounds, secret garden and superlative surrounding walking country appeals to adults, while kids cannot fail to be impressed by the waterwheel – the most powerful one still in use in Europe. A five-minute walk from the mill, the restored Apprentice House shows what life was like for the diminutive child workers brought in from the workhouse to toil in the mill. The tours are led by costumed actors, bringing a potentially dull slice of the country's industrial history into lively, involving focus for children.
Quarry Bank Mill *Styal, Wilmslow, Cheshire SK9 4LA (01625 445896/www.nationaltrust.org.uk).*

727 Make a mouse bookmark

Cut out a card oblong, about 8cm by 2cm. Remove the corners off one end to make the mouse's pointy nose. Take some black button thread – four 12cm lengths – and knot it in the middle, then glue it to the tip of the nose to make whiskers. Stick a 15cm length of string to the other end of the oblong to make a tail. Cut out two semi-circular ears to stick on, about a centimetre above the whiskers, then add two googly eyes (available from craft shops and Paperchase) between the ears and whiskers.

728

Trek on Exmoor ponies

In conservation terms, Exmoor ponies are rarer than giant pandas. Edinburgh University has a whole herd of these lovely creatures, though, and offers treks through the Pentland Hills between September and June, and from Glendevon in Perthshire in summer. Children must be eight years and above for the half-day or day-long treks, and under-12s must be accompanied – though the pony unit can provide shorter lead rein rides for younger children (four and overs). If you have no car, a pick-up can be arranged from the town of Penicuik for the Pentland rides, but this must be pre-booked. Staff will also do their best to help you get to the Glendevon base if transport is an issue, but can't promise miracles.

It's a blissful treat for pony-mad kids and parents – providing you're under the 79kg weight limit. Prices start at £20 for an evening or day trek, rising to around £35 in high season.
Edinburgh University Exmoor Pony Trekking Section *Royal (Dick) School of Veterinary Studies, University of Edinburgh, Easter Bush Veterinary Centre, Roslin, Midlothian EH25 9RG (07866 309677/http://ponytrek.eusu.ed.ac.uk).*

729

Saddle up for Bike Week

For anyone wanting to get their kids off the starting block and on to the road, Bike Week (www.bikeweek.org.uk), held annually in June, is the logical place to start. Local cycling clubs set up road safety courses and free on-the-spot bikes checks in parks across the nation, while cycle fairs roll up to showcase the best new bikes as well as the more weird and wonderful shapes such as Christiana's children's transporter trikes, tandems and trailers. It's also a chance to dip a toe into the social side of the two-wheeled world, with picnics and barbecues, off-road family days out and help planning local cycle route outings. For the showman (or girl) in the family, there are classes for kids to learn BMX skills.

ENO

On Family Days at the English National Opera (ENO), children attend workshops related to a current production (if it's suitable). They combine singing with drama, as in the real thing, write songs, design sets and, dress up. They may also tour the Coliseum, the biggest of all the West End theatres, ENO's home since 1974. In the 1960s it was a cinema and before that a freak show featuring 7ft 11in Fräulein Brünnhilde, 'the world's tallest pianist'.

English National Opera *St Martin's Lane, London WC2N 4ES (020 7632 8484/www.eno.org).*

Royal Opera House

The Royal Opera and Ballet companies are keen to welcome families, particularly those who have never been to anything at the Royal Opera House before, and those with blind or partially sighted children. You need an invitation from the ROH – which requires filling in an online application. The invitation entitles guests to attend family matinées of operas or ballets.

Royal Opera House *Covent Garden, Bow Street, London WC2E 9DD (020 7304 4000/www.roh. org.uk).*

Opera North

This award-winning Leeds-based opera company runs Little Movers, a weekly workshop for zero to four-year-olds and their carers. Run in partnership with Yorkshire Dance, these creative sessions encourage parents and children to take part in fun-filled activities that embrace movement, music and song. It's a busy programme that allows young children to meet new friends while making a song and dance about it.

Opera North *Grand Theatre, 46 New Briggate, Leeds LS1 6NU (0113 243 9999/www.opera north.co.uk).*

Scottish Opera

Sing Up Saturdays are weekly Glasgow workshops run by Scottish Opera for three- to ten-year-olds (term time only). Participants learn about specific operas, the techniques of performing opera and the countries of opera's birth, Italy and Spain. They are also taught stagecraft, and present a devised opera at the close of the summer term.

Scottish Opera *39 Elmbank Crescent, Glasgow G2 4PT (0141 248 4567/www.scottishopera.org.uk).*

English National Opera

734 Grow your own ginger

You can make an attractive houseplant and culinary aid from a piece of fresh ginger. In late winter or early spring, buy a 'finger' of ginger from your local shop. Choose a piece that has a shoot bud (like a little horn) developing. Take a sharp knife and cut off a 5cm section, including the horn. Bury it in a small pot of compost, with its shoot bud pointing upwards. Store the pot in a warm place, moving it to the window sill as the bud develops into a shoot. Keep the compost moist. As your ginger plant grows, you'll have to feed it with pot plant food and then transplant it into a bigger pot.

Once summer is over you can start drying out the plant; this will encourage it to form rhizomes (ginger roots), which you can them use for cooking. If you're in love with the plant and don't want to cut up its roots, you could try tending it through the winter. It's a difficult job, though, because we just don't get enough light. Note that ginger plants can't survive outdoors.

735 Join a tribe

During the summer months, Lower Upcott Farm in Devon rings with the sounds of whoops and war cries from the young braves taking part in the Kids' Indian Tribal Day (£80). 'I want to get kids excited about being outside and doing fun things, like building camps and using their imagination,' says organiser Ben May. Youngsters are initiated into the tribe with war paint and given an Indian name and bandana, then it's off to learn about tracking. This is followed by sneaking through the long grass in the meadow before going into a patch of woodland to build a camp and get a fire going for that all-important tribal lunch. In the afternoon, children can help hitch Shire horses Tom and Pip to the wagon. With 18 hectares to romp in and plenty of organised fun and games, your children, like the Famous Five, will come home tired but happy.

Forest Crafts *Lower Upcott Farm, Hatherleigh, Okehampton, Devon EX20 3LN (01837 811123/ www.forestcrafts.co.uk).*

736 Make waves at Wicksteed

Founded in 1926 as one of the UK's first theme parks, Wicksteed in Northamptonshire is a giddy whirl of fairground delights: mini-ferris wheels, rollercoasters, carousels and dodgems. For a truly unique thrill, though, head down to the lake to the park's oldest ride. The waterchute is the grandaddy of white knuckle rides, having celebrated its 80th birthday in 2006. It's brilliantly unsophisticated – sitting in a giant skip, nervous passengers speed down a steep ramp and plunge into a pond. If your legs aren't too wobbly afterwards, have a go on the pedal cycle monorail, which winds around the lake. The site also encompasses a narrow-gauge railway, rowing lake and parkland – and one of the largest free playgrounds in Europe, bristling with swings, see-saws and climbing frames.

Wicksteed Park *Kettering, Northamptonshire NN15 6NJ (0870 062 1193/www.wicksteedpark. co.uk).*

737 Tuck into Jaffa jellies

Orange jelly, mandarin segments and Jaffa Cakes are a match made in heaven. Take all three ingredients (canned mandarins are fine). Follow the making instructions on the jelly packet, then take four ramekins and divide the liquid jelly between them. Stir in a few mandarin segments. Place a Jaffa cake chocolate side up on top of each one. Chill for a couple of hours and serve with cream.

738 Dance the disco pavements

By day, the world's largest mirrorball proves a hypnotic draw, reflecting sea, sun, Prom and promenaders in a vast kaleidoscopic image measuring seven metres across. But it's by night that Blackpool's 50,000-mirror revolving artwork comes into its own, illluminated by a flickering, hi-tech coloured lightshow. Bring your own Abba.

739

Turn the seasons

The sinister but fascinating Museum of Witchcraft in the lovely old Cornish town of Boscastle has some really unusual treasures. A few of the creepier aspects of the collection, such as the creepy witch mirror inhabited by a spirit, or the coffins containing poppet dolls and spells or the horrible scold's bridle, shackles, skulls and cauldrons might alarm youngsters of a nervous disposition, but many children revel in it all.

For us, the most fascinating exhibit relates to the Wiccan and Neopagan year. The wheel of the year is mounted in such a way that you can turn it to view the Sabbats, or seasons. You can see symbols, activities and characters that represent the eight seasonal festivals, beautifully represented: Samhain (Hallowe'en, with pumpkins and candles); Winter Solstice (mistletoe and holly); Imbolc (Candlemas, around Valentine's Day); Spring Equinox (Easter; eggs); Beltane (May Day, with maypoles and ribbons); Summer Solstice (around Midsummer Day; singing and feasting); Lammas (early August; herbs and first fruits); and Autumn Equinox (Michaelmas, harvest day; bread and grains). In our modern indoorsy world, where seasons have merged into a strange, non-specific mulch, it's lovely to have it all presented to you in this aesthetically pleasing fashion.

The Museum of Witchcraft *The Harbour, Boscastle, Cornwall PL35 0HD (01840 250111/ www.museumofwitchcraft.com).*

740 *Don your armour*

Located in the centre of London, the Wallace Collection is a gem of a museum that runs family-friendly tours and events throughout the year. Its collection runs from artistic masterpieces like Frans Hals' *The Laughing Cavalier* to exquisite porcelain and miniatures. There's also a swashbuckling array of armour; some 2,500 pieces in all. One free activity that's always popular is trying on replica armour from the 15th to the 17th centuries, available at all times in the conservation gallery.

Look out too for bookable activities such as Chinese helmet making and painting workshops; run by artists, sessions cost £4.

The Wallace Collection *Hertford House, Manchester Square, London W1U 3BN (020 7563 9500/ www.wallace collection.org).*

741

See the ultimate rock garden

Everything at Cragside is on a palatial scale, from the 103-room mansion to the Douglas fir (Britain's tallest) that towers over the pinetum. Its owner, Sir William George Armstrong, wanted the biggest and best of everything – and that included his rock garden. It's a Himalayan-inspired masterpiece, strewn with massive rocks and bisected by streams and cascades. Pretend you're on a mountain trek, exploring uncharted lands, then head back to civilisation and the tea room.

Cragside *Rothbury, Morpeth, Northumberland NE65 7PX (01669 620333/www.nationaltrust. org.uk).*

742-747 *See a show with strings attached*

If the word puppet conjures up painful memories of beachfront domestic violence à la Punch and Judy, it's time for a rethink. Puppetry is now officially cool, and organisations from the Royal Shakespeare Company to the English National Opera are using it in their productions. There's no better way to introduce kids to theatre than by visiting one of Britain's six dedicated puppet venues, many of which also allow children to get some hands-in experience of puppetry.

Biggar Puppet Theatre, Scotland

Biggar is the home of Purves Puppets, a professional touring company that regularly performs throughout Europe, Asia and the Middle East. The company uses large-scale puppets manipulated in the Japanese bunraku style, where multiple puppeteers work on each puppet. Most productions take place in 'black light', with the puppets and scenery glowing in fluorescent paint. Puppet-making workshops are available for groups, and the theatre also caters for birthday parties.

Puppet Tree House, Broughton Road, Biggar, Lanarkshire MI12 6HA (01899 220631/ www.purvespuppets.com).

Harlequin Theatre, Wales

Puppetmaster extraordinaire Chris Somerville started working at the Harlequin in the '50s and, following the deaths of its founding members, has kept the theatre going single-handedly without any outside investment. One-man marionette pantomimes, fairytales, operas and even circus shows are performed in the theatre's ornate auditorium, which opens up during school holidays and can also be hired for private performances.

Rhos on Sea Promenade, Colwyn Bay, North Wales LL28 4EP (01492 548166/ www.puppets.uk.com).

Little Angel Theatre, London

A picturesque, winding passage through a graveyard in the heart of Islington leads to a temperance hall-turned-theatre which, for almost 50 years, has been putting puppets

Little Angel Theatre

rather than people centre stage. More than 25 productions take place each year, with an emphasis on classic long-stringed marionette shows. Highlights include magical Christmas productions of favourites such as *The Little Mermaid* – voiced by Judi Dench and Michael Gambon – and *The Snow Queen*, with all the puppets made in the adjacent workshop. The latter opens on weekends for a range of Saturday morning puppet clubs, at which children aged from two to 11 are invited to make their own puppets and devise a show for performance over the course of a term. A Puppet Academy, on Tuesday evenings, caters for older children.
14 Dagmar Passage, London N1 2DN (020 7226 1787/www.littleangeltheatre.com).

Norwich Puppet Theatre, Norfolk

The UK's largest theatre devoted solely to puppetry, Norwich offers around 30 shows a year and specialises in more contemporary styles such as object manipulation (where performers create puppets from unlikely items). A recent production of *Snow White and the Seven Dwarfs* had the whole cast

made from candles, while *The Crazy Kitchen Crew* brought corkscrews, potato mashers and spoons to life. Children aged five and over can attend the one-off workshops in puppet-making, held on Saturdays and during the school holidays.
St James, Whitefriars, Norwich, Norfolk NR3 1TN (01603 629921/www.puppettheatre.co.uk).

Puppet Theatre Barge, London

For 25 years, Juliet Rogers and Gren Middleton have been ferrying their puppet theatre productions up and down the River Thames, enchanting audiences from London to Oxford. Their small-scale marionette shows are for all the family and range from Shakespeare plays to adaptations of classics such as *Brer Rabbit* and specially commissioned new writing from the likes of Howard Barker and Wendy Cope. The Puppet Barge is moored in Little Venice from November to June and tours during the summer – see the website for details. Backstage visits can be arranged on request.
Blomfield Road, London W9 2PF (020 7249 6876/www.puppetbarge.com).

Scottish Mask & Puppet Centre, Scotland

A professional centre dedicated to the arts of mask, mime, puppetry and physical theatre, SMPC also has an 80-seat studio theatre that opens on Saturday afternoons for public performances from visiting companies, such as fellow Scots Clydebuilt Puppets and Kid Gloves Puppets, as well as occasional visits from outfits that have brought their shows from as far afield as Brazil, Indonesia, Japan and India. The centre also runs around eight seasonal puppet-making workshops, and can host birthday parties.
8-10 Balcarres Avenue, Kelvindale, Glasgow G12 0QF (0141 339 6185/www.scottishmask andpuppetcentre.co.uk)

748
See a silver swan come alive

Everyone is entranced by the silver swan at the Bowes Museum in the heart of the Pennines. A musical automaton, built in 1773, it's the jewel in the museum's magnificent art collection. Every day at 2pm the swan springs into action, as onlookers gawp in amazement. First, it gracefully turns its head to preen its feathers, before spotting a fish swimming in the rippling water (made from twisting glass rods). Inclining its neck, the swan seizes the wriggling fish and gulps it down – all in under a minute.

Bowes Museum *Barnard Castle, County Durham DL12 8NP (01833 690606/www.thebowesmuseum. org.uk).*

749
Go wild at Hebden Bridge

This small Yorkshire town, whose citizens once declared it a plastic-bag free zone, further proves itself to be one of the most eco-aware places in the country with its annual Big Green Weekend (www.biggreenweekend.org.uk). There are green-themed films in the cinema, as well as street theatre, storytelling, market stalls and musicians all singing from the same environmentally friendly hymn sheet.

750
Touch an iceberg

You can experience the sights, sounds and smells of a volcano, try to control the ultimate fate of this planet, or shudder at an earthquake at Our Dynamic Earth. Eleven multi-sensory galleries of audiovisual and interactive exhibits take you on an incredible journey that spans 15,000 million years, so there should be something for every young explorer – including a play area for under-tens and the ubiquitous café and gift shop.

Our Dynamic Earth *112 Holyrood Road, Edinburgh EH8 8AS (0131 550 7800/ www.dynamicearth.co.uk).*

751
Spot a cetacean

The Sea Watch Foundation studies whales, dolphins and porpoises (cetaceans) around the British coastline, monitoring trends in their numbers and species – and it needs your help. Anyone can get involved in its annual nine-day National Whale & Dolphin Watch by scanning the seas and reporting any sightings on a form downloaded from www.seawatchfoundation. org.uk. There are likely lookout points all over the country: the Shetland Islands are great for minke and killer whales, while bottlenose dolphins prefer Brighton harbour and porpoises favour Penzance. For details of these and other hotspots, check the Sea Watch website, which also lists manned watches where you can join trained observers (which are free) and boat observation trips (for which there is a charge).

752
Go letterboxing

If your kids shudder at the mere mention of 'a nice walk', gripping the TV remote with wild-eyed alarm, then a spot of letterboxing might be the key to putting roses into their cheeks. Invented in the mid 19th century, it's a tantalising mixture of orienteering, puzzle solving and patience. The aim of the game is to seek out a hidden box by following clues, recording your find by stamping your logbook with the rubber stamp tucked inside the box – proof that your search was successful. Boxes also contain a visitors' book, so you can also print your own personal stamp in there.

Letterboxes are stashed across the country, from the Isle of Man to the North York Moors, but the scene centres on Dartmoor; it's estimated that there are between 10,000 and 40,000 letterboxes tucked into its nooks and crannies (www.dartmoorletterboxing.org). According to the informal rules, once you've hunted out 100 letterboxes you become a member of the Letterbox 100 club (www. userfriendly-devon.com/100club).

753-758 *Reel around the fountains*

For many city centres, a post-millennium wash and brush up involved installing public water features that give their willing victims a thorough soaking: most refreshing on a hot day. The huge success of the dancing fountains at Somerset House (Strand, London WC2R 1LA, 020 7845 4600, www.somerset house.org.uk) led to a rash of copycat waterworks in London and beyond. We've spent many an afternoon in damp clothing following a playdate outside City Hall (www.london.gov.uk/gla) on Bankside or on the Duke of York's Square, tantalisingly close to the delicious ice-cream purveyor just outside Gelateria Valerie on Chelsea's King's Road.

Our favourite place to cool our toes in the capital, though, is a rather more horizontal water feature. The Diana, Princess of Wales Memorial Fountain, near the Serpentine Gallery in Hyde Park (020 7298 2000, www. royalparks.gov.uk) is a granite channel filled with running water, where children just can't wait to strip down to vest and pants. They should paddle with care, however; the water feature, designed by Kathryn Gustafsen, caused much controversy when it opened as its base became a bit slippy.

Bristol's swanky Millennium Square, intended as a showcase for the city's visitor attractions, also has its fair share of watery thrills. Aquarena, by William Pye, is a feature whose elements can be programmed to operate in a wide variety of different combinations. Children love to splash and paddle in the square, although they're not really supposed to.

The most impressive water feature in the land, however, is not some computer-programmed source of civic pride. The many fountains at Chatsworth House (Bakewell, Derbyshire DE45 1PP, 01246 565300, www. chatsworth.org), cascade, flow, gurgle and spout with glorious abandon. They were built in the 17th century by William Cavendish. The most delightful is the Willow Tree fountain, which shoots water high into the air when visitors get too close. The young Princess Victoria loved it, apparently, and called it 'the squirting tree'. The less surprising, but terribly impressive water cascade, meanwhile, flows down a series of 24 steps, then goes on to feed another elegant fountain, called the Sea Horse. Another notable fountain here, designed in the 19th century by Joseph Paxton, is the grand, gravity-fed Emperor.

759 Shin up a chimmney

Victorian schools were full of sadists, as children discover in the National Trust Museum of Childhood's replica classroom. 'Pupils' sit in 19th-century desks and write on roof slates, as directed by a strict, costumed teacher. Most of the lesson is devoted to discussing punishments – both corporal (with a vicious, bendy cane) and psychological (with a humiliating dunce's cap). Parental consent? You're having a laugh. Not going to school was just as grim: the Museum has a chimney you can force your urchins up and hands-on games such as 'jacks', the deadly rules of which are too elaborate to divulge here.

National Trust Museum of Childhood *Sudbury Hall, Sudbury, Ashbourne, Derbyshire DE6 5HT (Hall 01283 585305/Museum 01283 585337/www.nationaltrust.org.uk).*

760 See the country's oldest map

Drawn on an enormous sheet of vellum (calf skin), the 13th-century Mappa Mundi is much more exciting than modern maps. Dull geographical precision doesn't get a look-in: Jerusalem is at the centre of the world, while the Garden of Eden lurks on the edge. The Red Sea is (very sensibly) penned in red ink, while drawings of strange beasts, biblical characters and different peoples of the world cavort across the countries. It's far more enlightening than a standard map, providing experts with all sorts of insights into how medieval scholars saw the world, and how we humans fitted into it.

At home, have a go at drawing your own world map. Imagination is more important than getting every country in its correct place: you may wish to add a sea monsters or shipwrecks in dull corners of the ocean, or some lost tribes in undiscovered jungles. Personal touches are even better: you could draw your sunburnt dad on the beach where you went on holiday. Once you've finished, take your parents on a tour of the world, pointing out locations of note.

Hereford Cathedral *5 College Cloisters, Cathedral Close, Hereford HR1 2NG (01432 374200/ www.herefordcathedral.org).*

761 Feel the miners' pain in Cornwall

For almost 300 years, Cornish tin was mined below the cliffs at Geevor, and out under the Atlantic seabed. After shutting down in 1991, as the price of tin plummeted, the mine became a heritage centre – and, for the first time, visitors were allowed to explore its underground workings. The evocative subterranean tour takes you through the cramped 18th-century mine workings in single file. Spare a throught for the men who toiled down here in the darkness, day after day.

Geevor Tin Mine *Pendeen, Penzance, Cornwall TR19 7EW (01736 788662/www.geevor.com).*

762 Get your brain in gear at the Launch Pad

The Launch Pad is the what the Science Museum in London calls its 'hands-on, brains-on gallery'. During the holidays it is a seething mass of eight- to 14-year-olds, finding out that finding out can be fun. Experiment with stretchy water, bubble walls, icy bodies of solid carbon dioxide subliming on a watery surface and colours bouncing off light beams – and never forget to keep asking 'why?', because that's what gives your brain a workout. There are scientists and demonstrators on hand to make sure the 'whys?' get answered.

Science Museum *Exhibition Road, London SW7 2DD (0870 870 4868/www.sciencemuseum.org.uk).*

763 See damsels and dragons

Dragonflies and damselflies evolved before the dinosaurs. On a sunny day, Wicken Fen in Cambridgeshire is alive with these brightly coloured ancient beauties. What's the difference between a damsel and a dragon? Dragonflies hold their wings in a perpendicular position, damselflies keep theirs tucked neatly behind.

Wicken Fen *Lode Lane, Wicken, Ely, Cambridgeshire CB7 5XP (01353 720274/ www.wicken.org.uk).*

764 Keep it up!

Take time over the holidays to hone your keepie-uppie skills. For the uninitiated, this is the art of keeping your football in the air using any part of your body except your arms and hands.

Bruce, our resident 16-year-old soccer star (129 keepie-uppie record) says it's all about practice. 'To really master the art of keepie-uppies, also known as kick-ups, you need something like a six-week break from school to practise until your legs are in knots. If the first thing you do every morning is kick a ball, then by the new school year you'll be scoring hat tricks all over the shop.'

Practise with a friend. The secret of fine kickupability is perfect balance on either leg. Get a partner to lob you the ball, chest it down, then bounce it from your left foot to right knee, then left knee to right foot.

Martinho Eduardo Orige of Brazil managed to keep a regulation football in the air for 19 hours and 30 minutes using only his head, feet and legs. The feat was accomplished on 2 and 3 August 2003, according to the *Guinness Book of Records*.

765-767 Meet a Viking

York was once the site of a mighty Viking settlement. Jorvik Viking Centre (Coppergate, YO1 9WT, 01904 543400, www.jorvik-viking-centre.co.uk) occupies the site where archaelogists unearthed 40,000 objects during the excavation of an old sweet factory in 1979. Here, you can travel down below York in a pod through reconstructed streets evoking AD 975.

Archeologists who are under 12 can combine their Jorvik ticket with a visit to Dig (St Saviour's Church, St Saviourgate, York YO1 8NN, 01904 615505). Professional archeologists provide a trowel and guidance while their pupils excavate Roman, Viking, medieval or Victorian remains.

Children with a Viking obsession should drag their parents to York during February half-term, when the city erupts with Viking fever in a rousing five-day festival. The streets fill with warriors itching to demonstrate their battle drills, training routines and sword fights. Visitors can also take part in the 'have-a-go' sword combat or make a resplendent beard for the best beard competition. On the Saturday, Anglo-Saxon and Viking warriors prepare for battle in Museum Gardens, then process through the streets to Clifford's Tower for a sound and light spectacular as they fight the Normans. Information from Jorvik Viking Centre's website, or call 01904 615505.

768 Let 'em loose at Bramley's

Bramley's Big Adventure was one of the first indoor playgrounds in London with its playframe slides, dens and ball pools. Three pleasing extras make it a cut above. First, there's no time limit, so once you've paid (from £2.50 for under-twos to £3.50 to over-fives for members; membership £15/year), they can play all day. Second, the café specialises in fairtrade and organic food. Third, free Wi-Fi means parents can work while the children tear about. **Bramley's Big Adventure** *136 Bramley Road, London W10 6TJ (020 7960 1515/www.bramleys big.co.uk).*

Go twitch

*Derek Hammond **joins a new generation of birdwatchers.***

In recent years, there's been a sharp upswing in youthful awareness of our feathered friends, thanks in no small part to Bill Oddie and the BBC's *Springwatch* and *Autumnwatch* eco-fests. But if sitting on the sofa worrying over nestfuls of fluffy chicks has done wonders for boosting ornithology's image among young people, there's nothing quite as inspirational as a day out in the field, face to face with the critters.

At the Lodge, the rural Bedfordshire HQ of the RSPB (Royal Society for the Protection of Birds), there's a year-round programme of events and activities designed to take our growing interest in birds to a whole new level. The aim is the same at every RSPB reserve, big or small, up and down the country – and there's a nationwide programme of smaller events to snare your attention in the most unexpected of settings.

To mark the occasion of national Feed the Birds Day in autumn, marquees are set up in the garden at the Lodge. Kids' competitions and attractions include making your own bird-feeder, rustling up fat cakes to feed garden birds, getting sneaky in heathland hides and walking in the woods, from the depths of an old quarry to the peak of a recently excavated Iron Age hill fort. But there's no doubt about the main attraction. Children and parents alike gather around a long trestle table set up among the marquees, peopled by RSPB ornithologists.

'Ah, a blue tit,' says the studious Dr Guy Anderson, gently extracting one of the birds caught safely in nets strung around the gardens from a small cloth bag. Holding its head between his fingers, he measures its beak and wings, and shows us how to identify the bird. Meanwhile, the tit pecks furiously at the professor's fingers, most indignant at being turned upside down and popped into a film-holder for weighing.

'Eight grammes of pure anger,' the doc says of the little fellow, astonishing us with the fact that even a £1 coin weighs in at 9g. Finally, he pincers a light aluminium numbered ring on the bird's leg for identification and tracking

purposes. Someone gets to stroke the tiny bird's head and touch its powerful, outspread wing. Then it's hands up for who would like to hold the bird in their hands and set it gently free – me! me! – from which sweaty position it swoops straight up into the safety of the pines.

What's next up? Aha, a not-so-common-or-garden nuthatch – a greenish-grey 'mini woodpecker', as Sarah Dawkins, the next expert in line, calls it. 'It's resident in the UK all year round, and spreading north into Scotland as the climate changes. See how its beak is shaped to wheedle out grubs from tree bark?' She explains how it can make a hole in a tree and hollow out a nest, which it lines with oak leaves instead of the feathers and animal hair favoured by the tit. The nuthatch can also recycle old nestholes, resizing the hole to its own specifications, using beakfuls of hard-drying mud.

The kids take it in, looking at the nuthatch with new respect. Today started out as a walk in the great outdoors, but it's become properly fun. It's like a mixture of Pokémon and pets and football stickers, they later decide, where you learn the unique powers of each garden creature and how you can help to look after them – then set out to tick off the whole checklist.

'A Million Voices for Nature' is the RSPB's strapline. That's the number of members the charity relies on to spread its conservation message. And this is how it enthuses so many people – by giving the public access to wildlife it might otherwise overlook.

Inside the Lodge, over a bowl of soup in the canteen, I spoke to Richard Bashford, whose role is to set up these activities countrywide. 'Connecting People With Nature,' is the umbrella title of many of the events he organises, along with 'Aren't Birds Brilliant!'

Of course, there are year-round events at the bigger RSPB nature reserves – Rainham in Kent and Minsmere in Suffolk, to name but two. Held every August at Rutland Water, the British Birdwatching Fair is the biggest single bash, a three-day festival that has been described as the birdwatcher's Glastonbury. But just as important to Richard are the reserves that might offer just a single information post, or those devoted primarily to single species such as the red kite, or the puffin in North Wales.

'There are also the bird events that we like to set up where people least expect them. Hopefully in the summer we'll be able to set up again in the middle of Manchester. We go up to people and ask "would you like to see a falcon?", give them binoculars and information and point them up at the "R" on the sign of the Arndale Centre, where they nest. The same goes for the Embankment in London, where we've been able to point out falcons from July to September, on top of Tate Modern's chimney.'

You can also birdwatch even closer to home, he says. 'January's Big Garden Birdwatch is our largest single event, with 400,000 members joining in. The garden is a great place to start birdwatching, because things are always changing from season to season.'

Back at the Lodge, the species logged by the twitchers (birdwatchers who tick off sightings of as many different birds as possible) include a robin, chaffinch, wren, dunnock, greenfinch and goldcrest (which weighed in at just 5g – it's Britain's smallest bird).

'A swift can stay in the air for two years,' I'm reliably informed by Frances Hammond, aged nine. 'They sleep and eat in the air.' 'And I held a greenfinch,' chips in her seven-year-old brother Jimmy. 'He was so soft. I could feel him squiggling to get away. He weighs the same as ten Smarties.'

770-779 *Play the craziest golf*

Adventure Golf

All sorts of unexpected jumps and bumps can send balls careering off course at Blackpool's crazy golf attraction. Watch out for the water hazards on six and 11.
Blackpool Pleasure Beach *Ocean Boulevard, Blackpool, Lancashire FY4 1EZ (0871 222 1234/www.blackpoolpleasurebeach.com).*

Adventure Island Mini Golf

There are two indoor courses to tackle at this plush adventure golf centre. Kids love the tropical island surrounds, with parrots, rocky outcrops and tiki villages; get a hole-in-one on the 19th and you win a free round.
Adventure Island Mini Golf *Star City, Watson Road, Birmingham B7 5SB (0121 328 7474/ www.adventureminigolf.co.uk).*

Jurassic Encounter

Don't let the roaring mechanical dinosaurs distract you from your swing at this 18-hole outdoor course, where playful pterodactyls and T-Rexes oversee the action.
World of Golf *Beverley Way, New Malden, Surrey KT3 4PH (020 8949 9200/ www.jurassicencounter.com).*

Paradise Island Adventure Golf

Manchester's Trafford Centre is an unlikely venue for this indoor course – an over-the-top jungle themed affair: think tiki huts, totem poles, fake rocks and plastic fantastic foliage. Kids will be spellbound.
Paradise Island Adventure Golf *The Dome, The Trafford Centre, Manchester M17 8AA (0161 202 9544/www.paradiseislandgolf.com).*

Pirate Island Adventure Golf

Special effects abound at this glossy golf adventure. As you putt your way around 18 holes, you'll encounter an erupting volcano, a giant skull and a pirate galleon.
Codona's Amusement Park *Beach Boulevard, Aberdeen AB24 5NS (01224 595910/ www.codonas.com).*

Planet Hastings Crazy Golf

If you're after no-frills crazy golfing thrills, this one's a winner. There are no fibreglass frivolities, but tricky angles and unexpected undulations ensure its 18 holes are addictive.
Planet Hastings Crazy Golf *White Rock Gardens, St Leonards-on-Sea, East Sussex TN34 1LD (www.phcgc.com).*

Rylstone Gardens Crazy Golf

The flower-planted crazy golf course at Rylstone Gardens exudes old-fashioned charm. After tackling the course, adjourn to the tea rooms or wander by the bandstand to see if Shanklin's brass band is in residence.
Rylstone Gardens *Shanklin, Isle of Wight PO37 6RG.*

Sandbanks Crazy Golf Course

Deep in the heart of millionaires' mile, this mini-golf course has the spiralling Whirlygig and exasperating On the Piste, both of which demand precision putting. If you're determined to win, there are insider tips on tackling each hole on the website.
Sandbanks Crazy Golf Course *Sandbanks, Poole, Dorset BH13 7QD (01202 706561/ www.sandbankscrazygolf.com).*

Strokes Adventure Golf

Dotted with water features and palm trees, this floodlit 18-hole course is one where would-be champs can practise – it's twice hosted the British Open Championships.
Strokes Adventure Golf *Westbrook Promenade, Westbrook, Margate, Kent CT9 5BJ (01843 294970/www.strokesadventuregolf.com).*

Treasure Island

The 18-hole course at this pirate-themed park has testing bridges and tunnels. Then there's all the fun of Long John Silver's ship, with its zip slide and walkways.
Treasure Island *Royal Parade, Eastbourne, East Sussex BN22 7AA (01323 411077/ www.treasure-island.info).*

780 See art in the sand

Rookie sandcastle builders can pick up tips at the UK National Sandcastle Competition, held on the glorious sandy expanses of Woolacombe beach in North Devon every July. On each 7sq m plot, teams of six have three hours to transform a pile of sand into a finely crafted sculpture. Spider-Man, enchanted woods, polar bears, dolphins, space ships and giant turtles emerge as teams mould, sculpt, smooth and paint their designs, before the guest judges make their final decisions. Cost of entry is £75 per team, which goes to the North Devon Hospice. Spectators enjoy the sculptures, bands, face painting and general fun and games that accompany the event. With two miles of beach to play on, those inspired by what they see can get creative in the sand for free.

Woolacombe Bay *Woolacombe, Devon EX34 7BG (www.northdevonhospice.org.uk).*

781 Shop by torchlight in Bermondsey Market

When the old Caledonian Antiques Market moved to Bermondsey Square in 1948, it took advantage of a medieval *marché ouvert* decree, which meant it was legal to sell dodgy goods during the hours of darkness. A weekly carte blanche was big news for thieves and fences, and it was nearly 50 years before Mrs Thatcher put an end to the shenanigans. Starting around 6am every Friday morning in the redeveloped square, you can still snatch a bargain by torchlight, though many dealers are on their way with their pickings earlier than that. Stalls are piled with useless riches – tarnished silver cutlery, Victorian china chamber pots, chandeliers and brooches. It's an adventure as much as a shopping trip, delving into south London's backstreets before rush hour, but rest assured you'll soon be bantering and bartering for treasures you never knew you needed. A World War II entrenching tool. Spectacles on a stick. Stuffed blackbird going cheap, guv?

782

Brush up your bushcraft

There's not a lot of wilderness left in the UK, but the Cairngorms National Park is wild and woolly enough (and sometimes arctic enough) to be the setting for the unique and exciting Bushcraft Ventures (01339 886855, www.bushcraftventures.co.uk). Run by a team of extremely rugged folk, including qualified bushcraft instructor Lawrence Clark, erstwhile apprentice to Ray Mears, BV runs a variety of bushcraft courses for family groups and children. As well as being lots of fun, the courses teach you how to be resourceful in the wild: building fires to cook your dinner, working with knives (in the whittling, skinning sense), tracking animals and identifying wildlife are all on the agenda. The courses include a meal around the open fire and accommodation in the National Park. The courses are open to accompanied children over five, and cost from £140.

783

Be a Young Gun

The rolling countryside around the Surrey Hills makes for perfect mountain biking terrain. Long, winding trails weave through the woodland, and there's a tempting series of gentle descents around Pitch Hill, Holmsbury and Leith Hill (the highest point in the South-east). It's a designated area of outstanding natural beauty, so there are splendid views to be appreciated while you pause to catch your breath and rest your weary pedalling legs.

Mountain Bike Guiding (07976 353963, www.mountain-bike-guiding.co.uk) run four-hour Young Guns training sessions for eight to 16s, with core skills, confidence-building and a chance to put their newly acquired skills to the test on the tracks. At £45 a go it's somewhat pricey, but it's a great way to get kids' ability up to speed if you want to do any serious biking as a family. Courses run in the holidays and on selected weekends.

784

Be spooked by a garden...

The locked gates at Alnwick's Garden carry a warning: a plaque bearing a skull and crossbones, and the words 'These plants can kill'. It's spine-chilling stuff for kids; who knew botanicals could be so beastly? Guides lead visitors around the flame-shaped flowerbeds, telling stories about each plant's sinister properties and the legends that surround it. Belladonna, mandrake, hemlock and strychnine are among the inmates. Once you've looked round (no touching, mind), escape to the treehouse tea room or Bamboo Labyrinth.

Alnwick Garden *Denwick Lane, Alnwick, Northumberland NE66 1YU (01665 511350/ www.alnwickgarden.com).*

785

...or pleasantly surprised

Don't be startled if you hear the odd shriek coming from behind a high yew hedge in the eastern corner of Burghley's deer park. Behind it, through an elegant wrought-iron gate, are the Gardens of Surprise. Children love the mirrored maze and moss house and getting soaked in the water jets, watched over by busts of Roman emperors; keep a close eye on them, because they may have a surprise in store too.

Burghley *Stamford, Lincolnshire PE9 3JY (01780 752451/www.burghley.co.uk).*

786 Crawl into a chamber of secrets

From a distance, it looks like a mere hummock in the hillside – but Stoney Littleton Long Barrow in Somerset is one of the country's finest Neolithic tombs. Kids love crawling through the gloomy entrance to the burial chambers; bring a torch, and prepare to get muddy. Back in the fresh air, see who can spot the giant ammonite on the tomb's exterior. More details on www.english-heritage.org.uk.

787-789

Take one jar...

...for research purposes

A jar with a screwtop lid (with air holes punctured in it) makes an excellent temporary viewing container for young entomologists. Put a thin layer of soil in the bottom, a few leaves, then gather your bugs, grubs, ants, worms or caterpillars and watch them in the jar, making notes and drawings. Please release them exactly where you found them after an hour or so.

...for jolly gift ideas

Decorate your jar with glue, glitter, stickers, dried flowers, ribbons, glass paint, sparkly pipe cleaners and more, then fill it with pretty antique buttons, dried fruit and nuts or sweets for a one-of-a-kind handmade gift.

...for decorative effect

Make a snowglobe by glueing a simple scene into the lid of a round-shaped jar – a tiny penguin or a Santa Claus if you're making a Christmas scene. Let the glue dry, then fill the jar up to its neck with water, adding a couple of spoonfuls of silver or gold glitter. Screw the lid on very tightly. Turn the jar upside down, and give it a shake to make it snow.

You can be more adventurous by turning your jar into a lava lamp. Fill the jar three-quarters full with water, add a few drops of food colouring, then top up the water with vegetable oil. Let the oil and water settle, then add a teaspoonful of salt, which will make the oil gloop about. Adding more salt makes the oil move again. Set a torch behind your jar to get the full lava lamp effect.

790 Frame your family

If you go to car boot sales and charity shops you can pick up picture frames for next-to-nothing. Clean and decorate the frame, polish the glass and insert your own picture or photograph. Those of people are best. You can create a family gallery in this way.

791
Make a paper aeroplane

Step 1
Take an A4 sheet of paper, fold in half lengthways, then open it out again.

Step 2
Fold the two top corners to the centre line to make a triangle shape at the top.

Step 3
Fold this top triangle over so that the paper turns into a square shape.

Step 4
From this square, fold in the top corners again, letting their points touch at the centre line, leaving a slim triangle in the middle.

Step 5
There's a tiny triangle shape poking out at the bottom of the two folded-in corners: fold that up and over the corners.

Step 6
Now fold along the centre line again, making sure the tiny triangle is on the underside of the plane, making this shape.

Step 7
Make a diagonal fold from the 'nose' of this shape along to the back, about 2cm away from the top corner, as shown. Do this on both sides, trying to make your wings equal.

Step 8
Now open the plane slightly and fold a small triangle shape into the nose, tucking it in between the wings. This acts as a slight weight and stabiliser.

Step 9
And now you're ready to make that plane fly.

792

Visit the Berkshire tropics
Totally tropical, whatever the weather, the Living Rainforest (01635 202444, www.theliving rainforest.org.uk), contained within two enormous glasshouses just outside Newbury, is a steamy home to snakes – such as this emerald tree boa – as well as bird-eating spiders, monkeys, a dwarf crocodile called Courtney and free-flying exotic birds and bejewelled butterflies. There's also a giant Amazon waterlily; it once grew a great platter-like leaf with a spread of 2.5 metres, before it was decimated by a fugitive colony of leaf-cutting ants.

793 Have a creative Sunday afternoon

The Design Museum's year-round creative workshops for five- to 11-year-olds are legendary. They're led by a team of visiting designers and held in the handsome, child-friendly riverside studio. The theme changes monthly, depending on current exhibitions, so the discipline covered might be architecture, fashion or interior design, but they always offer children top-notch materials, excellent tuition from industry professionals and the chance to make something really special to take home. Booking is essential.
Design Museum *Shad Thames, London SE1 2YD (020 7403 6933/www.designmuseum.org).*

794 Mark the Martyrs

At the end of July every year, a festival to celebrate the lives and achievement of the Tolpuddle Martyrs takes place in the Dorset village that bears their name. The six farm labourers' crime was to dare to form a trade union; their sentence, deportation to the harsh penal colonies of Australia. After a huge public outcry, their sentences were rescinded and the trades union movement was born. The festival welcomes children for storytelling events, music workshops, fancy-dress parties and instructions on how to strike. For details, visit www.tolpuddlemartyrs.org.uk.

795 Translate poetry

Work out what a foreign-language poem is saying in English, and you can enter the annual Stephen Spender poetry translation prize (www.stephen-spender.org). Yes, you can use dictionaries. The poem can be any length and from any language. There are under-15 and under-19 categories, and the current holder of the former won with her version of a Spanish poem a good GCSE candidate could understand. There are book tokens to be won.

796 Peep behind the privy at Boscobel...

Children visiting Boscobel House in Staffordshire are invited to climb inside the priest-hole behind the toilet on the first floor. A priest-hole is the ultimate hide-and-seek cranny; a tiny space used in times of religious persecution for concealing priests. The stink from the toilet (fortunately, no longer in use) would have foiled the sniffer dogs.

A second priest-hole, hidden behind some panelling in the attic, once sheltered royalty. After his defeat at Worcester in 1651, Charles II hid here from Cromwell's Roundheads, spending his first night hidden in an oak tree and his second in the priest-hole; in the gardens, a descendant of the original oak still stands on the spot the wounded king took refuge.
Boscobel House *Boscobel Lane, Bishops Wood, Staffordshire ST19 9AR (01902 850244/ www.english-heritage.org.uk).*

797 ...then see another smelly hideway

For their occupants to evade capture, priest-holes had to be ingeniously disguised. The stakes were high: discovery could mean death and torture for the priests, and serious punishment for the families who had sheltered them. At Baddesley Clinton (Rising Lane, Baddesley Clinton, Warwickshire B93 0DQ, 01564 783294, www.nationaltrust.org.uk), there are three hidey-holes, two of which you can peer into. The first is in the moat room; you can't crawl inside, but there's a mocked-up priest-hole for children to try for size. The second, built into a drain, is even grimmer; as well as the cold and damp, the priests had to contend with foul-smelling sewage and waste.

Still, anything was better than discovery. Found hidden in one of his own hides at Coughton Court (Alcester, Warwickshire B49 5JA, 01789 400777, www.coughtoncourt.co.uk), priest-hole builder extraordinaire Nicholas Owen was taken to the Tower of London, and tortured on the rack until his stomach burst; the Catholic Church later made him a saint.

798 *Revel in your youth at Underage*

No parents, or guardians, or non-teens are allowed at Underage, the world's first 'credible' music festival for ages 14 to 19. The day belongs to youth, and it all kicks off on an August Sunday at east London's Victoria Park. If parents are alarmed at the idea of thousands of teenagers rocking out unsupervised, the website (www.underagefestivals.com) has a parents' page to set minds at rest. Note there are no beer tents at Underage – soft drinks and food only. Tickets are £23 plus booking fee.

Bruce Jones, a 16-year-old veteran, has this to say about Underage: 'If you're looking for a one-day music festival, this is the best option by a country mile. The standard of music is exceptional and the food isn't too bad either; pizza, chips, samosas, tapas, the works! The bands that play there are almost all relatively high on the fame scale. In 2008, for example, there were the Gallows, the Maccabees, Foals and Dizzee Rascal to name a few, accompanied by groups that will be on everyone's lips within the next few years.

'If you get bored with the food and music, there are plenty of other attractions: a double-decker bus full of places to show off your skills with a spray can, or a musical workshop led by John and Mary, two Ghanaians who demonstrated how to play the bongo drums. Next to that was a chill-out zone – an idea that has never really appealed to me, but on this occasion the beanbags and relaxing music drew me in like a moth to a flame. There's also a station within this zone where you write various things on colourful circular stickers and attach them to a wall.'

Underage

799 Start wobbling at the lights

No prizes for guessing the ingredients for traffic light jelly: three packs of jelly, in red, orange and green. Make the red jelly according to the instructions, and pour it into a large bowl to set. Add the orange jelly and, once that's set, the green – so when you turn the jelly out of the bowl, the red will be at the top. Up the treat factor by arranging some foil-wrapped chocolate cars around your masterpiece.

800 See a very quiet show

Now in its fourth decade, the annual London International Mime Festival (020 7637 5661, www.mimefest.co.uk) runs for two weeks every January. It invites companies from around the UK and abroad to perform circus skills, mask, mime, clown and theatre shows for audiences of all ages.

801 Earn your spurs in the Wild West

In the south-western tip of the Isle of Wight, Blackgang Chine fantasy park clings to a gaunt ravine; indeed, the further reaches of its rambling garden look as if they might drop on to the naturist beach below. It opened in 1843 as fashionable pleasure gardens for Victorian holidaymakers; since then, all manner of rides, attractions and wonders have mushroomed across the site. Smuggling, pirates, fairy tales, wizards, myths and legends are all honoured with a ride or sideshow. Many have a whiff of nostalgia about them – not least Frontier Land, a Wild West cowboy town with its own saloon bar, grocery store, railroad station and nearby native American encampment, peopled by slightly alarming life-size models. Parents tend to sit about supping tea while children rush around playing cowboys and injuns and firing cap guns; there's panning for gold too.
Blackgang Chine *Chale, Isle of Wight PO38 2HN (01983 730052/www.blackgangchine.com).*

802

Go on a snorkel safari

The shallow waters at Kimmeridge Bay in Dorset are perfect for snorkelling. From May to September, a 400-metre snorkelling trail leads you through a range of habitats, where you can peek at iridescent blue-green seaweed, spider crabs, sea anenomes, barnacles and blennies. Reaching a maximum depth of 3.5 metres on high spring tides, it's ideal for beginners and (accompanied) children. Bring your own snorkelling gear or hire it for a fiver – plus £20 deposit – from the Marine Information Centre, which also sells fish-friendly crabbing lines for a reasonable £1.50. **Purbeck Marine Wildlife Reserve** *Kimmeridge, Wareham, Dorset BH20 5PF (01929 481044/ www.dorsetwildlife.co.uk).*

803

Test your soil for signs of life

Garden soil is full of living things: insects, worms, grubs, fungi and bacteria. To see how alive your soil is, take a trowel of earth, a funnel, a large jar and a torch. Place the funnel on top of the jar, then pop your soil sample into the funnel. Shine your torch over the soil and see what drops into the jar (creatures will try to escape the light and move downwards). Examine your haul, then put the soil and creatures back into the garden.

804

Watch supermen wrestle and run

Grasmere's historic Sports Day (www.grasmere sportsandshow.co.uk) takes place on the last Sunday in August. It's a highly energetic event, involving Cumberland wrestling, hound trails and the Fell Race, in which musclebound men (whose bulging sinews look like reinforced steel cable) run straight up the fellside in their vests. Then there are the gun and sheepdog displays, junior races, mountain bike dashes and a tug of war. Beer tents abound for adult refreshment.

805

Take Britain's most audacious train ride

Pioneering Victorian engineer Isambard Kingdom Brunel famously claimed that 'Nothing is impossible for an engineer' – and when he was asked to build the South Devon Railway, he avoided the obvious route. Instead of tunnelling through the hills inland, Brunel decided to run the tracks beside the sea. The most thrilling stretch is the six kilometres along the purpose-built Dawlish Sea Wall, which runs right over the beach. In good weather, you feel as if you're skimming the waves; on wild and windy days, the sea can rear above the wall and threatens to swallow the train whole. It's a miracle that the route has survived this long – though during particularly fierce gales, services are suspended (0845 700 0125, www.firstgreatwestern.co.uk).

806

Learn Bronze Age culinary skills

In the 1980s, an enormous 3,500-year-old monument, used by the Celtic fen people as a place of worship and ritual, was discovered at Flag Fen, its timbers perfectly preserved in the Peterborough mud. The site has now grown into an archaeology park, taking visitors back to the Bronze Age in style with its Celtic roundhouses, farmsteads and gardens. During the school holidays, volunteers run workshops in weaving, flint-knapping and charcoal drawing, but the foodie activities are the most fascinating.

Children might be introduced to the culinary and medical uses of various herbs, grown in the Roman gardens, or shown how grain was ground on a quernstone. Soay lamb, bred on site, is sometimes cooked over an open fire in a suitably Bronze Age-style receptacle. Visitors can assist both with preparing, and tasting, when the time is right. Check the website for details of the next cook-up, and look out for the Flag Fen Food & Drink festival, held in August. **Flag Fen** *The Droveway, Northey Road, Peterborough PE6 7QJ (01733 313414/ www.flagfen.com).*

807
See the birdmen take flight

Each year, plucky contestants at the Birdman competition (www.birdman.org.uk) hurl themselves into the sea from a great height, hoping that their home-made flying machines will achieve lift-off. There's a £30,000 prize for the furthest flight over 100 metres – though to date, the record stands at 89.2 metres. Some competitors dress up as penguins or giant bugs, others build elaborate winged contraptions; whatever the design, everyone ends in the waves with a mouthful of seawater. The event takes place in Bognor or at Worthing in Sussex.

808
Roll with it

If you can tell your agates from your oxbloods and your cat's eyes from your peewees, visit what is reputed to be the largest collection of marbles in the world at the House of Marbles. This factory, museum and shop on the edge of Dartmoor is dedicated to traditional games and glass. The Marble Museum has marbles of all sizes and ages, from medieval to modern. Fine marble runs include the gigantic Snooki, the largest in Britain, with marbles the size of a fist. Buy marbles, games, toys and puzzles in the shop; children's hands and feet can be cast in glass at the factory. Entry is free.

Marble Museum *The Old Pottery, Pottery Road, Bovey Tracey, Devon TQ13 9DS (01626 835 285/ www.houseofmarbles.com).*

809
Ride the wheel

Lucky under-fives go free on the London Eye (0870 990 8883, www.londoneye.com), though you'll need to fork out for the rest of the family. It's worth it, though, as you make the magical 135-metre ascent. Progress is stately, giving you plenty of time to spot London's landmarks. Views stretch for 40 kilometres on a clear day – as far as Windsor Castle, if your eyes are sharp.

810-814
Dough try this at home

You don't have to buy playdough from the shops; just follow the recipe. We've used a cup as a measure. It doesn't matter whether it's a teacup or a mug, as long as the ingredients are mixed in the correct proportions.

Basic dough

Use half a cup of salt to one-and-a-half cups of plain flour, mixing it with water until a decent dough consistency is achieved. Get modelling.

Glittery colourful dough

Make up the basic dough recipe, then add glitter and food colouring as you roll it to make pretty decorative models.

Scented dough

Make up the basic dough recipe, then add a few drops of vanilla, peppermint, almond, lemon or rose essence.

Baked dough

Use one cup of salt to one quarter of a cup of water. Mix together in a saucepan. Stir over the heat until the mixture bubbles, then remove from the stove and add one cup of cornflour and another half-cup of water. Knead well. You can use this dough to make models or jewellery. Create beads by rolling the dough into small balls, then push a cocktail stick through each ball to make a small hole. Leave them to air-dry or bake in a slow oven. When they're hard, paint and string them, and wear your handiwork as a necklace.

Edible dough

This fudgy, chocolatey dough tastes nice in small doses (it's really sweet). Take one cup of cornflour, two cups of icing sugar, six tablespoons of cocoa, three-quarters of a cup of milk powder, half a cup of liquid glucose or golden syrup, one teaspoon of vanilla essence and 100g of butter (at room temperature). Mix all the ingredients into a dough using your fingers, adding a drop of water if it seems too dry. Make your models with clean hands if you plan to tuck into them later.

815-818
Go fly a kite

Come summer, kite festivals across the country fill the skies with high-flying beauties – from classic, single-line diamonds to spectacular stunt kites. In June, check out the action at Blackheath Common in London: past festivals have brought delicate, dragon-shaped Chinese paper kites, synchronised kite-flying displays and Japanese fighter kite demonstrations. Bristol's International Kite Festival, held in late summer, is an equally colourful shindig, with all manner of large-scale kites and inflatables: nine-metre giant monkeys and mermaids swoop overhead, while at ground level there are kids' kite-making workshops and daredevil stunts from power kiting pro-riders. Britain's windswept shores are also ideal for kiting: in early summer, Weymouth's kite festival is a classic, while the season generally close with daring displays over the waves down in Margate.

For details of these and other festivals across the country, contact the Kite Society (01206 271489, www.thekitesociety.org.uk).

819 *Learn to sign*

In Sign Language, you use your hands, face and body to communicate. One hand, usually the right, is primary, the other secondary. A single wave with the primary hand means hello, while closing the same hand is goodbye. A gesture as if pinging one's braces with both hands means 'How are you?' Hold a two-fingered pistol to your head, turn it into a scout salute, waggle a single finger, point at someone and you have 'What's your name?' Fan your face with both hands, fingers outspread, then thumb a lift with the primary hand and you can say 'Lovely weather for the time of year.'

Some sign language 'words' have transferred into ordinary conversation: for example, 'Would you like a drink?' is signed by holding an imaginary glass to the lips and tipping it back. To say that you would like a Coca-Cola, make a letter 'C' with your primary thumb and finger and move it to the right as if there were two of them. For water, strangely, you must pretend, to take a cigarette from your mouth with thumb and forefinger. What's a cigarette? Ask your parents.

International Kite Festival, Bristol

820 Go foraging for Christmas decorations

Fairylights and tinsel are lovely, of course, but there's much to be said for the natural look when it comes to decorating the house for Christmas. It's easy to do. From autumn onward, every time you go on a country walk, or to the park, pick up decorative bits and bobs. Look out for fir cones (these can be left as they are, or painted or touched up with glitter), twigs of berried shrubs (rosehips, hawthorn, the winter heads of hydrangea and honesty and cotoneaster all look pretty), teazles, interestingly shaped pieces of wood or bark and tangly twigs that can be painted with gold paint. Your spoils can be artistically grouped and used for table arrangements or on the mantelpiece in a big vase. A shallow glass bowl filled with fir cones, tangerines, cinnamon sticks and glass baubles looks really good. Experiment with different rustic arrangements, and don't forget to bring in plenty of holly (and other evergreens such as ivy, bay and conifer) with which to deck the halls.

821-822

Make your first movie

Feel you may possess Spielberg-like stirrings of cinematic genius? Enrol on a film-making course at west London's Young Film Academy (20 Fitzroy Square, W1T 6EJ, 020 7387 4341, www.youngfilmacademy.co.uk). Aimed at seven- to 16-year-olds, the tutored courses last from one to four days and involve participants in all aspects of film-making, from writing and acting to shooting and editing. They're taught by industry pros.

London-based fledgling film-makers might also enjoy the holiday courses, workshops, animation days and backstage BBC visits offered by Film Steps (0870 024 2522, www. filmsteps.com). Two-day animation courses create two-minute films using stop-motion techniques with the help of a professional animator. Film-making courses for seven- to 16-year-olds last up to four days and conclude with a red-carpet screening.

823-827

Take a ferry 'cross...

...the Mersey

Old-timers will know the song, while their children will just enjoy coming along for the ride. You pay £1.40, hop on board and admire the Liverpool cityscape. The ferry takes about ten minutes to cross between Seacombe on the Wirral and Pier Head in the city (0151 330 1444, www.merseyferries.co.uk) – just long enough to teach that famous song by Gerry and the Pacemakers to the kids.

...the Thames

Here's a great London river trip for cheapskates. The free Woolwich ferry (020 8921 5965, www.greenwich.gov.uk) runs every ten minutes between the terminal, just near the Woolwich Waterfront leisure centre on the south bank over to the north shore.

...Bristol Harbour

The inexpensive Bristol Ferry (from £1.10 single) gives you an eyeful of this fine old city's maritime sights – so works well as both a commuter ferry and a tourist attraction. Bristol Ferries also runs longer trips out and about on the Severn Estuary (0117 927 3416, www.bristolferry.com). The popular Gorgeous Gorge trip takes you under the Clifton Suspension Bridge to Pill and Avonmouth, passing dramatic scenery along the way.

...Langstone Harbour

The shortest ferry ride on our list, with tickets priced at £2.50 for adults, the historic Hayling Island Ferry (02392 482868, www.hayling ferry.com) is a jolly jaunt across Langstone Harbour from Portsmouth to Hayling Island (www.hayling.co.uk), which is a delightful beachside resort, and the home of windsurfing. There's a modern road bridge if you'd rather take a car full of beach gear across.

...Poole Harbour

A fleet of yellow-painted ferries plies the route between Poole Harbour and Brownsea Island (01929 462383, www.brownseaislandferries.com), with family tickets for the round trip from £14. Pack a picnic, then spend the afternoon spotting sika deer, woodpeckers and red squirrels.

828 *Feed a lamb*

Come to Seven Sisters at 11.30am or 3.30pm in the Easter or summer holidays to feed lambs with a bottle. Terry Wigmore's flock is made up of more than 40 British breeds, and his farm's visitors' centre is set in a pair of old barns in East Dean, Sussex. The farm is open from March to the beginning of May, and from July to September. Added attractions include shearing, wool spinning and weaving demonstrations, ewe-feeding and tractor rides. **Seven Sisters Sheep Centre** *Gilberts Drive, East Dean, East Sussex BN20 0AA (01323 123302/www.sheepcentre.co.uk).*

829 *Travel across an aqueduct*

Designed by Thomas Telford and opened in 1805, the Pontcysyllte Aqueduct soars above the River Dee in North Wales. Despite being over 36 metres high, it's only three metres wide. Crossing by narrowboat, it feels as if you're flying; all that stands between you and a dizzying drop is the low cast-iron lip that holds the water in. Walking across on the towpath offers the same vertiginous views. The experience is even scarier when you read the aqueduct's history: the mortar holding it together is made from ox blood, lime and water, while the joints were caulked with a mixture of flannel, lead and boiling sugar. For more information, visit www.waterscape.com.

830 *Orienteer!*

Orienteering involves following a map to find your way around an outdoor course, completing it in the fastest possible time. You don't need to be brilliant at sport; smart route planning and navigational skills pay dividends. Events for all ages occur across the country, and there are permanent courses you can sample any time; see www.britishorienteering.org.uk.

831-833 *Pitch camp*

Sausages sizzling on a stove; toes stubbed on tents pegs with much muffled swearing; waking in a heap thanks to an evil-sloping pitch: of these things are family memories made.

For proper old-fashioned camping, pitch your tent amid the trees at Burnbake (Rempstone, Corfe Castle, Wareham, Dorset BH20 5JH, 01929 480570). The site has slides and tyre swings, but there's a far better playground just around the corner – Studland's glorious beach.

Stubcroft Farm in Sussex (Stubcroft Lane, East Wittering, PO20 8PJ, 01243 671469 www.stubcroft.com) is another beauty, well within reach of the beach. It's an eco-friendly affair, with recycling bins and six eco loos. When the kids weary of cooing over the lambs and spotting wildlife in the hedgerows, walk to the sheltered sands at West Wittering, or hire bikes and explore.

Those with traumatic memories of collapsing canvas should consider a tipi instead of a tent. Shelters Unlimited (Rhiw'r Gwreiddyn, Ceinws, Machynlleth, Powys SY20 9EX, 01654 761720, www.tipis.co.uk) has two types: basic models or furnished with futons and blankets, set on a peaceful hillside. Each tipi has an open fireplace at its centre, keeping the interior wonderfully snug.

Shelters Unlimited

834 *Take the high way*

If you're over ten and have a good head for heights, you can experience the thrills of this extensive high-ropes course in Norfolk. The wood where it's set has some of the highest trees in eastern England; signs give details of the species you're swinging through. Participants can clamber up rope ladders, teeter on high walkways and whizz down a 300-metre zip wire. A smaller walkway and tyre swings area is set up for under-tens, while sedentary adults can retreat to the picnic pavilion, where a log fire crackles in chilly weather.

Extreeme Adventure *High House, Weasenham All Saints, King's Lynn, Norfolk PE32 2SP (01328 838720/www.extreemeadventure.co.uk).*

835 *Kip on a ship*

Experience life on the ocean wave without leaving dry dock with a Golden Hinde Living History Experience. Children aged between six and 12 must bring an adult to act as a 'tall sailor' when they stay overnight on this replica of Sir Francis Drake's square-rigged ship, moored next to the Thames in London. It costs £39.95 per person to stay from 5pm to 10am the next morning. All you require is a sleeping bag; period clothes, sea shanties, stories and grub (we have it on good authority that it's not hard tack and watery rum) are provided. Birthday boys and girls might also like to have their party on board – we're not sure, however, if walking the plank is an acceptable party game.

The Golden Hinde *St Marie Overie Dock, Cathedral Street, London SE1 9DE (0870 011 8700/www.goldenhinde.org).*

Extreeme Adventure

836
Hatch some butterflies

With a bit of luck, you can see the very hungry caterpillar story unfold before your eyes. If you want to do it on the cheap, you must look for butterfly food plants, such as cabbages, nettles and nasturtiums. You can either collect leaves that have eggs on, or kidnap any caterpillars that might be munching their way through the leaves. Place the leaves in a wide-mouthed jar, along with your eggs or caterpillars, then cover it with muslin or a well-punctured lid. Don't put too many caterpillars in one container; two or three is fine.

Be sure to have easy access to the food leaves, as the caterpillars get through a lot. Place a damp paper towel in the container and keep it clean of frass (insect droppings). As the caterpillars grow, which takes two to four weeks, place some twigs in the container for the pupation stage. After that, wait for about a week until your butterfly emerges, at which stage release it into the garden and wave it a fond farewell.

Alternatively, buy a butterfly kit online from Green Gardeners (www.greengardener. co.uk), which gives you a mesh garden, five caterpillars and everything else you need to keep them alive.

837
See reindeer roam

The Cairngorms National Park (01479 873535, www.cairngorms.co.uk) is utterly unlike anywhere else in the country. Its sprawling terrain ranges from arctic mountains – it has four of Scotland's highest peaks – and age-old granite hills to primeval forest. This dramatic landscape includes a rare type of pinewood seen only in Norway and Scotland, and heather moorland. It's home to an incredible 25 per cent of the UK's endangered bird, animal and plant species, including golden eagles, ospreys, otters and pine martins. Non-native species also live here; if you're lucky, you might spot the free-roaming reindeer herd, whose ancestors moved here from Lapland in 1952.

838
Make bones about it

Old Sarum, the remains of an Iron Age hill fort in Wiltshire, is the venue for the Festival of British Archaeology, which takes place in the summer holidays (01722 334956, www.english-heritage.org.uk). It's a hands-on spectacular, and part of the fun occasionally involves making shapes and skeletons with assorted old bones.

Even if you can't make it along to the festival, we reckon it's possible to make skeletal reconstructions at any time of year; there are enough old bones lying around, particularly at the seaside, to create the most fanciful monsters. First, amass a collection. It is quite important, of course, to pick up bones that have been scoured and bleached by time and tide. Do avoid bones that still have flesh on. Then arrange them on the ground as if you had just lifted them from an archaeological site. You can go further if you're handy with a skewer or bradawl, and carefully pierce holes in each bone so as to join them with knotted pieces of string. Wrap the skeleton in cling-film. Now wash your hands.

839
Visit Jersey's wartime tunnels

Take thick jumpers if you're visiting Jersey's War Tunnels – a series of subterranean passages and rooms that are chilling in more ways than one. Displays in the Captive Island exhibition explain how German troops occupied the island during World War II, and what life was like for the islanders. You'll also learn about the appalling conditions endured by the prisoners who built the tunnels; mostly Russians, they were seen by the Germans as *untermenschen* (sub-humans), and treated like slaves. The tunnels make for a vivid, albeit disturbing, snapshot of history; after your visit, take a moment to sit in the Garden of Reflection, whose plaques commemorate islanders who died during the conflict.

Jersey War Tunnels *Les Charrieres Malorey, St Lawrence, Jersey JE3 1FU (01534 860808/ www.jerseywartunnels.com).*

Litte green fingers

Allotmenteer Kate Fuscoe *praises the community veg patch.*

Allotmenteering has become the height of chic in these credit-crunched times, up there with camping and being creative with leftovers. Increasing numbers of families are donning wellies (flowery Boden ones, by preference) and getting down 'n' dirty. With all the benefits of growing your own organic veg and getting a workout at the same time, what's not to like?

Children, with their destructive tendencies, may at first be eyed with suspicion by older allotment holders. But careful rule setting means they may be treated to 'sweeties' (aka raspberries) by an elderly neighbour and can experience the kind of freedom many adults enjoyed as kids: playing in a safe environment with lots of folk looking out for you and letting you know when you cross a boundary. One of the most unexpected pleasures of allotment holding is the chance to interact with all manner of people of all ages. The gift of advice, a few courgettes or a little chat is particularly cherished among city dwellers more used to being cold-shouldered by their neighbours.

Allotment waiting lists are getting longer, particularly in urban areas. There's much variation, though, so don't be deterred. For example, Stourbridge Grove in Cambridge had a waiting list of just ten people at the time of writing, whereas East Finchley Allotment Association had a list of hundreds. Plots are generally re-allocated in January – so get down there and get your name down, ideally at a site that's within walking distance of your home. This allows for emergency watering missions, or a spot of lettuce-picking just before tea. You may also have to transport quite a few tools. Tip: leave the football at home.

It takes commitment: in the admittedly unlikely event of a hot summer, you might need to be there every evening. Allotments are measured, rather quaintly, in 'rods'; half a plot (usually five rods) is preferable at first, as there's pressure to keep things neat and this can be hard with very small children in tow. Measuring how fast the plants grow and what helps them to flourish is tremendously exciting

for kids, particularly with speedy growers like kohl rabi or radishes. Counting seeds and measuring rows brings maths into the equation, while the more gruesome minded will enjoy learning about the goodies and baddies of the insect world. Squashing snails and picking off asparagus beetles or distributing ladybirds and worms to do their work can be absorbing.

Have a look at www.kidsgardening.com for more age-appropriate activities – or just let the kids grub about and get on with it. Mine can happily spend a couple of hours hacking down brambles and poking in the compost heap. Expect little in the way of productive work and you may be pleasantly surprised. Mini-tools are fun to use and widely available, though from the age of about five, children do love to use real tools. If your nerves aren't strong enough to contemplate steel prongs, distract them with a dibber; a clever and far less hazardous device for making seed holes.

So what's best to plant? For starters, try beans and peas: they're easy to grow and care for, as well as good to eat. Sweetcorn and sunflowers are also fun and suitably dramatic in terms of size. Potatoes are an excellent starter for ground clearance, and nothing beats the pleasure of digging up your own spuds and counting them out; the taste too is sublime. Strawberries, although spurned by many seasoned allotmenteers for their relatively poor space/yield quotient, are a must for kids. Some parents recommend giving kids their own section, though mine are happy enough to work on our plot and generally take ownership of it all – especially when it succeeds.

As well as teaching children about the importance of seasonal eating, own-grown produce can persuade fussy youngsters to be more daring at dinner time. While they may still baulk at certain veggies, leaves, shoots and roots they've grown themselves are always more attractive than the supermarket variety. 'Allotment soup' is always an option for sneaking in a multitude of goodies. Though children's interest may wane in less clement seasons, keep the approach laid-back and you won't be disappointed. Just being on the allotment is fun enough for most kids.

To find your nearest allotment, which may be run by your local authority or by an allotment association, visit www.nsalg.org.uk.

841 Watch a meteor shower

These celestial firework displays occur when the Earth's orbit takes it through the meteor stream left behind by a comet's tail. Most of the debris in this cloud trail is smaller than a grain of sand and it enters the Earth's atmosphere at high speed, vapourising and leaving a streak of light in the night sky like a firework. The Leonids is described as the king of meteor showers, because every 33 years it brings a mega storm, with hundreds of thousands of bright meteors filling the night sky around 17 November. As the next big storm is 2032, the Perseids is your best bet for a good show. This annual shower, visible from mid July, is most active between 8 and 14 August, peaking on 12 August with 60 or more meteors per hour. All you need is a clear night so you can enjoy this amazing natural display.

842

Get back to nature on Bardsey

From one end to the other, the remote island of Bardsey (www.bardsey.org) in North Wales measures just two and a half kilometres. Nonetheless, there's a remarkable amount of history crammed into its Lilliputian domains. In the Middle Ages, its monastery was famed throughout the land, and pilgrims flocked here – until the 16th century, when Henry VIII decided to dissolve all the monasteries and seize their wealth. Sinners replaced saints on the island, with lawless pirates and buccaneers muscling in on the territory.

These days, though, it's birds that find refuge here: herons, choughs, shearwaters, gannets, razorbills and shags. Day-trippers are another common species in these parts, catching the ferry across from Pwllheli or Porth Meudwy (0845 811 3655, www.enlli charter.co.uk). If you're really keen to absorb the island's tranquility, there are seven holiday houses to rent out. It's all brilliantly back-to-basics, with gas and candle lighting, 'cold running water from a mountain spring or well', and outside (chemical) loos.

843

Cheat at ice-cream making...

Chef Gary Rhodes suggests an easy way to make ice-cream in his book *Short Cut Rhodes*. Take a carton (about 425g) of ready-made custard (we prefer the fresh stuff you find in the cream department of the supermarket). Fold into this 150ml of whipped cream, add a dash of vanilla essence, then spoon it into an clean ice-cream container and freeze. Keep returning to the mixture to give it a stir so that ice crystals don't form.

844-846

...then top it

Make sauces and toppings to create a luscious sundae from your ice-cream. Pour over one of the sauces below, then sprinkle with hundreds and thousands, chocolate chips, chopped nuts or mini-marshmallows. Serve in a tall glass with some whipped cream and the odd piece of fruit to give a semblance of healthy eating.

Chocolate sauce

You need:
  50g butter
  50g soft brown sugar
  25g cocoa powder
  3tsp milk
Stir all of the above in a pan until combined and heated through, then melt in some good quality dark chocolate to make it taste more 'real'.

Raspberry sauce

Take a punnet of raspberries, wash them in a sieve, then push the fruit through the sieve into a clean bowl. Add a couple of dessertspoons of icing sugar and stir well.

Toffee sauce

Melt 40g butter and add 70g soft brown sugar and 25g of golden granulated sugar. Add three tablespoons of golden syrup. Heat slowly until the ingredients have dissolved. Take the pan off the heat, then stir in 90ml of double cream and a drop of vanilla essence.

Any sensible modern orchestra is keen to cultivate audiences of the future, and has an education department charged with devising schemes to engage the attention of the young. Many children have never even seen a musical instrument close up, so players often supervise workshops at pre-concert events.

BBC National Orchestra of Wales

The *Dr Who* orchestra presents family concerts based on its contribution to the cult TV show, as well as 'Songs from the Shows' concerts at reduced prices in the brand-new Hoddinott Hall. *Hoddinott Hall, Wales Millennium Centre, Bute Place, Cardiff CF10 5AL (0870 040 2000/ www.bbc.co.uk/wales/now).*

BBC Philharmonic, Manchester

Parents are encouraged to bring eight to 14s to evening concerts at Bridgewater Hall – first, by putting on child-friendly programmes; second, by offering reduced rate tickets; and third, by not minding if they only stay for half the show. *Bridgewater Hall, Manchester M2 3WS (0161 907 9000/www.bridgewater-hall.co.uk).*

Bournemouth Symphony Orchestra

The country's second oldest orchestra (established in 1893) operates a 'kids-for-a-quid' scheme and organises summer picnic-and-fireworks concerts. *2 Seldown Lane, Poole, Dorset BH15 1UF (01202 669925/www.bsolive.com).*

City of Birmingham Symphony Orchestra

Family concerts take place on intermittent Sundays at 3pm in Birmingham's Symphony Hall, with pre-concert workshops and meet-the-orchestra intervals. The CBSO also has Notelets concerts and workshops for pre-schoolers. *CBSO Centre, Berkley Street, Birmingham B1 2LF (box office 0121 780 3333/ 0121 767 4050/www.cbso.co.uk).*

Hallé Orchestra, Manchester

The nation's oldest orchestra runs a children's choir for eight- to 13-year-olds. All that's required is that participants should have some experience of singing, and enjoy a challenge. Singers may eventually graduate to the Hallé Youth Choir, which takes part in many of the orchestra's prestigious concert series. *Bridgewater Hall, Manchester M1 5HA (0161 237 7000/www.halle.co.uk).*

London Symphony Orchestra

Quarterly Family Discovery Concerts take place in the afternoons, with colouring-in and instrument-playing workshops in the morning. The orchestra also runs the St Luke's Youth Choir for over-eights who live or go to school in the City, Islington or Hackney, with term-time rehearsals one evening a week under conductor Gareth Malone. *Barbican Centre, Silk Street, London EC2Y 8DS (020 7638 8891/www.lso.co.uk).*

Philharmonia Orchestra, London

Occasional Family Music Days for five- to 11-year-olds begin at 10am with craft, percussion and dance sessions, before the concert begins at 11am in the Royal Festival Hall. *The South Bank Centre, Belvedere Road, London SE1 8XX (0800 652 6717/www.philharmonia.co.uk).*

Royal Liverpool Philharmonic Orchestra

Monthly 'fidgeting allowed' family concerts for four to 11s are on Saturdays at 2.30pm in the Philharmonic Hall. Past themes have ranged from 'Bugs!' to 'Music from Outer Space'. *Philharmonic Hall, Liverpool L1 9BP (0151 709 3789/www.liverpoolphil.com).*

Southbank Sinfonia, London

Saturday Spectaculars at Cadogan Hall start at 10.15am with 45 minutes of activities before an 11am concert. Musicians demonstrate their instruments, and the event finishes at noon. *Cadogan Hall, Sloane Terrace, London SW1X 9DQ (020 7730 4500/www.southbanksinfonia.co.uk).*

856 Cosy up to the mutes...

The ancestors of mute swans living the life of Riley at Abbotsbury in Dorset represented a banquet for a bunch of monks. They farmed the swans for meat at St Peter's monastery in 1040. The Dissolution did for St Peter's in 1539, but the swans stayed. There are about 600 living here, and wandering among them is a delight. Time your visit to catch a feeding session (noon and 4pm). Mid May to late June is the best season, because that's when the downy cygnets hatch. You can walk up and down the paths humming the Danny Kaye classic under your breath so as not to offend mother mutes.

Abbotsbury Swannery *New Barn Road, Abbotsbury, Dorset DT3 4JG (01305 871858/ www.abbotsbury-tourism.co.uk).*

857 ... then whoop it up with the whoopers

The whooper swan is quite a different bird to the mute swan, the most common kind you see in park ponds across the land. The whooper holds its thin neck erect, has more yellow on its beak and it emits a loud whoop-whoop sound, whereas the mute prefers a quieter honk, true to its name. Whoopers sound fantastic when they fly, as their wings make quite a din too. The best time and place to see them is from October to April in the towers of the Peter Scott Observatory at WWT Caerlaverock Wetland Centre. Wild swan feeds take place daily at 11am and 2pm. It's quite a spectacle.

WWT Caerlaverock Wetland Centre *Fastpark Farm, Caerlaverock, Dumfriesshire DG1 4RS (01387 770200/www.wwt.org.uk).*

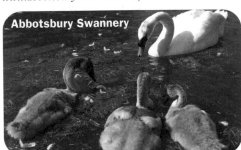

Abbotsbury Swannery

858

*Ride upside down
at Cantelowes*
*Camden's 'world class'
skate park (www.cante
lowesskatepark.co.uk) is
probably the coolest
concrete park in the land,
and certainly the most
ambitious in design. Its
witty combination of banks, street areas and bowls includes a
worrying-looking feature called a cradle, which lets skaters and
BMXers ride upside down. Hear the parents cry: 'Wear a helmet!'*

859

Make merry in the Botanics

Take a weekend wander through Edinburgh's Botanic Garden, and you might find yourself designing leaf lanterns, making a shadow puppet, creating a bug hotel from garden waste or going on a wildlife crossword treasure hunt – and most events are free. Look out for the storytelling sessions, some of which are held as part of the International Storytelling Festival. On chilly days the Victorian palm house and Rainforest Riches glasshouse, where orchids, tropical palms and pineapple plants flourish and tree frog croak, seem a sensible refuge.

Royal Botanic Garden Edinburgh *20A Inverleith Row, Edinburgh EH3 5LR (0131 552 7171/ www.rbge.org.uk).*

860

Write a secret note with invisible ink

Want to keep a message secret? Then inscribe it in invisible ink. The easiest invisible ink is lemon juice; use a cocktail stick as a nib to write your message. The acid in the lemon juice weakens the paper, so after it dries it leaves an imprint that can only be seen when heat is applied to the paper. To read the message, put the paper on a radiator, iron it or hold it briefly over a light bulb. Any mildly acidic liquid will work: try vinegar, diluted cola, milk, orange or apple juice. Prisoners of war used their own sweat or saliva, which also contain acid.

861

Patch up a puncture

Most local authorities now run classes to teach adults bike maintenance, but there are surprisingly few places for children to learn – so it's up to parents to instruct them. Older kids (14s and above) can, however, join regular Cycle Repair & Maintenance courses held by the Cycling Tourist Club (CTC, www.ctc.org. uk). The two-day courses on home bicycle maintenance deal with issues such as roadside repairs, punctures or slipped chains.

862

Show off your socks at Spinnaker Tower

Measuring 170 metres from top to bottom, Portsmouth's Spinnaker Tower dwarfs Nelson's Column. On a clear day, the views stretch all the way across the Solent to the Isle of Wight; at night the lights of Portsmouth and the south coast twinkle alluringly. Wear your best socks if you're paying a visit; if you want to walk across the dizzying glass floor on observation deck one, you have to take your shoes off. Even higher up is deck three, known as the Crow's Nest; it's out in the open air, and will take your breath away on blowy days.

Spinnaker Tower *Gunwhark Quays, Portsmouth, Hampshire PO1 3TT (023 9285 7520/ www.spinnakertower.co.uk).*

863

Have a flutter

The speed and power of racehorse and jockey as they thunder past the rails is an awesome spectacle. At most racecourses, accompanied under-16s go free, and Sundays are often family days with fairgrounds, bouncy castles and brass bands. The people-watching, the bookies taking your bets and the thoroughbreds in the parade ring and winners' enclosure is what it's all about. Find your nearest racecourse at www.britishhorseracing.com

864

See the floodgates closed

The Thames Barrier, which looks like a series of silvery fins poking up out of the river, has saved London from flooding at least 67 times. The floodgates are tested partially every month, but every September (usually on a Sunday) there's a full-scale testing, and all the gates are closed for a couple of hours. This event has become a family funday, and a great time to learn more about the barrier. To catch a piece of the action, ring the learning centre (1 Unity Way, London SE18 5NJ (020 8305 4188, www.environment-agency.gov.uk).

865 *Make cress heads*

This is a great make if you happen to enjoy egg and cress sandwiches. All you need is a packet of cress seeds, an egg, some cotton wool and water. When you next have a boiled egg, be sure to take the top off cleanly and eat every scrap inside. Once that's done, wash out the eggshell, let it dry, then use felt tips to draw a face on it. Fill it almost to the brim with cotton wool, then moisten the wool and sprinkle a layer of cress seed on its surface. Place your egg head in an egg cup on the windowsill. Make sure you keep watering the cotton wool, as it dries out quickly. After a few days, your cress will germinate. Let the seedlings grow quite tall to allow your egg head to achieve quite a 'do before you lop it off and stick it in your sandwiches.

866 *Hang out with primates*

Hugely popular since its TV exposure, Monkey World has no shortage of fans. Everyone wants to see our closest relatives monkeying around, and dense crowds around the enclosures often mean little ones have their view blocked. It pays to arrive early at this, one of Dorset's most talked-about attractions. Avoid feeding times, which really pull in the hordes, and head for a quieter area where you can observe the monkeys in greater comfort. The resident chimpanzees, orangutans, gibbons and monkeys were all rescued from various environments: laboratories, smugglers and cruel 'entertainment' acts, and they hail from all over the world. The centre also has a fabulous play area, with some challenging apparatus; it's much nicer to take a picnic to eat in the vicinity of this play area, the better to avoid the overcrowded café. The shop sells appealing posters, fridge magnets and other souvenirs – but we reckon that adopting a monkey is the most worthwhile memento of your visit.
Monkey World *Longthorns, Wareham, Dorset BH20 6HH (01929 462537/www.monkeyworld.org).*

867 *Practise your grass whistling*

Select a blade of grass. Thin blades work well, but they must have a wide, flat surface. Press one end of the blade of grass between the sides of your thumbs, up by your nails, then bend both thumbs and press them together at the base, catching the other end of the grass. Carefully straighten your thumbs to pull the blade of grass taut. Purse your lips slightly, put them right up against your thumbs and blow so that the air rushes between them and over the blade of grass. It should make a high-pitched whistling sound if you play your grass right.

868 *Hit the target with the Pandas*

The Panda Bowmen archery club (www.panda-bowmen.org.uk) flex their elbows at the West Park Leeds RFC ground at Sycamores, Bramhope, North Leeds, LS16 9JR. Their business is target shooting – all distances – and clout shooting, when you aim your arrows at a faraway flag, is a speciality. Children who want to join in with this sport are often told to go away and come back when they're 16, because this is a tricky sport to monitor at junior level. The Pandas, however, run 'Have a Go' classes for youngsters aged over ten, who can also enrol in the popular beginner courses; check the website for details. The Pandas run occasional fun shoots run throughout the year.

869 *Be the walking wounded*

The Royal Shakespeare Company's 'Gallery Active' workshops in Stratford upon Avon allow participants to taste and experiment with fake blood, create an authentic-looking black eye and wield some props that are not all they seem. Workshop leaders describe the history of stage properties, while youngsters revel in the glorious gore.
Royal Shakespeare Company *Stratford upon Avon, Warwickshire CV37 6BB (01789 403444/ www.rsc.org.uk).*

Rescue me!

Ronnie Haydon **ferrets about at Wood Green Animal Shelters.**

Here's some great news for any child who's ever pestered their parents for a pet – living with animals makes you healthier. That's according to research by health psychologist Dr June McNicholas, whose study of four- and five-year-olds found that those whose families kept pets had fewer days off sick from school. She concluded that pets may help boost a child's immune system – the theory being that early exposure to potential allergens may help prevent allergies developing in later life.

That's great ammunition for children embarking on a full-scale psychological assault on parents who are allergic to the idea of keeping pets. And here's some more. Bonding with pets makes children more responsive to the needs of others, and ultimately has a positive effect on their happiness, because they derive a great deal of emotional support from their furry friends. Allegedly.

Before such positive press sends you scurrying to the nearest pet shop, however, consider the finer points of animal husbandry.

Any animal, from a humble stick insect to a bouncing labrador puppy, needs regular care and attention. True, the former needs little more than a supply of bramble and a nursery for its copious offspring, whereas the latter needs daily walks and a deep wallet for the vets' bills, but they're both a responsibility and should never be an impulse purchase.

Marie Channer, who deals in 'small animal welfare' at Wood Green Animal Shelters' HQ at Godmanchester, Cambridgeshire (0844 248 8181, www.woodgreen.org.uk), couldn't agree more. 'Buying a pet must be a whole-family decision, and not the indulgence of what turns out to be a passing phase – with the result that the pet ends up neglected and resented.'

Marie should know, she cares for hundreds of unwanted pets – rabbits, guinea pigs and hamsters mostly. About 100 rejected rabbits are currently on the waiting list for a place in the centre's Bunnery (that's the place where bunnies are kept) and there are 30 living here at any one time, hoping to be rehomed.

Perfect pets

Tamed young, the fancy rat is a clever, characterful friend who sits charmingly on your shoulder and snuffles deliciously in your ear. Rats are best kept in same-sex pairs (many think two boys are best). Ferrets also make brilliant pets; inquisitive and intelligent, they're delightfully playful and easy to train.

If you're not convinced, how about a pair of guinea pigs? It takes time to win their trust, but perseverance pays dividends, and glossy, cuddly guineas that munch celery happily on your knee is the reward.

Dogs and cats, of course, can be a life-enhancing addition to the family, and there are any number at Wood Green Animal Shelters that would love a happy family home. The truth about cats and dogs is, however, that investing in them (and they are a huge drain on income) must be a whole-family decision – and once you have them, they have to be treated as one of the family. If the whole family is out of the house all day, or go off on holidays and short breaks a good deal, making provision for a dog (and, to a lesser extent, a cat) can be a headache.

Not a great bet

A relative newcomer to the pet scene in the UK, degus breed quickly and are spreading fast. They look like a cross between a gerbil and a chinchilla and are quick, immensely destructive and scream when crossed. They can't be tamed.

Hamsters are a classic pet, but they too can bring complications. Syrian hamsters (pet shop staples) prefer to sleep during the day – which means they'll keep you up at night with their incessant wheel-running and manic cage-bar chewing. The smaller Roborovski hamsters, sold by specialist breeders, have their downside. They're lightning fast as well as tiny, making them difficult to handle. They're also impossible to sex, so breed prodigiously.

Exotics, such as Madagascan hissing cockroaches and giant land snails, make fascinating pets for children with a feel for natural history who love observing animal behaviour. Generally, though, anything that needs a complicated vivarium and live food, and especially anything that can deliver a nasty bite (think geckos, spiders and snakes) are best left to adult experts.

Wood Green Animal Shelters were founded in London in 1924 by Miss Louisa Green, who was concerned for the welfare of homeless pets running around in the capital after World War I. Today the charity's three shelters take in more than 8,000 animals a year. The Godmanchester outpost sits in 21 hectares of farmland and has, alongside the bunnery, a cattery, paddocks, playgrounds, café and an arena for events. It's as much a grand day out for animal lovers as a refuge for the objects of their affection. The shelter is also a first stop for families that are thinking about buying a pet.

It's a far, far better thing to invest in a rescue pet than to buy an expensive unknown quantity from a pet shop. Your average rabbit will set you back £25 at a pet shop, and that's before you've bought it a hutch, never mind had it vet-checked, vaccinated and neutered. And it might not even be the rabbit you thought it was.

'We've a flemish giant in here that was sold to a family as a dwarf lop,' sighs Marie (the difference between the two breeds being about three kilos of rabbit). 'It grew too big, and they didn't want it.'

'The rabbits waiting for homes in the bunnery are vaccinated, neutered and checked by vets. They've been handled by our experts and we can help a family – especially children – learn how to handle them. It takes patience; we had a little girl who came to see us every day before she took her rescue rabbit home. She'd sit in the bunnery and let the animal get used to her, until eventually it would take food from her hand, then allow itself to be taken on to her lap.'

'Without the sort of help we at the shelter can give them, children will typically get their rabbits, guinea pigs or hamsters home, then chase or grab at them – they're so desperate to hold them,' says Marie. 'The animal nips, the child is discouraged and loses interest.'

Learning more about animal behaviour, it seems, is the key to contented pets. Did you know that guinea pigs love being in herds, for example, or that both rabbits and guineas are prey animals? 'That means that they shut down when they're injured,' explains Marie. 'They just suffer in silence.'

Such insights help people become better pet owners. It's all freely given at the shelters, so if you're warming to the idea of a four-legged addition to the family, contact Wood Green and make some small animals very happy.

Baby Loves Disco

871 *Love disco*

Once there was a mum who wanted a bit more pre-school cool for her tots. Her name was Heather, and she became the co-founder of the biggest dance craze for people still in nappies this world has ever known. Baby Loves Disco (www.babylovesdisco.co.uk), which has its roots in Philadelphia, in the States, but is now huge in this country, is an afternoon dance party for infants (six months to seven years) and their parents. Expect feelgood tracks and groovy extras like bubble machines, baskets of instruments, a chill-out room (with tents, books and puzzles), nappy-changing facilities and healthy snacks and drinks. Discos take place in clubs and halls nationwide; for details of your nearest, check the website.

872 *Make a ribbon corsage*

Take four equal lengths of two different colours and/or textures of ribbon, and four lengths of thinner ribbon. Fold each piece in half and sew along the short edges to make a loop. One by one, take each loop and place one on top of the other, moving them slightly around like a clock face to make a flower. You will find it easy to hold the flower in the centre while you're doing this. Secure the flower in place with a few running stitches pierced in the centre, to make sure you work through all the layers.

Repeat the criss-crossing with the narrower ribbon, and secure on top of your larger flower. To decorate the centre, glue bits and bobs such as plastic flowers and beads or sew on a button. Attach a safety pin to the back to make a brooch.

873

Lose the parents in Sussex...

Some children like to kick their heels without the Aged Ps slowing them down. School-holiday activity camps give them the chance to try out different sports and activities, make new friends and run wild (in controlled conditions). One of the jolliest is Sussex-based Wickedly Wonderful (0794 123 1168, www.wickedly wonderful.com), which offers treats such as jelly fights and beachside campfires, as well as watersports, riding, climbing and other ways and means of exhausting the heck out of the kids before handing them back to their parents. The three kinds of camps – multi-activity, pony and sailing – run from Mondays to Fridays.

874-875

...and elsewhere

Many holiday activity centres have a mostly sporty and outdoorsy nature, like Somerset's Mill on the Brue (01749 812307, www.millon thebrue.co.uk), a farm-based centre that offers canoeing and other river-based tomfoolery, as well as archery, climbing, camping and woodland crafts. Others provide more cerebral activities such as film-making and language learning alongside the sports. PGL (08700 551551, www.pgl.co.uk) has sites up and down the land, from the Little Canada centre on the Isle of Wight to the forest centre on the River Tay in Perthshire. It also runs driving courses for little petrolheads who can't wait until they're old enough for their provisional licence.

Wickedly Wonderful

876-883 *Cling to a climbing wall*

Less fearful than lily-livered grown-ups, kids make great climbers. Indoor climbing centres across the country run lessons and taster sessions; visit www.thebmc.co.uk for details.

The Castle, London

With its striking towers and turrets, the Castle started life as a Victorian water pumping station. These days it's devoted to the noble art of climbing, with some superbly high walls and gravity-defying overhangs. The website has details of the two kids' climbing clubs that operate in the centre, open to children aged nine and above. Be warned that the clubs and classes here are extremely popular, so you may have to join a waiting list.
Green Lanes, Stoke Newington, London N4 2HA (020 8211 7000/www.castle-climbing.co.uk).

Craggy Island Climbing Centre, Surrey

This centre is dedicated to bouldering: climbing along and up low-level walls with no ropes and harnesses (instead, giant crash mats cover the floor). Over-sevens can climb the walls to their hearts' content, or don a helmet and head torch to explore the 50-metre cave labyrinth. Stalactites, cave paintings and a secret ball pit await.
Oaks Sports Centre, Woodmansterne Road, Carshalton, Surrey SM5 4AN (0844 8808 866/www.craggy-island.com).

The Edge, Sheffield

Two-hour 'Rockstars' sessions at this busy climbing centre instruct intrepid seven to 13s in all the essentials; they'll be soon be shinning up scarily lofty walls with confidence, then signing up for the more advanced Edgemasters club, where they learn the finer points of the sport.
John Street, Bramall Lane, Sheffield S2 4QU (0114 275 8899/www.sheffield climbing.com).

Edinburgh International Climbing Arena

Built around a disused quarry, this is reputedly the world's largest indoor climbing arena, with impressive facilities for top-level climbers. It's also child-friendly, with soft play areas and climbing clubs for little kids.
Ratho, South Platt Hill, Newbridge, EH28 8AA (0131 333 6333/www.edinburghleisure.co.uk/list-291).

Rope Race, Stockport

A converted Victorian cotton mill now dedicated to climbers of all ages. Taster sessions run in school holidays; the Geckos club for under-18s offers an awards scheme.
Upper Hibbert Lane, Marple, Stockport SK6 7HX (0161 426 0226/www.roperace.co.uk).

Undercover Rock, Bristol

School holidays bring taster sessions for children and good-value family lessons; seven- to ten-year-old regulars can join the Rockhopper club. Staff look out for kids with raw talent to be coached to competition level.
St Werburghs's Church, Mina Road, Bristol BS2 9YT (0117 941 3489/www.bristol climbingcentre.com).

Summit Centre, South Wales

The climbing wall is one of the biggest in Europe. Ten and overs adore the high ropes course: an aerial adventure with rope bridges, balance beams and zip wires.
The Old Drift Mine, Trelewis, South Wales CF46 6RD (01443 710749/www.summit centre.co.uk).

Westway Sports Centre, London

Bookable and drop-in sessions for kids and families take place year round at this centre. Cling to the bouldering wall like a limpet, or tackle more towering climbs.
1 Crowthorne Road, London W10 6RP (020 8969 0992/www.westway.org).

884 *See cliff-edge drama*

Performances at the Minack Theatre in Penzance have to be good, as they're competing with the show-stealing view. The open-air theatre is set on a rocky outcrop overlooking the sea – a magnificent backdrop to the operas and Shakespearean dramas played out on stage every summer. There's more obviously family-friendly fare too; *Mowgli*, say, or *Treasure Island*. Spend the day on Porthcurno Beach, then climb the 90 steps up the cliff to the theatre. If it's raining, the show goes on; these thesps only cancel for a force ten or similarly extreme conditions.

Minack Theatre *Pothcurno, Penzance, Cornwall TR19 6JU (01736 810181/www.minack.com).*

885 *Peep out from behind a waterfall*

Waterfalls Country, a thunderously attractive section of the Brecon Beacons National Park, is a glorious place for a walk. To help you choose a route to ramble, it has its own visitors' centre, in the village of Pontneddfechan, near Glynneath. Start a waterfall walk from here, and don't miss the thrilling experience of stepping carefully behind the curtain of water at Sgwd yr Eira (Waterfall of the Snow).

Waterfalls Centre *Pontneathvaughan Road, Pontneddfechan, Neath Port Talbot SA11 5NR (01639 721795/www.breconbeacons.org).*

886 *Write a haiku*

A haiku is a Japanese verse form with only 17 syllables in three lines, and can be written on a postage stamp in tiny script. It's ideal for people who like to spend a lot of time writing, without writing much. The inventor and greatest master of haiku was the 17th-century poet Basho, who perfected such poetry as: 'Clouds appear/And bring to men a chance to rest/From looking at the moon.' Make your haiku relevant and thoughtful, as he did. 'You and I wonder/How to spend our idle hours/So we buy *Time Out*.'

887 *Follow the Five*

To fans of Dick, Anne, Julian, George and Timmy, the ruins of Corfe Castle (The Square, Wareham, Dorset BH20 5EZ, 01929 481294, www.nationaltrust.org.uk) may look strangely familiar. That's because its crumbling remains were the inspiration for Enid Blyton's Kirrin Castle. Peeping through its arrow slits and murder-holes and rolling down the grassy slopes outside is thirsty work, so head to the Ginger Pop Shop (The Town House, The Square, BH20 5EZ, 01929 477214, www. gingerpop.co.uk). Blyton fans will be in seventh heaven here. Not only is there a fine view of the fortress, but there are lashings of ginger beer. Buy bottles of the stuff, or pick up a kit to make your own at home. Open from the end of March until the end of October, the shop also sells old-fashioned toys and gadgets, along with the author's works; don't forget to leave a message in the Enid Blyton appreciation book.

888 *Climb the leaning spire of Chesterfield*

The 14th-century spire at St Mary & All Saints is the tallest in Derbyshire – but it twists and tilts at an alarming angle. According to legend, a local blacksmith agreed to shoe the Devil, but accidentally drove a nail into his foot: as Lucifer leapt away, he gave the spire a kick. Others say the Devil stopped to rest on the church, then sneezed as incense from Mass rose and tickled his nose. About to fall, he wrapped his tail around the spire and twisted it out of shape. The third story is the rudest: a virgin was getting married here, much to the amazement of the spire, which twisted round to have a look. In truth, the contortion was caused by the weight of the lead tiles on an unseasoned timber frame – and a shortage of craftsmen in the aftermath of the Black Death. The verger runs tours to the spire's base on Bank Holiday Mondays and most Saturdays; call to arrange a visit.

St Mary & All Saints *Church Way, Chesterfield, Derbyshire S40 1XJ (01246 206506/ www.chesterfieldparishchurch.org.uk).*

889-892

Visit a village fête

Innocent Village Fête

Remember coconut shies and tug o' wars, or cow pat bingo? (You need a cow, and a field divided into squares: work it out.) Fêtes are great for keeping kids amused and getting involved with your local community, with the added allure of bargain-priced homemade cakes and plenty of cider to sample.

For a modern take on the fête, Londoners should head for the Innocent Village Fête (www.innocentvillagefete.com) in Regent's Park. It offers a huge array of activities, of the quirky-chic variety: think kids' yoga, ferret racing and enthusiastic jiving in the alfresco ballroom. There's also a village green area, with welly-wanging and morris dancing.

To sample a truly traditional fête, though, with cream-slathered scones and bunting a-flutter in the breeze, you're best off in more rural parts. Innocent's website has a page where local fêtes across the UK post details of their events. Check what's going on in your neighbourhood, then start training Spot for the waggiest tail contest.

In the Berkshire village of Cookham Dean, the fête is held on the cricket common, usually on the third weekend in September (01628 528475, www.cookham.com). Once a local dignitary has declared it officially open, the fun begins. Canine competitors line up for agility trials, dads take aim at the hoopla stand and kids delve into the bran tub, all to the strains of a local brass band.

Over in Essex, meanwhile, the village of Hadstock (www.essexinfo.net/hadstock) is another bastion of the Great British Fête. The village centre becomes a joyful jamboree of bric-a-brac browsing, face-painting, and bunting: try your hand at tug o' war, listen to the silver band or lend your support to the wonderful cake stall.

Norfolk is also famous for its sumer fêtes, with tombolas and coconut shies dusted off and cranked into action at every opportunity. Hardingham Fête (http://eoe.xarg.co.uk/fete) is a cracker: a small but perfectly formed nostalgic shindig with skittles, sack races and a Women's Institute flower show.

A few of my favourite things

893-907

Camila Batmanghelidjh, founder and director of Kids Company

We look after and educate children aged as young as three and four, right up to 16 and 17. Many are severely traumatised lone children whose parents are unable to function as caring adults – so Kids Company (www.kidsco.org.uk) becomes a substitute parent. Many of the children are hyperactive, so we have to invent a lot of things for them to do, alongside taking them out on excursions. If we take them somewhere like the London Aquarium (County Hall, Westminster Bridge Road, London SE1 7PB (020 7967 8000, www.londonaquarium.co.uk), we make sure there's another element to the trip, such as having a picnic in a nearby park, so that they can burn off some energy.

The best projects involve lots of movement and activity, as well as an element of danger – such as building a go-kart. It's easy and fun. You can buy little wheels from a bike shop, then take a plank and screw the wheels underneath, drilling a hole in the front to attach a rope.

Active children get a kick out of rollerblading; the Italian champion teaches at Kids Company. Boxing is another physical way of letting off steam, so we also have boxing instructors. Children love learning circus skills too. Instructors help them do that.

Parks are a safe bet. Holland Park Adventure Playground (Holland Park, London W8 6LU, 020 7471 9813, www.rbkc.gov.uk) is terrific. Little ones prefer Regent's Park and the Princess Diana Playground (Hyde Park, London W2 2UH, 020 7298 2141, www.royalparks.org.uk).

A very successful, busy and tiring trip out involves ice skating and bowling at the Queens venue in Bayswater (17 Queensway, London W2 4QP (020 7229 0172, www.queensiceandbowl.co.uk), then popping along to Whiteleys (151 Queensway, W2 4YN, 020 7229 8844/www.whiteleys.com) for a bite to eat before going for a swim in nearby Porchester Baths (020 7792 2919).

If we take the children out of London, it's for the snowy experience at Xscape in Milton Keynes (602 Marlborough Gate, Buckinghamshire MK9 3XS, 0871 200 3220, www.xscape.co.uk) although that's quite a pricy treat.

Many of our kids enjoy a trip to Vauxhall City Farm (165 Tyers Street, London SE11 5HS, 7582 4204, www.vauxhallcityfarm.info), where they're known pretty well. We also had a really successful camping trip in a farmer's field one summer. The kids enjoyed every aspect of the holiday – putting up the tent, outdoor living and playing at camp. They loved gathering firewood to make a blaze: it turned into a therapeutic activity.

Sometimes we go to the seaside – Brighton (www.visitbrighton.com) is a favourite, because you can combine the beach with all the activities on the pier.

We have 15 general artists and 30 arts therapists working with our children. They introduce the materials and let the kids come up with ideas. One activity was to decorate old chairs and tables and use them to hold a dinner party. They invited everyone to dinner, to eat food they had made and to sit on the furniture.

Another successful art activity was making a little council estate with shoeboxes. Each child furnished a box and told a story about the home they had made. Others like the physical side of art – hurling or spraying paint at sheets strung up on the walls. Designing wallpaper – customising rolls of lining paper – also goes down well.

Whatever the artwork, giving children the chance to show their creations is good. You could curate your own art exhibition and invite friends and family along.

Designing your own clothes is another great way to get creative. Kids Company has its own fashion label, called Bare Threads. We recently put on a fashion show that was opened by Gwyneth Paltrow.

908

Have a Rummage

Stowed in the basement of Liverpool's National Maritime Museum is Seized! – devoted to the sharp-eyed officers of HM Revenue and Customs, and their work. Seized goods on display range from a Kommando machine gun to a guitar made from an endangered turtle's shell – but why did customs officers seize the harmless-looking dancing Coca-Cola can? Top marks to any smartypants who can guess. Children can also put their sleuthing skills to the test during the free 'Rummage' events, searching a replica ship's cabin for 25 suspect packages. They're stowed away in the unlikeliest hiding places, so you'll have to keep your wits about you.

Merseyside Maritime Museum *Albert Dock, Liverpool L3 4AQ (0151 478 4499/www.liverpool museums.org.uk).*

909

Be a pirate

Shiver me timbers! Every Thursday during the summer holidays, the fishing port of Brixham is overrun by pirates, under the command of Cap'n Blood 'n' Guts of the Brixham Buccaneers (01803 850382, www.brixhambuccaneers.co.uk). Pirate mania takes over the town, with skull and crossbones decorating many of the shops. Proceedings kick off with the quayside Pirate Parade at 10am, followed by various buccanneer-based events: splat the pirate, nautical knot instruction, jolly pirate language lessons, face-painting, storytelling and a treasure hunt. Dress up in pirate regalia and have your picture taken in front of a lifesize replica of Sir Francis Drake's *Golden Hinde* (The Quay, Brixham, Devon TQ5 8AW, 01803 856223), then go aboard for a taste of life on a 16th-century sailing ship. Finish the day off with an exciting pirate cruise with Captain Jack Sparrow (not that one) – details on 01803 844010, www.greenwayferry.co.uk.

910

Go wassailing on Twelfth Night

Celebrated in cider orchards across the South West, apple wassailing is a tradition with pagan roots – though these days, it's all about getting the community together for post-Christmas fun. Crusts of bread or cake, sometimes soaked in cider, are hung from apple trees or laid on the roots as a gift for the robin that represents the tree's spirit. Cider is poured over the tree roots in a blessing ceremony for a good crop.

In the Devon village of Bishopsteignton, the whole community gathers at the Millennium Community Orchard to wake up the sleeping tree spirits by banging drums and saucepans by the light of flaming torches, and an obliging farmer fires blank cartridges into the trees to rid them of witches and evil spirits. Keep an eye on your local cider orchard around 6 January to see if they'll be wassailing, or check Orchard Link's site at www.orchardlink.org.uk

911

Meet some mad scientists

The chemistry experts at Catalyst Science Discovery Centre are never happier than in the school holidays, when they can test their experiments on kids. Marvel at exploding icing sugar or custard powder, find out how to blow a square bubble, or test your grey matter with some giant brain-teasers. Tickets are allotted on a first come, first served basis. Afterwards, get in the glass lift and zoom around four floors of interactive galleries and a rooftop observatory.

Catalyst *Mersey Road, Widnes, Cheshire WA8 0DF (0151 420 1121/www.catalyst.org.uk).*

912

Clear up the beach

Beachcombing is a wonderful activity – found objects like wave-smoothed driftwood, shells and pebbles are treasures to take home and enjoy. But consider this: if everyone filled a carrier bag with rubbish (either their own or someone else's) and disposed of it, the beach would be an even better place.

913

Blow some eggs...

Take an egg and give it a wash, then make a small hole in the big end with a pin. Turn the egg and make another hole in the narrow end; this time, use the pin to chip away a little more shell so the hole is slightly larger. Use a skewer to pierce the membrane inside the egg and swirl it gently to mash up the contents. Put the smaller hole to your lips and, holding the egg over a bowl, blow steadily. Once all the egg seems to be out, rinse the shell in warm soapy water and leave it to dry before you paint it. You can make both holes bigger and thread thin ribbon through, so the egg can hang from a tree.

914

...and make an Easter tree

Cut a twiggy branch from a tree; about 60cm is a good length. A piece from an apple, pear or cherry tree is ideal if it has blossom buds on it that will open in the warm. Place the branch in a tall vase of water, with sand in the bottom if the weight threatens to tip it over. Hang your blown, painted and threaded eggs on the twigs. Rabbits, chick and egg shapes cut from card and decorated with paints, glitter glue or offcuts of fabric also look good. Make a hole in the top to attach a thread or ribbon to hang them from the tree. Do the same with foil-wapped mini chocolate eggs. You can arrange more eggs around the base too.

915-916

Meet some high fliers

The giant halls and hangars at the Royal Air Force Museum (Grahame Park Way, London NW9 5LL, 020 8205 2266, www.rafmuseum. org.uk) house a stupendous collection of aircraft, parked at ground level or swooping from the rafters in the Milestones of Flight building. In the Aeronauts Interactive Centre, children can try out a hand-glider simulator, and the school holidays bring activities such as making helicopters or hot-air balloons, or re-enacting life as a wartime evacuee.

More magnificent men and their flying machines can be admired further north in Cambridgeshire, at the Imperial War Museum Duxford (Duxford, Cambridgeshire CB22 4QR, 01223 835000, www.iwm.org.uk). To see some of its collection in action, come to one of the air shows. Expect aerial derring-do from stunt pilot display teams, and oohs and aahs from the crowd.

917

See a West End show, for free

SOLT, the Society of London Theatres, provides a great introduction to Theatreland with Kids Week (www. kidsweek.co.uk). During the last two weeks of August, children aged five to 16 can attend popular West End shows such as *The Lion King* and *Les Misérables* for free, provided each is accompanied by a paying adult; up to two additional children can get in at half-price. They can also go backstage, meet the stars and take part in workshops. For more on Kids Week and the best family-friendly theatre information in London, subscribe to the free family bulletin on the SOLT website at www.officiallondon theatre.co.uk.

918-922 *Seek red squirrels*

Since grey squirrels from North America began muscling in on their territory, Britain's native reds have had a tough time. Squirrelpox (a virus that the greys carry, but are immune to) has exacerbated the situation.

Red squirrels still hold sway in some strongholds. Midwinter is a good time to spot them. In Cumbria, Whinlatter Forest Park (01768 778469, www.forestry.gov.uk) is now a Red Squirrel Refuge, where cameras are trained on the feeding stations, so even if you don't make any sightings from the Squirrel Scurry woodland trail, you can catch some live footage in the visitors' centre.

Another haven is Formby Point Squirrel Reserve, north of Liverpool (01704 878591, www.nationaltrust.org.uk). Around 1,000 squirrels live in the coastal pine woods; follow the 5.5-kilometre squirrel walk and see how many you can spot.

In Northumberland, Kielder Forest (01434 250209, www.forestry.gov.uk) is home to the UK's biggest red squirrel population. Creep quietly, and you might spot a shy roe deer too.

In Scotland, try Scolty Woodland Park (01466 794161, www.forestry.gov.uk), where squirrels play high in the tops of trees, or descend to the forest floor to gather fungi in autumn. In Perthshire, the Loch of the Lowes Visitor Centre & Wildlife Reserve (01350 727337, www.swt.org.uk) is a good bet: reds can be spotted here playing in the treetops or lunching at the feeders.

923 *See the sunset from Clevedon Pier*

While other once-mighty Victorian piers, like Brighton's West Pier, have crumbled into the sea, Clevedon's, in North Somerset, still stands strong (01275 878846, www.clevedonpier.com). The wrought-iron beauty has been saved from demolition and restored to its former glory. Hire a rod and fish, take a paddle steamer trip or just admire the lovely views over the Severn Estuary – at their best at sunset, when the pink-and violet-dappled sky seems to stretch forever.

924 *Have a monster beauty contest...*

Go shopping for fake blood, face-paints, scars, boils, rotten teeth, brown fingernails and hair gel for dramatic spikey hairdos. Get out the dressing-up box and charge your camera. Tell the children there's a prize for the best gurning. Buy some postcard mounts and have the kids send monstrous pictures of themselves to their godparents.

925 *...then see how the professionals do it*

The World Gurning Championships, held at the Egremont Crab Fair in the Lake District, takes place every September. The tradition dates back to 1266. Competitors are required to pull faces through a horse's collar, and winners are chosen according to the amount of applause their monster face earns. Other events at the fair include Cumberland wrestling, greasy pole climbing and apple chucking. Visit www.egremontcrabfair.org.uk to find out more.

926

Make popcorn

Heat three tablespoons of oil with a high smoke point (rice bran oil works well) in a large, heavy saucepan with a well-fitting lid – preferably see-through so you can observe what's going on. When you think the oil is hot enough, drop in a few corn kernels to make sure they pop. Once they have done so, add about 70g of kernels in an even layer, remove the pan from the heat and count slowly to 20, then return it to the heat. The corn should pop like mad (don't open the lid, but do shake the saucepan and occasionally slide open the lid slightly to let the steam out). Once the popping noise slows right down, so you can count a few seconds in between pops, take the pan from the heat, lift the lid and put your popcorn in a bowl. Melt a knob of butter together with some sugar or salt in the hot pan, pour over the popcorn and stir it all in. Then eat!

927-929
Learn the offside rule...

...in football
You are offside in soccer if someone passes to you when there are no defenders between you and the goalkeeper. Defenders try to catch attackers out by creeping past them so that they will be caught 'in the offside trap'. In this respect the offside rule is a variation on the parlour game Grandmother's Footsteps.

...in rugby union
Anyone who is in front of the ball is offside. If you immediately retire behind the ball, you incur no penalty. When the ball disappears into a scrum, the scrum itself becomes the ball. Anyone not in the scrum must be behind the back foot of the hindmost scrummager. If you leave the scrum and do not retire to where the backs are, you are also offside. If you manage to get yourself on the wrong side of the ball on the ground in the middle of a scrum and cannot get out because the opposition have their boots bearing down on your neck, you are still offside.

...in cricket
Offside in cricket is not an offence, but a part of the field. It is opposite the leg side, determined by the way the batsman stands at the stumps – left-handers one way, right-handers the other. If you have left- and right-handed batsmen playing at the same time, the leg and off sides of the field are constantly changing, which is a headache for the fielders. Understand?

930
Keep an eye on Earth's atmosphere
The Spaceguard Centre (Llanshay Lane, Knighton, Powys LD7 1LW (01547 520247, www.spaceguarduk.com) monitors the threat posed by 'near Earth objects' – that is, asteroids, comets and space debris that could hit the Earth. Its camera obscura, telescopes, planetarium, satellite weather station and a collection of meteorites are all explained entertainingly during tours that run from Wednesday to Sunday, May to October only.

931
Know your lucky seven
Sure enough, the old Newcastle mill occupied by the children's book museum Seven Stories has seven storeys. The name comes not only from the number of floors, but from the idea that there are only seven basic stories in the world (though thousands of ways of telling them). Seven Stories tells as many as it can by holding exhibitions, curated around a book, an author or a theme. The themes change weekly during the summer holidays. For the record, the seven stories are: 1) voyage and return, 2) rags to riches, 3) overcoming the monster, 4) the quest, 5) rebirth, 6) tragedy and 7) comedy.
Seven Stories *30 Lime Street, Newcastle upon Tyne NE1 2PQ (0845 271 0777/www.seven stories.org.uk).*

932
Seek Arthur's sword...
The quest to track down Excalibur, King Arthur's sword, takes you to the boggy, wastes of Bodmin Moor, to seek out Dozmary Pool (www.visitnorthcornwall.com). It was beside this lake, some say, that the king lay dying after being wounded in battle; at his request, Sir Bedivere hurled Excalibur into the waters. The Lady of the Lake stretched out her hand to take it, and the sword was never seen again.

933
...then enter a magic cave
Merlin is reputed to have lived in a cave that can be reached by scrambling down the rocks from Tintagel Castle (Tintagel Head, Cornwall PL34 0HE, 01840 770328, www.english-heritage.org.uk). This is a quest for older children and adults only, as the cave can only be entered at low tide; at high tide it's full of seawater. For more on Cornish Arthur legends, visit the Arthurian Centre (Slaughter Bridge, Camelford, Cornwall PL32 9TT, 01840 212450, www.arthur-online.com).

934 Grow your own blackcurrants...

Blackcurrant bushes are easy to grow from hardwood cuttings, so if you know someone with bushes, ask if you can take a few cuttings from a mature plant. Otherwise you can buy a plant from a garden centre, and take some cuttings from it once it's established. Take hardwood cuttings during the dormant season, in the winter, cutting a piece of stem about 20cm long. Make a slit in the ground with a spade, push the cutting in and cover the stick with soil to half its length. Then just leave it ouside for a year, making sure that the ground doesn't dry out in the summer. When your cutting has grown leaves, it's ready to dig up and move to where you want it in the garden.

935 ... and make blackcurrant squash

When your blackcurrant plantation yields fruit, you can brew up a refreshing vitamin C-rich beverage. Simmer 500g blackcurrants with about a cup of water. When they're soft, squish them with a potato masher, then simmer again for a few minutes. Pour into a jelly bag (available from kitchen shops) and strain over a bowl to catch the juice. Once you've collected all you can, add some sugar to the warm juice and let it dissolve: how much sugar depends on the sweetness of the teeth involved. Keep your squash in the fridge, and dilute before drinking.

936 Ride an electric bike

The pretty Suffolk coast is perfect cycling terrain: not too hilly. To maximise your family's pedal power, hire some sleek electric bikes from Light Electric Vehicles (0845 602 6652, www.electricbikehire.co.uk) and spend a few days exploring. With recharging points dotted around some of Suffolk's loveliest seaside towns, you can stop to see the sights while the batteries are boosted, then set off again. Electric bikes are recommended for 14 and overs, but you can hire models with tot seats.

Natural History Museum

937 See some weird specimens

The Natural History Museum is a holiday treat that shouldn't be missed. Dinosaurs, earthquake simulators, a blue whale and creeping arthropods – they're all big thrills for small kids. Older ones, however, should be introduced to the specimens stored in the Darwin Centre (due to re-open in September 2009), where they can explore the natural world in truly hi-tech surroundings.
Natural History Museum *Cromwell Road, SW7 5BD (020 7942 5725/www.nhm.ac.uk).*

938 Dial the hotline for starling staring

Bill Oddie and his mates have started a starling craze among their younger viewers. Having seen the multi-starling formation flying on the telly, they're mad to witness the drama for themselves. Binoculars at the ready, then, and set your sights on Avalon marshes in the Somerset Levels. Thousands of starlings roost in various sites here in autumn. To make it easier for visitors to locate them, the RSPB (Royal Society for the Protection of Birds), Natural England and Somerset Wildlife Trust have set up a starling hotline: call 07866 554142 for a newsflash on starling movements, and instructions about visiting the sites.

939

Buzz on Down to Darwin's inspiration

There has never been a better time to acquaint yourself with Down House, Charles Darwin's imposing home in Kent (01689 859119, www.english-heritage.org.uk). A new permanent exhibition opened here in 2009, marking 200 years since the great naturalist's birth and 150 years since his groundbreaking On the Origin of Species – written at Down – was published. The house is a glorious collection of curiosities, both personal and professional. The most absorbing thing about it for children, however, is in the garden laboratory. Here, English Heritage has reconstructed an observation beehive just like the one Darwin used to study bees' honeycomb building habits, having a lightbulb moment for his theory of evolution as he did so.

940 Force a hyacinth into bloom

In autumn, take a small flower pot (an 8cm one will do) and place a few shards of broken crockery over the drainage hole. Fill it half full of compost, then pop in a hyacinth bulb. The tip should reach the rim of the container, so adjust the level of the soil as you fill it. Water the soil.

Place the pot in a cool, dark place, such as a garden shed. Over the next six weeks, check it periodically to make sure that the soil is damp. When the shoot is about 3cm above the soil, and white roots are emerging from the drainage hole, bring the pot out of cold storage and move it to a slightly lighter, cool place, like a porch. Keep it watered. Turning the pot every day or so keeps the flower stem straight and strong. In a week or two, the stem will lengthen and the bud become plump.

When the foliage and bud are developed, move the pot to a bright window sill. Hyacinths will bloom fragrantly for nearly two weeks. After flowering, cut the flower stems and store the bulb in a cool, dry place until late summer, when it can be planted in the garden.

941

Be bowled over at Ripley's

The extraordinary exhibits to tour at Ripley's Believe It or Not! have been well documented – all those shrunken skulls, dinosaur eggs and artworks made out of tumble drier fluff – but our favourite bit of the experience has to be the Topsy Turvy Tunnel. This looks innocuous enough – a bridge with hand rails that takes you through a slowly spinning kaleidoscopic tunnel. Trouble is, the combination of the moving surroundings and the bridge to cross causes a feeling of disorientation so intense you end up staggering drunkenly across the bridge, grabbing helplessly at the railings. The knack is to bound across as confidently as you can, ignoring all diversions. Needless to say, children are much better at this than adults.

Ripley's Believe It or Not! Museum London *Pavilion, 1 Piccadilly Circus, London W1J 0DA (020 3238 0022/www.ripleyslondon.com).*

942-943

Make like Robin Hood

To those of an adventurous spirit, Sherwood Forest can mean only one thing: Robin Hood. The arrow-shooting, tights-wearing champion of the poor and oppressed lives on in these parts, with a week-long festival held in his honour every August at the Sherwood Forest Visitor Centre (Edwinstowe, Mansfield, Nottinghamshire NG21 9HN, 0844 980 8080, www.robinhoodfestival.info). Jesters, jousters, costumed characters and wandering minstrels provide the entertainment, while green hats and tunics are de rigueur.

You can also catch up with Robin in October, at the colourful two-day pageant held at Nottingham Castle (off Maid Marian Way, Nottingham NG1 6EL, 0115 915 3700, www. nottinghamcity.gov.uk). Broadswords ring on bold-painted shields as Robin rides out against the rascally Sheriff, fire-eaters breathe out blazing infernos, and the Merry Men tell stories of derring-do; for £1 you can hold a magnificent raptor and feel like king of the forest.

944 Walk the walls

A five-kilometre walk atop York's medieval city walls (the best preserved in Britain) is a great way to get a feel for this wonderful city. Pick up a guide and a rubbing kit at the visitor information centre and start at Bootham Bar, one of five gateways to the city. Take a rubbing from its plaque; collect all nine along the way, and you finish with a complete map of the city walls. Look out for the portcullis and 14th-century gatehouse at Monk Bar and the bullet holes and cannonball scars in Walmgate that date from the English Civil War. Micklegate Bar, the monarch's entrance to the city, has a small museum (01904 634436) with a gory display of models of the heads of rebels and traitors, skewered on pikestaffs and left to be pecked by passing crows.

Visitor Information Centre *De Grey Rooms, Exhibition Square, York YO1 7HB (01904 550099/www.visityork.org).*

945 Believe in the Unicorn

According to Caryl Jenner, who founded this legendary children's theatre company in 1947, a unicorn exists only if you believe in him – a notion that children adore. Fortunately, thousands of people do believe in the Unicorn; enough to raise, over several decades, the £13m needed to create this purpose-built children's theatre, set by the Thames in London.

Jenner decided in 1970 that children needed their own theatre in the heart of the capital, but died before the dream could be realised. The light, bright theatre standing proud today, with its pure white unicorn sculpture rearing up in the foyer is the result of many years of campaigning and a three-year collaboration with local schoolchildren, whose ideas were incorporated into the design.

Unicorn Theatre for Children *147 Tooley Street, London SE1 2HZ (020 7645 0560/www.unicorn theatre.com).*

946 Venture inside the Devil's Arse

It's a better experience than it sounds. The Peak Cavern (its politer name) is a stunning part of Derbyshire, near a village called Castleton. You approach the cavern, buried deep in a limestone cliff, via a lovely riverside walk. En route, you'll see the old miners' cottages: a whole community lived in and around this giant cave. Ropemaking was their trade, displays of which are still put on for visitors who take the tour.

Tours around the Arse itself last about an hour, with October half-term a popular time to visit, for Hallowe'en purposes. Why is it called the Devil's Arse? Ask your guide, but here's a clue – think of a strange cavern acoustic that sounds like something that rhymes with 'art'.

Devil's Arse *Peak Cavern, Castleton, Derbyshire S33 8WS (01433 620285/www.peakcavern.co.uk).*

Unicorn Theatre

Chinese New Year

947 *Make a quill pen...*

You may need the help of an obliging adult, as the cutting involved is quite tricky, and requires a sharp craft knife.

Take a medium-sized, stiff-spined feather (duck, pheasant or turkey feathers work well), then cut the end at a steep angle with a craft knife. If the plumes extend all the way down the feather, cut them away so that there's room for you to hold the quill when writing.

Carefully cut a small slit in the angled point of the quill. Turn the quill over and cut out a fingernail-shaped scoop from the back, then cut two scoops at each side of the slit to make a nib. (It helps to use a fountain pen nib as a model to copy.) Dip the quill pen in ink, blot it on some newspaper, then see if you can write with it.

948 *...then inscribe an ancient parchment*

This is great for making a treasure map look like the real thing. First, you need some rough recycled paper – the more uneven and coarse, the better. Next, using some cotton wool soaked in cold tea, lightly dab the paper to turn it a nice aged brown. Leave it to dry, then ask an adult to singe the edges with a candle to give it a jagged, curling-edged look. Now all you have to do is draw your map, and mark the X.

949-951 *See in the Chinese New Year*

Kung hei fat choi! Say that often enough around the end of January and beginning of February and you'll win friends in Chinatown. Chinese New Year celebrations are held around this time of year (depending on when the new moon falls). The celebrations are the biggest event in the Chinese calendar and a terrific spectacle for all ages; children are particularly entranced by the lion and dragon dances, which parade the streets bringing in good luck and noisily warding off evil with drums and cymbals.

In the capital, festivities are organised by the London Chinatown Chinese Association (www.chinatownchinese.co.uk) and begin with the lighting of lanterns in Oxford Steet and a parade through the Strand to Rupert Street, with further performances, stalls, food and fireworks in Trafalgar Square. In Liverpool (www.visit liverpool.com), which has one of the oldest Chinese communities in Europe, the New Year is welcomed in at the Chinese Arch on Nelson Street with firecracker performances, dancers and t'ai chi demonstrations. In Manchester (www.visitmanchester.com), the party includes an impressive Golden Dragon Parade from Albert Square to Faulkner Street. The day ends with a firework finale in Chinatown, then dinner at one of the many restaurants offering special menus in honour of the occasion.

952-954

Have a souper cook up

Introduce a morning's soup making with the story of the wise hen who outfoxed the fox.

A little hen is out walking when a fox leaps out and threatens to eat her. She persuades the wily one that she would taste better in a soup, then picks up a stone, telling the fox that stone soup is the tastiest there is. The pair go to the hen's cottage, where she sends the fox to dig up potatoes, carrots, onions and other vegetables, and to complete a series of exhausting chores while she cooks. He is so desperate for the soup that he complies. When the soup is ready, the fox is so hungry he gobbles it all up, saying he will eat the hen afterwards. But he is so full that he cannot manage a chicken dinner. The climax of the story comes as the fox leaps up – to grab the stone. He carries it off, convinced it is the secret ingredient for truly delicious soup.

Stone soup (without the stone)

Take a selection of vegetables: a couple of potatoes, four carrots, an onion, half a swede and a leek is about enough for a litre. Wash, peel and chop the veg into chunks. Warm two tablespoons of oil in a pan, add the veg and stir. Sauté on a low heat for about ten minutes. Once the vegetables have softened, add a litre of vegetable stock and two tablespoons of tomato purée. Bring to the boil, then simmer for about 30 minutes. Add more stock and seasoning to taste. Use a handheld blender to purée, but leave a few chunks as it adds to the appeal.

Alphabet soup

Sauté an onion and a clove of garlic, then add three chopped carrots and two sticks of finely chopped celery. Stir in a tin of chopped tomatoes, a handful of frozen peas and sweetcorn, a tablespoon of tomato purée, a sprinkle of salt and pepper and about 750ml of vegetable stock. Simmer the soup for about ten minutes, then add 50g of alphabet pasta (you can buy this from supermarkets and health food shops). Cook for a further 15 minutes or until the pasta is al dente. Serve with grated cheddar (or parmesan, if your children don't insist it smells of sick).

Stinger soup

Stinging nettles make a gentle and cleansing soup – though you can only cook it in spring, when the plants are young. Children are so fascinated by the idea of eating stingers, they always give it a try.

If you're a wildlife gardener, you may already have a fine crop of nettles in the yard for butterflies; otherwise you'll have to find your nettles in parks or woods (make sure they're away from any main roads). Wearing thick gardening gloves, pick the young spring nettles – only the tender tops, not the coarse stems. You need about 200g, which is quite a lot.

Bring the leaves home, give them a good wash and chop them with some spring onions. Cook 400g of potatoes for ten minutes, then drain and chop. Melt 25g of butter in a heavy-bottomed pan and sauté the chopped nettles, spring onions and potatoes. Add a litre of vegetable stock and simmer for about ten minutes. Purée the mixture with a handheld blender and serve with a grind of black pepper and an artistic swirl of cream.

955 Sell the family junk

One family's trash is another's treasure. Give yourselves a month and set aside an area for everyone to put items they have not used for, say, five years. Be ruthless. Look for car boot sale adverts in the local press. Fill car boot and arrive early. Use a trestle table to display your junk (sorry, goods). You will be amazed both at what you can shift and what you can make.

956

Ride a penny farthing

School holiday events at Erddig, a grand stately home in Wrexham, are always a blast – but the best fun comes with the Victorian days. Staff wear appropriate dress, and an antique bicycle specialist is brought in to give lessons on how to ride the old schoolmaster's penny farthing. It's just as difficult as it looks. Give it a try.

Erddig *Wrexham, Wales LL13 0YT (01978 315151/www.nationaltrust.org.uk).*

957

Join the cavemen

Feel, smell and experience the life of our prehistoric ancestors in the palaeolithic cave system they once called home – the dark depths of Kents Cavern in Torquay. Take an hour-long guided tour of the caves, then create your own cave painting of a woolly mammoth in the activities area. Walk in the footsteps of Cavog the Caveman and his tribe on the Stone Age Woodland Trail and look for food – but watch out for sabre-tooth tigers and cave lions. Budding archaeologists will love the Dig, where they can excavate a shark's tooth or uncover an ammonite.

Kents Cavern *89-91 Ilsham Road, Torquay, Devon TQ1 2JF (01803 215136/www.kents-cavern.co.uk).*

958

Compose a symphony

Now in its 11th year, the BBC Proms Inspire Young Composers' Competition (020 7765 2679, www.bbc.co.uk/proms) is an unmissable opportunity for young composers.

The winning pieces are commissioned, recorded, broadcast and (most thrillingly) performed live at a Proms concert. The piece can be in any style, whether it be classical, jazz, experimental or rock, use any instruments and last up to five minutes. The only condition is that it must be written down so other people can play it. Entrants compete in two age categories: 12 to 16s and 17 to 18s.

'Composer Labs', designed to assist hopefuls with their compositions, take place in London, Glasgow, Manchester and Cardiff in the run-up to the competition closing date, which is usually at the end of May. Be inspired by professional musicians and composers, meet other young music-makers, then get down to the serious business of composing your own miniature masterpiece. For details of times and dates, check the BBC Proms website.

959 *Explore Scotland's oldest house*

As the oldest continuously inhabited house in Scotland, Traquair is historic with a capital H, with loads of intriguing artefacts. Highlights include the concealed priest stairs, a lady's list of potential husbands (and their shortcomings) and the famous Bear Gates, adorned with ursine sculptures. After mooching round the house, you can stroll around the woodland, play on the junior adventure course or be bamboozled by the beech tree maze.

Traquair also hosts the annual Traquair Medieval Fair, and there are seasonal events at Easter, Hallowe'en and Christmas.

Traquair House *Innerleithen, Peeblesshire EH44 6PW (01896 830323/www.traquair.co.uk).*

960 *Be a vole in a hole at Muncaster*

Life can be tough when you're just over six centimetres tall, as you'll discover at Muncaster Castle's Meadow Vole Maze. It's an indoor interactive trail through a surreal, large-scale set, with two-metre high blades of grass and daisies bigger than dinner plates. Your job is to guide young Max the meadow vole home to safety before dusk falls, past the hungry predators that lie in wait along the way. There are some dark areas, so under-fives may find it slightly scary.

Muncaster Castle *Ravenglass, Cumbria CA18 1RQ (01229 717614/www.muncaster.co.uk).*

961

Surf on an artificial reef

Surfing should be the number one attraction in Boscombe (www.bournemouthsurfreef.co.uk), once the UK's first artificial reef, being worked on as we went to press, is up and running. The structure acts as a ramp, pushing waves upwards, doubling their size and improving their quality. Zip on that wetsuit, grab your board and head for the south coast – surf will be up... a lot.

962 Let off steam with the Marsh Boggles

The crazy creatures at Bewilderwood (01603 783900, www.bewilderwood.co.uk), a wild adventure park set in woodland near the Norfolk Broads, believe children should be running around outdoors 'climbing trees, exploring and scraping your knees'. To that end they've constructed a paradise from sustainably sourced wood, and dreamed up a cast of woodland characters – Twiggles, Marsh Boggles, the strange Thornyclod and the Wood Witch – to stir up wild imaginings. Children can shoot down zip wires, explore the treetop village, build dens and launch themselves down the Slippery Slope. Special events, such as bonfire parties and flower-planting days, go on throughout the school holidays, but mostly this is all about fresh air and physical play, which can only be a good thing.

963 *See mice in the hice...*

Battersea Park Children's Zoo is the perfect, pint-sized attraction. Its small-scale charms include a mynah bird that talks back, meerkats whose enclosure you can share via a tunnel and viewing domes, and impossibly comical otters. Then there are the benign goats, sheep and Shetland ponies, who amble over good-naturedly for a pat. No mini-animal adventure would be complete without some mice, however, and this little zoo sees them right. There are many, of various types, living inside their own mouse mansion, with cars outside to 'drive' and furnished rooms inside to scuttle through and play hide and seek with their admirers. It's all very Beatrix Potter. **Battersea Park Children's Zoo** *Battersea Park, London SW11 4NJ (020 7924 5826/www.batterseazoo.co.uk).*

964 *...then make sugar mice*

Take a packet of fondant icing sugar and follow the instructions for 'modelling icing'. We used half the pack (250g) and a tablespoon of water to make a soft paste, adding extra water a drop at a time; too much water means melting mice. We coloured a third of our paste with a drop of red food colouring, a third with cocoa powder (knead it in well for an even colour) and left the rest white. Shape the sugary paste into rodent shapes, then use a cocktail stick to make holes for the eyes (we used silver cake-decoration balls) and slits to insert ear shapes, fashioned from icing or tiny marshmallows. Make a hole in the mouse's bottom and then insert a clean piece of string to act as a tail. Leave to set.

965 *Peer through a squint*

The mansion at Lyme Park is the largest in the county of Cheshire, owned by the Legh family from 1346 to 1946. The 16th-century house is full of portraits that reveal how well connected they were. The Black Prince hangs in the entrance hall. His portrait swings out to reveal a 'squint' or spy-hole into the drawing room, formerly the dining room. This was either used for political eavesdropping or so that cook could check how many were coming to dinner. The gardens were laid out in the 19th and 20th centuries – and include the lake in which Mr Darcy so memorably took a dip in the BBC's *Pride and Prejudice*. The estate was taken over by the National Trust in 1946, so that children from everywhere could enjoy its deer, stream and adventure playground. **Lyme Park** *Disley, Stockport, Cheshire SK12 2NR (01663 762023/www.nationaltrust.org.uk).*

966

Be a tableau vivant

Your mission, should you accept, is to try to recreate a picture from an art gallery. Michiel Nouts' *A Family Group*, painted around 1656, is a good one. You can see it in the National Gallery in London, or on its website.

First, gather the props (the quill pen you made for No.947 – *see p290*, the tray of cups, the prayer book, the wooden doll and so on) and improvise the costumes (the long skirts, the black tights, the stiff, white collars, Dad's tall hat). Next, summon your family and friends, dress them up smartly and command them to pose as in the picture. Do your best to emulate the facial expressions too.

Take a snap, then put the original and the photograph side by side. How many differences can you spot?

National Gallery *Trafalgar Square, London WC2N 5DN (020 7747 2423/www.nationalgallery.org.uk).*

967 *See a Shetland Pony Grand National*

The thunder of hooves, the roar of the crowds: there's no doubt that the Shetland Pony Grand National is a highlight of the Olympia Horse Show (01753 847900, www.olympiahorseshow. com). Held each December, it raises thousands of pounds for charity. The doughty ponies and their young jockeys (aged nine to 13) chase at speed over brush fences around the ring. The qualifying races, held outdoors at summer shows (the season kicks off with Windsor Show) are faster than the big one in the Olympia arena, because the ponies have more space to gallop.

The ponies and children who race are members of the Shetland Pony Stud Book Performance (SPSB) Awards Scheme, and have to compete for a year before taking part in a variety of disciplines, including dressage, cross-country and gymkhana. To find out where to watch the qualifying races, or even how to get involved, visit the SPSB's website at www.shetland performance.com. To see how it feels to ride the race, watch the riders' eye view via the hat-cam footage on www.horseandhound.co.uk.

Shetland Pony Grand National

968 *Appraise pyrotechnics*

For two nights in mid August, the night sky around Plymouth Hoe, Devon, is lit up by the biggest professional firework competition in the UK (www.britishfireworks. co.uk). The 2006 British Firework Championships entered the record books when 56,645 rockets simultaneously took to the air, and the displays just get better and better each year. By 9.30pm, when the display starts, thousands have gathered along the waterfront to watch the finalists pit their pyrotechnic talents against each other. Competitors are judged on rhythm, continuity, pattern and creativity, as tonnes of fireworks are set off in this annual showdown in the sky.

969-981

Ride the rollers

Most of the rollercoasters below require riders to be 1.4 metres tall; throwing a tantrum or standing on tiptoes won't get you anywhere.

Colossus

There are no less than ten vertical loops on this monster – before the quadruple corkscrew twist at the end. One for intrepid teenagers.
Thorpe Park *Staines Road, Chertsey, Surrey KT16 8PN (0870 444 4466/www.thorpepark.co.uk).*

GForce

Whisks you through loop-the-loops. Small kids prefer the Troublesome Trucks runaway coaster.
Drayton Manor Theme Park *Drayton Manor Park, near Tamworth, Staffordshire B78 3TW (0870 872 5252/www.draytonmanor.co.uk).*

Grand National

Two cars thunder along parallel tracks on this 1930s wooden rollercoaster in a tense race.
Blackpool Pleasure Beach *525 Ocean Boulevard, Blackpool FY4 1EZ (0870 444 5566/www.blackpool pleasurebeach.com).*

Green Dragon

The gravity-powered Dragon takes you on a swooping ride through the trees.
Greenwood Forest Park *Y Felinheli, Gwynedd LL56 4QN (01248 671493/www.greenwoodforest park.co.uk).*

Jubilee Odyssey

The Jubilee has an inverted track, so you spend some time upside down before being flung around a series of corkscrews and loops. The slow climb at the start ramps up the tension.
Fantasy Island *Sea Lane, Ingoldmells, Skegness, Lincolnshire PE25 1RH (01754 615860/ www.fantasyisland.co.uk).*

Ladybird

If you're a metre tall you can ride this children's coaster; try to grab the front seat if you can.
Lightwater Valley *North Stainley, Ripon, North Yorkshire HG4 3HT (0870 458 0040/ www.lightwatervalley.co.uk).*

Megafobia

This Welsh white-knuckler is one of the biggest wooden coasters we've ever seen. It gives a rollicking ride, even though the maximum speed is a modest 80kph.
Oakwood Theme Park *Canaston Bridge, Narbeth, Pembrokeshire SA67 8DE (01834 861889/ www.oakwoodthemepark.co.uk).*

Pepsi Max Big One

Climb to 65 metres on Britain's tallest coaster, then swoop back down to earth at over 112kph. Best save the hot dogs for afterwards, unless you've got a stomach of steel.
Blackpool Pleasure Beach *See Grand National.*

Rita: Queen of Speed

When the lights turn green, off she goes – accelerating from zero to 160kph in just two-and-a-half stomach-churning seconds. Not surprisingly, it's unsuitable for young 'uns.
Alton Towers *Stoke-on-Trent, Staffordshire ST10 4DB (01538 703344/www.altontowers.com).*

Roller Coaster

The oldest roller on our list has an on-board driver controlling the brakes – so you'd better hope he's paying attention. Small fry are allowed on with an accompanying adult.
Pleasure Beach *South Beach Parade, Great Yarmouth, Norfolk NR30 3EH (01493 844585/ www.pleasure-beach.co.uk).*

Stealth

Towering over Thorpe Park and visible for miles around, Stealth is one for serious speed fiends, reaching 130kph in just two seconds.
Thorpe Park *See Colossus.*

The Ultimate

With 2.5 kilometres of twisting track, this is Europe's longest rollercoaster. With some seriously step drops and bone-shaking bends, it's designed for older children and adults.
Lightwater Valley *See Ladybird.*

Zipper Dipper

With no height restrictions, this classic wooden rollercoaster with steep, sudden dips was designed for thrill-seeking tots (more portly parents may struggle to squeeze into the seats).
Blackpool Pleasure Beach *See Grand National.*

Shore thing

Treasures of the deep dot Britain's shorelines, says Teresa Trafford.

Come rain or shine, beachcombing is a timeless pleasure. The waves yield countless tiny treasures, which children are far quicker than adults to recognise. All that's needed is a little imagination. You see a bedraggled length of rope; they may see a mermaid's sun-bleached hair or a giant's grizzly beard. A broken pedal is a rich prize – ripe for transformation into a robot's eye or a spaceman's foot. Sometimes, nature does all the work: look at a sea-polished, knobbly piece of timber from the right angle, and you might find an old man's craggy face peering back out at you, or the contours of a hump-backed camel.

Taking time to walk along the water's edge and sifting through the detritus washed up by the sea is an activity that children of all ages enjoy – and can provide the starting point for a wonderful model, sculpture or picture. Encourage children to look beyond shells and stones and gather less predictable objects: battered containers, bits of net, frayed ends of cable, pieces of wood, curved animal bones or

discarded floats. The sea can turn the most humdrum of materials into something rich and strange; even a plastic box, coated with algae and buffeted by the sea can inspire a young artist.

Lal Hitchcock, a Dorset-based artist, runs arts workshops involving found materials for adults and children. She's a firm believer in letting your inner creativity guide you. 'I don't want to dictate what people make,' she explains. 'I'd much rather each person finds their own starting point. A certain piece might suggest an animal, or a body part, and could inspire them to find other bits to make their sculpture.'

The best approach, she's found, is to assemble a treasure trove of different materials, then lay them out on the beach. Explore the different textures and shapes, then see where your imagination takes you. 'The object itself should be the starting point,' she says. 'The idea is to be led by the materials, not to say "I want to make a dinosaur," and then have to try to find the relevant bits.'

Lal prefers to see parents letting their children work independently, offering a little help if requested, but not taking over. She believes the creative process is personal, and the creator needs time to try out ideas and experiment with different materials.

Twelve-year-old Susannah Felstead (pictured below with her masterpiece) was a recent participant in one of Lal's events at Kimmeridge beach. Her sculpture began with a float, which she embellished with a number of other found objects from the beach. Lal provided basic tools and joining materials such as wire and string, and from the motley array of scrap and odds and ends, a chicken slowly emerged.

'There were lots of materials to choose from, and I liked the idea of using things that had been found along the beach,' said Susannah. She also liked it that Lal was on hand to offer advice when she got stuck, but let her work through her own ideas. Susannah was delighted with her chicken – named 'Chucky', as it was made from things that had been 'chucked away'. Since the course, she's been inspired to embark on her own beachcombing expeditions.

The beauty of beachcombing lies in its universal appeal. Anyone can get involved, from toddlers to teenagers (think striking sculptures or driftwood photograph frames). All you need to start you off are a few simple tools and joining materials.

The best time to go beachcombing is after a high tide, when flotsam and jetsam will have washed up around the high tide mark. Storms and blustery weather can stir up all sorts of long-forgotten treasures from the sea bed too, so it's worth venturing on to the beach the next day in your wellies and sou'wester, and seeing what's come ashore.

When it comes to making beachcomber art, the important thing is to let children get creative with a minimum of parental meddling. Instead, stand back and let your child discover the delight of making something wonderful from the materials they have stumbled across – a treasure they'll cherish all the more if it's of their own invention.

For information on events held on Dorset beaches during the summer holidays, visit www.coastlink.org.

Natural treasures

One of the weirdest things you'll find washed up on the seashore is a mermaid's purse. A gnarly-looking thing, it's roughly rectangular in shape, but with a bulge in the centre. It's the discarded egg case from a ray, skate or shark; the tough, leathery casing protected the baby fish during its months of gestation, while the curly tendrils at each corner anchored the egg in the patch of seaweed where it was laid. They're certainly not like any purse we've ever seen – but who knows what mermaids carry their cash in? If you find one, the Shark's Trust would like to know about it for its national database: log on to www.eggcase.org, which also has a handy species identification guide.

If you don't come across a shark's egg case, you may get lucky and find one of its gnashers instead. Fossilised shark's teeth, millions of years old and blackened by age, are a thrilling find. Bracklesham Bay in Suffolk (keep off the clay and mud flats), Herne Bay in Kent and Barton-on-Sea in Hampshire are all likely spots to find one.

Another unusual find is a cuttlefish bone. The live cuttlefish is an elusive beast – a squid-like mollusc that hides on the seabed and is related to the octopus. Look out, though, for cuttlefish skeletons on the beach: little ovals of white, porous bone. Check to see if there are any teeth marks, which indicate how your cuttlefish met its end.

983
Catch a fish supper

'Kids double, dogs free,' says the website for All My Sons (01947 840278, www.sea-angling-staithes.co.uk), a sea-angling charter boat based in the little harbour at Staithes, north of Whitby. Don't believe a word of it. Skipper Sean Baxter has fished round the world and takes out serious sea anglers on all-day fishing trips, but he also has two kids and a dog of his own and is just as happy to transport families on sessions of two or three hours. He supplies all the gear, fixes the hooks, untangles the lines, dispatches the fish and even guts it ready for the pan. Mackerel is almost guaranteed, with cod and ling the heftier prizes.

984-987
Pedal like an Olympian

Inspired by Olympic champs like Chris Hoy and Nicole Cook? Cycling clubs across the country can provide kids' coaching. The British Cycling website (www.britishcycling.org.uk) runs a Go-Ride youth scheme and lists accredited clubs. Velodromes (indoor racing tracks) are also great places to get in training for gold. The steeply banked sides look scary at first, but the adrenaline rush is addictive.

Calshot Velodrome

South England's only indoor banked velodrome runs regular 90-minute taster sessions for over-12s, on what is invitingly called the 'wall of death'. The £14 charge includes bike, helmet and all other kit.
Calshot Activities Centre, Calshot Spit, Fawley, Southampton, Hampshire SO45 1BR (023 8089 2077/www.hants.gov.uk).

Herne Hill Velodrome

Herne Hill is London's only velodrome – and the sole remaining venue from the 1948 Olympic Games that is still in active use. Youngsters can train with a coach on the 450-metre track and learn the fine art of mastering the 30° banking.
Burbage Road, London SE24 9HE (www.vcl.org.uk).

Manchester Velodrome

Turn up on the right day and you might see Victoria Pendleton pedal past at this world-class track. Although it's in demand, the velodrome has a youth programme with taster sessions for over-12s on most days, and school holiday sessions for nine to 16s for a mere £5.50.
The National Cycling Centre, Stuart Street, Manchester M11 4DQ (01612 232244/ www.manchestervelodrome.com).

Newport Velodrome

Second only to Manchester in terms of excellence, Newport's velodrome is 250 metres long. Activities for eight to 16s include beginner sessions on Saturdays – for £2, with bike hire.
Newport International Sport Village, Velodrome Way, Newport NP19 4RB (01633 656757/ www.newportvelo.com).

988-997

Wendy Wason,
comedian
and actress

I do stand-up, so I'm always on the road, and I take my children (Isabella, six, and Maxi, four) all over the place. They've seen so much. When we're at home in London, we like to keep it simple. We like Kensington Gardens (Hyde Park, London W8 4PX, 020 7298 2100, www.royalparks.gov.uk) a lot. It's really beautiful in autumn. If you walk to the other side of the pond from the statue of Peter Pan, there is a bench from which you get a beautiful view right up the park to Kensington Palace (Kensington Gardens, W8 4PX, 0844 482 7777, www.hrp.org.uk). On that side of the park there is a much quieter play park for the children. The Gardens is also home to the Diana, Princess of Wales Memorial Playground (near Black Lion Gate, Broad Walk, London W8 2UH, www.royal parks.gov.uk), which has a massive pirate ship the children can crawl over. There is also a musical area where the kids can bang away to their hearts' content while the grown-ups grab a quick snog in the bushes. **On a Sunday you can spend a while looking at the artwork tied to the railings, but be prepared for little people to be quite loudly vocal about what they don't like.** Not far from Kensington Gardens, at the other end of Queensway, is Whiteleys shopping centre (151 Queensway, London W2 4YN, 020 7229 8844, www.whiteleys. com). This was a haven for me when the children were little and it rained – as it often does in London. You can let tinies run around in a vast enclosed space, then head up to the bookshop (020 7229 3865, www.borders.co.uk) and read some kids' books, then top the afternoon off with a pizza or some sushi, or just just a coffee and a muffin. Who knows – you can even push the boat out and take in a movie. **There are other freebie things you can do with the kids. Adults know Hamleys (88-196 Regent Street, London W1B 5BT, 0870 333 2455, www.hamleys.com) is a toy shop, but the kids don't know you're supposed to buy stuff. If you switch off the worrying about time, you can spend all day in there letting them play with the display toys. Around Christmas, there is a snow storm from the roof every day at 5pm.** Similarly, Selfridges (400 Oxford Street, London W1A 1AB, 0800 123400, www. selfridges.com) is fantastic over Christmas. It has the most amazing Santa Express, with – get this – more than one grotto, so the kids don't have to wait forever to tell Father Christmas what they want. Simple! On the children's floor there are craft tables where the kids can make treasure chests or jewellery boxes, and it's all free. (I say free, though I think it's assumed you'll spend a small fortune in the shop. Thankfully, you're not obliged to.) **I'm away from home for work so much that sometimes it's nice to just stay in and play – or make something arty, if you're up to the cleaning-up afterwards. The children love making papier-mâché and turning it into masks, or creating fairy books.** Away from London, we're always delighted to be by the sea at Paignton in Devon (www. englishriviera.co.uk). It has magnificent long, sandy beaches and is brilliant for exploring; the rockpooling is pretty good too. **I also like to float about in the Cotswolds (www.cotswolds.com) with the children, taking riverside walks, visiting ridiculously pretty villages and playing Poohsticks from suitable bridges.** If we go down to Dorset, we always take a detour to visit Monkey World (Longthorns, Wareham, Dorset BH20 6HH, 01929 462537, www.monkeyworld.org), a rescue centre that we all rate very highly. **Because of the nature of my job, we spend much of the summer in Edinburgh at the Festival (www.eif.co.uk); I'm performing my show on the Festival Fringe (www.edfringe. com). As far as the kids are concerned, though, the highlight is the Edinburgh Book Festival (www.edbookfest.co.uk); they have the best time sampling all the workshops, activities and events.**

998

Go to Crane School

There is so much to recommend a day out at the headquarters of the Wetlands Trust at Slimbridge, it's difficult to know where to start. The Duckery, the flamingo lake, welly boot land (a playground) and dramatic starling migrations in season are all wonderful for families. One part of the site you mustn't miss, however, is the Crane School.

In the summer holidays, small groups of children are invited to put on a special crane disguise to join experts as they teach the young hand-reared cranes in the school. (They dress up so that the chicks don't become too used to interacting with humans.) What are the cranes learning? How to behave, of course. The young cranes are taken for a walk through the marsh garden and taught how to feed, recognise and protect themselves from predators, and interact with their brothers and sisters to find their place among the other cranes.

WWT Slimbridge Wetland Centre *Slimbridge, Gloucestershire GL2 7BT (01453 891900/ www.wwt.org.uk).*

999

See a ship cut in half

Walk along the Thames Path to the Greenwich Peninsula and you can spot any number of fascinating landmarks. Just to the west of the O2 (www.theo2.co.uk), *A Slice of Reality* is a 20-metre high vertical cross-section of a sand dredger anchored to the riverbed, created by artist Richard Wilson. The ship has been cut through and sealed with reinforced glass, opening up its insides to the viewing public.

1000

Make someone breakfast in bed

By someone we mean parents or carers, obviously. After all this frantic activity, the poor old grown-ups could do with a treat, after all. Use a tray and don't be tempted to be too elaborate – cereal and toast are perfectly adequate. A fruit juice would be nice. Handy with the blender? Try this: five ice cubes, one cup of plain yoghurt, one cup of fruit juice, half a banana, a few strawberries, raspberries or other fruit. Blend them into a smooth liquid. Pour into glasses. Serve. Bask in congratulations.

WWT Slimbridge

County index

In addition to counties, major cities are also indexed.

Channel Islands

England

Advertisers' index

Please refer to relevant sections for addresses and / or telephone numbers

When you have run out of things to do why not visit...

Thematic index

A-Z index